International Perspectives on Lifelong Learning

Edited by
John Holford
Peter Jarvis
Colin Griffin

LONDON AND NEW YORK

YOURS TO HAVE AND TO HOLD
BUT NOT TO COPY

First published 1998 by Kogan Page

2 Park Square, Milton Park, Abingdon, Oxfordshire OX14 4RN
52 Vanderbilt Avenue, New York, NY 10017

Routledge is an imprint of the Taylor & Francis Group, an informa business

First issued in paperback 2020

Copyright © John Holford, Peter Jarvis, Colin Griffin and named contributors, 1998

All rights reserved. No part of this book may be reprinted or reproduced or utilised in any form or by any electronic, mechanical, or other means, now known or hereafter invented, including photocopying and recording, or in any information storage or retrieval system, without permission in writing from the publishers.

Notice:
Product or corporate names may be trademarks or registered trademarks, and are used only for identification and explanation without intent to infringe.

British Library Cataloguing in Publication Data

A CIP record for this book is available from the British Library.

ISBN 978-0-7494-2869-3 (hbk)
ISBN 978-0-367-60512-4 (pbk)

Typeset by Kogan Page

Contents

Preface vii
The Contributors and Editors xi

PART I: INTERNATIONAL POLICY 1

1. **Edgar Faure After 25 Years: Down But Not Out**
   Roger Boshier 3

2. **Public Rhetoric and Public Policy: Analysing the Difference for Lifelong Learning**
   Colin Griffin 21

3. **Lifelong Learning and the European Union: A Critique from a 'Risk Society' Perspective**
   Barry Hake 32

4. **Critical Perspectives and New Beginnings: Reframing the Discourse on Lifelong Learning**
   Michael Collins 44

PART II: LIFELONG LEARNING IN THE LEARNING SOCIETY 57

5. **Paradoxes of the Learning Society**
   Peter Jarvis 59

6. **Persuasive Discourses: Learning and the Production of Working Subjects in a Post-industrial Era**
   Elaine Butler 69

7. Lifelong Learning for Social Responsibility: Exploring the Significance of Aesthetic Reflectivity for Adult Education
   Theo Jansen, Matthias Finger and Danny Wildemeersch   81

8. Lifelong Learning Through the Habermasian Lens: Providing a Theoretical Grounding to Adult Education Practice
   Brian Connelly   92

PART III: LIFELONG LEARNING AND POLITICAL TRANSITIONS   101

9. From Apartheid Education to Lifelong Learning: Assessing the Ameliorative Potential of Emerging Education Policy in South Africa
   Bobby Soobrayan   103

10. Lifelong Learning: A Cure for Unemployment? From *Betriebsakademien* to *Beschäftigungsgesellschaften* in Germany
    Marion Spöring   115

11. Schools Run by Social Forces: The Development of the Private Sector for Lifelong Learning in China
    Xiao Fang   124

12. 'Through-Life' Perspectives and Continuing Education in Hong Kong: Policy Review and Policy Unformation
    John Holford   137

PART IV: LEARNING, MARKETS AND CHANGE IN WELFARE STATES   153

13. Demands and Possibilities for Lifelong Learning in Market-Oriented Society: A Finnish Perspective on Public Policy and Reality
    Jukka Tuomisto   155

14. **Market Oriented Policies and the Learning Society: The Case of New Zealand**
    Michael Law — 168

15. **An Analysis of Lifelong Learning Policy in Japan**
    Hiromi Sasai — 180

16. **Can User Choice Contribute to Lifelong Learning? Implications of the Australian Experience**
    Fran Ferrier — 186

17. **A Market For Lifelong Learning? The Voucher Experience in the City Of London**
    Peter Jarvis, Colin Griffin and John Holford — 198

PART V: LEARNING AND CHANGE IN EDUCATIONAL STRUCTURE — 211

18. **How Can University Work-based Courses Contribute to Lifelong Learning?**
    David Boud — 213

19. **What Would Lifelong Education Look Like in a Workplace Setting?**
    Paul Hagert and David Becket — 224

20. **Towards the Learning Society: An Italian perspective**
    Aureliana Alberici — 236

21. **Sentencing Learners to Life: Retrofitting the Academy for the Information Age**
    Cliff Falk — 245

22. **The Role of the Public Library in Lifelong Learning: Can Cinderella go to the Ball?**
    Matthew J Williamson and Margaret K Wallis — 256

PART VI: LEARNING AND CHANGE AT WORK — 267

23. **Beyond the Threshold: Organizational Learning at the Edge**
    Paul Tosey and John Nugent — 269

24. **Creating Contingency Workers: A Critical Study of the Learning Organization**
    Fred M Schied, Sharon L Howell, Vicki K Carter and Judith A Preston — 280

25. **Consultative and Learning Approaches in the Context of Organizational Process Innovations**
    Annikki Jarvinen — 291

26. **Promoting Learning Networks For Small Business: How Can Group Learning Facilitate Change?**
    Sue Kilpatrick — 303

PART VII: AIMS, ETHICS AND SOCIAL PURPOSE IN LIFELONG LEARNING — 315

27. **The Liberal Instrument**
    Evan Alderson and Mark Selman — 317

28. **Teaching/Learning and Decision-Making: The Face-to-Face Versus the Interface, Some Implications for Ethical Practice**
    Del Loewenthal and Robert Snell — 326

29. **Lifelong Learning: The Path to Lifelong Liabilities for Women?**
    Venitha Pillay — 337

30. **Education of Employees and Business Social Responsibility: the Question of Political Utilitarianism**
    Janko Berlogar — 349

Index — 359

Preface

It seems today that everyone believes in 'lifelong learning'. Managers, gurus, teachers, counsellors, television presenters and trades union leaders all tell us that schooling is not enough: change is so fast, we must continue to learn throughout our lives. They are backed up by an impressive array of supporters. From the European Commission to UNESCO, inter-governmental organizations sing its praises. National governments follow the same score. Policy papers appear in profusion: and their authors' political colour never seems to dampen the enthusiastic endorsement they give to the 'vision'. The British Conservative government, for instance, issued *Lifetime Learning* in 1995; the new Labour government issued *The Learning Age* less than two years later. The refrain echoes through the policy world. Across the world, university grants committees, state governments, school boards and local education authorities, universities, colleges, schools – however lacklustre their past or present attitudes to adult or continuing education – endorse the new creed.

Enthusiasm for learning through life is much to be welcomed. But this volume seeks to move beyond the 'hype' which too often passes for analysis. Falling between a number of rather distinct research traditions, lifelong learning has been ill-served by scholarship. Educationalists have focused on the school years. Recently, they have given some attention to higher education, but adult education has long been, in scholarly as well as financial terms, a 'poor relation'. For sociologists and psychologists, too, learning has been chiefly a matter of the early years of life. Sociology of education, with few exceptions, has concentrated on schools as agencies of socialization and of distribution of social and economic opportunities. Economists, political scientists and students of public policy have likewise concentrated on the initial education sector – if only because part-time, post-initial education has been a trivially small element of the activities of most governments' educational activities. There have, of course, been some valuable exceptions – not least the recent interest sociologists and economists of labour have shown in workplace training – but by and large the scholarship of education and training has mirrored the contours of public educational provision itself.

This is natural enough. It means that as lifelong learning burgeons in practice, those who seek to shape or study it proceed with few established models or traditions to guide them. In both professional and academic terms – as a field of practice and of scholarship – lifelong learning is relatively uncharted territory. Of course, this provides opportunities. Experimentation is relatively untrammelled by professional standards or academic sclerosis. New ideas abound. But there are also risks. Too often, professionals must invent anew procedures and approaches which may not have been tried and tested elsewhere. Few principles of practice are generally established. Lifelong learning, for instance, has few of the broadly accepted ethical standards associated with school teaching, education or counselling. Similarly, diversity of theory, orientation, and method sometimes makes scholarship in the field diffuse to a point where potentially important issues or unsatisfactory findings are allowed to pass unchallenged.

The contributors to this book stem from a range of intellectual backgrounds, nationalities and cultures. They address a number of issues and areas in different national and institutional contexts, employing a number of approaches and sometimes competing theoretical positions. They share a commitment to developing scholarship and research in what is at the same time a fast developing area of professional endeavour, and an area with important implications for social, economic and political development.

The book falls into seven parts. These address some of the key areas in which we believe debate and analysis of lifelong learning should develop. The first examines the development of lifelong learning policy internationally. Roger Boshier sets the scene by analysing how the notion of lifelong learning has evolved since the Faure Report of 1972. He sees contemporary lifelong learning discourse as a 'mugged' and 'wounded' version of Faure's lifelong education. Colin Griffin sees lifelong learning as a 'policy ensemble' of 'rhetoric' and 'reality' which casts it as both desirable and unavoidable. Barry Hake examines the evolution of European Community policy: he sees the much-vaunted 'learning society' as a 'risk society' in which individuals must learn to survive lifelong. Finally, Michael Collins argues that while the 'lifelong education' agenda of the 1970s has by no means been realized, experience over the past three decades has generated knowledge – about the importance of connecting school and community, for instance – that 'lifelong learning' must not ignore.

Peter Jarvis starts Part II: Lifelong Learning in the Learning Society, by discussing how the notion of a 'learning society' has been used, and some of its ambiguities and paradoxes. Elaine Butler presents a powerful case that lifelong learning is a discourse designed to produce workers for 'new local global worksites'. Theo Jansen, Matthias Finger and Danny Wildemeersch, however, develop a case that despite the fragmentation of postmodern life, certain forms of educational practice can strengthen social responsibility, while

Brian Connelly shows how the work of Jürgen Habermas can contribute to the social theory of learning and education.

Parts III and IV examine the politics of lifelong learning from the perspective of societies in various forms of transition. Part III looks at societies which have been marked by major political transitions. Bobby Soobrayan sees lifelong learning as attractive in South Africa because of its 'conceptual malleability' – it allows both radical and functionalist discourses. His discussion is of far wider significance, and raises in a different form some of the concerns expressed by Roger Boshier in Chapter 1. Marion Spöring discusses how lifelong learning opportunities have fared in the process of German reunification, Xiao Fang looks at how a market-based private sector of lifelong learning has emerged in China, while John Holford examines the fate of 'through-life' perspectives on learning and education in 1990s Hong Kong. Part IV examines lifelong learning in what are (or were formerly) broadly 'welfare' societies. Analytical and policy chapters on Finland (Jukka Tuomisto) and New Zealand (Michael Law), and a chapter on policy development in Japan (Hiromi Sasai), are followed by two more detailed studies of attempts to introduce market systems or 'user choice' into lifelong learning: in Australia and London.

A recurring tendency in discussion of lifelong learning is to use the term as though it means post-compulsory education and training. The chapters in Part V provide useful correctives to this. David Boud, David Beckett and Paul Hager look in various ways at the relationship between work-based learning and more traditional forms of education. Aureliana Alberici, using Italian experience, argues that lifelong learning requires major changes in school systems. Cliff Falk develops a postmodern critique, arguing that changes in education designed to fit the information age are designed to produce 'malleable but disciplined' workers. Finally, Matthew Williamson and Margaret Wallis explore how public libraries must adapt to meet the needs of lifelong learning.

Lifelong learning is often seen as a policy for enthusiastic pursuit of educational and training opportunities by individuals. But an important element of the discourse is the notion of collective learning. Thus we encounter not only learning communities and societies, but learning organizations. The chapters in Part VI examine aspects of the relationship between learning, work organizations and change.

Paul Tosey and John Nugent use a case study to suggest the existence of a learning organization 'threshold'. This, they argue, is linked to individuals' ability to shift from a problem-solving approach to an 'inquiring' one, 'integrating systematic research with personal development'. The organizational paradigm, they believe, will change only if we also change our learning paradigm. A different and more uncompromising critique of the learning organization literature is offered by Fred Scheid, Sharon Howell, Vicki Carter and Judith Preston. Companies may speak of learning, co-operation and trust, but when workers abandon hard-earned rights in return, their well-being is seldom enhanced. Anniki Jarvinen contributes to knowledge of learning in organizations by examining how new organizational forms are shaping the organization of learning, while at the same time, new approaches to lifelong learning are shaping changes in organizational processes. Sue Kilpatrick considers the problems of developing learning in a small business. Her lens focusses on Australian farms: the key, she believes, is providing opportunities for group interaction and collective support.

Finally, the four chapters in Part VII examine return to some of the issues of ethics and purpose first raised in Part I. Evan Alderson and Mark Selman argue that central aspects of the 'liberal' approach need to be preserved in any lifelong approach to learning. Del Loewenthal and Robert Snell assert that vital elements of learning can only be achieved in face-to-face settings. Venitha Pillay suggests from South African experience that gendered perspectives are central to a fuller understanding of lifelong learning. And from Slovenia, Janko Berlogar argues that there are profound impediments on the road to lifelong learning, stemming from the unequal power relations of the workplace.

The chapters which compose this book all originate in papers presented at a conference, 'Lifelong Learning: Rhetoric, Reality and Public Policy', held at the University of Surrey in July 1997. We are grateful to the various authors for revising their papers, in some cases very substantially, to fit the requirements of the present book. The conference played a very valuable role in identifying and exchanging issues and perspectives in this emerging field, and we should like to thank all those who participated in or helped to organize it. Its continuing value is indicated not only by the chapters in this book, but by the *International Journal of Lifelong Education* special issue on 'Lifelong Learning' (Volume 18, No. 2, 1999), which also consists of papers which originated there.

This book is offered as a contribution to collective scholarly engagement in the analysis of lifelong learning. The various contributors continue this work around the world. At the University of Surrey, the Lifelong Learning Research Group, of which the editors were founding members, remains committed to theoretical and empirical research to shape understandings and perspectives in the field. We have incorporated lifelong learning perspectives in our recent book, *The Theory and Practice of Learning* (Kogan Page 1998), as well as in our continuing work.

John Holford
Peter Jarvis
Colin Griffin

Guildford
June 1998

The Contributors and Editors

Aureliana Alberici is Professor of Adult Education in the Educational Sciences Department, University of Rome Three, Italy. Her research has concentrated on educational systems and educational policy. Formerly Vice-President of the Italian Senate's Standing Committee on Education, she is now a member of National Scientific Committee for achieving the SIALS in Italy.

Evan Alderson is Associate Professor at Simon Fraser University, Canada. He has held numerous administrative positions at Simon Fraser, among them founding Director of the School for the Contemporary Arts, founding Director of the Graduate Liberal Studies Program and Dean of the Faculty of Arts. He is currently on assignment at SFU's downtown Vancouver campus, developing specialized programs for adult learners. He has published in the fields of American literature, cultural policy and dance studies.

David Beckett is a Lecturer in Vocational Education and Training at the University of Melbourne, Australia. He is author of several works on the philosophy of education, such as 'Critical Judgement and Professional Practice' in *Educational Theory* (Spring 1996), and he is co-writing a book (with Paul Hager) on the postmodern practitioner. His current areas of commissioned research are workplace learning in aged care facilities, management learning, and schooling and vocationalism.

Janko Berlogar has an MSc in Communicology and is a doctoral candidate in Human Resource and Social Management, just now finishing his dissertation on organizational ethics. He works on educational programmes research and development in the Department for Development and Counselling at the Slovene Adult Education Centre, Ljubljana, Slovenia.

Roger Boshier is Chief Executive Officer of Gulftow Salvage and Marine Safety Ltd and Professor of Adult Education at University of British Columbia, Vancouver, Canada. He was formerly a Director of the New Zealand campaign to stop atmospheric testing of nuclear weapons in the Pacific and, in 1996, was a New Democratic Party candidate for election to the BC legislature.

David Boud is Professor of Adult Education at the University of Technology, Sydney, Australia. He is Editor of Studies in Continuing Education and has written and edited widely on adult and continuing education.

Elaine Butler lectures in Work Studies at the Department of Social Inquiry (Centre for Labour Studies), University of Adelaide, Australia. Her research focuses on the interrelationships between work and work-related learning. Of significance are issues relating to equity; power/control and worker subjectivity; and the changing nature of work. She has an active interest in post-structuralism, feminisms, epistemology and critical pedagogies.

Vicki K Carter is an Instructional Designer and doctoral candidate in Adult Education at the Pennsylvania State University, USA.

Michael Collins is Professor and Co-ordinator of Graduate Studies in Adult and Continuing Education at the University of Saskatchewan, Saskatoon, Canada. He has worked as an adult educator in the UK and the USA as well as Canada, and is the author of *Competence in Adult Education: A New Perspective*, *Adult Education as Vocation* and *Critical Crosscurrents in Education*.

Brian Connelly works at Hackney Community College, London. In 1997 he was awarded a PhD by the University of Surrey for a thesis which analysed the relevance of the theories of Jürgen Habermas to adult education.

Cliff Falk is a doctoral student in curriculum studies at Simon Fraser University, Vancouver, Canada. His work concerns institutional responses to demands for educational change. He is especially interested in a comparative analysis of the contemporary demands for change with the demands placed on the project of mass education during its inception.

Xiao Fang is an Assistant Registrar at the University of Hull, UK. Previously, she worked as a Lecturer in the Research Institute for Higher Education Science at Xiamen University in China. She obtained her PhD degree

THE CONTRIBUTORS AND EDITORS xiii

from the University of Sheffield. Her research interests are in international comparison in adult and higher education.

Fran Ferrier is a Research Fellow in the Centre for the Economics of Education and Training, a joint venture of Monash University and the Australian Council for Educational Research, in collaboration with the University of Melbourne. Her current areas of research include equity and the economics of vocational education and training and new developments in postgraduate education.

Matthias Finger is a Professor of Public Management in Lausanne (Switzerland). He has lectured in adult education at Columbia University (NY). His research focused on adult education and social responsibility, social and ecological movements, social learning and management practices. He is involved in consultancy activities for various transnational organizations, including the reconstruction of the Swiss postal services.

Colin Griffin is Associate Lecturer and a member of the Lifelong Learning Research Group in the School of Educational Studies, University of Surrey. He is author of *Curriculum Theory in Adult and Lifelong Education* (1983), *Adult Education as Social Policy* (1987) and editor of *Empowerment through Experiential Learning: Explorations of Good Practice* (1992, with John Mulligan). With Peter Jarvis and John Holford, he is author of *The Theory and Practice of Learning* (Kogan Page 1998).

Paul Hager is an Associate Professor in the Faculty of Education at the University of Technology, Sydney, Australia. He has published books and research papers on the philosophy of adult education and vocational education and training, on workplace learning, on critical thinking and on professional competence. He is currently writing a book with David Beckett on the postmodern practitioner.

Barry J Hake is Senior Lecturer in the Centre for Learning and Communication in Organizations, Leiden University, the Netherlands, and Secretary of the European Society for Research into the Education of Adults (ESREA).

John Holford is Senior Lecturer and a member of the Lifelong Learning Research Group in the School of Educational Studies, University of Surrey. His books include *The Theory and Practice of Learning* (with Peter Jarvis and Colin Griffin), *Union Education in Britain* and *The Hong Kong Adult Education Handbook* (with David Gardner and Jennifer Ng). He is also Reviews Editor of the *International Journal of Lifelong Education*.

Sharon L Howell is an Assistant Director for Student Aid and a doctoral candidate in Adult Education at the Pennsylvania State University, USA.

Theo Jansen is a senior lecturer of adult and continuing education at the University of Nijmegen in the Netherlands. His research over the last years has focused on the relationship between adult education and social responsibility, adult education in the context of the risk society, social movements and social learning, experiential learning, postmodernity, etc.

Annikki Jarvinen is a Professor in Adult Education, specializing in professional continuing education, at University of Tampere, Finland. Her special research interests are professional development, reflective thinking, consultative work and adult learning at work contexts.

Peter Jarvis is Professor of Continuing Education and a member of the Lifelong Learning Research Group in the School of Educational Studies, University of Surrey. He is author and editor of many books on education and learning; among his more recent ones are *Ethics and the Education of Adults in Late Modern Society* (NIACE 1997) and *The Teacher Practitioner and Mentor in Nursing, Midwifery, Health Visiting and the Social Services* (with Sheila Gibson). In 1998 he became Joint Editor of the *International Journal of Lifelong Education*.

Sue Kilpatrick is Associate Director of the Centre for Research and Learning in Regional Australia at the University of Tasmania, where she also lecturers in Adult and Vocational Education. Her recent research has been into the impact of education on change and profit in small business, effective training delivery methods and labour mobility.

Michael Law is a Senior Lecturer in Labour Studies at the University of Waikato, Hamilton, New Zealand. His primary teaching and research interests include contemporary social theory, comparative labour studies, and workers' education and training. He has been actively involved in adult education, especially workers' education, since the late 1960s.

Del Loewenthal is a Senior Lecturer in the School of Educational Studies at the University of Surrey. Co-editor of the *European Journal of Psychotherapy, Counselling and Health* (Routledge), his recent publications include 'The Saviour in the Gap: a Comparison of Lacan with Freud and Laing', (with J Wall) and 'A Case Study Investigation: Is Therapy Possible with a Person Diagnosed With Dementia?' (with D Greenwood). He is particularly interested in the implications of continental philosophy for educational practice and research.

THE CONTRIBUTORS AND EDITORS xv

John Nugent is an independent consultant in the field of personal and organizational transformation. He has completed successfully the MSc in Change Agent Skills and Strategies (University of Surrey), with research into change agents' experiences of spirituality. He has special interests in Torbert's 'action inquiry' as a mode of consulting, which he has applied in major UK companies.

Venitha Pillay is a Lecturer in the Department of English at Springfield College of Education, Durban, South Africa. Her main areas of research interests are gender equity and gender and education management. She is currently serving on the editorial collective of *Agenda*, the only feminist journal in South Africa.

Judith A Preston is Training Manager for the West Company in Williamsport, Pennsylvania, USA, and a doctoral candidate in Adult Education at the Pennsylvania State University, USA.

Hiromi Sasai is Associate Professor at Hokkaido University, Japan, and a member of the Research Division for Lifelong Learning in the University. He specializes in is continuing higher education and lifelong learning policy. Until 1994 he worked for Japan's Ministry of Education.

Fred M Schied is Assistant Professor of Adult Education at the Pennsylvania State University, USA. He was awarded the Cyril Houle Prize for Adult Education for his book, *Learning in Social Context: Workers and Adult Education in Nineteenth Century Chicago* (1993).

Mark Selman is Associate Dean of Continuing Studies at Simon Fraser University, Canada. He is a co-author of *The Foundations of Adult Education in Canada* and is known for his work in the development of innovative degree programmes for mid-career students and on inner-city community education projects. His major research interests involve attempts to rethink liberal education and the mandate of universities in the light of social, economic and technological changes.

Robert Snell is currently Staff Tutor in Counselling and Psychotherapy at the University of Surrey, and a student counsellor and therapeutic and writing group facilitator at the University of Sussex. He trained as an art historian at the University of London and subsequently taught widely in art colleges. He is author of *Theophile Gautier: A Romantic Critic* (Oxford University Press 1982), contributes on art to *The Times Literary Supplement*, and is Reviews Editor of the *European Journal of Psychotherapy, Counselling and Health*.

Bobby Soobrayan is Senior Lecturer in the School of Education, University of Natal, Durban, South Africa. His major teaching, research and publication involvement has been in the areas of education policy and the economics of education.

Marion Spöring is Lecturer in Continuing Education at the Institute for Education and Lifelong Learning at the University of Dundee, Scotland. She is responsible for the Modern Languages programme and for the postgraduate Certificate in Teaching Modern Languages to Adults. With a German educational background, she has been teaching and researching both in Germany and Britain in the secondary and tertiary sector.

Paul Tosey is Lecturer and member of the Lifelong Learning Research Group in the School of Educational Studies, University of Surrey, UK. He joined the School's Human Potential Research Group in 1991. He was responsible for validating and co-ordinating for five years the highly successful MSc in Change Agent Skills and Strategies. His research interests include energy and spirituality in organizations, organizational transformation and transformational learning.

Jukka Tuomisto is Associate Professor of Adult Education in the Faculty of Education, University of Tampere, Finland. He is a member of the editorial staff of the *Yearbook of Adult Education*, the Vice-President of the Adult Education Research Society and a member of the ESREA steering committee. His main area of research is the theory and history of adult education, lifelong learning in the postmodern society.

Margaret Wallis is Principal Lecturer in the School of Information Management at the University of Brighton, England. In 1995 she was a member of the team which carried out the Review of Public Libraries in England and Wales for the British government.

Danny Wildemeersch is a professor of social pedagogy and andragogy at the universities of Nijmegen (Holland) and Leuven (Belgium). His research has focused on experiential, biographical and social learning in the context of adult and continuing education, of social movements and of organizational transformation.

Matthew Williamson is a Researcher in the School of Information Management at the University of Brighton, England. He holds a British Academy Professional and Vocational award and is researching the role of the public library in information service provision to jobseekers.

PART I
INTERNATIONAL POLICY

Chapter 1

Edgar Faure After 25 Years:
Down But Not Out

Roger Boshier

Going out with strangers

Go to the annual meeting of shareholders in just about any multinational corporation, settle into a soft seat in the rented hotel ballroom and, before too long, the smiling assistant will hand you the annual report. But, what's this, profit and dividends are on the back pages? Instead of such mundane matters, the front pages trumpet the virtues of lifelong learning. Some companies even disguise their business. Instead of being a bank they're a 'learning organization'.

Everyone has heard the story. Being a learning organization or engaging in lifelong learning is now essential to economic health. It enables organizations to compete in the global economy. Moreover, by properly deploying technology such as the worldwide web, individuals can all be linked into learning networks. Now everyone has access to education without having to endure the indignities of admissions procedures, let alone authoritarian and disciplinary teachers.

The adult educators who helped UNESCO and others build an architecture for lifelong education must be delighted. Their ideas have moved out of church basements, extension offices, institutes of adult education and community groups and into corporate boardrooms. As this book demonstrates, there is considerable enthusiasm for lifelong learning which, in its most exaggerated or utopian elaborations, is touted as the New Jerusalem which leads to a bountiful and promised land.

Much discussion around lifelong learning is infused with uncritical and utopic notions such as these. There is another side to this story and, in this opening chapter, the task is to examine the roots of lifelong education in the Faure (1972) Report and disentangle the threads of lifelong learning. At the centre of this analysis is the notion that lifelong education, as envisaged by Faure, is an entirely different creature to the one parading through corporate boardrooms dressed up as lifelong learning. For Gustavsson (1997) contemporary European notions of lifelong learning are a disguise for recurrent education. In our view, lifelong learning is recurrent education or human resource development (HRD) in drag. It might look splashy and alluring, it can preen and prance and strut its stuff. And it goes out at night. But what you see is not necessarily what you get. Remember what your mother said about going out with strangers?

Interests served

Learning To Be (Faure, 1972) the UNESCO report that proposed lifelong education as a master concept, was a response to the ferment of the 1960s. Constructed as a blueprint for educational reform in industrialized and so-called developing countries, it was launched on a wave of protest spawned by student activists, grave concerns about ecological catastrophe, crisis in French education and politics and the toxic remnants of the Vietnam war. At the time there were provocative critiques of formal education by innovative thinkers like Ivan Illich, John Holt, Everett Reimer, Paul Goodman, Paulo Freire and others whose work was nested in Anarchistic-Utopian or neo-Marxian perspectives (see Boshier 1994, Paulston 1977, 1996).

But now, 26 years after Faure, education is being transformed by neo-liberalism and architects of the new right have hijacked some of the language and concepts used while ignoring actions proposed by Faure. UNESCO deployed the notion of lifelong education as an instrument for developing civil society and democracy. In some ways the Faure Report echoed the British Ministry of Reconstruction 1919 Report, also billed as a 'design for democracy' (Waller 1956).

The OECD, which earlier made Herculean attempts to erect an architecture for recurrent education, now proposes lifelong learning (not education) as the strategy for the 21st century. The European Union has also co-opted lifelong learning into a neo-liberal way of thinking where it is an instrument to enhance economic effectiveness. Hence, the first sentence of the European Union (1993) White Paper that led to the Year of Lifelong Learning asked

'Why this White Paper?' The answer – The one and only reason is unemployment. We are aware of its scale, and of its consequences too. The difficult thing, as experience has taught us, is knowing how to tackle it' (1993: 1). If lifelong education was an instrument for democracy, lifelong learning is almost entirely preoccupied with the cash register.

Roadside mugging

The central point of this chapter is that Faure was mugged on the road to the 21st century. Bruised and abused by architects of the new right, Faure's language is in use but the emancipatory potential of the report is wounded. Worse still, this was not an isolated mugging or sneak ambush on a dark road. Everywhere Faure's concepts and language have been stolen by advocates of a form of globalization which has everything to do with corporate élites and economics and, in stark contrast to what Faure was saying, appears untroubled by the erosion of civil society and democratic structures. At the centre of this analysis is the notion that, despite the advancing age of Faure's commissioners and the tendency to dismiss their work as unduly utopian and impractical, the original report is still an excellent template for educational reform. It is one of the outstanding adult education texts of the 20th century and, moreover, some of the surviving authors have not bent to the winds of globalization (Rahnema and Bawtree 1997).

In an attempt to revive some of the Faure ethos, UNESCO recently commissioned another enquiry into the future of education. The Delors (1996) report, entitled *Learning: The Treasure Within*, rectified some of the imbalances in the Faure commission processes. For example, whereas all seven of the Faure commissioners were men, five of the fifteen Delors commissioners were women. But the ink was barely dry on the Delors book when the OECD, the European Union and several other national or international organizations issued their own reports on lifelong learning (eg DfEE 1995, Dohmen 1996, Tuckett 1997).

Making the Faure Report

In December 1965 UNESCO's International Committee for the Advancement of Adult Education received a paper from Paul Lengrand on continuing education and recommended that the organization endorse the notion of lifelong education. After the French riots of 1968 and the worldwide critique of higher education, René Maheu, Secretary-General of UNESCO, created an International Commission on the Development of Education. These days it would not be acceptable to ask seven men to undertake a worldwide enquiry into the state of education. However, despite the absence of women, Maheu attempted to secure commissioners who would represent contrasting cultural sets.

One of the Faure commissioners was Majid Rahnema, who had been a career ambassador for much of his life. In 1967 he was asked to form Iran's first Ministry of Science and Higher Education. Later he founded an Institute for Endogenous Development inspired by the work of Paulo Freire and other advocates of bottom-up development. As a cabinet minister he was vulnerable, but left Iran before the revolutionary upheavals that led to the demise of the Shah. After a period as a UNDP Representative in Mali, René Maheu invited Rahnema to join the International Commission for the Development of Education. At the time, he was living in France and able to accompany Chairman Faure to Latin America and other places (Boshier 1983).

Faure and Rahnema travelled to several countries, sometimes with other commissioners or members of the UNESCO secretariat. They received submissions from government sources and made special efforts to meet critics of education. As well, UNESCO commissioned papers from leading scholars, some of whom were staunch critics of formal education. *Learning To Be* was prepared at the UNESCO secretariat. Rahnema did more writing than others because he had more time than other Commission members. The Commissioners acted as individuals, not as representatives of their various governments.

Edgar Faure's appointment to chair the commission was intriguing. Before his death in 1988 he occupied every important post in the French government except the Presidency. He was one of France's most progressive Ministers of Education and, after the student revolts of 1968, masterminded sweeping reforms of higher education. Something of a renaissance man, he also wrote musical scores and detective novels. At the age of nineteen he had earned a doctoral degree. Later in life he had an old-fashioned sense of honour. Once, after having had his motives questioned in print by a magazine reporter, he challenged the writer to a duel. Notoriously near sighted, he was waving the pistol when a colleague talked him out of it. He was also something of a father figure and, in France, known affectionately as Edgar. Maheu's decision to ask Faure to head the International Commission was most fortuitous.

Concepts

There is no doubt that 1972 was a halcyon year for educational reform and at about the time delegates met at the Tokyo conference on adult education, UNESCO released *Learning To Be* (Faure 1972). 1972 was also the year of the influential UN Conference on the Environment, held in Stockholm, where delegates considered the Blueprint for Survival, assembled by the editors of the *Ecologist* (Goldsmith *et al.* 1972) and the Club of Rome Report *Limits to Growth* (Meadows *et al.* 1972). It was also the year of the progressive Worth (1972) Report in Alberta, influenced by recurrent education (Kallen 1979) and the Wright (1972) Commission Report (in Ontario) on the need for a 'learning society' (Pawlikowski 1998).

The architecture of the Faure Report was organized around three concepts, which concern the vertical integration, horizontal integration and democratization of education systems. A vertically and horizontally integrated and democratized system of education would result in what Faure called a learning society.

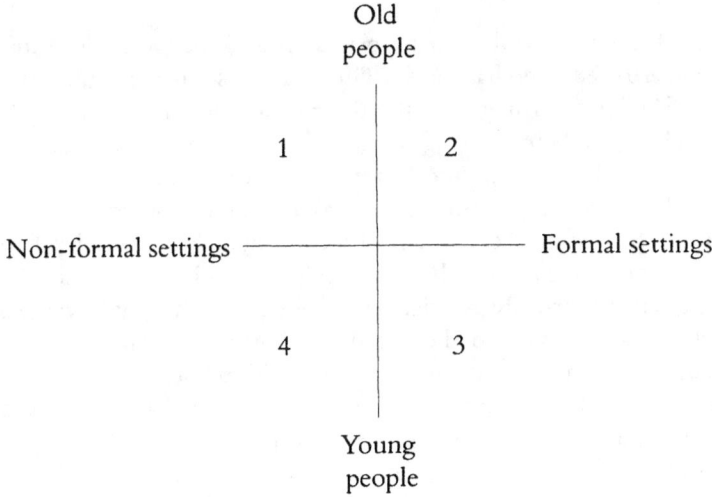

Figure 1.1 *Dimensions of lifelong education*

Figure 1.1 is our rendering of what the Faure commissioners were talking about. Extant educational systems assign an undue emphasis to the education of young people in formal settings (Quadrant 3). In a learning society, there would be a more equal distribution of resources and emphasis on each quadrant. Hence, there would as much emphasis on the education of young people in non-formal (Quadrant 4) as in formal settings (Quadrant 3). As well, there would be a considerable emphasis on the education of older people (adults) in formal (Quadrant 2) and non-formal settings (Quadrant 1). Each quadrant is the same size as every other. This is because in a learning society there would be a more or less equal amount of emphasis on education in each of the four quadrants. Moreover, although the vertical and horizontal lines in Figure 1.1 look solid, in a learning society they would be permeable. A child or adult learner would be able to swim back and forth, much like a fish, securing education in a formal setting today and a non-formal one tomorrow. The emphasis would not be on where a learner gets educated. Rather, the focus would be on the quality of what is learnt. As well, there would be a more relaxed attitude about prerequisites. Systems or, as Rahnema prefers to say, unsystems, would accept that learning does not always occur in linear ways and learners could secure access to higher levels without always having done the so-called prerequisites (Boshier 1983).

Learning and education

In parts of this book and in many places around the world, learning and education are used interchangeably. This can be a source of confusion. The notion of lifelong learning has little theoretical juice since learning (as an internal change in behaviour) is an inevitable corollary of life. Some advocates of lifelong learning specifically reject the use of 'learning' to label a psychological construct and, instead, use it as a gerund to describe an array of behaviours that sound very much like education. For example, Tough's (1971) adult learning projects have precisely the kind of deliberate and systematic qualities normally associated with education. It is, however, easy to understand the motivation of those wanting to promote learning. In the public mind, education is so indelibly identified with schooling that it becomes necessary to invoke a term that doesn't trigger all the bad thoughts about school. Having barely survived teacher incompetence and the brutality of Hastings Boys' High School in New Zealand, the author understands why some people want to use learning to distance it from schooling.

But practitioners should be wary because lifelong learning denotes a less emancipatory and more oppressive set of relationships than does lifelong education. Lifelong learning discourses render social conditions (and inequality) invisible. Predatory capitalism is unproblematized. Lifelong learning tends to be nested in an ideology of vocationalism. Learning is for acquiring skills that will enable the learner to worker harder, faster and smarter and, as such, enable their employer to better compete in the global economy. These days, lifelong learning often denotes the unproblematized notion of the savvy individual consumer surfing the Internet (Boshier *et al.* 1997, Boshier, Wilson and Qayyum 1997).

Education is the optimal (and usually systematic) arrangement of external conditions that foster learning. Education is a provided service. Lifelong education requires that someone – often government or other agencies –

develop policys and devotes resources to education that will preferably occur in a broad array of informal, non-formal and formal settings. Deliberate choices must be made. Hence, whereas lifelong learning is nested in a notion of the autonomous free-floating individual learner as consumer, lifelong education requires public policy and deliberate action. Lifelong learning is a way of abdicating responsibility, of avoiding hard choices by putting learning on the open market. If the learner as consumer doesn't decide to take advantage of available opportunities, then it is his or her fault. It is easier to blame the victim than overcome structural or psycho-cultural barriers to participation.

Learning and schooling

As well as distinguishing education from learning it is necessary to differentiate both of these from schooling. One consequence of not making these distinctions was observed when Ohliger (1974) compared lifelong education to a kind of life sentence of schooling. He noted that schools and even adult education institutions had the unhappy proclivity to 'define people as inadequate, insufficient, lacking and incomplete' and worried about the extent to which teachers, headmasters and all the other, not always welcome, attributes of formal education were now going to be foisted on adults for an entire lifetime.

Like the Faure commissioners, Ohliger preferred learning in natural settings – particularly from poets, folk-singers and actresses – and was a staunch admirer of Illich and his proposals for deschooling. In the 1970s his apprehensions appeared to stem from the idea that schooling is often a synonym for education, which it is not. Lifelong education opens access to a plethora of settings, of which the school is only one. Education concerns the deliberate arrangement of conditions that foster learning and educators are capable of placing value on education provided in out-of-school settings. Indeed, Rahnema, Ohliger and Tough (1971) all exemplify an anarchist-utopian tradition which, to this day, informs some vibrant forms of adult education (Paulston 1977).

Dimensions of lifelong education

The Faure Report made 21 major recommendations that pertained to four concepts – vertical integration, horizontal integration, democratization and the notion of the learning society.

Vertical integration

The vertical dimension of Figure 1.1 refers to the life-span aspect of lifelong education – the idea that education should occur throughout life, from cradle to grave. There are profound psycho-social and structural barriers that impede the ability of people to opt in and out of education throughout their lives. In a vertically integrated system, structural barriers would be removed by passing appropriate legislation (such as on paid educational leave). However, equal opportunity does not automatically translate into equal participation, because audiotapes inside people's heads send negative messages about returning to education as an adult. For this reason, it is naïve to think that merely facilitating access (as in distributed learning) will overcome the historic tendency for formal education to reproduce unequal power relations. Access, by itself, is not enough because it fails to overcome adverse psycho-cultural factors that impede participation (Boshier 1973). Faure's notion sparked extensive research on who participates in education and why but, as Rubenson (1996) observed, no such tendency is visible in recent constructions of lifelong learning. These days there is little evidence of concern with any need for equity.

Horizontal integration

Horizontal integration (or interaction) refers to the need to foster education in a plethora of non-formal as well as formal settings. The architects of lifelong education believed it is intolerable to have a situation where education secured in formal settings results in status and credentials, and that gained in non-formal, let alone informal settings, secures few credentials and no status. If someone needs to learn how to pilot their fishing boat, file their taxes, run their computer or get along better with their kids or spouse, does it matter if these things are learnt in school or in non-formal (out-of-school) or informal settings? What counts is what is learnt, not where it was learnt. There should be a more relaxed attitude about the value of what occurs in non-formal and informal settings. Such an approach should not necessarily lead to the banality of 'prior learning assessment' and the pedantry of assessing 'competencies'.

Typically, education in formal settings is paid for by government, is well organized, assigned adequate resources (despite what teachers and others say) and results in the award of widely recognized credentials. Education secured in non-formal settings is largely unorganized, struggles with meagre resources, is regarded as outside the mainstream and has a stigma attached to it. What Faure envisaged was not a dismantling of formal settings. Rather, the report proposed developing a more pluralistic and accessible array of opportunities for education throughout the life cycle. Integration or interaction is needed.

At present, formal and non-formal settings are like two parallel railway lines. Both cross the landscape but never touch. Formal settings have little to do with the non-formal. Hence, schoolteachers know little about the education children secure at their Scout or Guide group, at the summer camp, at the community centre or in other non-formal educational settings. As for informal settings, try and pull your kid out of school to take a trip to an exotic foreign country and listen to the headteacher complain. Learning in informal settings is not 'real' education.

There are informal, non-formal and formal settings for education. It is confusing to speak of formal or non-formal education because it suggests formality of processes is the issue. There are many non-formal educational settings (such as in prisons) where the processes are as rigid as those found in formal settings such as universities. The intent of this tripartite distinction is to portray education as something that occurs throughout society.

Educators, particularly those in formal settings, should not have a monopoly on education. Perhaps the worst thing that could happen to education is to have it fall into the hands of educators. In this analysis, formal settings are those age-graded credential-awarding schools, colleges, universities and similar settings, usually under the control of the Ministry of Education. Non-formal are 'out-of-school' educational settings such as community centres, churches, prisons, workplaces and suchlike. The instructional processes employed in non-formal settings may be quite formal. Finally, people also learn in informal settings through exposure to the media, through conversations, casual and incidental encounters in community settings, trade shows or public awareness campaigns. Although people learn in informal settings – and in AIDS-awareness and other campaigns it is important they do so – this is not education.

Democratization

Cutting across the need for vertical and horizontal integration is the need for democratization. In this context, democratization refers to the need to remove barriers that impede access to education and the more widespread involvement of learners in the design and management of their educational processes. These are linked. Simply creating access does not represent much progress unless learners become more extensively involved with creating their educational agenda.

Learning society

Lifelong education is utopian and calls for more than a mere tinkering with education systems. As the first recommendation of the Faure Report noted, it requires a restructuring of education systems. Ironically, it is probably easier to implement in countries where formal education is not well developed. A successful application of the principles of lifelong education would result in creation of a learning society (see Boshier 1980, Husén 1974, Edwards 1997, Wright 1972). Education, and access to it, would be an inalienable human right, as fundamental as clean water and a roof over your head.

Since 1972, the meaning ascribed to the notion of a learning society has paralleled neo-liberal restructuring and the ascendancy of the free market and, in this book, readers will find it constructed in a variety of ways. In his postmodern reflection, Edwards (1997) claimed there are now at least three different discourses which differentially construct the learning society.

1. *As an arena for citizenship* In this discourse there is an emphasis on providing opportunities for people to understand their roles as citizens in a social democracy. It is assumed that progress is possible, respectful communicative action desirable and it is the responsibility of citizens to learn what they need to know in order to take action to build a society that benefits the entire populace. In Canada, this conception was deftly described by Welton (1997). Support for it comes from professional groups such as the remnants of the Canadian Association for Adult Education or left-lobbies like the Council of Canadians. This is a discourse of education.
2. *As a learning market* In this discourse, institutions provide learning opportunities for individuals as part of their participation in and development of a market economy. Lifelong learning is a key instrument to foster economic development. Learning opportunities are put on an open market and individual learners, motivated by a need to update their skills – by unemployment, threat of redundancy or restructuring – 'rationally' choose from an array of offerings, taking advantage of those that appear to best meet their vocational needs. In Canada, support for this conception comes from right-wing think tanks like the Fraser Institute, the Conference Board or the Business Council of Canada. There is an unproblematized endorsement of technology and the web as the way to ensure that learning occurs. This techno-rational discourse assumes there is an objective reality and learners engage in rational decision-making. This is a lifelong learning discourse.
3. *As an arena for participation* Learning pervades life and, in this discourse, groups of learners, tribes or collectives have it as the centrepiece of an

active and socially-engaged lifestyle. People belong to overlapping networks or, as Edwards (1997) explains, neo-tribes. The notion of the market or even the idea of citizenship is displaced by the idea of education as a central activity through which collectivities pursue a wide assortment of goals. There is respect for organic intellectuals and the wisdom of ordinary folk. Education pervades society and is no longer the monopoly of formal settings or educators. Societies adjust structures so as to facilitate a commitment to learners and, in pre-adult education, there is a greater emphasis on information seeking and learning how to learn. This is a discourse of education.

In these discourses there is a shift from the provision of education (as a provided and planned service) to one of learning (as an individual activity driven by 'choice'). While different meanings are embedded in each discourse, the dominant idea in the second discourse is the notion of a market that allegedly responds to learner needs. Whether these are the 'real' needs of learners or designed to make them better cogs in the machinery of global competitiveness is not a subject of much debate. This is a far cry from what Faure was talking about.

Applications

There has been a shift from a neo-Marxist or anarchistic-utopian template for reform (the Faure Report) to a neo-liberal, functionalist rendition (OECD) orchestrated as a corollary of globalization and hyper-capitalism. As Rubenson (1996) noted: 'lifelong learning has become the *élan vitale* of economic life ... The erosion of a commitment to equality and the total dominance of the economic imperative is very evident ... With this perspective (of lifelong learning) ... accountability, standards, relevance to the needs of the economy and cost effectiveness have become the key issues, not equality.'

With the Minister of Finance now talking about lifelong learning more than the Minister of Education it has also become fashionable to claim that, although Faure was theoretically suggestive, there was no template for implementing lifelong education as a master concept. For example, Rubenson (1995: 3) claimed: 'the discussion on lifelong education and lifelong learning was a strange mixture of global abstractions, utopian aspirations and narrow practical questions which often lost sight of the overall idea.' Gustavsson (1997) mounts a similar critique.

After elaborating the theoretical underpinnings of lifelong education at the Second UNESCO World Conference (in Montreal, 1960) and aspects of 'application' at the Third (in Tokyo, 1972) there was an effort to implement

Faure's ideas. After 1972 the UNESCO Institute of Education in Hamburg produced a large amount of material and hosted many activities designed to foster the implementation of lifelong education (eg Dave 1976, Cropley 1977, 1979, 1980, Cropley and Dave 1978) and published special issues of the *International Review of Education* (eg 1974, 4 and La Belle 1982). In Scandinavia, Husen (1974) elaborated the concept, while similar work occurred in British Columbia (Niemi 1974), the UK (Griffin 1983), Australia (Crowley 1975, Duke 1976) and many other parts of the world. Hence, despite Rubenson's recollections of the 1970s and 80s, many UNESCO member nations took the Faure seriously and progressive policies were put in place.

For example, in Aotearoa/New Zealand one index of the seriousness attached to it was the fact more than 60,000 citizens participated in the Educational Development Conference (EDC) which had lifelong education as a centrepiece. After Faure and the Third UNESCO Conference on Adult Education, the New Zealand Education Amendment Act (1974) made clear the fact continuing education embraced vocational and non-vocational forms. Within the Farm Road and other branches of the Labour Party adult educators insinuated *Learning To Be* into political arenas. The impetus was utopian and infused with possibility (Boshier 1980). These days what Dakin (1996) called the 'optimism of the 1970s' has evaporated. As Benseman, Findsen and Scott (1996) showed in their recent analysis of the New Zealand situation, the emancipatory potential of Faure has been extinguished by the excesses of the new right, what Kelsey (1995) labelled 'The New Zealand Experiment'. By 1998 the government had embarked on a plan to turn universities into profit-making enterprises.

Contested meanings

Throughout the 1970s the UNESCO secretariat that produced *Learning To Be* laboured not far from policy researchers at the Centre for Educational Research and Innovation in the Paris headquarters of the OECD. While UNESCO researchers explored the labyrinths of lifelong education, those at OECD promoted the notion of recurrent education. Like VHS and Beta, it was probably inevitable that one would prevail at the expense of the other. Nevertheless, the extent to which the January 1996 OECD statement foregrounds lifelong learning and dismisses recurrent education as an 'earlier' but no longer useful way of thinking is stunning. There were only a few tips of the hat in the direction of Faure. Instead, the emphasis is on means whereby OECD members can prevail in the global economy. Look closely at the OECD rendering of lifelong learning and the name 'recurrent education' is clearly visible under the new paint on the bow. Moreover, the flag of OECD at the masthead remains unchanged.

The OECD renunciation of recurrent education in favour of lifelong learning was nothing less than stunning. The OECD blueprint was fuelled by concern about the global economy, workplace and individual learning. In the OECD work there was barely a hint of the democratic vision proposed by *Learning To Be* and not much that will help developing countries. Faure had a collectivist and anarchistic-utopian vision, wanted to legitimize learning in non-formal and informal settings and increase respect for organic intellectuals and learning from life.

OECD ministers foregrounded school and school-like settings. Secondly, their version of lifelong education is firmly welded to the world of work, competition and the exigencies of global competitiveness. Thirdly, the discussion on partners contains a threat to further erode public education. The state will have to become more 'strategic ... and set goals and targets ... towards gaps in provision' (OECD 1996: 4). If the desire to secure partners for lifelong learning had emanated from Faure an emancipatory perspective could be assumed. But when issuing from OECD ministers it means abandoning what have been state responsibilities to those of the free market. Hence, 'governments will seek to establish an environment that encourages individuals to take greater responsibility for their own and their children's learning and, where appropriate, permits a choice as to where they acquire the learning they need' (OECD 1996: 6).

Tuckett's (1997) *Lifelong Learning in England and Wales* was a British response to the European Year For Lifelong Learning. The discourse shaping this glossy publication was displayed in the opening paragraph: 'There is now a widespread consensus that it is going to be central to the economic well being of the UK for us to create a learning society. The arguments are familiar. In an increasingly global economy there is supposedly a marked economic advantage for societies with skilled, adaptable and learning workforces.' Then followed 34 pages about vocational training, workplace learning and qualifications. Despite a slight nod in the direction of homelessness, authors of *Learning To Be* would be hard-pressed to find anything recognizable in partnerships, mentoring, access and information technology.

Faure foregrounded the legitimacy of learning from life, recognized the importance of indigenous ways of knowing, resisted the metanarratives of western scientism and education and was committed to participation and democracy. *Learning To Be* did not ignore the importance of work-life and learning at work but nor did the UNESCO commission raise it to the kind of fetishistic levels of recent elaborations of lifelong learning. Whereas Faure foregrounded the needed for collectivity, conviviality and learning in groups, recent reports place an extreme emphasis on individual learning within an era of further cuts to public education.

Hazardous futures

It is sobering to note that within three years of the Faure Report, Lowe (1975) issued a prophetic warning about the dangers of lifelong learning: 'Governments may be tempted to concentrate ... on post-school formal education and occupational training, directing their attention to man as a producer and neglecting his family and civic functions' (1975: 29). Secondly, the disadvantaged, a traditional focus of adult education, 'are the people most likely to be even more neglected than they are now in the event of the introduction of a sophisticated system of lifelong education' (1975: 30).

Romantic yearnings

It would be easy to dismiss this chapter as romantic yearning for the utopianism of the 1960s and 70s or just another 'story' deployed to stiffen the sagging bulwarks of adult education. This possibility is worth examining because Edwards (1997), amongst others, claimed adult education is a closed field, now displaced by the more open discourse of lifelong learning. From his UK vantage point, adult education might seem closed but in Canada (and plenty of other places) its boundaries are more open and permeable than ever before, even though its professional organizations are disintegrating.

Adult education

Lengrand (1970) and Parkyn (1973) clearly demonstrate how lifelong education depended on adult education. Now Edwards and Usher (1996) are deeply suspicious of adult education 'stories' and evocations of (particularly male) tribalism. A postmodern perch nailed into something as dubious as lifelong learning is not a secure place from which to take pot-shots at adult education. But before adult educators deny or throw earlier commitments into a fragmented and market-driven postmodernism, it is salutary to remember the historic adult education preoccupation with equity. There are also trails blazed by the likes of RH Tawney, who thought nothing of riding a bike 60 miles to lecture miners in the coalfields and then, late at night, hoisting a leg for the long ride home. As well, there are Canadian women and men who organized desperately poor people into housing and marketing co-operatives and credit unions. It does not suffice to dismiss such material events as patriarchy or 'stories'. Whether adult education is considered open, closed or enormously confused, it is vastly premature to jettison lifelong education in the name of technocratic efficiencies and corporatism nested in lifelong learning.

Adult education is a highly multifarious phenomenon. Despite what Edwards might think or what Usher says when he reads from written conference papers (Bryant and Usher 1997) adult education is not grounded in some singular universal metanarrative. True, a profound process of balkanization is underway. But if any metanarrative is visible, it is the commitment to social justice. Adult educators need not apologize. Instead of rebutting Edwards it is better to pin our colours to the mast, trim the sails and sail off to the next struggle. Although it is increasingly difficult to stay on the course of social justice this is not the time to abandon the voyage.

In contrast to adult education, lifelong learning is a more singular (and, in our view, unsavoury) construction. Edwards and Usher (1996) suggested that those who can't give up their 'tribal affiliation' in adult education and get with the new metanarrative − postmodern lifelong learning − will resist by stridently restating their affiliations but might be better advised to seek counselling. They wonder if the tendency to strident behaviour might be 'gender-specific' − an act of resistance by recalcitrant males who yearn for the good 'old days of liberal education with a smattering of social justice'. Those in Britain now have an additional challenge, the Labour government 'style offensive' which is replacing village cricket, tea and scones, Beefeaters and grouse hunts with 'images of pulsing telecommunications, global business transactions, information technologies and buccaneering entrepreneurs' ('Cool Britannia! It's Goodbye Old and Traditional, Hello Young and Modern', *Vancouver Sun*, 14 November 1997, A21). If everything fails there is always counselling, a commodified kind of friendship.

International reach

Lifelong education is attracting considerable attention and constitutes a powerful template for educational reform. As authors of the remaining chapters demonstrate, it is a concept that can be viewed from many angles. It is sufficiently comprehensive and multifaceted to avoid being dismissed as just another metanarrative or totalizing discourse. Moreover, as Lengrand (1970) pointed out, there is no one 'pattern' for lifelong education since every country has its own forms and traditions. Nevertheless, the language of lifelong education (and learning) is spoken in places as far apart as East Africa (Nyrere 1976), Japan (Thomas *et al.* 1997, Wright 1997), Latin America (Torres 1990), Scandinavia (Larsson 1997), Australasia (Boshier 1980, Crowley 1975, Duke 1976), South Africa under the ANC (Gustavsson 1997) and many other places throughout the world.

This book, and the conference that preceded it, are important because they bring together authors from contrasting cultural backgrounds who share an interest in evolving conceptions of lifelong education or lifelong learning. In just about every place there is a focus on the vertical and horizontal dimensions and, in some parts of the world, the democratization of education. The dimensions of lifelong education are greatly shaped by the context in which they are applied and, as subsequent chapters demonstrate, much can be learnt by examining the way they play out in different settings.

References

Benseman, J, Findsen, B and Scott, M (Eds) (1996) *Adult and Community Education in Aotearoa/New Zealand*, Dunmore, Palmerston North.

Boshier, RW (1973) 'Educational Participation and Dropout: A Theoretical Model', *Adult Education*, 23, 4: 255-282.

Boshier, RW (Ed.) (1980) *Towards a Learning Society: New Zealand Adult Education in Transition*, Learningpress Ltd, Vancouver.

Boshier, RW (1983) *The Faure Report After Fifteen Years: A Television Interview With Majid Rahnema*, UBC Access Television, Vancouver.

Boshier, RW (1994) 'Initiating Research' in RD Garrison (Ed.) *Research Perspectives on Adult Education*: 73–116, Krieger, Malabar.

Boshier, RW, Mohapi, M, Moulton, G, Qayyum, A, Sadownik, L and Wilson, M (1997) 'Best and Worst-Dressed Web Courses: Strutting Into the 21st Century in Comfort and Style', *Distance Education: An International Journal*.

Boshier, RW, Wilson, M and Qayyum, A (1997) 'Education and American Hegemony on the World Wide Web: Old Wine in New Bottles'. Paper Presented at the Annual Conference of the Comparative and International Education Society (Western Region), University of Southern California, Los Angeles, 18 November.

Bryant, I and Usher, R (1997) 'The Personal and the Particular: Adult Educators, Post-Modernity and the Problem of Localised Knowledge', *Proceedings of the Crossing Borders – Breaking Boundaries Conference:* 80–84, University of London.

Cropley, AJ (Ed.) (1977) *Lifelong Education: A Psychological Analysis*, Pergamon, Oxford.

Cropley, AJ (Ed.) (1979) *Lifelong Education: A Stock-Taking*, Pergamon, Oxford.

Cropley, AJ (Ed.) (1980) *Towards a System of Lifelong Education: Some Practical Considerations*, Pergamon, Oxford.

Cropley, AJ and Dave, RH (1978) *Lifelong Education and the Training of Teachers*, Pergamon, Oxford.

Crowley, D (1975) 'The Role of the Government in Lifelong Education', *Unicorn* (Bulletin of the Australian College of Education), 1, 2: 38–49.

Dakin, J (1996) 'Looking Back' in J Benseman B Findsen and M Scott (Eds) *The Fourth Sector: Adult and Community Education in Aotearoa/New Zealand*: 21–37, Dunmore, Palmerston North.

Dave, RH (1976) *Foundations of Lifelong Education*, Pergamon, Oxford.

Department for Education & Employment (DfEE) (1995) *Lifetime Learning: A Consultation Document*, UK Department of Education & Employment, Sheffield.

Delors, J (Chair) (1996) *Learning: The Treasure Within*, UNESCO, Paris.

Dohmen, G (1996) *Lifelong Learning: Guidelines for a Modern Education Policy*, Federal Ministry of Education Science, Research and Technology, Bonn.

Duke, C (1976) *Australian Perspectives on Lifelong Education*, Australian Council for Educational Research, Melbourne.

Edwards, R (1997) *Changing Places: Flexibility, Lifelong Learning and a Learning Society*, Routledge, London.

Edwards, R and Usher, R (1996) 'What Stories Do I Tell Now? New Times and New Narratives for the Adult Education', *International Journal of Lifelong Education*, 15, 3: 216–229.

European Union (EU) (1993) *White Paper on Growth, Competitiveness and Employment* [http://europa.eu.int/en/record/white/c93700/preamble.html], European Union, Brussels.

Faure, E et al. (1972) *Learning To Be*, UNESCO, Paris

Goldsmith, E, Allen, R, Allaby, M, Davoll, J and Lawrence, S (1972) *Blueprint For Survival*, The *Ecologist*, London.

Griffin, C (1983) *Curriculum Theory and Adult and Lifelong Education*, Croom Helm, London.

Gustavsson, B (1997) 'Life-Long Learning Reconsidered', in S Walters (Ed.) *Globalization, Adult Education and Training*: 237–249, Zed Books, London.

Husén, T (1974) *The Learning Society*, Methuen, London.

Illich, I (1970) Deschooling Society, Harper and Row, New York.

Kallen, D (1979) 'Recurrent Education and Lifelong Learning: Definitions and Distinctions' in T Schuller and J Megarry (Eds) *Recurrent Education and Lifelong Learning*: 45–54, Kogan Page, London.

Kelsey, J (1995) *The New Zealand Experiment*, Auckland University Press, Auckland.

La Belle, T (1982) 'A Holistic Perspective on Lifelong Learning', *International Review of Education*, 28, 159–175.

Larsson, S (1997) 'The Meaning of Lifelong Learning', in S Walters (Ed.) *Globalization, Adult Education and Training*: 250–261, Zed Books, London.

Lengrand, P (1970) *An Introduction to Lifelong Education*, UNESCO, Paris.

Lowe, J (1975) *The Education of Adults: A World Perspective*, UNESCO, Paris.

Meadows, DH, Meadows, DL and Behrens, WW (1972) *The Limits To Growth: A Report For The Club of Rome's Project on the Predicament of Mankind*, Universe Books, New York.

Niemi, J (1974) *The Meaning of Lifelong Learning*, Association for Continuing Education, Vancouver.

Nyrere, J (1976) 'Liberated Man: The Purpose of Development', *Convergence*, 9, 4, 9–17.

OECD (17 January 1996) *Press Release Concerning Meeting of the Education Committee At Ministerial Level – Making Lifelong Learning A Reality For All*, OECD Press Division, Paris.

Ohliger, J (1974) 'Is lifelong education a guarantee for permanent inadequacy?', *Convergence*, 7, 2, 47–58.

Parkyn, GW (1973) *Towards A Conceptual Model of Life-Long Education*, UNESCO, Paris.

Paulston, R (1977) 'Social and Educational Change: Conceptual Frameworks', *Comparative Education Review*, June/October, 369–395.

Paulston, R (Ed.) (1996) *Social Cartography*, Garland Press, New York.

Pawlikowski, G (1998) *1972: A Good Year for Adult Education*, Unpublished MA thesis, University of British Columbia, Vancouver.

Rahnema, M and Bawtree, V (Eds.) (1997) *The Post-Development Reader*, Zed Books, London.

Rubenson, K (1995) *Lifelong Learning: Between Utopia and Economic Imperatives*. Paper Presented at the 1995 Nordic Conference on Adult Education, Gothenburg, Sweden.

Rubenson, K (1996) 'Lifelong Learning: Between Utopia and Economics', in D Kelly and J Gaskell (Eds.) *Debating Dropouts: Critical Policy and Research Perspectives on School Leaving*: 30–43, Teachers College Press, New York.

Thomas, JE, Takamichi, U and Schuichi, S (1997) 'New Lifelong Learning Law in Japan: Promise or Threat?', *International Journal of Lifelong Education*, 16, 2, 132–140.

Tough, A (1971) *The Adult's Learning Projects*, Ontario Institute for Studies in Education, Toronto.

Torres, C (1990) *The Politics of Nonformal Education in Latin America*, Praeger, New York.

Tuckett, A (1997) *Lifelong Learning in England and Wales*, National Institute of Adult Continuing Education, Leicester.

Waller, RD (1956) *Design For Democracy: An Abridgment of a Report of the Adult Education Committee of the British Ministry of Reconstruction Commonly Called the 1919 Report, With an Introduction 'The Years Between'*, Association Press, New York.

Welton, M (1997) 'In Defence of Civil Society: Canadian Adult Education in Neo-Conservative Times', in S Walters (Ed.) *Globalization, Adult Education and Training*: 27–38, Zed Books, London.

Worth, W (1972) *A Choice of Futures: Report of the Commission on Educational Planning*, Queens Printer, Edmonton.

Wright, DT (1972) *The Learning Society: Report of the Commission on Post-Secondary Education in Ontario*, Ontario Ministry of Public Services, Toronto.

Wright, M (1997) *Lifelong Education in Japan*. Paper Presented at the Annual Conference of the Comparative and International Education Society (Western Region), University of Southern California, Los Angeles.

Chapter 2

Public Rhetoric and Public Policy:
Analysing the Difference for Lifelong Learning

Colin Griffin

Now that lifelong learning has emerged on the stage of public policy new analytic issues arise, and this paper is intended to address the issue of how we think of lifelong education as an object of public policy.

The comparatively short journey from the universal, humanistic and visionary concept of its earliest exponents (Faure 1972, Lengrand 1975) to its current incorporation into national and international policy documents (DfEE 1996, European Commission 1995) has been accompanied by a certain amount of ambiguity, so that terms such as lifetime learning, life-span learning, or the learning society are sometimes used. But the basic form of the concept remains essentially the same, and it has during the last quarter century been explored from a wide variety of perspectives within philosophy, social science and education (Knapper and Cropley 1985, Wain 1987, Smith *et al.* 1990, Candy 1991, Duke 1992).

This journey, however, has not been linear, so that we cannot say the concept of lifelong learning has somehow ceased to be a concept and become a policy of governments and international organizations. Lifelong learning remains suspended, perhaps some might say stranded, between the two. For example, the visionary concept remains associated with its origins in international organizations such as UNESCO (1996) at the same time as scholarly journals such as the *International Journal of Lifelong Education* and *Lifelong Learning in Europe* explore lifelong learning both as concept and policy.

As in the case of other desirable social objectives, there is often a perceived gap between the ideal and the reality, the theory and the practice, the promise and the performance, or whatever. To speak of rhetoric and reality in the public policy of lifelong learning is to draw attention to just such a disjunction.

But what is the significance of this gap or disjunction? Is it inevitable? Can we do anything about it? Above all, does it matter? In order to address these questions, the significance of rhetoric for public policy needs to be analysed and its function in the public policy process needs to be reviewed. This is necessary because, for example, the pejorative associations of 'rhetoric' are of comparatively recent origin in the context of politics, and also because the policy process itself is much more problematic than the simplistic vision of 'closing the gap' between ideal and reality would seem to convey. We need to contemplate rhetoric as an intrinsic element of democratic politics, and policy as the outcome of a particular discourse as much as of the distribution of power in society.

There is no doubt that, nowadays, 'rhetoric' has negative connotations. Thus, although the *Shorter Oxford English Dictionary* defines it in neutral terms as 'the art of using language so as to persuade or influence others', and refers to 'elegance or eloquence of language', it also defines it as 'language characterized by artificial or ostentatious expression'. Nowadays, the word is often used to convey persuasive selling of some commodity or idea, with implications of insincerity, bad faith or even deception. At the same time, persuading people of the need for public policies, such as those which might bring about, for example, a universal system to support lifelong learning, would seem an inevitable consequence of believing in the concept in the first place. At least, this has to be the case in democratic societies. The fact is, that the literature of adult and lifelong education has always incorporated a major element of advocacy, persuasion and rhetoric. It has even been argued (Evans 1987) that the rhetoric of 'political millenarianism' on the part of some adult educators had the reverse effect of stimulating opposition to their ideals. Persuading politicians that lifelong learning should be an object of public policy entails the use of rhetoric on the part of all those who believe in it as a concept. The question is, what rhetorical strategies are most likely to succeed, and what kind of understanding of the policy process is necessary to grasp the significance of rhetoric in it?

The rather diverse sources for the following analysis consist of Aristotle's *The 'Art' of Rhetoric* (1975), which provides a typology of rhetoric as valid now as it was when it was written in c. 330BC, and Stephen J Ball's *Education*

Reform: A Critical and Post-structural Approach (1994) which provides an important framework for distinguishing policy as text and policy as discourse. These two sources, taken together, provide a powerful tool for investigating the function of rhetoric in relation to the policy process of lifelong education.

One of the most significant contributions of an Aristotelian analysis is that it reminds us that the meaning of 'rhetoric' has been determined by historical conditions. As the editor of the scholarly edition points out:

> 'Rhetoric, in the general sense of the use of language in such a manner as to impress the hearers and influence them for or against a certain course of action, is as old as language itself and the beginnings of social and political life' (Aristotle 1975: xi).

No claims to classical scholarship are being made here, of course: the *Rhetoric* is not regarded as one of Aristotle's important works, and indeed there has been doubt concerning his authorship. Moreover, there are other interesting issues touched upon which have a contemporary resonance, such as the relation between rhetoric and sophistry, but which cannot be pursued here.

For our purposes, what is relevant is the division of the work into three books, each of which more or less treats a different type or category of rhetoric. Having broadly defined rhetoric as 'the faculty of discovering the possible means of persuasion in reference to any subject whatever' (Aristotle 1975: 15) he identifies the following forms which such persuasion may take:

1. Rhetoric as logical proof

This type of rhetoric takes the form of a dialectical or syllogistic proof. It is the kind of persuasion which appeals to our reasoning faculty, whether inductive or deductive, so that the speaker presents a case based upon the consequences of doing something or not as though these followed logically. It is, of course, the persuasiveness of this form of argument that is the concern of the speaker, and it is certainly not being suggested by Aristotle that people could always be swayed by reason or logic alone. Indeed, in the first book of *The 'Art' of Rhetoric* he is at pains to argue that the appropriateness of the rhetorical form is determined by the kinds of public being addressed. These may be 'judges of the future', 'judges of the past' or simply disinterested observers of an orator's rhetorical skill (Aristotle 1975: xxxvii).

Rhetoric as the appeal to reason is one of the commonest forms underlying advocacy of public policy, and the reasons for this must be of interest in any attempt at policy analysis. Judging the audience, or making assumptions about what is likely to be an appropriate form of persuasion, is a major factor affecting likely outcomes. For example, it could be argued that the overwhelming majority of policy documents in the field of lifelong learning are intended to be read by those already convinced of the logical and political arguments in favour of it. What policy analysts call the 'policy community' is often constituted exclusively by a professional body, and it is the gap between the policy community and the other communities constituting society that is the cause of the gap between rhetoric and reality. The gap is a consequence of the social division which this implies, expressed as it often is by the phrase about 'preaching to the converted'.

The rhetoric of lifelong learning policy may thus take the form of logical proof or demonstration, that is, Aristotle's rhetoric which is a kind of syllogism. The technical definition of 'syllogism', according to the *Shorter Oxford English Dictionary* is:

> 'An argument expressed or claimed to be expressible in the form of two propositions called the premisses, containing a common or middle term, with a third proposition called the conclusion, resulting necessarily from the other two.'

There then follows an example in Latin. Fortunately, we do not need Latin to understand the significance of all this for the analysis of the function of rhetoric in the public policy process. Quite simply, this is the kind of argument that confronts us with the logical necessity of a particular outcome, given the conditions out of which the situation arises. So, for example, given conditions such as population growth or economic growth, or technological growth, then policies for the environment or lifelong learning and so on, are the only logical alternative to ecological or social disaster. Or, given the 'globalization' of the world economy and the information revolution, every society needs to institute a lifelong learning system in order to compete or even survive in these conditions. The form of the persuasive argument is therefore either/or, or from necessity. As will be seen, much of the policy rhetoric of lifelong learning takes this form.

Nevertheless, although its appeal is to reason and necessity, this remains essentially rhetorical. For one thing, the premisses, relating to matters of fact rather than logic, can always be challenged; so that, for example, government policies which threaten the interests of powerful groups are frequently challenged by such groups with respect to the factual premises upon which they are put forward. Also, the necessity for any particular policy solution can be challenged by an alternative policy to achieve the same desired outcome, in what Aristotle would call a political society. So the argument from syllogistic or dialectical reasoning can always be rejected by challenging the logic of either/or or necessity. In this sense, some kind of gap between rhetoric and reality might appear inevitable, and the function of rhetoric in the policy process would seem to be assured. We have in the doctrine of dialectical materialism a prime example of the argument from necessity, together with its associated triumph of force over political rhetoric.

2. Rhetoric as moral persuasion

Aristotle has reminded us that rhetoric can be based upon an appeal to reason, but in the second book of *The 'Art' of Rhetoric* he deals with a more familiar modern perspective: its appeal to our emotions and feelings. Since the model of classical Greek political life was oratory, the analysis does not directly engage with the moral systems which have since evolved in Western or other cultures, so we must understand 'virtue' as having a significance which cannot be exactly matched today. But Aristotle's point is that rhetoric must appeal to our emotional nature and needs:

> 'For the orator to produce conviction three qualities are necessary; for, independently of demonstrations, the things which induce belief are three in number. These qualities are good sense, virtue and goodwill; for speakers are wrong both in what they say and in the advice they give, because they lack either all three or one of them' (Aristotle 1975: 171).

By 'demonstrations' here, he is alluding to the logical proofs of the rhetoric of reason, as analysed in the first book. The pejorative implications of rhetoric, which were alluded to at the outset as characterizing our modern meaning of the term, are surely connected with an absence of these qualities identified by Aristotle, in particular goodwill. We suspect rhetoric because we do not attribute goodwill to those who are trying to persuade us of something, whether this is to buy something, do something or believe in something. In the case of much public policy rhetoric, it is no doubt the case that we are unconvinced that politicians are sufficiently committed to the policies they do lip-service to: there is a sense that policy commitments may be inauthentic or not entered into in good faith. In other words, the gap between rhetoric and reality is a credibility gap between policy-makers and ourselves. However, it has to be said that the policy process is fraught with possibilities for ambiguity and conflicts of meaning: how do we know that politicians, professionals and public share common meanings and understandings? This important aspect of the policy process will be analysed again in the context of Stephen Ball's concept of policy as discourse, later in this paper. Clearly, whilst there can be credibility gaps, there can also be gaps and discontinuities of meaning: the gap between rhetoric and reality may take many forms, and this needs to be acknowledged in any attempt to analyse the policy process itself.

We suspect the rhetoric of the market-place, of buying and selling, because it is often characterized by the 'artificial or ostentatious expression' of the dictionary definition. The political rhetoric of public policy may be cast in a more refined language but its essential purpose is the same. There is, of course, a moral dimension to the rhetoric of public policy which is absent from that of the buying and selling of the market-place, and although Aristotle's term 'virtue' is not the same thing as what we would now refer to under the name of morality, nevertheless there is frequently the appeal to general moral principles such as equity, justice, freedom, citizenship and so on. This appeal may be relatively open, or it may be unstated, which is why contemporary policy analysis invokes a concept such as discourse in order to disclose the problematic and ambiguous elements of the policy process itself: the same policy may be advocated from a variety of moral perspectives. The policy of rewarding successful enterprise may be couched in the same rhetoric as that of increasing employment; that of investing in education may invoke a moral rhetoric of equal opportunity for individuals at the same time as one of community solidarity.

In looking at the policy literature of lifelong learning, therefore, we should expect to find some rhetoric of moral persuasion. A common pattern is for the rhetoric of reason to be balanced by a degree of moral persuasion. So, not only is lifelong learning necessary for skill development and competitiveness, it is desirable for the sake of freedom and civilization itself:

> 'Lifetime learning also plays a key part in our wider social and cultural activity, yielding benefits extending beyond the economic field. The preservation and acquisition of knowledge and the ability of individuals to fulfil their personal capacity to learn are vital signs of a free and civilized society' (DfEE 1995: 6).

This mixture or balance of rational and moral persuasion is characteristic of the way in which lifelong learning, and before that adult education, have been advocated, both on the part of governments and professional bodies. In other words, both types of rhetoric have entered into policy literature and practice, which has been to the effect that adult and lifelong learning is rendered inevitable by the conditions in which we live, and that it is also desirable on moral and political grounds. An interesting by-product of this arises from the question of why, if lifelong learning is rendered inevitable by human and social conditions, does it need to be an object of policy in any case? This point has already been made. In a lecture given at Goldsmiths College, University of London marking the European Year of Lifelong Learning, Sir Charles Carter argued that:

> 'Life-long learning' ought to have no significance as an object of policy, for it is like "life-long breathing" – something which we cannot avoid while remaining conscious' (Carter 1997: 9–10).

Raising this issue, that of advocating something which must, of necessity, come to pass anyway, directs our attention towards an aspect of rhetoric which Aristotle introduced and which has come to be of considerable relevance in contemporary policy analysis. This is a view of rhetoric in its own right or for its own sake. Rhetoric, in other words, has its own meaning independent of its function as advocacy or persuasion in the policy (or any other) context.

3. Rhetoric as style

In the third book of *The 'Art' of Rhetoric* Aristotle discusses, less thoroughly than the other types, perhaps, the issue of the function of style in the rhetoric of persuasion, and in this comes closest to a contemporary or postmodern perspective on it. This implies a concern with form rather than substance or the medium rather than the message. As he says:

> '...it is not sufficient to know what one ought to say, but one must also know how to say it, and this largely contributes to making the speech appear of a certain character' (Aristotle 1975: 345)'

The form nowadays is less likely to be the speech of the orator of the city-states of ancient Greece and more likely to be that of the official paper or document. Nevertheless, these are just as likely to be couched in the rhetoric of style: 'for written speeches owe their effect not so much to the sense as to the style' (Aristotle 1975: 349). It could indeed be argued that modern communications, in whatever medium, are converging upon a rhetoric of style, or to be more precise, format. Format analysis of policy documentation or communication may itself contribute to a perception of a gap between rhetoric and reality, the style and the substance. The glossy format of policy documentation corresponds to the rhetorical flourishes of oratory, and policy analysis increasingly needs to take this into account.

Postmodern analysis focuses precisely upon such issues in communication, so that the whole idea of a 'gap' between rhetoric and reality itself becomes problematic. From a theoretical point of view, the opposition of rhetoric and reality in policy discourse is based on a particular set of assumptions associated with structuralism and which are challenged by more contemporary thought:

> 'Unlike the structuralists who confined the play of language within closed structures of oppositions, the poststructuralists gave primacy to the signifier over the signified, and thereby signalled the dynamic productivity of language, the instability of meaning, and a break with conventional representational schemes of meaning. In traditional theories of meaning, signifiers come to rest

in the signified of a conscious mind. For poststructuralists, by contrast, the signified is only a moment in a neverending process of signification where meaning is produced not in a stable, referential relation between subject and object, but only within the infinite, intertextual play of signifiers' (Best and Kellner 1991: 20–21).

What we now call postmodernism is a movement whose origins lie partly at least in poststructural theory, and its focus upon language and meaning in the construction of reality can be related to precisely those raised by the analysis of rhetoric as style: the discourse of rhetoric is a constituent of reality itself. For Aristotle, the rhetoric of the political orator was only a manifestation of 'the dynamic productivity of language'; from a postmodern perspective, the rhetoric is the reality and there cannot be a 'gap' in any meaningful sense between them.

This argument will now be pursued by turning to just such a poststructuralist analysis in the context of education policy. In this context, Stephen Ball distinguishes between policy as text and policy as discourse. Policy as text represents a structuralist approach, which text is 'read' as an appeal variously to logical argument or moral persuasion, these being the final justification for that 'authoritative allocation of values' which public policy is traditionally taken to represent:

> 'Here, somewhat under the influence of literary theory, we can see policies as representations which are encoded in complex ways (via struggles, compromises, authoritative public interpretations and reinterpretations) and decoded in complex ways (via actors' interpretations and meanings in relation to their history, experiences, skills, resources and context)' (Ball 1994: 16).

Policy as text and policy as discourse

Ball proposes an alternative way of approaching policy, one which reflects Aristotle's intimation that the rhetoric constitutes the reality of politics, and this he does citing Foucault's concept of discourse:

> '...we need to appreciate the way in which policy ensembles, collections of related policies, exercise power through a production of "truth" and "knowledge", as discourses. Discourses are practices that systematically form the objects of which they speak ... Discourses are not about objects; they do not identify objects, they constitute them and in the practice of doing so conceal their own invention' (Ball 1994: 21).

PUBLIC RHETORIC AND PUBLIC POLICY

Lifelong learning is precisely such a 'policy ensemble' or 'collection of related policies', and the rhetorical element in its construction as policy discourse is central to our understanding of it. In other words, the rhetoric of lifelong learning is the reality of it, and in this sense there is no 'gap' between one and the other.

The rhetoric of lifelong learning may be constituted according to Aristotle's typology, that is by way of logical argument or moral persuasion, or it may be constituted by style or discourse, as these concepts have been developed in postmodernism. Between them, it is argued, these provide us with a framework for analysing lifelong learning as public policy. This may be illustrated by analysing three diverse but current policy-related documents.

First, considering them as text, there are the arguments from need, necessity or inevitability, corresponding to Aristotle's rhetoric as logical proof:

> 'Rapid technological and organizational change mean that, however good initial education and training is, it must be continuously reinforced by further learning throughout working life. This must happen if skills are to remain relevant, individuals employable, and firms able to adapt and compete' (DfEE 1995: 6).

> 'Life's rapidly changing challenges and demands necessitates skill-developing lifelong learning. However, using traditional forms of instruction as the primary format for literally life-long learning is not feasible, affordable nor desirable. The objectives pursued by responsible, adult learners demand a form of self-directed learning that is more active and open to real life' (Dohmen 1996: 94–95).

> '...the countries of Europe today have no other option. If they are to hold their own and continue to be a reference point in the world, they have to build on the progress brought about through closer economic ties by more substantial investment in knowledge and skills' (European Commission 1996: 1).

> 'This country needs to develop a new learning culture, a culture of lifelong learning for all. It is essential to help the country and all of its people meet the challenges they now face, as they move towards the twenty-first century' (NAGCELL 1997: 3).

This is the rhetoric of need and necessity in the context of policy as text. In the same sources, we can trace the rhetoric of moral persuasion:

> 'Alongside the economic motivation, individuals have a powerful incentive in the wider benefits learning can bring. And for society at large there are social benefits which can spread far beyond individual learners' (DfEE 1995: 20).

'...since we are social beings, we must continue working together to develop more flexible community structures that will ensure our survival, just as we must seek sensible new paths that will lead us out of this acute impasse in a peaceable, humane and democratic way' (Dohmen 1996: 2).

'...social exclusion has reached such intolerable proportions that the rift between those who have knowledge and those who do not, has to be narrowed' (European Commission 1996: 30).

'For the nation, learning will be the key to a strong economy and an inclusive society. It will offer a way out of dependency and low expectation towards self-reliance and self-confidence. In doing so, it will be at the heart of the Government's welfare reform programme. We must bridge the 'learning divide' which blights so many communities and the widening gap, in terms of employment expectations and income, between those who have benefited from education and training and those who have not' (DfEE 1998: 3).

The European Year of Lifelong Learning in 1996 resulted in policy texts such as these, in which the rhetoric of logic and that of moral persuasion were balanced, and such quotations as these also clearly demonstrate lifelong learning as what Ball calls a 'policy ensemble', rather than a policy as such.

But there is also a policy discourse here, which can similarly be related to Aristotle's concept of rhetoric as style, which has to do as much with our own responses to policy as to its texts: 'We read and respond to policies in discursive circumstances that we cannot, or perhaps do not, think about' (Ball 1994: 23). In accepting the historical inevitability and embracing the moral imperatives of lifelong learning as public policy, we should bear in mind that rhetoric is intrinsic to the discourse, and the gap between the rhetoric and the reality can never be closed.

References

Aristotle (1975) *The 'Art' of Rhetoric*, Loeb Classical Library Aristotle Vol XXII, Harvard University Press, Cambridge, Mass.
Ball, S (1994) *Education Reform: A Critical and Post-structural Approach*, Open University Press, Buckingham.
Best, S and Kellner, D (1991) *Postmodern Theory: Critical Interrogations*, Guilford Press, New York.
Candy, PC (1991) *Self-Direction for Lifelong Learning*, Jossey-Bass, San Francisco.
Carter, C (1997) *Recognising the Value of Informal Learning*, Learning From Experience Trust, Chelmsford.
Delors, J (Chair) (1996) *Learning: The Treasure Within*, UNESCO, Paris.

Department for Education & Employment (DfEE) (1995) *Lifetime Learning: A Consultation Document*, DfEE, London
Department for Education & Employment (DfEE) (1996) *Lifetime Learning: A Policy Framework*, DfEE, London.
Department for Education & Employment (DfEE) (1998) *The Learning Age: A Renaissance for a New Britain* (Green Paper; Cm 3790), The Stationery Office, London.
Dohmen, G (1996) *Lifelong Learning: Guidelines for a Modern Education Policy*, Federal Ministry of Education, Science, Research and Technology, Bonn.
Duke, C (1992) *The Learning University: Towards a New Paradigm?*, SRHE/Open University Press, Buckingham.
European Commission (EC) (1995) *Teaching and Learning: Towards the Learning Society* (White Paper on Education and Training), EC, Brussels.
Evans, B (1987) *Radical Adult Education: A Political Critique*, Croom Helm, London.
Faure, E et al. (1972) *Learning To Be: The World of Education Today and Tomorrow*, UNESCO, Paris.
Knapper, C and Cropley, A (1985) *Lifelong Learning and Higher Education*, Kogan Page, London.
Lengrand, P (1975, revised edition) *An Introduction to Lifelong Education*, Croom Helm, London.
National Advisory Group For Continuing Education & Lifelong Learning (NAGCELL) (1997) *Learning for the Twenty-First Century* (The Fryer Report), NAGCELL, London.
Smith, R et al. (1990) *Learning to Learn across the Lifespan*, Jossey-Bass, San Francisco.
Wain, K (1987) *Philosophy of Lifelong Education*, Croom Helm, London.

Chapter 3

Lifelong Learning and the European Union:
A Critique From a 'Risk Society' Perspective

Barry J Hake

Lifelong learning has recently re-emerged as a hot topic on the policy agendas of inter-governmental organizations, multinational enterprises and national governments. Since the early 1990s the European Union (EU) has demonstrated growing interest in lifelong learning and it is now the core principle of EU education and training policies. This chapter offers a critique of EU policies on lifelong learning in terms of sociological theories of globalization, reflexive modernization and risk society. It is argued that EU policy priorities fundamentally ignore the dynamics of social and cultural (re-) production in post-industrial societies at the structural, organizational and individual levels.

Lifelong learning on the EU agenda

An important milestone in EU policy development was the *Memorandum on Higher Education* (CEC 1991a), while other documents dealt with vocational training (CEC 1991b) and open distance learning (CEC 1991c). The *Memorandum* made ambitious proposals for universities to 'support an expanding knowledge-based economy' and proposed that universities should contribute to the single labour market for highly qualified personnel, widen access to higher qualifications, and offer opportunities for regular updating and renewal of knowledge and skills.

This was taken up in the 1993 White Paper on *Growth, Competitiveness and Employment* (CEC 1993). Given the single European market and increasing mobility of capital, goods and services and labour, attention focused upon Europe's capacity to innovate, to introduce new knowledge and know-how in the market place and effective applications of new technologies. A key element was the low level of education and training of the European workforce. The White Paper proposed that:

> 'All measures must therefore necessarily be based on the concept of developing, generalising and systematising lifelong learning and continuing training. This means that education and training systems must be reworked in order to take account of the need ... for the permanent recomposition and redevelopment of knowledge and know-how' (CEC 1994: 136–137).

Similar formulations are found in documents on social policy. With a view to 'preserving and developing the European social model' of social partnership and cohesion as the basis of the quality of life, the EU pointed to the creation of 'a transparent and dynamic system of lifelong learning' as a key priority in order to secure high levels of employment and promote social cohesion (CEC 1994).

The 1995 White Paper *Teaching and Learning* (CEC 1995) offered a baseline for the EU's general approach to education and training policy. It appeared on the eve of the European Year of Lifelong Learning (EYLL) in 1996. EYLL involved consciousness-raising activities to put lifelong learning on the policy agenda throughout the EU and comprised conferences, seminars, exhibitions, festivals and adult learners' weeks. It sought to inform governments, organizations and individuals of the need for lifelong learning and their own responsibility for investing in education and training. Lifelong learning was also a central feature in the Green Paper on the information society (CEC 1996) and *Accomplishing Europe through Education and Training* (CEC 1997a). EU policies on lifelong learning are driven by economic globalization and Europe's competitiveness. They are based upon recognition of global competition and specific European problems including the single internal market, high levels of structural unemployment, labour immobility, and recognition of an education and training lag. The core of EU policy is an almost aggressive post-Fordist understanding of technologies applied to the production of goods and services. This has major implications for its understanding the organization of work in post-industrial society and an instrumental approach to lifelong learning. Deregulation policies are increasingly extended to the workplace and involve flexibilization of working conditions and workplace learning (CEC 1997b). The key words are deregulation, flexibility, employability and individual responsibility for investments in education and training. Information and communication technologies are regarded as the motors of the knowledge/information/learning society. EU policies assume that the knowledge and skills to enhance employability are now available to individual consumers in the globalized market place for open and distance learning. This is now the chorus of every policy paper at European and national level.

Lifelong learning and late modernity

There might seem to be some similarity between the EU's view of the challenges presented by global competition for lifelong learning and the literature on late modernity. A more sophisticated view of lifelong learning can be distilled, however, from theories of late modernity, which examine globalization in terms of reflexive modernization, de-traditionalization and risk situations. In Western Europe, this demands at least a rudimentary acquaintance with the core ideas associated with the work of sociologists such as Beck, Bourdieu and Giddens, whose ideas contribute challenging insights about globalization and lifelong learning in late modern societies. Three core ideas guide their understanding of the dynamics of late modernity and the centrality of lifelong learning:

1. the globalization of access to communication and information
2. the de-traditionalization of social life
3. the need for continuous reflexivity in all aspects of life in the 'knowledge society'.

Giddens (1994) views globalization as characterized by the emergence of instantaneous communication without regard to national borders and the availability of knowledge without respect for space and time. He argues that increasing availability of knowledge leads to the de-traditionalization of social life when distant sources of information may exert more influence than traditions associated with the nation, region or locality. Social life is consequently disembedded from tradition as globalization of knowledge erodes local values and habits. Giddens argues that routine application of knowledge to social life is the most dynamic feature in the organization and transformation of social life. When the application of knowledge becomes the constitutive element of late modern societies this leads to 'institutionalized reflexivity'.

Giddens' discussion of the structural necessity of reflexivity provides one way of understanding why learning is a permanent feature of social life in late modern societies. His case is that globalization, de-traditionalization and institutionalized reflexivity lead to the centrality of learning in all social relations. Reflexivity and learning become inherent to all forms of social interaction; learning comes to pervade all of society. Late modern societies are typified by learning challenges and necessity of lifelong learning as a structural characteristic. Beck has introduced a key new dimension to our understanding of the necessity of learning in late modernity. There is now no question of opting out if one is to survive in the learning society. Globalization confronts societies, organizations and individuals with new learning challenges as they struggle to cope with and survive in a rapidly changing and unstable environment. For Beck this means that late modern society is a 'risk society' in which institutions, organizations and individuals are 'at risk' with respect to their chances of survival in the face of change and uncertainty. This directs attention to possibly negative consequences of the all-persuasive emphasis upon learning in late modern social formations. Access to learning opportunities and survival skills may be unevenly available in late modern social formations. This has important consequences for those 'at risk' and carries with it the potential of social exclusion.

The social distribution of lifelong learning: social allocation mechanisms and social space

The construction of national educational systems as mechanisms for social allocation was inherent to the modernization of European society from the late eighteenth century onwards. Late modernity has apparently lost faith, however, in the grand narrative of modernization associated with the Enlightenment project. Globalization and individualization seem to lead inevitably away from collective interventions associated with national educational systems towards the deregulation of markets, consumer choice and individual flexibility as the keys to social allocation (Bisovsky and Stifter 1996).

Recognition of the social allocation function of adult and continuing education first entered the policy sphere in Europe during the late 1960s and early 1970s. It became an important aspect of government policy as a compensatory social (re-) allocation mechanism through second chance general education for adults. This was part of the broader temporary alliance between social-democratic reformism and the capitalist drive to modernize both itself and society. In this sense education and training for adults became an integral part of educational expansion as 'simple modernization' (Beck 1986). Its relationship to vocational education and on-the-job-training remained indistinct, however, and manifested itself at best in arrangements for paid educational leave for employees in a number of European countries. Reformist initiatives of the early 1970s contributed to the expansion of opportunities for social mobility and the opening up of social space in Western European (Bourdieu 1979). This produced new structures of social allocation which modified the opportunities for significant segments of the population to secure a place in an expanding labour market. An end came to this process during the 1980s, when growing unemployment and educational cuts effectively worked towards a closure of social space and the structures of opportunity provided by public education.

Western European societies seem to be now entering a period when the management of social space and opportunities for social mobility are increasingly associated with radical changes in mechanisms for social allocation and access to the labour market. On the one hand, social structure continues to demonstrate a remarkable conservatism in terms of inequalities of educational opportunities between the social classes. Nonetheless, the coherence of the social classes is less distinctive than in the past as new cleavages have appeared. These cleavages within social classes are marked by the differentiation between traditional and modernizing milieus with their own distinctive habitus, which include different ways of 'thinking' about the importance of education and learning (Vester et al. 1993). On the other hand, class origins no longer provide individuals with a clear sense of social destination, while the new emphasis upon self-realization, also by way of education, enhances the need for individual reflexivity. Social origin now provides but one of the many sources for working upon individual modernization and no longer provides a guarantee of social integration in late modern society (Vester et al. 1992).

It is at exactly this point that changes in social allocation mechanisms assert their importance in the distribution of opportunities and risks. Greater stress upon the market and individual choice lead to increasing differentiation in the capacities of individuals to manage their own social allocation as part of the 'individual modernization' process (Beck 1986). This can threaten social integration and the potential implications for social exclusion are expressed in the 'one-third, two-thirds society' debate (Berger and Sopp 1995). For one part of the population, individualization leads to greater opportunities to make choices, to the differentiation of life worlds, milieus and lifestyles, and to greater variety in individual life courses. For another part of the population, the necessity of individual choice turns into a risk situation. Detachment from traditional sources of individual identity can give rise to disorientation and anomie which Beck has termed 'anti-modernity' (Beck 1993). In conditions of economic, political and social transformation and dislocation, especially in the ex-Communist societies, we find this most clearly reflected in the retreat to pre-modern sources of identity such as nationalism, regionalism, localism, racism, ethnicity and xenophobia. This ambivalence of late modern social formations raises the issue as to whether post-industrial society, on the one hand, creates new forms of social participation and identity formation or, on the other hand, is a source of social exclusion and the fixation of traditional identities. Of interest here is the question as to the empirical distribution of these opportunities and risks in a structured and institutionalized manner, and in particular the contribution of education and training to social allocation throughout the life course.

When lifelong learning demands a radical rebalancing of investments in education and training throughout the life course, attention must be focused on the development of new social allocation mechanisms which emphasize the market, individual choice and a consumerist orientation towards education and training. Research must devote far more attention to opportunity and allocation mechanisms, whether within or outside the workplace, which facilitate or hinder the access of adults to learning opportunities. Given demographic pressures, this should also focus on older workers who will no longer be excluded from work and for whom new arrangements are required in most work organizations. All this requires studies of learning taking place outside of formal education, the accreditation of work-based learning, and flexible learning routes for adults.

The learning organization as an arena for social allocation

Differentiation of social allocation mechanisms is increasingly manifested in organizations as increasingly important locations for learning associated with organizational reflexivity. The 'learning organization' now commands the high ground in discourses about organizational learning. Significant here is that many examples of the learning organization have often been drawn from the area of civil society – such as voluntary organizations and (new) social movements (Eyerman and Jamison 1991) – rather than from governmental organizations or business enterprises (Field 1995). Indeed the worlds of business and government organizations are specific and limiting instances of learning organizations.

From Schon onwards, the 'learning organization' has been considered as a 'socio-cognitive structure' which organizes learning and generates knowledge (Schon 1971). There is a significant move towards a permanent interface between productive and learning processes in organizations. Handy (1990, 1992) has described the 'learning organization' in terms of:

> '...organizations which encourage the wheel of learning, which relish curiosity, questions and ideas, which allow space for experiment and for reflection, which forgive mistakes and promote self-confidence.'

Emergence of the 'knowledge organization' is the specific manifestation of globalizing tendencies (Winslow and Bramer 1996). The rise of the knowledge sector, knowledge organizations and knowledge workers entails that social organizations become powerful learning environments where learning becomes the central unifying focus, indeed the lubricant, of organizational activities (Gibbons *et al.* 1994). This 'educationalization of organizations' is manifested in permanent activities which support both organizational and individual learning.

The learning organization becomes a key arena for social allocation with distinctions between three groups of employees in work organizations:

1. the permanent core
2. the contractual fringe
3. the flexible periphery (Nasta 1993: 21).

This intra-organizational division of labour has consequences for the distribution of learning opportunities among different categories of employees and can be regarded as the new class structure of post-industrial society. There is a tension here between investment in lifelong learning and trends in the reorganization of work, flexibilization of employment practices and emphasis upon individual 'employability'. Changes in employment practices lead towards the flexibilization of employment with fixed-term contracts, part-time work and reduced rights to training. This generates an emphasis upon 'employability' which is predicated upon the willingness of employees to accept their individual responsibility for investing in education and training.

These developments have negatively affected investment in older workers, especially among men, whose participation in work has significantly declined in the last decade. Growing participation by women in the labour force has been manifested above all in part-time work, on short-term contracts, without rights to paid holidays, pensions and training. Furthermore, in many European countries significant barriers prevent minorities from gaining access to the labour market. In both public and private enterprises, there is widespread evidence of discrimination in recruitment, promotion and investment in their education and training (Glastra and Schedler 1996). In a broader sociological perspective, these exclusionary social allocation mechanisms in organizations manifest the development of risk situations associated with marginalization processes affecting the contractual and flexible fringes in organizations.

Attention must not be restricted to those most at risk of social exclusion from participation in learning organizations, such as less-qualified young adults, especially young men, those with the least formal education, men in 'non-work' situations (Wilson 1996), re-entering women, ethnic minorities, migrants and older (working) adults. It is increasingly important to focus on emergent risks among those whose qualifications were traditionally thought to provide 'bureaucratic' career security but who now have to plan for 'flexible' careers (Brown 1995). They increasingly find themselves in risk situations at the cutting edge of the knowledge society and learning organizations.

Learning to survive in the learning society

A corollary of organizational reflexivity is intentional learning as a vehicle for 'individual reflexive modernization' (Beck 1986). The dynamics of late modernity give rise to new risk situations when identity and biography become reflexive projects for individuals (Giddens 1991: 53). Institutionalized socialization into standard biographies has been disrupted by individualization processes. Individual biographies understood as 'trajectories in social space' (Bourdieu 1987) lose their sharp contours as class, gender, religion and ethnicity as traditional sources of identity are denuded by the expansion of biographical resources. Individuals increasingly have to assume personal responsibility for formulating their identities and life courses. This leads to the expansion of risk situations.

Institutionalization of the life course, with key transitions between the 'preparation phase in education', the 'activity phase in employment' and the 'withdrawal phase in retirement' have become increasingly recognized as risk situations. The youth phase has been progressively extended through longer formal schooling, while the 'late adulthood phase' has been both brought forward and thus prolonged. The active phase of employment has declined in importance within the life course. Late modernity adds to the number of transitions in the life course and introduces new risk situations. Combinations of periods of work and non-work are becoming increasingly significant for adults. Structural unemployment among men, together with increased participation by women in education, paid employment, particularly in part-time and less qualified work, is enhancing this development. Complexity and differentiation in women's employment careers are becoming the norm for men (Dausien 1996). The lives of the elderly appear to manifest a growing heterogeneity in life courses, which are enhanced by trends towards variable engagement in employment and retirement. Such developments contribute to the expansion of the number of transitions, status passages and risk situations in late modern societies.

Globalization introduces a profound transformation of daily life where individuals can chose between diverse sources of identity. Globalized mediation of lifestyles is counteracted, however, by processes of the local and differential reception and interpretation which may undermine or reinforce available sources of identity. Biographical resources required 'to work' on the construction of individual biography are of paramount importance in strategic life-planning (Pineau 1995). According to Dominice (1990), the life course appears to be turning into an experimental sphere where 'biographical skills' have to be developed without the help of known curricula. Alheit (1995) argues that the fundamental provocation within an understanding of 'biographical learning' is its insistence on a different way of learning in relation to the transitions characteristic of late modern society. Alheit (1992) defines this biographical competency as 'The ability to attach modern stocks of knowledge to biographical sources of meaning and, with this knowledge, to associate oneself afresh'.

Despite the universal distribution of threats and risks posed by modernization, individuals differentially develop the capacity to independently organize their biographies. This 'biographical competency' is perhaps *the* key compentency which can enable individuals to cope with the risks associated with transitions and critical life events. Biographical competency becomes the key competency to ensure individual survival in late modernity (Antikainen *et al.* 1996). This directs attention to the relationships between learning in transitions and 'biographical work', where individuals make use of intentional learning in coping with transitions and risks. Whether in institutional or informal settings, intentional learning can become a biographical resource for individuals in the strategic planning of individual life courses. This can focus upon the diversity of learning in a variety of settings varying from formal education, mutual learning in groups, and self-directed learning. Increasing differentiation of learning settings also contributes to diverse learning careers and complex 'educational biographies'. This conjunction of learning settings and educational biographies can throw much light upon the utilization of intentional learning as a biographical resource in transitions and risk situations.

Conclusions: learning to survive in the learning society

Lifelong learning has been embraced by the EU as 'the solution' to the competitiveness of European economies in the global market-place. Its calls for flexibilization, employability and individual responsibility effectively ignore, however, the dynamics of 'risks' at the structural, organizational and individual levels of the learning society. Structurally, the emergence of increasingly differentiated arenas for the management of social allocation in late modern societies demands continuing research on policies for lifelong learning and the organization of opportunity structures and allocation mechanisms at the European and national levels. It is necessary to critically examine these structures in the degree to which they differentiate between the public and market sectors in the creation of structures of opportunity to acquire qualifications and access to the labour market. This involves differences in the respective responsibilities of governments, firms and individuals for investment in education and training.

The relevance of this analysis will be directly obvious with regard to current public debates about government and employers' responsibilities in response to flexibilization of employment, and the growing emphasis on the individual's responsibility for investment in education and training in order to maintain their 'employability'. Much more attention has to be directed to the learning organization as an arena of social allocation and exclusion where social space is increasingly fractured at the organizational level. Despite rhetoric about the threat of social exclusion, current EU policies on education and training fail to recognize the Europeanization of labour markets, largely on the basis of immigration from outside the EU. Ethnic responses to 'the other' in labour market and training policies have to be examined in terms of their effects on the closure of social space, displacement and social exclusion. Participation in intentional learning is, furthermore, far from equally distributed and available as a biographical resource.

This becomes a vital factor with regard to the educational biographies which will be developed by individuals in response to the new emphasis upon employability and individual responsibility for education and training. It is also necessary to focus on the role of learning in relation to other forms of social participation and the development of educational biographies associated with non-work careers. If education and training as key biographical resources continue to be unequally distributed, this means that the capacity to 'learn to live a life' in changing and uncertain times will become a vital factor in determining social exclusion. In other words, the biographical work required to learn to survive in the learning society is a risk situation which confronts an ever-growing number of Europeans. The learning society is a risk society.

References

Alheit, P (1992) 'The biographical approach to adult education', in W Mader (Ed.) *Adult Education in the Federal Republic of Germany: Scholarly Approaches and Professional Practice*: 186–221, University of British Columbia, Vancouver.

Alheit, P (1995) 'Biographical learning. Theoretical outline, challenges and contradictions of a new approach in adult education', in P Alheit *et al.* (Eds) (1995) *The Biographical Approach in European Adult Education*, : 57–74, ESREA, Vienna.

Antikainen, A *et al.* (1996) *Living in a Learning Society: Life Histories, Identities and Education*, Falmer, London.

Beck, U (1986) *Risikogesellschaft. Auf dem weg in eine andere Moderne*, Suhrkamp, Frankfurt.

Beck, U (1993) *Die Erfindung des Politischen, Zu einer Theorie reflexiver Modernisierung*, Suhrkamp, Frankfurt.

Berger, P and Sopp, P (Eds) (1995) *Sozialstruktur und Lebenslauf*, Opladen.

Bisovsky, G and Stifter, C (Eds) (1996) *Wissen fur Alle: Beitrage zum Stellenwert van Bildung in der Demokratie*, Edition Volkshochschule, Vienna.

Bourdieu, P (1979) *La Distinction*, Editions de Minuit, Paris.

Bourdieu, P (1987) 'The biographical illusion', *Proceedings of the Centre for Psychological Studies*, Volume 14.

Brown, P (1995) 'Cultural capital and social exclusion: some observations on recent trends in education, employment and the labour market', *Work, Employment and Society*, 9, 1, 29–51.

CEC (1991a) *Memorandum on Higher Education in the European Community*, Luxembourg.

CEC (1991b) *Vocational Training in the European Community in the 1990s*, Luxembourg.

CEC (1991c) *Memorandum on Open and Distance Learning*, Luxembourg.

CEC (1993) *Growth, Competitiveness and Employment: The Challenges and Ways Forward for the 21st Century*, Luxembourg.

CEC (1994) *European Social Policy: A Way Forward for the Union*, Luxembourg.

CEC (1995) *Teaching and Learning: Towards the Learning Society*, (Luxembourg.

CEC (1996) *Living and Working in the Information Society: People First*, Luxembourg).

CEC (1997a) *Accomplishing Europe through Education and Training*, Luxembourg.

CEC (1997b) *Partnership for a New Organization of Work*, Luxembourg.

Dausien, B (1996) *Biographie und Geschlecht*, Donat, Bremen.

Dominice, P (1990) *L'histoire de vie comme processus de formation*, Harmanttan, Paris.

Eyerman, R and Jamison, A (1991) *Social Movements: A Cognitive Approach*, Polity Press, Cambridge.

Field, J (1995) 'Citizenship and identity: the significance for lifelong learning of Anthony Gidden's theory of life politics', in M Bron and M Malewski (Eds) *Adult Education and Democratic Citizenship*: 31–46, ESREA, Wroclaw.

Gibbons, M *et al.* (1994) *The New Production of Knowledge*, Sage, London.

Giddens, A (1991) *Modernity and Self-Identity: Self and Society in the Late Modern Age*, Polity Press, Cambridge.

Giddens, A (1994) 'Living in a post-industrial society', in U Beck A Giddens and S Lash *Reflexive Modernization*, Polity Press, Cambridge.

Glastra, FJ and Schedler, PE (1996) 'Opportunities, obligations and the market imperative', *New Community*, 22, 3, 539–544.

Handy, C (1990), *Inside Organizations*, BBC, London.

Handy, C (1992) *Managing the Dream: The Learning Organization*, Gemini, London.

Nasta, T (1993) *Change Through Networking in Vocational Education*, Kogan Page, London.
Pineau, P (1995) 'Life histories considered as an art of existence', in P Alheit *et al.* (Eds), *op cit.*, 44–56.
Schon, DA (1971) *Beyond the Stable State*, Temple-Smith, London.
Vester, M *et al.* (1992) *Neue soziale Milieus und pluralisierte Klassengesellschaft*, Hanover.
Vester, M *et al.* (1993) *Soziale Milieus im gesellschftlichen Strukturwandel*, Bund, Koln.
Wilson, WJ (1996) *When Work Disappears*, Knopf, New York.
Winslow, C and Bramer, WL (1996) *Future Work: Putting Knowledge to Work in the Knowledge Economy*, Free Press, New York.

Chapter 4

Critical Perspectives and New Beginnings:
Reframing the Discourse on Lifelong Learning

Michael Collins

'The transfer from the idea of initial training to that of continual education is the mark of modern pedagogy' (Faure *et al.* 1972: 117).

'Is not this the time to call for something quite different in education systems? Learning to live, learning to love the world and make it more human; learning to develop in and through creative work' (Faure *et al.* 1972: 69).

Vision and rhetoric

A quarter of a century has gone by since UNESCO published the visionary Faure Report *Learning To Be: The World of Today and Tomorrow*. In the interim global geopolitical conditions have radically altered. We live in different times.

Broadly speaking, we can trace the reasons for this global restructuring to the effects of the neo-conservative ascendancy on the one hand, and the virtual collapse of state capitalist command economies ('socialism as it has already existed') on the other. These historically significant eventualities were not anticipated by the utopian Faure Report and similar visionary publications of the era, such as *No Limits to Learning: Bridging the Human Gap* (Botkin et al. 1979) and *The Learning Society* (Husén 1974), which embraced lifelong learning as a guiding principle for global development. And in the meantime, lifelong learning, or lifelong education (the terms are used interchangeably), has become little more than a catchphrase within the conventional discourse on education.

The terms lifelong learning and lifelong education tend to be used interchangeably. Often one term (more often it seems to be lifelong learning) also stands in for the other. This is the case for this chapter and, no doubt, for other chapters in the book. In somewhat stricter usage, lifelong learning refers to the actual experience of the individual learner or that of groups of learners. The focus then is on what psychological characteristics, social settings, classroom practices, curriculum formulations and so on come to bear in shaping actual learning experiences in their immediacy-as specific attributes and events in specific individuals (or groups) and in particular contexts.

In a broader sense, one that would be more aptly defined as lifelong education, lifelong learning as it is used in this chapter also refers to the nature of the educational vision, state policies and forms of institutional restructuring which effect the way relevant educational opportunities can be made more or less accessible to us over our entire life span. From this more encompassing definition a political role for the adult educator, though not necessarily for the detached observer of lifelong learning as a mere object of study, re-emerges around the critique and transformations required to make lifelong learning a central feature of the global learning society envisaged by Faure (1972), Husén (1974) and Botkin et al. (1979).

The lifelong learning concept is now invoked, even enthroned, as the guiding principle in identifying the needs of young adults as a special demographic category, particularly with regard to the problem of 'school failure' (King 1992, Oran 1993). References to lifelong learning occur with regularity in contemporary studies on educational philosophy, life-span transitions, educational assessment, civic learning (citizen education), socio-economic development, spirituality, the arts, outdoor education, the environment and international perspectives. And such studies are not confined to publications concerned primarily with developments in our schools, colleges and universities.

Of critical interest here are commentaries on lifelong learning which argue for the need to foster a new dialogue on the relationship between initial education and adult education (Belanger 1991) and, by the same token, for connecting schools and community organizations (Heath 1994). Another critical insight developed within the discourse on lifelong learning has to do with 'learning to unlearn' (Rinne 1991). This perspective offers a thought-provoking variation on the popular theme, also prominent in lifelong learning discourse, around 'learning how to learn' (Smith 1982). The recent sources cited here are of significance in that they suggest how real substance might now be incorporated during the late 1990s to the rhetoric on lifelong education and lifelong learning in the schools.

The notion of learning to unlearn, for example, opens up possibilities for a new line of investigation within the discourse on lifelong learning. One of the axioms of modern adult education practice is that mature students typically bring something of relevance to any learning situation, whether or not they have much in the way of formal education, by virtue of their past experience. Thus, a primary task for the competent adult educator is to help students draw meaningfully on relevant aspects of their already acquired stock of knowledge (past experience) in the process of learning.

This pedagogical insight about the relevance of past experience makes sense. It confirms the view that significant learning can take place at any time during an individual's life span and it is the basis for encouraging adult students who have little or no formal education to have confidence in their capacity to learn. What this important insight has tended to overlook, however, is the extent to which past experience actually blocks the capacity to learn. (This concern about the negative aspects of past experience refers not only to content, but also to the time and circumstances of events that constitute negative experience.) Thus the dysfunctional aspects of past experience that hinder the capacity to learn need to be unlearnt before the potential for individual development can be fully realized.

The case for learning to unlearn can also be applied to social groups. For example, what is it about a social group's collective and distinctive past experience – its historically acquired stock of knowledge – that gets in the way of a clear understanding of what really impedes its development? The concept of learning how to unlearn can be usefully enlarged upon, and theorized, for social groups as well as individuals, with the emergence of a critically informed discourse on lifelong learning.

Given the enthusiastic endorsement of the lifelong concept since the appearance of Edgar Faure's *Learning To Be* (1972) and Torsten Husén's *The Learning Society* (1974), it is not surprising to encounter these days overwhelming advocacy for 'making lifelong learning a way of life'. Numerous professional associations and major educational conferences have adopted the term in their titles. It is almost two decades since a leading American adult educator of the time, Alan Knox, specified 'a positive attitude toward lifelong learning' as a key proficiency for adult educators (Knox 1979: 9). To the extent that this specification speaks to a commitment that can now be taken for granted among adult educators, they find themselves sharing a standpoint that claims our very existence, in all its dimensions, is a lifelong learning process.

The kind of commitment for adult educators envisaged here is one that can still be drawn from the aims of Thomas Hodgskin, co-founder of the mechanics' institutes movement, for whom 'the education of a free people will always be directed more beneficially for them when it is in their own hands' (Collins 1972: 37). This is the kind of pedagogical commitment described for us by Paulo Freire (1974) in *Pedagogy of the Oppressed*. It is the kind of political commitment identified by Raymond Williams (1990: 157) who viewed the emancipatory potential of adult education as 'part of the process of social change itself' – as part of history in the making – rather than as a mere reaction to social change in the larger society.

Adult Education, Inc. – the kind of adult education exemplified by management-oriented human resource development (HRD), government-sponsored mandatory training for the unemployed and programmes for the continuing career development of professionals – will look after itself. Though most adult educators must realistically earn a living within the enterprise of Adult Education, Inc., it has little real need for the moral and political concerns which vocationally committed adult educators bring to their work.

Yet Adult Education, Inc. occupies a large part of the arena in which the discourse on lifelong learning is played out. In this arena there is also a crucial alternative role for a critical practice of adult education. This is a role that can still be relevantly, and prudently, guided by Faure's vision of lifelong learning from the grounds defined for an adult education legacy by the likes of Thomas Hodgskin, Paulo Freire and Raymond Williams.

Critical commentaries

But what has been the practical import of the mounting lifelong learning discourse of the past two decades? No doubt educators and others who do not take education for granted are more attuned to the fact that significant learning is not confined to our schools, colleges and universities. Yet it cannot be reasonably asserted that these institutions, along with our other important public service agencies, have been systematically transformed in line with the livelong learning concept in the years since the Faure Report and Torsten Husén's recommendations for *The Learning Society*. Many seemingly impressive programmatic changes and add-ons to conventional curriculum formats may have been undertaken under the rubric of lifelong learning, but there have been no fundamental changes in the institutional structures that shape our schools, colleges and universities.

No doubt ongoing fiscal restraint has had something to do with re-enforcement of a traditional conservatism and the development of a survival mentality in these institutions which work against initiatives for radical transformations from within. Perhaps understandably, the tendency within our institutions has been more towards accommodation with outside pressures in the hope of 'saving the turf' rather than for creative, admittedly riskier, moves to bring about entirely new institutional arrangements. Clearly, something quite different is envisaged here to the now familiar kind of restructuring ('downsizing') that comes in reaction – as a perceived necessity – to budget cutbacks.

It is true that we have witnessed a widespread deployment of advanced technology to educational services of all kind in recent years. (The corporate sector is in favour of such innovation.) And in most Western and developing countries formal education is becoming more accessible to people of all ages and backgrounds. Organizations such as the British Open University, which was once rightly regarded as non-traditional, and educational institutions wedded from the start to alternative forms of distance education as their major commitment have become more widely accepted. However, the approaches of even these 'alternative' or 'non-traditional' institutions tend to legitimize their status with the same conventional trappings (formal examinations, standardized curriculum, degrees, certificates, continuing education units and organizational designations) as our mainstream institutions. The British Open University, once spurned by most of the academic establishment in the UK, is now very much part of that establishment. It competes rather successfully with other universities in a league table foisted on the university community by the government, having relinquished some of its founding commitments – most notably to making higher education more widely accessibly to working class adults (Tunstall 1974: ix). Though distinguished founding figures of the Open University made a relevant connection between their aims and those of the adult education movement, including the Workers' Educational Association, it was clear from the outset that legitimation as a recognized university was more of a central concern to them than the realization of educational egalitarianism (Perry 1977).

These 'alternative' institutions may offer something a little different in education, but they can hardly be viewed in their present form as the means of 'making lifelong learning a way of life', as far as the vast majority of people are concerned. The fact of the matter is that more than a quarter of a century after the Faure Report, and despite prolific discourse around the lifelong concept, the nature and organization of pedagogy today, our formal and informal systems of education and the preparation of teachers (especially) and other public service practitioners (in general) remain substantially unchanged.

Rather than embracing lifelong learning as a guiding principle for fundamental change, our educational institutions, public service agencies and workplaces have taken the concept on board largely as an add-on to existing approaches to curriculum formation and programme design, to teaching and counselling, and to views on learning and development. Accordingly, the term lifelong learning is routinely incorporated into conventional curriculum discourse as a sensible acknowledgement that what the schools have to offer should be followed by some form of further education.

We can look to mainstream literature on continuing professional education programmes, human resource development (HRD), and competency-based instruction for examples of how the conventional positivistic discourse on curriculum design and programme development persists (Rothwell and Cookson 1997). These programmatic responses to an imperative for skill training and for altering individual behaviour are increasingly advanced under the rubric of lifelong learning. For 'program leaders and visionaries centre their careers in lifelong education – and promote the fields of program planning and lifelong education' (Rothwell and Cookson 1997: 56).

Competency-based education (CBE) is virtually the paradigm case of an overly reductionist approach to programme planning, curriculum design and classroom organization. Critical analysis of CBE as it emerged in the USA, especially with regard to its manifestation in adult education (Collins 1983), focused on the practical shortcomings that an educational approach steered entirely by technical rationality entails. With a shift in focus to CBE's ideological role, its prevalence within the conventional discourse on lifelong learning can be viewed as having to do with the legitimation of *status quo* institutional arrangements and the constraining positivistic approaches to educational programme planning those arrangements manage to sustain. While it is important to know about their use, it is also important to recognize the extent to which conventional approaches to educational programme design emerge from a straight line functionalist perspective that evades more creative impulses and political strategies required for a radical transformation of our education systems.

Largely absent from this contemporary functionalist discourse around lifelong learning is any real sense of its moral and political implications. The critical debates around the issue of autonomy and control, especially as exemplified in the case of mandatory continuing education (MCE), are no longer a significant feature of the discourse on lifelong education. Thus the critical question posed by John Ohliger (1974) in his thought-provoking essay 'Is Lifelong Education a Guarantee of Permanent Inadequacy?' is not being addressed. Ohliger warned us to distinguish between the idea of lifelong education 'from cradle to grave' (Faure 1972: 8) and the very real prospects of schooling from cradle to grave as a means of surveillance and control. Though Ohliger drew critical attention to the link between mandatory continuing education (along with its coercive effects) and lifelong learning, the trend towards MCE has gained momentum in recent years. Opposition to the tendency, once advanced on moral and political grounds, is now scarcely discernible.

More significant is the absence from lifelong learning discourse of a political sensibility – of a willingness to discuss relevant political strategies – needed for real progress towards an emancipatory pedagogy of global proportions. It is as though liberal and progressive educators of the left have been thoroughly browbeaten by charges of 'political correctness' (a term that originated with the ideological new right in the USA to beat upon the 'radical' educational practices and policies introduced during the 1960s and early 1970s).

Political imperatives

Yet the work of Paulo Freire, from the internationally acclaimed *Pedagogy of the Oppressed* (1974) on, remains instructive for us. Education (and, hence, educators) cannot be neutral. It is significantly shaped by contesting ideological interests, in the course of political struggle. There is no neutral ground. Self-deluding educators who claim to be neutral are merely aligning themselves with the predominant ideological interest of the time. (Ironically, these ideological interests are currently supported by a deceptive rhetoric about the 'end of ideology' which now pervades mainstream conservative, liberal and social-democratic political parties alike.)

Dialogue is central to Paulo Freire's pedagogy. A problem-posing approach which examines crucial issues of everyday life as they are experienced by ordinary people worldwide challenges *status quo* arrangements and is inherently political. Dialogue as pedagogy finds theoretical expression, highlighting its relevance for fostering social learning processes, in the concept of communicative action (Habermas 1984, 1987). Thus, a view of lifelong learning that focuses on the acquisition of communicative competence as conceptualized by Habermas, and actually practised in the internationalist pedagogy of Freire, goes against the manipulative effects of marketplace advertising, mainstream media, soundbite messages, career politicians and professional 'spin doctors'.

In our very attempts to facilitate dialogue, the basis of genuinely democratic communicative action, we constitute a politicized counter-discourse that questions the way everyday events at local and international levels are presently determined. We are talking here about continuing education for the practice of democracy. It is through the inevitably politicized dialogue of Paulo Friere and communicative action as conceptualized by Habermas that democracy is learnt and the everyday lifeworld (or civil society), including aesthetic and spiritual as well as economic and political dimensions, can be sustained. This is what lifelong learning that matters should be about.

Within two days of the 1 May 1997 general election which Britain's Labour Party won in a landslide, representatives of teachers' unions demonstrated outside the new Prime Minister's official residence at Number 10 Downing Street. Their intent was to hold the Labour Party to very minimal commitments around its pre-election promise of making education a top priority. (The actual commitments included reducing class sizes and cutting back on public funding for selective private schools.) Clearly, there is more to direct political action than public demonstrations and government-lobbying, but we can hope that this kind of pressure on Britain's new social democratic government – 'You say education is a top priority, so show us' – prefigures more in the way of political action from educators at local and international levels.

In the months following the UK election it became clear that New Labour would endorse the private school sector (McLeod 1997). Meanwhile, prospects for publicly funded schools in socially deprived areas, especially in view of a teacher shortage, looked bleak. Hopes that the universities would receive more adequate funding after years of restraint under the previous government were shattered. University students not entirely supported by their parents have to take on a heavy debt load. Meanwhile, New Labour's welfare-to-work training schemes are merely a variation on an approach established under the previous administration. They turn out to be very much akin to the training programmes for welfare recipients and young unemployed people that have been deployed in North America for some time.

The point is that New Labour, like social democratic parties in power elsewhere (in the Canadian provinces of British Columbia and Saskatchewan, for example), has revealed itself to be thoroughly permeated with neo-conservative free-market ideology. In these circumstances, appropriate political work for those wedded to a notion of lifelong learning expressed by Faure and others should focus on pressing governments like New Labour, which claim the legacy of progressive social democracy, to allocate much-needed resources to expanding publicly funded education as the necessary precursor of creative transformations in prevailing educational systems.

Accessibility: connecting school to community

Ensuring widespread accessibility to its educational institutions is fundamental to the learning society envisaged by Edgar Faure and Torsten Husén. In advanced industrial countries the provision of elementary and secondary school education for young people is now virtually taken for granted. And in these countries, during the past three decades, the accessibility of post-secondary education has increased significantly. Yet the provision of elementary education as a right of all citizens has yet to be achieved for the vast majority of the world's population. In the 'developing' countries education at both secondary and post-secondary levels is reserved only for the elite and the very fortunate. For the majority, access to state-funded elementary schooling, to the extent that it exists, is still regarded as a privilege. This is the situation which prevails a quarter of a century after Faure in the Indian subcontinent (India, Pakistan and Bangladesh), in most of Africa and in much of South America.

Even in the most highly developed of Western countries, access to education varies significantly. Elementary and secondary schools for the children of the lower classes are not nearly as well-resourced as those attended by middle and upper-class children, who are more likely to go on to university education and get the better jobs. It is simple as that. For schooling is still very much a factor in reproducing class status, in social and economic terms, a fact which runs counter to claims that class analysis no longer has any relevance when it comes to looking at the structure of advanced capitalist societies. In view of the unevenness in the quality of publicly funded education that persists within most developed countries, studies informed by class analysis such as *Schooling in Capitalist America* (Bowles and Gintis 1976), *Reproduction in Education Society, and Culture* (Bordieu 1977) and *Education and the Working Class* (Jackson and Marsden 1966) remain instructive.

The question for our times concerning accessibility of post-secondary education is whether universities should or will continue to be regarded as the be all and end all. On this matter, The Faure Report (1972: 203) noted that 'in general, the concept of lifelong learning rules out any form of final, pre-mature selection' and then made the following recommendation:

> 'As educational systems become more diversified and as possibilities for entry, exit and re-entry increase, obtaining university degrees and diplomas should become less and less closely linked to completing a predetermined course of study' (1972: 203-4).

Improved access to educational institutions and the growth in non-traditional approaches are in keeping with an emerging discourse on the need for community involvement and inter-agency co-operation in creating a learning society. This emphasis on community and agency involvement in partnership arrangements with the educational establishment undoubtedly has a lot to do with the search for extra resources in these times of continuing budget cutbacks. Yet the renewal of a concern for connecting community development initiatives with education and the sense of collective identity entailed mark a departure from the political ideology of the Thatcher era, which disparaged notions of community and society as significant contexts for human action. From that ideological perspective there is no society in this collective sense (according to Mrs Thatcher, who had a marked influence on many of Reagan's policy advisers); rather it viewed the political economy as being made up of individuals who go out each day to compete with each other in the market-place and rely on home and family for support and sustenance. Now, at the end of the 1990s, the relevance of society and community, along with prospects for historical development, is returning to mainstream political discourse.

At the institutional level, the community school concept holds out a great deal of promise in terms of lifelong education and the development of a learning society. Community schools are intended to be accessible to all age groups and, since all schools are potentially community schools, they represent a considerable resource-base for their immediate neighbourhoods.

In these times, especially, it does not make economic sense to use publicly funded schools only during the hours when the conventional programme for children and young people from kindergarten to graduation is under way.

For the community school to fulfil its potential within a learning society, a wider role for the teacher in today's society, a new conception of classroom practices and a more creative approach to curriculum development in line with community needs are required. In addition to a familiarity with the usual classroom management techniques (a central preoccupation in most teacher education programmes), teachers should become conversant with strategies for developing a relevant learning programme in conjunction with other teachers and community representatives on school councils. At the same time, teachers should understand the need to forge partnerships with parents, community members and various human service organizations, as part of a collaborative process to define educational and community issues and to establish the most effective way to share resources. As key participants, teachers will need to become more committed to, and proficient in, the practice of community development as an educational and motivational process.

Community schools, though not a new idea, could well be integral to the defence of publicly funded education against the onset of privatized charter schools and other market-driven educational initiatives that foster the cult of competitive individual advancement. With the incorporation of adult education approaches – which call for focusing on the learning needs of teachers, parents and various community-based stake-holder groups as well as children – community schools can provide the catalyst for enabling the people to take education into their own hands. Further, in broadening its purpose to extend into the community while simultaneously bringing the community into the classroom, the publicly funded community school becomes a meaningful response to the radical 'deschooling society' polemic advanced by Ivan Illich (1970) against conventional schooling.

Renewing the commitment

Even if we cannot go home again to the utopian vision of the Faure Report and the other texts on the learning society it represents, they help us understand how lifelong learning calls for educators to align themselves with the practical day-to-day interests of ordinary people – with the need to foster civil society globally through an internationalist pedagogy.

> 'We remain convinced that the question of lifelong education, the decisions to take and the paths to follow in order to achieve it are the crucial issues of our time, in all countries of the world, even in those which have yet to become fully aware of this idea' (Faure *et al.* 1972: 182).

A quarter of a century beyond Faure, these are times for educators to adopt political strategies for adding substance to 'this idea'.

References

Belanger, P (1991) 'Adult education in the industrialized countries', *Prospects*, 21 (4), 491–500.
Botkin, J *et al.* (1979) *No Limits to Learning: Bridging the Human Gap*, Pergamon Press, Oxford.
Bourdieu, P (1977) *Reproduction in Education Society, and Culture*, Sage, London.
Bowles, S and Gintis, H (1976) *Schooling in Capitalist America*, Routledge, London.
Collins, M (1972) 'The mechanics' institutes: Education for the working man?', *Adult Education: Journal of Research and Theory*, 33 (1), 37–47.
Collins, M (1983) 'A critical analysis of competency-based systems in adult education', *Adult Education Quarterly: Journal of Research and Theory*, 33 (3) 174–183.
Faure, E *et. al.* (1972) *Learning To Be: The World of Education Today and Tomorrow*, UNESCO, Paris.
Freire, P (1974) *Pedagogy of the Oppressed*, Seabury, New York.
Habermas, J (1984) *The Theory of Communicative Action, Vol. I*, Beacon Press, Boston, MA.
Habermas, J (1987) *The Theory of Communicative Action, Vol. II*, Beacon Press, Boston, MA.
Heath, S (1994) 'The best of both worlds: connecting schools and community youth organizations for all-day, all year learning', *Educational Administration Quarterly*, 30 (3), 278–300.
Husén, T (1974) *The Learning Society*, Methuen, London.
Illich, I (1970) *Deschooling Society*, Harper and Row, New York.
Jackson, B and Marsden, D (1966) *Education and the Working Class*, Penguin Books, London.

King, E (1992) 'The Young Adult Frontier and the Perspective of Continuous Change', *Comparative Education*, 28 (1) 71–82.

Knox, A. (1979) *New Directions for Continuing Education, No. 1*, Jossey-Bass, San Francisco, CA.

McLeod, D (1997) 'Learning Curve', *Guardian Weekly*, 157 (20), 19 (16 November).

Ohliger, J (1974) 'Is Lifelong Education a Guarantee of Permanent Inadequacy?', *Convergence*, 7 (2), 47–59.

Oran, G (1993) 'Meeting the challenge', *Preventing School Failure*, 38 (3) 5–6.

Perry, W (1977) *The Open University*, Jossey-Bass, San Francisco, CA.

Rinne, R (1991) 'Learning to Unlearn: What can we Expect from Education?', *Life and Education in Finland*, 4, 8–13.

Rothwell, W and Cookson, P (1997) *Beyond Instruction: Comprehensive Program Planning for Business and Education*, Jossey-Bass, San Francisco, CA.

Smith, R (1982) *Learning How to Learn*, Cambridge Books, New York.

Tunstall, J (1974) *The Open University Opens*, Routledge & Kegan Paul, London.

Williams, R (1990) *Adult Education and Social Change. What I Came to Say*, Hutchinson Radius, London.

PART II

LIFELONG LEARNING IN THE LEARNING SOCIETY

Chapter 5

Paradoxes of the Learning Society

Peter Jarvis

Many metaphors have been employed in recent times to describe contemporary society, such as the 'information society' (Archer 1990, amongst others), 'knowledge society' (Stehr 1994), 'postmodern society' (Lyotard 1984, amongst others) and the 'learning society'. Metaphors seek to describe, or illustrate, a phenomenon - often by one or other of its salient features. The idea of the learning society has become almost taken for granted in a very short space of time and a multitude of publications have appeared assuming the metaphor to be a reality. There are a few scholars, however, who have endeavoured to probe beneath the surface and ask more fundamental questions about this concept; a brief paper by Edwards (1995) embarked upon this process and this paper follows a similar approach to the learning society, although the typology discussed here is different from his and was reached independently of his work.

One of the fundamental issues in the concept of the learning society is the concept of 'learning' which is so frequently confused with 'education', as will become apparent in the following discussion. Yet the idea of a society undertaking an individual, and indeed individuating, act is rather strange, since society is more than the sum of its individual members and learning is always individual. The fact that it does not appear strange is a problem to which this paper will return. However, it is necessary from the outset to make a clear distinction between the two concepts and, for the purposes of this paper, education is treated as a social institution which has been established by the state in most countries of the world to provide some organized learning opportunities for its citizens and for other residents within its domain; but in most instances this provision was only for the children of citizens or residents, so that adult educators have had to work very hard for a reform of the educational institution within their own society and to introduce a system of adult and then lifelong education (Yeaxlee 1929, Lengrand 1975). Education is, in this sense, a public phenomenon and provides public recognition for the learning that it provides (Jarvis 1996).

Learning, however, is broader than education and is something that everybody does - it is private; it is the process whereby individuals transform their experiences, whether they are educational or not, into knowledge, skills, values, attitudes, emotions, beliefs, senses, etc. It is universal and to some extent lifelong - and this has always been the case, although this has only become apparent as more opportunities for learning have emerged in rapidly changing society. In other words, learning is a human ability possessed by everybody, but it is a private activity.

Significantly, some theorists of the learning society have started with an educational perspective, whilst others have started from a broader sociological perspective in which individual learning is located; and this has resulted in considerably different pictures emerging in their writing. Indeed, for some the term 'learning' is not actually used although the implications of their writing are clearly about learning and these have been adopted by educationalists.

This paper falls into in two parts. The first explores three interpretations of the learning society: as an idealized conception of society – a futuristic ideal; as a reaction to social change – a reflexive society; and as a market phenomenon of the information society – a consumer society. The second part seeks to explore the paradoxes inherent within these three formulations and asks what conception of education has a place in such a society.

Interpretations of the learning society

In this section the three different ways of looking at the learning society that were mentioned above are discussed, commencing with the one which has the most public orientation.

The learning society as a futuristic society

When Hutchins (1968: 133) wrote his classic book on the learning society, he looked to a future and suggested that the learning society:

'would be one that, in addition to offering part-time adult education to every man and woman at every stage of grown-up life, had succeeded in transforming its values in such a way that learning, fulfilment, becoming human, had become its aims and all its institutions were directed to this end.'

For Hutchins, education would come into its own and the new learning society would be the fulfilment of Athens, made possible not by slavery but by modern machines. It was the realization of this computer revolution that led Husén (1974) to very similar conclusions. He (1974: 238) argued that 'educated ability will be democracy's replacement for passed-on social prerogatives'. He recognized that the knowledge explosion would be fostered by a combination of computers and reprographics and he (1974: 240) foresaw the possibility of 'equal opportunities for all to receive as much education as they are thought capable of absorbing'. Despite Sweden's long history of adult education, Husén still regarded the learning society as being educational and based on an extension of the school system.

More recently, a similar position has been adopted by Ranson (1994: 106) who has suggested that:

'There is a need for the creation of a learning society as the constitutive condition of a new moral and political order. It is only when the values and processes of learning are placed at the centre of the polity that the conditions can be established for all individuals to develop their capacities, and that institutions can respond openly and imaginatively to a period of change.'

Ranson's writing does not cite either of the earlier authors mentioned above although he also approaches the subject from a similar perspective, starting with school education rather than an adult or lifelong education framework. It is futuristic and rather idealistic. Boshier (1980), while still looking forward to a learning society, actually started from the position of an adult educator and recognized that it was more than school education – he explored the post-school institutions in New Zealand to discover the structural basis of such a society – but it was still an educational phenomenon.

In a sense, each of these foresaw an educative society and as such it was a phenomenon of which Illich and Verne (1976) were afraid. Significantly, they also start their analyses with one part of the public institution – the structures of society – and while it might be unwise to separate structure from agency, once the structures are loosened or weakened, then the agent becomes more significant - or individual learning assumes a more significant place than education - and herein lies the foundation for another approach to the learning society.

The learning society as a reflexive society

Reflective learning and reflective practice have become commonplace ideas among educators in recent years, echoing the work of Schon (1983). But reflective learning is itself a sign of the times; underlying this is another approach to society epitomized by Giddens (1990) and Beck's (1992) *Risk Society*. However, Giddens and others have argued that reflexivity is fundamental to the nature of modernity, for with its advent modernity overrode tradition of all forms. Giddens (1990: 38-39) writes:

> 'The reflexivity of modern social life consists in the fact that social practices are constantly examined and reformed in the light of incoming information about those very practices, thus constitutively altering their character. We should be clear about the nature of this phenomenon. All forms of asocial life are partly constituted by actors' knowledge of them. Knowing "how to go on" in Wittgenstein's sense is intrinsic to the conventions which are drawn upon and reproduced in human activity. In all cultures, social practices are routinely altered in the light of ongoing discoveries which feed into them. But only in the era of modernity is the revision of convention radicalized to apply (in principle) to all aspects of human life...'

Society has become reflexive and the knowledge that people acquire is no longer certain and established for ever – its value lies in its enabling them to live in this rapidly changing society. As society is changing so very rapidly, everybody is required to learn new things in order to keep abreast with the changes. This is very clearly the case with the knowledge-based occupations where, for instance, practitioners are required to keep abreast of the changes occurring within their occupational field. Hence, there has been a mushrooming of vocational education qualifications, often at higher degree level, and in this case the learning is certificated and public; but where the learning is non-vocational there is a tendency for some of it to be private and not to be recognized publicly. This tremendous growth in new information and the very rapid changes that are occurring in society might reflect the idea that the learning society is intrinsic to modernity.

Indeed, there has been a growth in learning networks, rather like those learning webs advocated by Illich (1973: 75–105); but then he was regarded as radical, although now these ideas are becoming more realistic with the development of the Internet and of all forms of electronic communication. This has led to greater opportunity for those who have the technological knowledge, skill and equipment to access up-to-date knowledge and for those who are knowledge producers to share their ideas and research.

But as some forms of knowledge change more rapidly than others (Scheler 1980) the process of learning is both individuating and fragmentary to society as a whole. Neither is it something which all individuals desire; they sometimes seek an unchanging world (Jarvis 1992: 206-207) and a harmony with their environment. Endeavouring to discover the certainty of an unchanging world is a reaction to the learning society, as it is to modernity itself.

From the perspective of rapidly changing knowledge, there is a fundamental shift in the conception of knowledge itself – from something that is certain and true to something which is changing and relative. This means that underlying this form of society lies experimentation itself, leading to people reflecting constantly upon their situation and the knowledge that they possess to cope with it. Constantly they need to learn new knowledge; but learning new things and acting upon them always contains an element of risk – for inherent in learning is risk but, paradoxically, learning is also a reaction to the risk, of not always knowing how to act in this rapidly changing world. Reflexivity is a feature of modernity (Beck 1992). Reflective learning is a way of life rather than a discovery made by educators and something to be taught in educational institutions. The learning society is not then a hope for the future but an ever-present phenomenon of the contemporary world.

The learning society as a consumer society

Contemporary society is also a consumer society and the history of consumerism can be traced back to the eighteenth century (Campbell 1987). Campbell traces it back to the romantic period in the eighteenth century, when pleasure became the crucial means of realizing that ideal truth and beauty which imagination had revealed and, significantly, this eighteenth-century Romantic Movement 'assisted crucially at the birth of modern consumerism' (Campbell 1987: 206), so that a longing to enjoy those creations of the mind becomes the basis for consuming new phenomena. In other words, there can be no market economy unless there are consumers who want to purchase the products that are being produced. Advertising plays on imaginary pleasure – and learning becomes fun! Now, as Usher and Edwards (1994) point out, one of the features of contemporary society is that of experiencing – it is a sensate society. This is nothing new, as Campbell has shown, but it is the type of society in which the longings of the imagination can be realized through consumption – so that the basis of advertising is the cultivation of desire.

Whilst learning was equated with the educational in people's minds, they remembered their unpleasant experiences at school when it was no fun to learn, a barrier to further education was erected and it was one which every adult educator sought to overcome. But once learning became separated from education, then learning could become fun – and there is a sense in which this has become a more popular thing to do in the United Kingdom since the creation of the British Open University. Now people could learn all the things that they had wanted to learn, and they did not have to go to school to do it. They could read books, watch the television, listen to the radio and go and talk with other people – if they wanted. The Open University marketed a commodity, and other organizations have followed. The Open University's foundation marked a crucial step in this process – it moved education of adults away from the school setting and into the consumer society. Now it is possible to learn all the things individuals have wanted to know – by purchasing their own multimedia personal computers and surfing the web, watching the television 'Learning Zone' programmes, buying their own 'teach yourself' books and magazines and, even, purchasing their own self-directed learning courses. But the providers of these learning materials are now not all educational institutions, and educational institutions are having to change their approach with a great deal of alacrity in order to keep abreast with a market generating information about all aspects of life every minute of the day, so that people have to choose not only what channel they are going to watch but what medium they are going to employ to receive their information! Knowledge production has become an industry, cultivating the desire of people to learn so that they can be regarded as modern.

The information society is now an information market. Significantly, information is a public commodity – contained in every form of media transmission – but learning remains a private activity and knowledge has become personal knowledge (Polanyi 1962). Herein lies a problem with private learning, since one of the features of the market is that the consumption has to be public – conspicuous consumption – and so educational qualifications now become an institutional activity and the public education institutions accredit learning from prior experience for educational qualifications! But for how long they will retain their monopoly remains another question. Judging by the direction of recent events, the answer will be that this monopoly will soon be broken and education will be but one more provider of information in the learning market and the educational qualification will become the public recognition of a very private process.

Paradoxes of the learning society

A number of issues appear in the above conceptualization that require further elaboration, some of which will be explored here: recognition of the learning society, access to learning, the fear of learning and 'real' learning.

Recognition of the learning society

Scholars have looked to the learning society as a futuristic ideal and even Ransom still sees it in this way. Campaigns for learning exist, as if they are sometime necessary in order to generate a learning society. Campaigners are still fighting a battle to introduce lifelong learning, as if it is still a futuristic enterprise. Yet this is a wrongly located battleground, for this battle has already been won. Modernity has created the necessary social conditions and the learning society has already arrived. Failure to recognize this is itself indicative of a restricted and institutional definition of learning, and the apparent current endeavours to 'create' a learning society seem to centre around efforts to control more learning opportunities through institutionalizing them in a redefined educational institution – learning! For as the learning society is a metaphor, and some of its exponents are introducing a new educational discourse focused on learning – they are trying to make a private phenomenon public – a point to which this paper will return. There is nothing wrong in these campaigns, but it is necessary to recognize that the learning society has arrived and the current discourses are about a new institutional phenomenon.

Access to learning

For many decades educators, especially adult educators, have campaigned for a reform in the institutional system so that adults could gain access to learning opportunities – the educational institution in many countries has been slow to reform and, in many cases, has resisted reform. Indeed, it is still resisting that reform in some countries in the world. This was a function of state monopoly and gradually, as that monopoly has been broken within the educational system itself and education has begun to embrace lifelong education, in just the way that scholars like Yeaxlee (1929) envisaged, education itself has been supplanted by the very thing that it offered – learning! At the heart of the learning society lies the very phenomenon that education offered, the opportunity to learn, but now education has no monopoly, it is but one provider in the market and opportunities to learn are multitudinous.

The privatization of education is a process that many educators would have opposed, and yet, paradoxically, the market has partially created a situation which those educators strove after. However, every time greater access is offered, a new form of social exclusion is generated and so those who cannot participate in the market-place of learning, for whatever reason, are denied access to its products and become a new poor. What is true, however, is that there are more opportunities to learn than ever before and this, it might be argued, is one of the major benefits of such a society – but this is not true for everybody all the time.

Fear of learning

Beck (1992) claims that this society is a risk society – it is reflexive society. It is a society which frees agency from structure. Non-learning (Jarvis 1992) through repetition is a way of staying within the familiar world of structures and not taking risks, but the learning agent is freed from the restrictive structures of society, and such emancipation always contains within it more than an element of risk. Reflective learning is a sign of living in a changing world, monitoring action and learning to cope with change – it is a process of being free to break away from the traditions and being free to act – but for some freedom is frightening (Fromm 1942). The fear of freedom is a fear of learning. Consequently, there is a social reaction to the learning society – a non-learning society. Some people are reacting against the learning society, they are seeking to recreate structures, to re-enact traditions and to create 'safe' social *milieus* for everyday life. For some, the learning society is a risky place and not always the utopia that some educationalists have sought.

'Real' learning

In the analysis in the first section, education and learning have been very clearly distinguished, and this is not accidental since this is a feature of the late modern society. Mass education has developed as a state provided institution – a public phenomenon – whereas contemporary developments about learning are private in nature. This is a continuation of the process of the 'transformation of the public sphere' about which Habermas (1989) first wrote in German in 1962. Now the private sphere has not been reduced to family (Habermas 1989: 154) but to the individual and to individual acts and processes. This privatization is significant, since activities in the public sphere are public and *de facto* of political significance, but once they have become individual and private they have become depoliticized. As Habermas (1989: 160–161) points out in his discussion of the way that public cultural debate was transformed into a private exercise:

> 'But as soon as and to the degree that the public sphere in the world of letters spread into the world of consumption, this threshold became levelled. So-called leisure behaviour, once it had become part of the cycle of production and consumption, was already apolitical, if for no other reason than its incapacity to constitute a world emancipated from the immediate constraints of survival needs. When leisure was nothing but a complement to time spent on the job, it could be no more than a different arena for the pursuit of private business affairs that were not transformed into a public communication between private people. to be sure, the individual satisfaction of needs might be achieved in a

public fashion, in the company of many others, but a public sphere did not emerge from such a situation.'

This process has occurred now in the learning society; education has become depoliticized and learning has become a process of consuming products of a new culture industry. Yet there is still need for public recognition and there appear to be two significant features about this: firstly, that learning that is vocationally orientated needs some form of public recognition because there is a sense in which its outcomes remain in the public domain – the world of work and the labour market; and, secondly, the capitalist enterprise of the mass media has penetrated the private sphere of individual leisure pursuits and de-privatized the sphere of interiority by creating a pseudo-public learning sphere (Habermas 1989: 162) through the medium of qualifications, since it is only the possession of educational qualifications that demonstrates that 'real' learning has occurred.

Conclusions

The learning society is a metaphor and there are many discourses about it. They are contradictory and they start with different premises. Contained within these are debates about agency and structure, private and public, and learning and education. In one sense, it is also about creating a pseudo-public sphere from a very private process. Learning remains the driving force of the human being, something that is individual and individuating - and it can only be applied to society because society is fragmenting and individuating. Perhaps the term the learning society only makes sense and can be taken for granted because it reflects the nature of contemporary society - an agglomeration of individuals – in which the nature of the social itself is undergoing change.

References

Archer M (1990) 'Theory, Culture and Post-Industrial Society', in M Featherstone (Ed.) *Global Culture*, Sage, London.
Beck U (1992) *Risk Society*, trans. M Ritter, Sage, London.
Boshier R (1980) *Towards a Learning Society*, Learning Press, Vancouver.
Campbell C (1987) *The Romantic Ethic and the Spirit of Modern Consumerism*, Blackwell, Oxford.
Edwards R (1995) 'Behind the Banner: Whither the Learning Society?', *Adults Learning*: 187–189.

Fromm E (1942) *The Fear of Freedom* (reprinted ARK paperbacks), Routledge, London.
Giddens A (1990) *Consequences of Modernity*, Polity, Cambridge.
Habermas J (1989) *The Structural Transformation of the Public Sphere*, trans. T Burger, Polity, Cambridge.
Husén T (1974) *The Learning Society*, Methuen, London.
Hutchins R (1968) *The Learning Society*, Penguin, Harmondsworth.
Illich I (1973) *Deschooling Society*, Penguin, Harmondsworth.
Illich I and Verne E (1976) *Imprisoned in a Global Classroom*, Writers & Readers, London.
Jarvis P (1992) *Paradoxes of Learning*, Jossey Bass, San Francisco.
Jarvis P (1996) 'The Public Recognition of Lifetime Learning', *European Journal of Lifelong Learning*, 1, 10-17.
Lengrand P (1975) *An Introduction to Lifelong Education*, Croom Helm, London.
Lyotard J-F (1984) *PostModern Society*, Manchester University Press, Manchester.
Polanyi M (1962) *Personal Knowledge*, Routledge and Kegan Paul, London.
Ranson S (1994) *Towards the Learning Society*, Cassell, London.
Scheler M (1980) *Problems of a Sociology of Knowledge*, trans. M Frings, ed. K Stikkers, Routledge and Kegan Paul, London.
Schon D (1983) *The Reflective Practitioner*, Free Press, New York.
Stehr N (1994) *Knowledge Societies*, Sage, London.
Usher R and Edwards R (1994) *Postmodernism and Education,* Routledge, London.
Yeaxlee B (1929) *Lifelong Education*, Cassell, London.

Chapter 6

Persuasive Discourses:
Learning and the Production of Working Subjects in a Post-industrial Era

Elaine Butler

> 'In a social structure of ever-increasing complexity like that of advanced capitalism, befogged by ideological murk, any claim to systemic knowledge appears as a flight of foolish fancy. Reality is opaque; but there are certain points – clues, signs – which allow us to decipher it' (Ginzburg 1980 in Donald 1985: 247).

Introduction: reading the signs

Discourse, as Bakhtin (1981) reminds us, is 'populated – overpopulated – with the intentions of others'. However, as participants within discourses, the potential exists for readings, interpretations, challenges and/or compliance. Readings of lifelong learning texts illustrate both their persuasiveness and the contradictory positions available within their discourses, eg:

> 'because of rapidly changing circumstances (particularly but not exclusively economic) there is a strong need for people to continue their learning – that is to be lifelong learners. The message is clear: the key to economic and social improvement lies in having a population that is adaptable, flexible, well educated and attuned to the need for lifelong learning' (NBEET 1996: 2).

Given the emphasis over the last decade for Australia to become a 'clever country', globally competitive with a highly skilled workforce, it is not surprising that the (policy) language used to 'sell' lifelong learning both privileges the economic and includes the social. Further, it centres desired attributes for citizenship that mirror those utilized in the portrayal of model workers engaged in post-industrial production – flexible, adaptable, ready and willing to engage in continual (self) improvement/learning. Benefits are to accrue both to the nation/economy, and to industries/enterprises, with the latter also charged with the task of 'learning':

> 'international competition and globalism of the economy, the introduction of new technologies and the intensive emphasis on quality in enterprises has accelerated the need for lifelong learning. Both individuals and enterprises need to adopt the underlying principles of lifelong learning ... The move to a knowledge-based society has led to calls for not only the creation of learning enterprises which are able to work smarter and engage in a process of continuous improvement but also more generally a "learning culture"' (NBEET 1996: 6).

The 'cost' of not heeding these persuasive invocations is great:

> 'the future now belongs to societies that organize themselves for learning. What we know and can do now holds the key to economic progress, just as command of resources once did. Everything depends on what firms can learn from and teach to their customers and suppliers, or what countries can learn from one another, or what workers can learn from each other and the work they do ... The prize will go to those countries that are organized on national learning systems, and where all institutions are organized to learn and act on what they learn' (Hood 1994: 2).

Drawing critically on such texts and on policy documents, I have argued elsewhere (Butler 1996) that discourses of learning, and especially learning for work, are colonized by the dominant discourse of globalization and discursive practices associated with global competitiveness and late capitalism. Such a stance calls into question the discursive interconnections between globalization, the changing nature, organization, management and distribution of work (and workers) and the knowledge practices and pedagogies associated with learning/work. In this paper I suggest that the production of working subjects for the new work order (Gee et al. 1996) is also located within these discourses.

Australia on the global stage

Australia embraced globalization as a response to shifts in global economic power that impacted negatively on its economy and international competitiveness (Sklair 1996), with crises framed in terms of productivity, competition and profitability (Watkins 1994). Policy responses were developed by representatives of the state (politicians, bureaucrats) and élites from industry and the labour movement, and a dual strategy was formulated – the construct of a 'postmodern' market and the development of a new vocationalism within education (Hinkson 1996). The following depiction (Table 6.1) by Hall and Harley (1995) best illustrates the Australian approach. It also regulates the 'new order' for education/learning and work in this country.

Table 6.1 *Dimensions of globalization*

Dimension	Historical trends	Ideological interpretations
Economic	Expansion of capital, labour and trade markets	Economic globalization demands competitiveness and efficiency of domestic industries without state regulation
Political	Mobilization of organizations, groups and forces beyond state jurisdiction and efficacy	Political globalization neutralizes state policies and necessitates tariff reductions, labour market deregulation and economic rationalism
Cultural	Development of means of communications and information technology encouraging transmission of ideas and information	Cultural globalization encourages international best practice, new production systems, HRM and flexible specialization

Globalization has been picked up as an organizing principle 'with enormous and uncritical enthusiasm by many businesses, management and human resource (HR) management researchers and practitioners' (Hall and Harley 1995: 71). The rhetoric for global competitiveness accompanies both the HR/management and contemporary training literature, shaping restructuring of labour forces, workplaces, work and vocational education and training

(VET). Education is positioned as both part of the problem and the answer (Butler 1997) with globalization used as a fact to justify the redesign of Australian education, including the social and organizational re-norming of education currently underway (Seddon and Angus 1997). Marginson (1994: 17) argues that:

> 'globalization, technological development and markets have broken open the national education systems but they have changed those systems rather than abolishing them. The government ordering of education is now located within global systems of control as much cultural as economic, in which international regulatory agents have increasing effects.'

Educators are excluded from top level decision making bodies, and are also under direct challenge as practitioners in the marketized VET system, with industry/enterprise defined by the state as both the 'driver' and the 'client' of the system. Policy initiatives continue to deregulate and marketize the provision of (commodified) education, further rewarding industry/enterprise as the pre-eminent site of learning, with the right and the resources to select curriculum knowledge (competency-based standards); and to select (or provide) trainers, training, assessment and certification. The message is clear – the aim of the national VET system is the provision (production) of an 'educated, skilled, flexible workforce to enhance Australian industry to be competitive in domestic and international markets, to effectively participate in employment' (to) meet Australia's labour market and industry needs (ANTA 1994, 1997: 3).

This then, is a partial map of the global-local context in which workplace learning is situated. It is a context in which people, when represented, are constructed as citizens/workers in gender/race-neutral terms. The key actors are corporate interests supported by the state. The elusive citizens are cajoled, in economically explicit and socially persuasive ways to embrace learning, for the economic good of their nation. Benefits to them remain illusory, framed in uncertain global visionings of emerging futures.

Hamilton (1996) contends that the benefits of globalization for 'ordinary' Australians have been elusive, with fewer jobs, longer working hours for those in full-time work, an increase in unpaid overtime, and job security becoming a thing of the past. While it is oversimplifying the complexity of labour processes in Australia by using the descriptor post-Fordism, there is general agreement that the nature, distribution and organization of work is changing rapidly, as are the ever-restructuring workplaces in which worker/learners are situated (eg Davis and Lansbury 1996: 11, Gollan *et al.* 1996). The profile of the labour force and patterns of (paid) work continue to change, including increase in women's labour-force participation; a decline in full-time (core) jobs, and an increase in part-time, casual (peripheral, precarious and marginalized) employment; a decline in manufacturing and increase in service work (reflecting the previous points); continuing high unemployment, including youth unemployment. Despite these shifts, patterns of segregation in the labour force, by gender and race/ethnicity, remain resilient to change.

Kelly (1995: 124) contends that 'discourse has played an important role in the conditioning of the environment in which workplace change has occurred over the last decade'. While the discourses of micro economic reform, restructuring and productivity provided the opportunity for industry/managers to embark on major reform campaigns, the language utilized in the discursive politics of change is that associated with new managerialism – participation, collaboration, teams/empowerment, improvement, flexibility, family friendly workplaces and so on. This is the language of the HR texts and practices – the so-called 'cultural' dimension of globalism as depicted by Hall and Harley (1995).

The 'cultural shift'

The use of the term 'culture' in the HR/management and related texts is both prolific and problematic. This cultural shift, which is also evident in discourses of lifelong/work-related learning, is best framed by what Stockley and Foster (1990: 312) describe as 'productive culture' – a culture being constructed through changing work orientation and practices, in which learning is centred to solve current economic and social 'crises'. Such a cultural shift calls for 'new' managers and 'new' workers, to populate the 'new' work order. Gee *et al.* (1996: 5) argue that:

> 'contemporary, globally competitive businesses don't any longer compete on the basis of their products or services *per se*. They compete, rather, on the basis of how much learning or knowledge they can use as leverage in order to expeditiously invent, produce, distribute and market their goods and services...'

Such an approach invests learning and knowledge with a production consciousness and culture, which assumes that managers trust workers, and are eager for worker consultation and participation (Lansbury *et al.* 1996). However, rhetoric and reality are far from congruent. The very poor record of consultation undertaken by Australian managers (Davis and Lansbury 1996: 11) informs the critique offered in the influential 1995 Karpin Report, that Australian managers lack managerial expertise. The report is structured around five management challenges as a template for change: develop a positive enterprise culture and better management skills; upgrade vocational education and training and business support; harness the talents of diversity; achieve best practice management development; reform management education and explore a new management paradigm.

The 'new' management paradigm stresses the need for enhanced people skills (enabling, empowering and entrusting), for better strategies for knowledge-based competition (lifelong learning) and for a world orientation (Kenway 1996: 19). Managers then, are to 'manage' lifelong learning within 'positive' enterprise cultures, as well as transform their own practices though lifelong education. Their task is to transform control oriented organizations to commitment driven enterprises (Cunningham *et al.* 1996). The 'new' workers are to be highly skilled, flexible risk-takers, who are able to tolerate fear, uncertainty, continual change and stress, while still being able, productive and creative (Martin 1995). They are to be 'empowered', to enhance their commitment and increase their enterprises' competitiveness (Cunningham *et al.* 1996). Enterprises are to be 'social networks of co-operative learning' whereby individual members of the organization 'embrace and explore each other's wisdom and concerns' (Hames 1994: 76).

Although the discursive practices associated with new managerialism have been demonstrated to act as regulatory disciplinary techniques, and are not so 'new' (eg Webb 1996, Kelly 1995, Townley 1994, MacDermott 1994), the discourse of productive culture continues to evolve, as do the practices that inform and shape it. Utopian depictions of learning organizations are numerous, as are telling statements such as 'our people are our most important asset' (Morgan and Smith 1996: 3); 'the ability to learn faster than your competitors may be the only sustainable competitive advantage left' (de Geusin in Hames 1994: 35). Perhaps the intent is best illustrated by Savellis (1995/96), who, after describing companies that are creating learning cultures, and becoming learning organizations, embedding (low-cost) learning as part of the industrial process, concludes that 'companies have found a way to keep control of the learning process and ensure that it is always linked to actual corporate needs and practical benefits'.

More and more, within this cultural shift, emphasis is placed on workers' attributes rather than skills, giving value to personality, temperament and flexibility/adaptability; openness to learning, development and retraining; initiative (Morgan and Smith 1996: 2); and motivation, communication skills, honesty and the ability to get along with others (Robinson 1996). The new workplace requires 'the whole person' (Morgan and Smith 1996), to labour willingly within its new (organizational-cultural) community, where members 'engage in learning on behalf of the organization and the results of their shared learnings become embedded in the organizations images of itself – its culture' (Hames 1994: 267–8).

Du Gay (1996: 41) contends that this contemporary turn to culture is linked to the production of social meanings – 'meaningful practices' – a prerequisite for the implementation of social learning practices:

> 'in order to compete effectively in the turbulent modern global economic environment, the foremost necessity is to remake meaning for people at and through work. 'Culture' is accorded a privileged position because it is seen to structure the way people think, feel and act in organizations. The aim is to produce the sort of meanings that will enable people to make the right and necessary attribution to the success of the organizations for which they work.'

In this way, the struggle for the hearts, minds and bodies of workers (the whole person) is located within discursive (cultural/learning) practices intent on producing model 'working subjects'. Through (continual) learning, the labouring/knowing subject, located within the 'culture' of a (learning) organization/enterprise 'adds value' to self and the enterprise's productivity. Casey (1995: 132) contends that:

> 'the new cultural discourses of production as manifest in the corporation's designed culture are now as essential to production as labour and machine technology were in traditional industrial production. ... A culture of feeling good at work by having apparently meaningful and energized team and family relations generates a simulated sociality that ensures the necessary human effort in production cultures.'

Culture, then, becomes a technology within the seductive discourses of both new managerialism and learning/work, through which workers can seek fulfilment as social subjects and working subjects, both through labour and through enterprise/organizational 'success'. In this way, culture is presented as an essentialized and gender neutral set of 'resource meanings', universally available for transformation of self, and of enterprises (Adkins and Lury 1996: 218).

Persuasive discourses?

Much has been written about subjectivity and work/labour (eg Knights and Willmot 1989, du Gay 1996). The discussions by Donald (1985) and Sakolosky (1992) are relevant here. Donald argues that the production of subjectivity is not the mirroring of social order by passive individuals, but rather 'the precarious ordering of symbolic categories ... an active process - not the least because such categories are never encountered in the abstract but are always formulated in discourse and deployed in social action' (1985: 245).

For Sakolosky (1992: 249), it is the relationship between discursive systems and disciplinary mechanisms of power which leads to the formation of labouring subjects at the workplace. Within these frames, it is possible to locate *inscribed* subjects, constructed by discourse and signifying systems (Usher and Edwards 1994: 25); *productive* subjects (Townley 1994: 126–131) and Casey's *corporate* subjects – defensive, colluded, capitulated (1995: 190–192).

I argue that discourses for lifelong/work-related learning are deeply implicated in the production of working subjects for new local global worksites – embodied subjects who know/learn/labour; who engage in self disciplinary practices; who are inscribed, productive, corporate. However, many contradictory subject positions are possible within these knowledge/power relations; the 'making up' (du Gay 1996: 110) of the working subject is reliant on the 'taking up'. Data from two research projects that foreground women, work and learning within contemporary Australian workplaces illustrates both compliance with and challenges to discursive attempts to produce 'model' working subjects.

The project 'Women work and training' (Butler *et al.* forthcoming) involved nationwide research that gathered information from women workers in feminized industries and occupations about their access to and knowledge of learning opportunities available through the national VET system. Women participants expressed particular concerns about their (lack of) access to both information and training in their workplaces; the perpetuation of existing structural and workplace discrimination against women workers; and concerns about the structures and procedures of assessment and accreditation of their learning/training. Overwhelmingly, participants were enthusiastic about the potential for increased access to training, accreditation of their knowledge/learning and career paths.

Many employers/managers had little formal knowledge or understanding of new training agendas; work-related training opportunities were often distributed according to the perceived status, role and worthiness of workers. In this way, 'learning' is used to allocate workers to specific roles and futures within their respective workplaces. Workers cited examples of being told they were 'too valuable to be released' for training, while at the same time employers utilize their expertise to train others and exploit their willingness to learn informally from others. The above is an example of managerial colonizing of learning and restricting learning opportunities that illustrates the illusory nature of depictions of shared loyalty, mutuality and trust between managers and workers. While such practices contribute to the production of capitulated corporate subjects, evidence also shows that a number of the women participants self-enrol in education and training programmes, in their own time and at their own expense, to 'learn their jobs' formally, both for their own benefit and that of 'their' enterprise. Such action can be read in contradictory ways – as resistance and as moving towards construction of self-motivating/self-disciplining working subjects.

Another interesting example is that of women expressing concern about the 'tap on the shoulder' technique of selecting individual workers for further training and career advancement. Responses to this technique included refusal of training; negotiation with team members about desired outcomes, through to collective negotiations for access by all team members to training, because of the potential to undermine the camaraderie and mutual support experienced in their work teams. In this case, while learning is seen as central, the (perceived) benefits of mutuality are (re)located by the workers/learners within their work team/s, rather than with 'management', illustrating Bakhtin's (1981) 'populated' discourse and differing readings of intent.

While the above examples make visible some of the complexity around subject positions available to workers, the study by Butler and Schulz (forthcoming), located in an Australian university, well illustrates the willingness of academic and general staff workers to engage with the discourses of workplace learning as inscribed subjects, within a worksite with a strongly enunciated mission statement/vision and goals. However, the project also illustrates the ability of the women to 'seize the rules' (Comay in Sakolosky 1992: 247), to utilize the discursive practices to challenge masculinist discourses within the institution.

The institution under review is a 'new' university created by government intervention in the period of micro-economic reform and globalism discussed earlier. Like most Australian universities, the institution, in its brief 'new' history, continues to undergo massive changes, due to funding restrictions, accountability requirements, globalization, socio-cultural and economic political imperatives and expectations. Dramatic work intensification, a spilling over of 'work into life' were evident. So too was the 'loyalty' and 'dedication' (albeit often couched in realist/pragmatic and cynical terms) contributed by the (model) workers.

Although it can be argued that this institution provides the ideal site for viewing the production of working subjects through the discourses under review, counter discourses are also evident. Workplace learning was categorized as 'work'. Worker contributions to the mission statement, goals and associated practices were identified and again very firmly categorized as 'work'. Here, the definitions of work were challenged and extended, by corporate subjects.

As this institution is still experiencing turbulent change, the 'story' about production of working subjects is both complex and still in the making.

Concluding comments

This paper has interrogated the notion that the discourses of lifelong learning, through their interrelationships with globalism and new managerialism, are deeply implicated in the production of working subjects. The discourses are both persuasive and powerful. However, within the textual representations, learners/workers are often absent. The absence can be linked with Lowe's description of the body as Other to late capitalism. However, as he contends, the 'body' is 'always an embodied-being-in-the-world, constructed and realized within social practices to satisfy changing needs' (1995: 74–75).

Workers/learners are embodied subjects, gendered, heterogeneous, compliant and/or resistant, but never neutral. While managers and workplaces may well seek 'knowing' labour (Casey 1995), labour also 'knows' and learns. As we know, learn, labour and live, we can continue to read the signs. In this way, the struggles for different futures continue.

References

Adkins, L and Lury, C (1996) 'The Cultural, the Sexual and the Gendering of the Labour Market', in L Adkins and V Merchant (Eds) (1996) *Sexualising the Social: Power and the Organisation of Sexuality*, MacMillan Press, Hampshire.

Australian National Training Authority (ANTA) (1994) *Towards a Skilled Australia: A National Strategy for Vocational Education and Training*, ANTA, Brisbane.

Australian National Training Authority (ANTA) (1997) *Australian Training*, 4, 1.

Bahktin, M (1981) *The dialogic imagination: four essays*, ed. M Holquist trans. C Emerson and M Holquist, University of Texas Press, Austin.

Butler, E (1996) *Equity and Workplace Learning: Emerging Discourses and Conditions of Possibility*. Keynote paper for National Colloquium on Research Directions for Workplace Learning and Assessment, Sydney University of Technology, Sydney.

Butler, E (1997) *Beyond Political Housework. Gender Equity in the Post-school Environment. A Discussion Paper*. Commissioned paper prepared for Premier's Council for Women, Dept for Women, New South Wales.

Butler, E and Schulz, L (forthcoming) *More Than Just Work. Women and the Politics of University Work*, University of South Australia, Adelaide.

Butler, et al. (forthcoming) *Talking About Training. Women, Work and Training in Australia*, AGPS, Canberra.

Casey, C (1995) *Work, Society and Self: After Industrialism*, Routledge, London.

Cunningham, I, Hyman, J and Baldry, C (1996) 'Empowerment: The Power to Do What?', *Industrial Relations Review*, 27, 2, 143–154.

Davis, E and Lansbury, R (1996) 'Consultation and Employee Participation in Australian Workplaces: 1986–1995', in E Davis and R Lansbury (Eds) Managing

Together. Consultation and Participation in the Workplace, Longman, Melbourne.
Donald, J (1985) 'Beacons for the Future: Schooling, Subjection and Subjectification', in V Beechey and D James (Eds) (1995) *Subjectivity and Social Relations. A Reader*, Open University Press, Milton Keynes.
du Gay, P (1996) *Consumption and Identity at Work*, Sage, London.
Gee, J, Hull, G and Lankshear, C (1996) *The New Work Order. Behind the Language of the New Capitalism*, Allen and Unwin, St Leonards.
Gollan, P, Pickersgill, R and Sullivan, G (1996) *Future of Work: Likely Long Term Developments in the Restructuring of Australian Industrial Relations*, ACIRRT, Sydney.
Hall, R and Harley, B (1995) 'The Australian Response to Globalisation: Domestic Labour Market Policy and the Case of Enterprise Bargaining', in P Gollan (Ed.) (1995) *Globalisation and its Impact on the World of Work*, ACIRRT, Sydney.
Hames, R (1994) *The Management Myth: Exploring the Essence of Future Organisations*, Business and Professional Publishing, Chatswood.
Hamilton, C (1996) 'Workers in the Globalised World: the End of Post-war Consensus' in ACOSS Congress Supplement, *Impact*, December 1996.
Hinkson, J (1996) 'The state of Postmodernity: Beyond Cultural Nostalgia or Pessimism', in P James (Ed.) (1996) *The State in Question. Transformations of the Australian State*, Allen and Unwin, St Leonards.
Hood, D (1994) 'Why Learn?' in *Learn* April/May 1994, 1, 2.
Karpin, DS (1995) *Enterprising Nation: Renewing Australia's Managers to Meet the Challenges of the Asia Pacific Century*. Report of the Industry Taskforce on Leadership and Management Skills, Commonwealth of Australia, Canberra.
Kelly, R (1995) 'Total Quality Management: Industrial Democracy or Another Form of Management Control?', in *Labour and Industry*, 6, 2, 119–140.
Kenway, J (1996) 'The Karpin Report: Implications for Schools', in *Changing Education*, 3, 3, September 1996, 19–22.
Knights, D and Willmott, H (1989) 'Power and Subjectivity at Work: from Degradation to Subjugation in Social Relations', in *Sociology*, 23, 4, Nov 1989, 335–558.
Lansbury, R, Davis, E and Simmons, D (1996) 'Reforming the Australian Workplace through Employee Participation', in *The Economic and Labour Relations Review*, 7, 1, June 1996, 29–45.
Lowe, D M (1995) *The Body in Late-capitalist USA*, Duke University Press, Durham.
MacDermott, K (1994) 'Training for Women', in *Issues in Work-related Education*, Deakin University, Geelong.
Marginson, S (1994) 'Markets in Education: the Dynamics of Positional Goods and Knowledge Goods'. Keynote paper at *(re)Forming Post-compulsory Education and Training: Reconciliation and Reconstruction*, Griffith University, Brisbane.
Martin, E (1995) 'Flexible Bodies. Health and Work in an Age of Systems', in *The Ecologist*, 25, 6, Nov/Dec 1995, 221–226.
Morgan, R B and Smith, J E (1996) *Staffing the New Workplace: Selecting and Promoting for Quality Improvement*, ASQC/CHH, Milwaukee.
National Board of Employment, Education and Training (NBEET) (1996) *Lifelong Learning*, AGPS, Canberra.

Robinson, P (1996) 'Skills, Qualifications and Unemployment', in *Economic Affairs*, 16, 2, Spring 1996, 25–30.

Sakolosky, R (1992) 'Disciplinary Power and the Labour Process', in A Sturdy, D Knights and H Willmott (1992) *Skill and Consent: Contemporary Studies in the Labour Process*, Routledge, London.

Savellis, R (1995/96) 'Australian Industry: Learning to Learn' (source unknown).

Seddon, T and Angus, L (1997) 'Introduction' in *Reshaping Australian Education: Reshaping Australian Institutions Project*, RSSS/ANU, Canberra.

Sklair, L (1996) 'Who are the Globalisers? A Study of Key Globalisers in Australia' in *Journal of Australian Political Economy*, 38, December 1996, 1–30.

Stockley, D and Foster, L (1990) 'The Construction of a New Public Culture: Multiculturalism in an Australian Productive Culture', in *Australian and New Zealand Journal of Sociology*, 1990, 26, 3, 307–328.

Teicher, J and Grauze, A (1996) 'Enterprise Bargaining, Industrial Relations and Training Reform in Australia', in *Australian Bulletin of Labour*, 22, 1, March 1996, 59–80.

Townley, B (1994) *Reframing Human Resource Management. Power, Ethics and the Subject at work*, Sage, London.

Usher, R and Edwards, R (1994) *Post Modernism and Education*, Routledge, London.

Watkins, P (1994) 'The Fordist/post-Fordist Debate: the Educational Implications', in J Kenway (Ed.) (1994) in *Economising Education: the Post-Fordist Directions*, Deakin University, Geelong.

Webb, J (1996) 'Vocaubularies of Motive and the "New" Management', in *Work, Employment and Society*, 10, 2, June 1996, 251–271.

Chapter 7

Lifelong Learning for Social Responsibility:
Exploring the Significance of Aesthetic Reflectivity for Adult Education

Theo Jansen, Matthias Finger and Danny Wildemeersch

We have just concluded a three year study project called 'adult education for social responsibility: reconciling the irreconcilable?'(Wildemeersch *et al.* 1998) In it, we have argued that a major function for adult education today is the reinforcement and facilitation of public debate and action with respect to different social, political and economic scenarios for the future. We invited colleagues to investigate how far adult education can contribute to tuning local and personal concerns to a sense of collective and global responsibility for the 'common good'. We took into account the de-institutionalization and privatization of adult education, and the concomitant pluralization and diversification of learning needs and desires. But our main question was whether the fragmentation and the self-actualizing life-styles that are the hallmark of postmodern culture, still allow educational scenarios for social responsibility.

This question relates to the meaning that is currently inscribed into the concept of lifelong learning. In social policies, and in practices and theories of adult and continuing education, the concept of lifelong learning has become an important metaphor for individual processes of self-actualization in a market-oriented society. The subject that is addressed in the discourse of lifelong learning is an 'entrepreneur of the self', who has to make adequate provisions to (re)produce his or her own human capital, both as a worker and as a consumer (cf. du Gay 1996). Lifelong learning becomes synonymous with the permanent (re)shaping of one's own life project in response to changes in circumstances and to the likelihood of optimizing self-fulfilment. In this context, involvement in lifelong learning counts as an individual virtue, that differentiates responsible and autonomous identities from the ones that show a 'lack of enterprising capacities', and therefore become socially marginalized.

However, this discourse of lifelong learning raises questions about its limits. The individualized value of enterprise that is involved, relates the ethical capacities and engagement of the subject exclusively to the quality of a personal life project. The reduction of ethics to such a 'caring for the self' seems to imply severe limitations to human competencies and desires for social responsibility, caring and 'belonging'. The discourse of lifelong learning produces a learner identity that is emptied of any needs and capacities to engage in clear and meaningful social and political options, to connect self-actualization to issues of sociability and communality. It was exactly this elimination of issues of collective responsibility, identification and solidarity in so many practices and theories of current adult and continuing education that constituted the main concern of our project.

The fusion of modernity and postmodernity

Looking back at the different answers that were given to the basic question that gave direction to our project, we notice that many of them reflect a (con)fusion between modern and postmodern ways of conceptualizing the issues involved that seems typical for the eclectic and 'disembedding' processes that mark many academic and educational discourses today.

The main features of postmodernism can be summarized as the substitution of master-narratives by local knowledge and domestic niches, the dissolution of canonical judgements towards authenticity and self-directedness, the aestheticization of daily life and the de-centring of the subject (Featherstone 1995). Most of our contributors recognize and accept these postmodern dimensions in the conditions of social life today. On the other hand, they all clearly believe in the need and possibility to reconcile such dimensions with the function of adult education to strengthen the sense of social responsibility and competencies for social participation. Yet, in the concepts and theories proposed to accomplish this reconciliation, most of the contributions show a remarkable shift to the logic constitutive of the rationality of modernity. It looks as if the analysis of the problem at stake is 'contaminated' by the spirit of postmodernity, whereas the proposals for a solution show a tendency to stick to the more familiar ground of modernity. The rationality of the latter may be summarized as founded in a cognitive reflexivity, embedded in abstract institutions (Giddens 1990), and in the logic of an individualized development and identity (Grossberg 1996). These ingredients of modernity turn up in a good proportion of the arguments and ideas aimed at revitalizing the notion of collective responsibility.

The significance of cognitive reflexivity is emphasized by our contributors. They refer to the utopian aims of education in creating a moral society, to qualifications being inevitably intertwined with moral questions, to the mission of adult education to question the dominant economic discourse. It is also shown in the centrality of a self-critical reflection by participation in dialogue and public debate, and finally in a strong preference for the discursive understanding of notions such as democracy.

The supposed connection between responsibility, reflexivity and institutional participation is expressed, for instance, when learning processes are located in the possibility of taking part in professional communities, and 'career identity' is considered to be a key to personal and social responsibility; or, in another case, when institutionalized opportunities to exist and to act as citizens are recognized as central conditions for the democratization of public life.

The logic of individualized development and identity is manifest in the contributors' neglect of the social power dimensions when the issue of identity construction is at stake; but also in the fact that community education and community politics require a greater commitment of individual citizens. It is also reflected in the assertion that today individuals need to establish a meaningful connection between education, work and biography; or in the mission of adult basic education, ascribed by other authors, to strengthen the social and cultural identity of learners, or in the conviction that a life story approach links learning about environmental issues to fundamental processes of identity construction.

The (con)fusion of both modernist and postmodernist concepts and frameworks in the aims and tools of adult education today, seems a logical reflection of the situatedness of adult education in a world, that witnesses both the globalization of institutions that constitute the core of modernity (Giddens 1990), and the eroding legitimation of these same institutions because of their diminishing capacity to steer and monitor their own effects in social life (Beck 1992). In this sense our world can neither be grasped in terms of a continued modernity, nor in blind adherence to postmodern metaphors. We are involved in transformations that create new, unpredictable and unknown ways of life in which all kind of mixtures between the modern and the postmodern can and do evolve. Therefore, it is perfectly understandable that adult education, in its search for new ways to reconcile personal and collective responsibility and for new concepts and practices of communality and solidarity, fuses perspectives that are strongly indebted to a modernist rationality with analyses and descriptions of the world we live in influenced by postmodernist discourses.

Such a view, however, risks neglecting new forms of social responsibility and communality that cannot be grasped by the intellectual tools of modern rationality. Adult education's sensitivity to the many-sided, non-rationally inspired movements towards social responsibility and communality in society today seems rather low, and was indeed scarcely present in the contributions to our research. Contrary to the intuitions of many interpreters of current social practices, one could claim that the rise of the postmodern self-reflexive individual has heightened rather than diminished solitary social practices. Yet, the ways in which these acts of solidarity are organized and the meanings attributed to them, have drastically moved away from the forms and traditions which were characteristic of modernity. Therefore, we want explicitly to direct attention to what might be called the aesthetization of communality, and to its significance for adult education to promote social responsibility.

Aesthetic communities

According to Maffesoli (1995) the aesthetization of communality is the expression of an 'ethic of the aesthetic' that links the concerns and stylization of daily life to the imagery of communitarian desire and shared emotions. It draws attention to the persistence of affectual bonds that are the cause and medium of extra-logical communities that generate common feelings and an adherence to recognizable signs and shared symbols (Featherstone 1995). The communitarian ideal embodied in this aesthetic lifestyle expresses forms of being-together that are no longer oriented to the future, but are both the outcome and the medium of concrete, local practices and actions for managing the present.

These kinds of communities are to be found all over society. Maffesoli himself refers both to archaic manifestations in the fundamentalist attachments to religion, ethnicity and territory which today experience a renaissance, and to the emotionally charged demonstrations and gatherings of major sports events and music festivals. Yet, he also observes the aesthetic communitarian ideal in concerts for humanitarian causes, in the commitment to non-governmental and voluntary organizations, and in the recrudescence of 'good works' and charitable initiatives. To this, one could add the concept of the 'good life' with its concomitant ideas of consensual social relations and the lifeworld that, according to Eder (1993), plays a dominant role in middle-class culture and in the concerns of the new cultural movements that are rooted in this culture. Moreover, the bodily and emotionally inspired involvement and care that are expressed in patterns of communication and interaction among particular spiritual, self-help and personal-growth communities may figure as examples of aesthetic communities.

Maffesoli draws our attention to the specific qualities of the aesthetization of the communitarian ideal. First, it gives rise to an 'organic solidarity', a solidarity that lives rather than conceptualizes the engagement of the persons involved, and that enables them to involve themselves in actions that have direct repercussions on the community itself. The concern of the activity is affective rather than instrumental or rational, and related more to collective sentiments than to tangible results. Therefore, the results of actions that spring from this organic solidarity be neither grasped nor measured by the standards of instrumental reason and efficiency. Such actions derive their significance most of all from the possibility they offer to commit oneself, and by doing so, to come into touch with and be touched by the other.

Secondly, the togetherness of such communities is self-sufficient. It has no need for particular objectives to justify itself. It is a sociality without teleology or finality. But this does not imply that these communities are without significance. They represent cultural undercurrents that articulate alternative frameworks of values and ideals, less by argument than by their living and doing. They present a nuisance to the representatives of institutional and instrumental rationalities, and in many cases contribute to the erosion of mainstream culture (cf. van der Lans 1995). Therefore, Eder's (1993) analysis of the countercultural environmental movements might be valid for other aesthetic communities as well. They represent another model of 'morality' that cannot be grasped by the notions of equality and justice, that figure so prominently in modernist systems of morality. This alternative model rather has to do with notions of decency and sentience – ie a model of 'purity' with health, body and soul as its central symbolic values – in which a strong affective element is shown, that thematizes and challenges the symbolic basis of moral foundations and cultural meanings, that lie hidden behind their cognitive awareness.

Third, the way in which the desire to be with similar-minded people shapes these communities, goes together with a comprehensive relationism. The 'care for the self' and the experience of 'life as a work of art' that are involved, push the self toward or up against the other. The preoccupation with the quality of life can only be realized and derives its rights from the valorization of the other: the desire and pleasure of being with the other constitute an 'aesthetic of shared pleasures'. The aesthetic community revolves neither around individualism nor around egocentric hedonism, but situates the self in relation to the gaze and the empathy of the other. Its relationism even predominates when it excludes those who are different. Their competing images and mythologies, that often place different communities in opposition to each other, nevertheless presuppose a state of co-presence and have to accommodate themselves to the existence of the other ones. Be it in expressions of violence and aggression, of tolerance and solidarity, or of indifference and fatalism, the multiplication and diversity of aesthetic communities cannot but call for pluralist compositions, that constitute the social link of society. Even communities in which nationalist and racist sentiments flourish, and which at first oppose and exclude migrants and other 'strangers', after some time show patterns of equilibrium and adjustment towards the 'being there' of such 'outsiders' in their neighbourhoods and lifeworlds (van der Lans 1995).

Fourth, the lifestyle of the aesthetic community focuses upon the quotidian, the everyday experiences of the domestic niche. It is the quality of the immediate living conditions and the opportunities of a 'good life' in the present that are at stake, rather than concerns about institutional powers and promises of a better society in the future. This orientation is the expression of an awareness that in a society where political, economic and social institutions have gone out of control, and produce effects that cannot be foreseen nor governed, one can 'make the best' of life only by enjoying and (re)creating what is at hand in the conditions of daily life. Resisting the impositions of the institutional world is not waged in actions that seek to improve or to overcome the shortcomings of their instrumental rationality, but in the creation of a sociality that is founded on the shared feelings and affects that rule the domestic lifeworld: a culture of sentiment. Eder's observations (1993) of the new social movements also apply to aesthetic communities in general; that is that the issues they articulate are non-negotiable within the existing institutional frameworks and rationalities.

This does not, however, imply that the social repercussions of such communities are negligible. Their turn towards an aesthetic lifestyle of the quotidian seems to fit perfectly into a more general tendency to aestheticize social life today. In the world of production and consumption, image and design have become more and more important with the increase of symbolically coded material goods (Lash and Urry 1994). And in corporate culture, the relational, affective and creative factors are more and more interwoven with, and sometimes even outweigh, reality principles of organizational and economic rationality – witness the importance of affective team-building, the creation of quality-circles, the encouragement of semi-autonomous co-operatives on a human scale, etc. Similar observations also apply to established political, social and cultural institutions. One might very well conclude that the aestheticization of social life and the kind of communality this implies is increasingly shaping and styling many domains of social life. For that reason, the aesthetic community should be taken into account more seriously in reflections on what motivates people to move beyond their private interests in society today.

Implications for adult education

When adult education begins to understand aesthetic communities as another way of reconciling the rise of individualized desires and needs with a sense of social responsibility, it should no longer maintain a self-image built exclusively on support for modernist concepts like emancipation, democracy and justice. Its notions and practices should also be informed by the characteristics of such communities, ie address the non-rational desires and wants that are expressed in the ways of communication that are at the heart of their 'relationism' – like the significance of affectual bonds, a care for the self that requires the sharing of experiences and pleasures with the other, the predominance of the quality of opportunities to enjoy daily life and so on.

This does not imply, however, that adult education should take all kinds of aesthetic communities for granted, and should just 'follow the crowd'. After all, the non-rational sources of inspiration of these communities can easily evoke irrationality when they get stuck into fundamentalism or defensively reproduce the traditional rituals and habits of their lifeworld. In such cases the communication that is practised in aesthetic communities will not give rise to (collective) learning processes. A necessary precondition of learning in such communities consists of participants' competency and readiness to reflect on the moral sources of inspiration and the affective motives that lie behind the sociality of their peculiar associative practices, and to establish communicative relationships in which the significance of these practices is thematized. Orientating adult education towards the practices of aesthetic communities would necessitate investigating how learning processes can be constituted by aesthetically inspired forms of sociality and communication.

However, learning processes in aesthetic communities are based on a notion of communication different from the ability to make their practices the subject of argumentative debate and communicative conflict resolution. This latter definition of communication is predominantly obliged to the development and diffusion of processes of cognitive reflection, as in Giddens' concept of life politics or in Habermas' idea of communicative action. Yet, such definitions direct the attention too one-sidedly to a rational 'discourse of ethics'. They do not make allowance for the increasing pervasiveness of an aesthetic reflexivity in society today. And yet this kind of reflexivity constitutes exactly the starting-point to understand how learning processes may occur in aesthetic communities.

According to Lash and Urry (1994), and unlike its cognitive counterpart, aesthetic reflexivity neither entails monitoring a subject-object relationship of the self to itself, nor presupposes the prevalence of judgement over immersion and involvement. It is rather based upon prejudgements: interpretations of the self as a being-in-the-world, and of social practices that shape the background of its horizons. In relation to the sociality of aesthetic communities, however, the most significant element of aesthetic reflexivity consists of a reflexive creation and invention of the symbol-systems that appeal to feelings of togetherness and solidarity. In many cases the participants are very well aware of their creation of such symbol systems and consciously make use of them to express the singularity and the togetherness of the community. Yet it is exactly this awareness which permanently opens up choices and necessitates decisions whether to join or leave such communities. Therefore, the rise of the aesthetic community implies identity choices and new forms of identification. On the one hand the aesthetic style of sociality transforms the subject, previously conceived of as an autonomous being, into a heteronomous being, existing only through and thanks to her or his co-existence with the other. On the other, the possibility of aesthetic reflection upon the meaning of communities to take 'care of the self' attunes the subject to a wide range of experiences and sensations and enables rapid switches between an immediate immersion into a particular community, and a distantiation and detachment from the sociality it creates (cf. Featherstone 1995). For that reason, Maffesoli (1995) states that aesthetic communities fissure the identity of the subject into many places: they transform identification into identifications, that are more attached to a loose agglomeration of places than to the temporal development of a consistent identity.

The recognition of the emergence of new forms of identification throws another light on the trinity of social cohesion, collective responsibility and identity represented in the majority of modernist concepts and policies. In these, identities are thought of as the product and articulation of hierarchically inscribed historical positions within the social order. These both enable and restrict possibilities for (the representation and legitimation of) one's experiences, and the responsibilities for one's actions (cf. Grossberg 1996). As a consequence, issues of social responsibility and cohesion are more often than not linked to definitions of identity in terms of difference and deficiency (cf. Jansen and Wildemeersch 1996). However, Grossberg demonstrates clearly that postmodern forms of identification point to different planes of individuation and belonging. As a consequence, the modern unity of identity, social position (cohesion) and agency (responsibility), which would function as one single 'map' for the definition and production of identification and belonging, is falling apart today.

Agency pertains to possibilities of moving into particular sites of power and activity, and of belonging to them in such a way that one can 'make things happen', ie to wield transformative power. Questions of agency therefore have to do with one's access to and participation in specific kinds of places, and imply the structured mobility of people to move into and belong to the places where strategic possibilities to enact power and transform reality are created. From this point of view, participation in aesthetic communities is not a matter of identifying and identity, but of affiliation. It enables people to belong to a community that takes 'care of the self' by being together in a particular place, without ascribing a common identity to its participants. These places are temporary points of belonging, that define the forms of agency and of 'making history' that are available to particular groups, while going in and out of them. They are the intersection of various 'maps' of identity, meaning and desire, where different processes of individuation and of subjectivation are articulated. Participation in aesthetic communities calls for a concept of belonging without identity: how to find the way in and belong to a variety of places and practices that empower through its forms of being-together, without equating contextually and temporary defined involvement with the image of a complete and continuing identification.

Taking into account the significance of aesthetic reflexivity and its implications for questions of identification implies the need for a conceptualization of communication and collective learning, that is different from mainstream adult education. The aesthetic community does not seek an 'ideal speech community', nor for ethical justifications of self-actualisation in a globalized world. It is an expression of the desire to experience togetherness, as a condition 'feeling good' and enjoying life. Communication then is about the possibility of contacting and touching the other. And the aesthetic reflection upon such communication does not focus on the validity and the legitimation of the reasons for participation that are implied, but on the question where, when and for whom a particular community does signify such a sense of belonging. As a consequence, collective learning is not about the facilitation of argumentative discourses in and by these communities, but deals with their capacity to communicate in a sensible way the moral and affective significance of the symbol-systems and lifestyles, that are implied in the forms of sociality they create.

Adult education, then, is challenged with respect to both its possible contribution to the promotion of aesthetic communication and reflection, and to its facilitation of learning processes that are aesthetically informed. These challenges point to a twofold orientation of adult education: a social learning orientation and a biographical learning orientation. On the one hand adult education has a role to play in furthering access to and participation in places where people take care of themselves by the common enactment of transformational power. On the other hand, adult education has a mission in facilitating people's involvement in different and successive communities. Adult education may play a role here, by its support of learning processes on how to make sense of new images and modes of living, and how to overcome the fears and threats these may imply. But it may also have a function in creating conditions and experiences that enable people to get in touch with different places and to live through a variety of affiliations, without risking a complete loss of control over their emotions and desires by the incoherence of a steady flow of sensations and images.

Such a 'mission' stands in opposition to communitarian ideals that confine the sociality of people to the borderlines of imagined communities and discourage border-crossing between different communities. It is also contrary to neo-liberal options that leave it to the 'negative freedom' of the individual autonomously to find a way through the unpredictable and chaotic conditions of postmodernity yet neglect its desire for 'positive freedom' (expressed in the ever-changing choices to be and to act together with like-minded people). It rather implies the articulation of a different notion of social cohesion and social participation. This notion would situate communication and interaction not in the ethical and rational foundation of reasons, and in the tension between consensus and dissension this involves, but in the extended reflectivity related to the enactment of lifestyles and symbol-systems. Cohesion and participation are situated in aesthetic processes of affective involvement and detachment that connect the self to others in different contexts and in various places, and thereby give rise to new blends of social engagement and respect on the one hand, and care for the self and social distantiation on the other.

Such a view of cohesion and participation makes clear that the 'entrepreneurial identity' that is implied in dominant concepts of lifelong learning, conceives of the learner in a very one-sided way. Ethical qualities and concerns of learning subjects are far more complex and diffuse than is imagined in concepts of lifelong learning that declare the rational calculating, market oriented 'entrepreneur of the self' the alpha and omega of all spheres of social life. Such images too easily neglect that the rationality of entrepreneurialism originates from and belongs to the life order of the market. Its diffusion to different domains of public life not only suppresses and undermines the peculiar ways of life and the particular mentalities of these domains. It also collides with wants and desires of human beings that hide from the enterpreneurial view, but that represent a substantial part of the 'postmodern' condition: the rising need for an aesthetization of communality.

References

Beck, U (1992) *Risk Society*, Sage, London.
Eder, K (1993) *The New Politics of Class*, Sage, London.
Featherstone, M (1995) *Undoing Culture*, Sage, London.
du Gay, P (1996) *Consumption and Identity at Work*, Sage, London.
Giddens, A (1990) *The Consequences of Modernity*, Polity, Cambridge.
Grossberg, L (1996) 'Identity and Cultural Studies – Is That All There Is?', in S Hall and P du Gay (Eds) *Questions of Cultural Identity*, Sage, London.
Jansen, T and Wildemeersch, D (1996) 'Adult Education and Critical Identity Development', *International Journal of Lifelong Education*, 15 (5), 325–340.
van der Lans, J (1995) *De onzichtbare samenleving*, Nizw, Utrecht.
Lash, S and Urry, J (1994) *Economies of Signs and Space*, Sage, London.
Maffesoli, M (1995) *The Contemplation of the World*, University of Minnesota Press, Minneapolis.
Wildemeersch, D, Finger M and Jansen T (Eds) (1998) *Adult Education for Social Responsibility: Reconciling the Irreconcilable?*, Peter Lang, Frankfurt.

Chapter 8

Lifelong Learning Through the Habermasian Lens:
Providing a Theoretical Grounding to Adult Education Practice

Brian Connelly

Introduction

Adult educators are increasingly recognizing the importance of Habermas' ideas for their theory and practice. However, they do not explain these sufficiently in Habermasian theoretical terms, nor recognize their full significance for education and society. In particular, these interpretations do not sufficiently recognize Habermas' developmental account of rationality nor his discussion of the relationship of the state and the public sphere. These Habermasian themes demonstrate that adult education has a lifelong, educational and political role, which is important to the advancement of a more democratic and open society.

Habermas' theory of communicative action

Habermas has developed an interdisciplinary macrotheory of communicative action based on a long-term critical engagement with, and modification of, theories of philosophy, sociology, politics, psychology and linguistics. Two motifs underpin this communicative theory: the increasing dominance of purposive rationality in society, and the need to develop a communicatively-based rational challenge to this (Habermas 1979, 1988c, 1991). Purposive-rational action is an ends-oriented action, involving either instrumental action to influence the external world or strategic action to influence others. It is with the former that Habermas is primarily concerned. Communicative rational action is process-oriented: ends are attained through a process of reaching an agreement based on mutual respect and understanding. Habermas asserts that it is in the distinction between these two rationalities that the development and structure of society can be explained.

Habermas argues that communicative action is implicit in the speech act and language, as the very attempt of taking part in discussion implies recognition of the possibility of achieving a consensus. In the 'ideal speech situation' this consensus should be achieved on rational grounds only, and thus be free of external constraints and influences. Such an ideal speech situation is counter-factual in that it is unlikely to be achieved in the real world; nevertheless, it acts as a standard against which to assess existing argument and practice.

This standard of communicative rationality requires the raising, testing and validation of universal validity claims. Habermas argues that in speech acts people take up a relationship with one or more worlds. Each of these actor-world relationships is characterized by a validity claim. The objective claim of truth relates the speaker to the cognitive-instrumental world of external reality and science; the subjective claim of truthfulness relates the speaker to the aesthetic-expressive world of authenticity, meaning and intention; the social claim of normative rightness relates the speaker to the moral-practical world of agreed norms and values.

Habermas (1979, 1988a, 1991) asserts that the lifeworld performs three functions which correspond to these worlds. The lifeworld reproduces the culture, social integration and processes of socialization necessary to the continuation of society. In our everyday social life the claims associated with these functions are not challenged, as they occur within a shared lifeworld of consensual background knowledge and action. Indeed, this undisputed lifeworld historically characterized traditional, archaic society. However, as society has evolved and become increasingly complex, economic and political-administrative institutions split off from the lifeworld to form a more purposive-rationally oriented systems world. These institutions are no longer primarily steered by communicative considerations but by instrumental considerations of money and power. Habermas recognizes that this development was functionally necessary, but argues that now this systems world has become too dominated by purposive-rationality.

Further, the systems world is also increasingly invading and 'colonizing' the lifeworld and attacking its communicative values and institutions. Habermas (1991) refers to the increasing 'juridification', or welfare state bureaucratization and monetarization, of the institutions of the family and education as an example of this.

Habermas is concerned to identify communicatively-informed institutions in the lifeworld which can challenge this colonizing and instrumentalizing process. At different times in his writings he identifies a public sphere of reformed, democratized political parties and pressure groups (1989b), the student movement (1987c), the women's movement (1992) and new social movements (NSMs) (1987b, 1992) as potential vehicles for this communicative challenge. More recently, Habermas (1996) has extended his notion of the public sphere, or civil society, to argue that a range of political institutions and associations may challenge and influence the state institutions of the systems world.

Interpretations of Habermas

Habermas' analysis resonates strongly with adult educators who perceive this instrumentalizing process increasingly affecting their institutions and practice. Equally, Habermas' belief in a communicative challenge based on democratic, rational, dialogical action resonates with educators who associate these qualities with practice and theory in adult education – whether this theory and practice is informed by a more liberal or radical approach. The three major promoters of Habermas' ideas in adult education theory are Mezirow, Collins and Welton. Mezirow (1990, 1991) bases his theory of perspective transformation on the linguistic aspects of Habermas' communicative theory. Perspective transformation is a process of transformative critical, dialogical reflection on the constraining psycho-social assumptions which form identity. This process primarily emphasizes individual autonomy, perception and transformation, although it may also lead to collective action. The social aspects of Habermas' theory are not considered: Mezirow (1991, in Welton 1995) briefly recognizes Habermas' system-lifeworld thesis, and the implications for adult education of the colonizing trend, but does not analyse this within Habermas' structural, developmental context.

For Collins (1991, in Welton 1995) this structural context is also important: the colonization of the lifeworld is central to an understanding of the increasing instrumentalizing of adult education by neo-conservative governments and ideologies. This instrumentalizing takes such forms as the increasing technicization, accreditation and professionalization of adult education. Collins argues that adult education must adopt Habermas' critical, discursive mode of practice to oppose this developments. This opposition must take place in the institution through the encouragement of critical discourse and democratic practices in areas such as professional relationships, the curriculum and teaching practice. But the communicative attitude should also be encouraged at a wider social level through the co-operation of adult education with important social movements, such as those concerned with women's, peace and environmental issues, which are concerned to preserve and foster the communicative constituents of the lifeworld. Collins' analysis reflects Habermas' concern about the growth of neo-conservatism (1989a, 1991) and his identification of the possible, oppositional role of NSMs (1987a, 1992).

Collins limits his discussion of the structural features of Habermas' theory primarily to the colonization process. Welton (1991, 1995), however, demonstrates a stronger analytical understanding of both the systems-lifeworld structure and its underlying evolutionary dynamic. Welton (1993, 1995) also emphasizes more strongly than Collins the role of NSMs. These NSMs are the major vehicle through which adult educators can work towards a more democratic society. The role of critical adult education, in co-operation with these NSMs, must be 'to preserve the communicative infrastructure of the lifeworld and extend communicative action into state or economic institutions' (1995: 156).

These interpretations contribute to a Habermasian-informed theory of lifelong learning. Mezirow (in Welton, 1995) proposes the development of a learning society characterized by a reflective critical community, while Collins (1991) emphasizes the role of the adult educator in promoting critical practice in educational institutions and in arenas of emancipatory action. Welton (1995) proposes a critical social learning paradigm which emphasizes 'developmental citizenship', a collective learning which takes place primarily through political engagement with state and economic institutions. However, these interpretations are limited: they do not recognize the full potential of Habermas' theory for educational and political practice.

Further themes in Habermas' social theory

Habermas' account of the communicative potential of the institutions and traditions of the lifeworld provides theorists of adult education with descriptive and normative interpretations of the role of adult education. However, omissions exist in these interpretations which prevent a fuller recognition of adult education's potential communicative, lifelong role. First, Habermas' evolutionary schema offers more than a phylogenetic description of the development of rationality at the societal level. Habermas (1979, 1990) also proposes an ontogenetic biographical account: this posits the development of cognitive-moral rationality through a number of stages in the individual to a post-conventional stage of universalistic principles and values. It is at this post-conventional stage that communicative discourse and action can take place.

Second, at the more structural, phylogenetic level adult educators who celebrate the new social movements as the major vehicle for the furtherance of transformatory adult educational practice do not recognize Habermas' (1992) ambivalent attitude towards NSMs. Habermas asserts that these may possess particularistic, illiberal as well as universal, progressive qualities. More importantly, this celebration of NSMs by adult educators ignores Habermas' (1989b, 1996) recognition of the communicative potential of other institutions and associations in the public sphere or civil society. Habermas asserts that 'peripheral' political institutions and associations of the public sphere 'give voice to social problems, make broad demands, articulate public interests or needs and thus attempt to influence the politic process' (1996: 355). This periphery is essential to the legitimacy of the political institutions and the law; the latter, if they wish to retain their legitimacy 'must be steered by communication flows which start at the periphery and pass through the sluices of democratic and constitutional procedures' (1996: 356).

Third, the negative, colonizing view of the state presented by adult educators in their celebration of NSMs is not an accurate reflection of Habermas' representation of the communicative role and possibilities of the advanced welfare state. Habermas' (1987b, 1989a) view of the welfare state has been more ambivalent. He argues that the social welfare state represents the most communicative level of institutionalized law so far achieved: despite its capitalist-legitimating and lifeworld-colonizing role, the welfare state also represents a legal, moral and democratic advance in terms of the universalistic principles underlying the legal rights and entitlements of its citizens. In sum, the welfare state possesses both communicative and instrumental features.

Further, this earlier ambivalent view of the state's role has become more positive in Habermas' more recent works. The earlier Habermas (1988a) argued that the legitimacy of the state relied on its ability to maintain capitalism through the fostering of instrumental values in the public and private spheres of the lifeworld. Habermas (1996) now argues that the social-welfare state draws its legitimacy from the maintenance and protection of popular sovereignty and civil and political rights. Thus Habermas asserts: 'The institutions of the constitutional state are supposed to secure an effective exercise of the political autonomy of socially autonomous citizens' (1996: 176).

Lifelong learning in the public sphere

The recognition of these themes in Habermas' theory provides a fuller and more important role for adult education in lifelong learning than has so far been recognized. At the ontological level of his thesis of developmental rationality, Habermas views the discursive post-conventional stage as the culmination of a psychological development which only or primarily adults can achieve. This provides a potentially distinct role for adult education practice in the fostering or utilizing of this communicative capacity. This role can be taken further. Habermas sees this ontogenetic development not in linear but in dialectical terms: the communicative-rational development of society and individual are mutually dependent on each other. Thus, adults are more likely to attain the post-conventional stage in a more advanced and democratic form of society; equally, society is more likely to develop on communicative lines if at least some of its members have attained the post-conventional stage. Habermas recognizes that this ontogenetic post-conventional stage is partly counter-factual, in that some adults never attain a discursive capacity. Nevertheless, the fact that Western societies are underpinned by the universalistic principles of constitutional law and social welfarism demonstrates that at least those individuals and institutions responsible for formulating and instituting these principles do possess this communicative quality.

This has clear implications for a role for adult education which extends beyond the rational advancement of the individual; this role can contribute also to the communicative, democratic advancement of society at the wider institutional and social levels. As Habermas (1996) recognizes, a core feature of adulthood in modern democratic societies is that adults are citizens with certain civil and political rights and responsibilities. Adult education, in both an educational and political context, can help adult learners *qua* citizens in their attempts both to attain the post-conventional stage, and thus advance their own rationality, and to contribute to the advancement of society's level of democracy and rationality through political discourse and action. Chambers asserts that this discursive procedure is intrinsically educational: 'A discursively formed public opinion can represent a process of *Bildung* or education in which citizens build better foundations to their opinions through discursive interaction' (in White 1995: 238).

Chambers also recognizes that this opinion-forming may need some assistance. Adult education can contribute to this process, particularly for those who may have to develop their skills and understanding if they are to play an effective part in the discursive process. This is important if discourse is to be open to all so that people can exercise their civil and political rights equally. In this sense adult education is important to democracy: it can facilitate access to discourse on more equal and effective terms, thus enhancing the capacity of the individual or the peripheral, 'opinion-forming' associations to influence the political process. To be effective this access must be on a lifelong basis. This can only be guaranteed if adult education is regarded as a social right: the state should grant legal recognition and provide the material resources for adult education to perform this important educational *qua* political role.

This lifelong role for adult education would take two forms. The communicative capacities of the individual may be enhanced within formal educational institutions through politically and dialogically informed curriculum and practice. These communicative capacities can also be encouraged in both the individual and the organization through wider, educational and political activity in the 'peripheral' public sphere institutions. This 'developmental citizenship' might take the form of participation in new social movements and pressure groups. However, it could also refer to the encouragement of other communicatively-informed political associations such as citizens' juries and policy analysis forums which would engage in critical discourse on proposed or existing policies and issues.

In conclusion, Habermas' thesis of the dialectical phylogenetic-ontogenetic advancement of rationality and democracy, and his account of the relationship of the state and the public sphere, demonstrates that adult educators can justify their practice on Habermasian-theoretical normative grounds. Adult education in the lifelong context can make an important contribution to individual and collective empowerment, democratic government and communicative advance. This role is so vital in a society increasingly dominated by instrumental practices and values that lifelong adult education should be recognized and guaranteed by the state. As Peukertruth states: 'How serious we are about democracy is revealed in how serious we are about education' (1993: 167).

References

Chambers, S (1995) 'Discourse and Democratic Practices', in SK White (Ed.) *The Cambridge Companion to Habermas*, Cambridge University Press, Cambridge.

Collins, M (1991) *Adult Education as Vocation: A Critical Role for the Adult Educator*, Routledge, London.

Collins, M. (1995) 'Critical Commentaries on the Role of the Adult Educator: From Self- Directed Learning to Postmodernist Sensibilities', in MR Welton (Ed.), *In Defense of the Lifeworld: Critical Perspectives on Adult Learning*, State University of New York Press, Albany.

Habermas, J (1979) *Communication and the Evolution of Society*, trans. T McCarthy, Heinemann, London.

Habermas, J (1987a) *The Philosophical Discourse of Modernity*, trans. FG Lawrence, Polity Press, Cambridge.

Habermas, J (1987b) *The Theory of Communicative Action. Vol. 2. Lifeworld and System: A Critique of Functionalist Reason*, trans. T McCarthy, Polity Press, Cambridge.

Habermas, J (1987c) *Toward a Rational Society*, trans. JJ Shapiro, Polity Press, Cambridge.

Habermas, J (1988a) *Legitimation Crisis*, trans. T McCarthy, Polity Press, Cambridge.

Habermas, J (1988b) *On the Logic of the Social Sciences*, trans. T McCarthy, Polity Press, Cambridge.

Habermas, J (1988c) *Theory and Practice*, trans. J Viertel, Polity Press, Cambridge.

Habermas, J (1989a) *The New Conservatism*, trans. SW Nicholsen, Polity Press, Cambridge.

Habermas, J (1989b) *The Structural Transformation of the Public Sphere*, trans. T Burger with assistance of F Lawrence, Polity Press, Cambridge.

Habermas, J (1990) *Moral Consciousness and Communicative Action*, trans. C Lenhardt and S Weber Nicholsen, Polity Press, Cambridge.

Habermas, J (1991) *The Theory of Communicative Action. Vol. 1. Reason and the Rationalization of Society*, trans. T McCarthy, Polity Press, Cambridge.

Habermas, J (1992) *Autonomy and Solidarity: Interviews with Jurgen Habermas*, Ed. P Dews, Verso, London.

Habermas. J (1996) *Between Facts and Norms: Contributions to a Discourse Theory of Law and Democracy*, trans. W Rehg, Polity Press, Cambridge.

Mezirow, J and associates (1990) *Fostering Critical Reflection in Adulthood: A Guide to Transformative and Emancipatory Learning*, Jossey-Bass, San Francisco.

Mezirow, J (1991) *Transformative Dimensions of Adult Learning*, Jossey Bass, San Francisco.

Mezirow, J (1995) 'Transformation Theory of Adult Learning', in MR Welton (Ed.) *In Defense of the Lifeworld: Critical Perspectives on Adult Learning*, State University of New York Press, Albany.

Peukertruth, H (1993) 'Basic Problems of a Critical Theory of Education', *Journal of Philosophy of Education*, 27 (2), 159–169.

Welton, M (1991) 'Shaking the Foundations: the Critical Turn in Adult Education Theory', *The Canadian Journal for the Study of Adult Education*, Winter, 5, 21–42.

Welton, M (1993) 'Social Revolutionary Movements: the New Social Movements as Learning Sites', *Adult Education Quarterly*, 43 (3), 152–164.

Welton, MR (Ed.) (1995) *In Defence of the Lifeworld: Critical Perspectives on Adult Learning*, State University of New York Press, Albany.

White, SK (Ed.) (1995) *The Cambridge Companion to Habermas*, Cambridge University Press, Cambridge.

PART III

LIFELONG LEARNING AND POLITICAL TRANSITIONS

Chapter 9

From Apartheid Education to Lifelong Learning:
Assessing the Ameliorative Potential of Emerging Education Policy in South Africa

Bobby Soobrayan

After having long thought of ourselves as special, South Africans are beginning to realize just how similar our 'home-grown' policies are turning out to be to those of the rest of the world. For a range of reasons which cannot be entered into here, much of the policy discourses in education in South Africa are being shaped by the international context. However, as Christie (1996) has argued, these discourses are being mediated and constituted in particular ways by forces in the South African context. This paper seeks to conduct an assessment of the ameliorative potential of emerging education policy in South Africa. I propose to focus this assessment largely on how the concept of 'lifelong learning' is being employed in the conceptualization and rhetoric of emerging education policy. The paper begins with a critical review of the major policies and discourses related to lifelong learning in South Africa. This is followed by an attempt to explore how contextual factors are shaping these discourses and related education policies in South Africa. Finally, I present some thoughts on the possibilities and constraints related to improving the ameliorative potential of education policy in South Africa.

Although 'lifelong learning' does not feature explicitly in policy debates, it is probably the touchstone of the overarching conceptual framework of emerging education policy in South Africa. In fact, direct references to 'lifelong learning' are not frequent and, where they do occur, often receive only brief reference. In the first comprehensive policy pronouncements, contained in the *Draft White Paper on Education and Training* of 1994 of the new Department of Education, there are two references made to lifelong learning in the section on goals and principles:

> 'Education and training is the major vehicle for human resource development. In the Reconstruction and Development Programme it is seen as a broad-based set of activities, without boundaries in time and place. The underlying goal is that South Africans should have access to lifelong learning. It should be available not just in schools and other educational institutions, but in homes and workplaces' (DoE 1994: 10).

and:

> 'The overarching goal of policy must therefore be to enable all individuals to have access to *lifelong education and training*, irrespective of race, class, gender, creed or age' (DoE 1994: 11).

Ever since lifelong education was advocated by UNESCO in the early 1960s as its 'master concept' for education planning (Wain 1987) it has spawned much debate in education circles and a significant body of literature (Wain 1987, Giere 1994). From its early formulations to the recent re-emergence of lifelong education in the education literature and even when it has been invoked to inform education policies of many countries, lifelong learning has been conferred with multiple meanings and interpretations (Giere 1994).

Similarly, in South Africa today lifelong learning assumes multiple meanings and interpretations in the way it is applied and articulated in policy discourses on education transformation. At one extreme, it is employed as a coherent conceptual framework which presents a comprehensive and particular understanding of education priorities, the strategies required to address these and a fundamental assertion of a radically different and distinct pedagogy. At another level, its more simpler expression places emphasis on the temporal plane, making education available throughout the life cycle. In this form, the major questions posed relate to access and provision rooted in a discourse of equity. In this latter dimension there is no explicit focus on pedagogy; the main emphasis being on expanding present education provision to more.

In its many formulations lifelong learning appears to be influenced by many discourses. I wish to expand on two of these discourses. The first is primarily an economic discourse which emphasizes the need to develop appropriate skills for the economy: 'The primary goal of the Skills Development Strategy must be to raise the competence, motivation and adaptability of the workforce, to support increases in productivity in the workplace and rising employability of the working age population' (Department of Labour 1997: 65). The second is an equity discourse which is predicated on the assumption that improved access of target groups to skills development will result in a more balanced distribution of skills across the population and, consequently, to a redistribution of employment and earnings. While these two discourses are often conflated in the rhetoric, they are analytically distinct and will be analyzed as such here. I will now turn to a more detailed analysis of how the concept lifelong learning is being expressed in emerging education policies in South Africa.

The process of formulating policy for an alternative to apartheid education preceded the political transition which began with the unbanning of popular political movements in 1990. Soon after the first democratic elections in 1994, the new government, with varying participation of various stakeholders from civil society, soon embarked on a comprehensive revision of education policy, the major tenets of which revolve around two interrelated but analytically distinct discourses: one focused primarily on economic growth and the other primarily on equity. Today, three years after the inception of democratic rule, the intention of promoting a system of lifelong learning has already found expression in some important policy pronouncement and legislation. Central to this process has been the establishment of a National Qualifications Framework (NQF), which explicitly seeks to increase learning opportunities throughout the life-cycle and to remove the barriers which militate against this. The proposals allow for the recognition of prior learning and intends to harmonize qualifications horizontally and vertically, throughout an integrated system of education and training, to allow for portability of learning between tracks and over time. Policy documents stress a shift from an emphasis on 'inputs' to one on 'outputs' or 'outcomes' as articulated in the emphasis on Outcomes Based Education.

Although Outcomes Based Education is, yet again, another construct that carries multiple meanings, it has at one level been employed as a logical extension of a National Qualifications Framework. By shifting the stress to outcomes and by institutionalizing the definition of outcomes associated with particular qualifications, the policy seeks to create enabling conditions for education and training to take place in multiple sites with no limiting prescriptions in respect of inputs or time. It provides an essential framework for the implementation of the recognition of prior learning; portability of credits between tracks, and the accreditation of institutions and qualifications.

'Outcomes-based learning makes it possible to credit learners' achievements at every level, regardless of the learning pathway they might have followed, and at whatever rate they may have acquired the necessary competence' (Department of Education 1996: 38).

At this level, Outcomes Based Education is invoked to perform a somewhat technical function of harmonizing educational qualifications and of separating qualifications from the process involved in obtaining the qualification. Consequently, it constitutes what I would call a minimalist view, one which calls on Outcomes Based Education to deliver on mainly administrative challenges of a National Qualifications Framework.

At another level Outcomes Based Education is being employed as a guide to curriculum change within a conceptual framework of progressive pedagogy. A further motivation often cited in policy documents for adopting an Outcomes Based Education is that the shift of focus to outcomes will necessitate a shift of focus to skills. In this context, skills are often implied to mean the ability of a learner to demonstrate a particular competence. It assumes that skills, if properly defined, will facilitate the achievement of a greater relevance between education and work or, more to the point, between education and economic development. Here, the discourse of economic growth features as a key focus of policy. The tendency to link Outcomes Based Education with progressive pedagogy has happened mainly in curriculum transformation of the public formal school system and is located in a discourse of transformation.

I have tried to demonstrate above that there are a number of analytically distinct discourses that overlap in the education policy nexus in South Africa. These discourses are used interchangeably in policy documents and the particular discourse drafted into service depends on the policy objectives being motivated for. Although the subject of much debate, some have argued that economic and equity imperatives can, and must, be reconciled if any country is to succeed in achieving a sustainable development path (Psacharopoulos and Woodhall 1985). Economic growth, if not a necessary condition for achieving equity, is certainly a facilitator – particularly in contexts where options for radical redistributive strategies are considered incompatible with the hegemonic view on the ideal economic growth model and on what would lead to the greatest political stability. However, there are many competing perspectives on whether economic and equity imperatives can be reconciled and, even for those who believe that this is possible, there has been competing perspectives on how best to achieve this.

My central contention in this paper is that factors in the policy context of South Africa is exerting a powerful and overriding mediating influence on the interplay between these different discourses and their impact on education policies. I will now turn to a brief analysis of what I consider to be one pre-eminent factor, the macroeconomic policies adopted by the new government, to assess its likely influence on education policies.

One of the most important mediating factors to influence the process of translating discourse into policy and outcomes can be found in the South African government's new macroeconomic policy. There are perhaps three reasons for this. First (and the more obvious reason), macroeconomic policy, especially monetary and fiscal policies, will influence the nature and extent of government financing of lifelong learning. In the policy world, this is always a sobering variable in the determination of what is possible and how ideals get translated into action plans. Second, it has become customary for economists and others charged with formulating strategies for improving economic development to look to education as the main instrument for a planned intervention. This raises tremendous expectations which education policy-makers are nervously aware of. The third reason is that macroeconomic policy often serves to interact dialectically with the dominant development discourses within which education policy-makers try to define the aims and goals of education.

Perhaps one of the central and most contested element of the government's present macroeconomic policy revolves around the strong emphasis on fiscal discipline and the consequent commitment to reduce the budget deficit. The pre-election and immediate post-election rhetoric of the governing party, the African National Congress, as enshrined in the Reconstruction and Development Programme, sought to bring about growth, reconstruction and redistribution within a Keynesian framework (NIEP 1996) and tended to highlight redistribution as a major policy objective and fiscal discipline as a means of achieving this in a sustainable way. However, the present policy appears to have raised fiscal discipline as an objective, with redistribution now enjoying much less prominence. The government's new authoritative pronouncements, as articulated in the Growth, Employment and Redistribution (GEAR) strategy, puts it thus:

> 'In response to the unsustainable fiscal situation that had developed by 1992/3, when the overall deficit reached 9.0 per cent of GDP, fiscal policy has been informed by the following goals:
> - to cut the overall budget deficit and the level of government dissaving
> - to avoid permanent increases in the overall tax burden
> - to reduce the general government consumption expenditure relative to GDP
> - to strengthen the general government contribution to gross domestic fixed investment' (Department of Finance 1996: 9).

After declaring (somewhat uncritically), that 'progress in education shows up consistently in comparative studies as a key determinant of long-run economic performance and income redistribution', it continues:

> 'With spending on education at nearly seven per cent of GDP there is a need to contain expenditure through reductions in subsidization of the more expensive parts of the system and greater private-sector involvement in higher education' (Department of Finance 1996: 15).

Considering that increases in government revenue consequent upon a growth of GDP will in all likelihood first be allocated in favour of bringing down the budget deficit, it is unlikely that government spending on education and training will increase in real terms even in a climate of moderate economic growth. The overwhelming portion of the education and training budget, which already accounts for 21 per cent of the overall budget, is used to run the formal schooling system. Around 75 per cent of the total education recurrent expenditure is presently being used for personnel costs (Hofmeyr and Hall no date). This leaves very little with which to meet the resounding demand for an increase in spending on non-teacher items. Therefore any additional vote of funding to education will immediately be absorbed to deal with what many consider to be a dire need in the schooling system. So, while the rhetoric of lifelong learning calls for education throughout the life cycle, government funding now and in the foreseeable future will not be available in any meaningful way beyond the conventional formal system.

The formal institution-based education system cannot be an appropriate vehicle for achieving equity objectives, because the majority of the target populations have neither the minimum educational entry requirement, the time nor the money to enrol at any of the formal post-secondary institutions. Given the above budgetary reality, even though the challenges associated with achieving equitable access to quality formal education are big, the more intractable problem is creating education and training opportunities for those who fall outside of the formal system. This is the major challenge for moving from the present system to lifelong learning in respect of its limited objective of access. Before assessing the government's proposals for responding to the education and training needs of the latter sector, it is first necessary to provide a brief overview of some salient socio-economic and labour market characteristics of this group.

Perhaps the most powerful reason for a strong equity focus in South Africa derives from the racial structure of employment patterns. Africans account for 75 per cent of the population who are not economically active (60 per cent of whom are women) and account for 87 per cent of the unemployed (55 per cent of whom are women) (Department of Labour 1996). The category 'self-employed' denotes very different realities for different racial groups: 35 per cent of economically active African women are self-employed, of which 69 per cent earn between R0 and R400 per month and only 4 per cent earn over R2000 per month (Department of Labour 1996). On the other end of the continuum, 20 per cent of white men are self-employed, of which 6 per cent earn R0-R400 per month and 82 per cent earn over R2000 per month (Department of Labour 1996). The majority of the self-employed African women and men tend to run enterprises in the informal economy, generally not out of choice but as a survival strategy in the face of unemployment and rural underdevelopment. These enterprises are generally on a micro scale and have very trying working conditions. Their fortunes are very unpredictable and cyclical.

The steadily increasing numbers of new jobseekers entering the labour market each year are faced with a stagnation of employment growth in the formal economy. The relative share of low-wage jobs in the labour market has increased from the 1970s to about one-third of total jobs and:

> '...a large pool of unemployed men and women, who earn no income or derive sporadic earnings from informal self-employment, make up about a third of the potential labour force' (Department of Finance 1996: 17).

In addition, growing unemployment in the country is being accompanied by a trend towards casualization of labour.

> 'Irregular, sub-contracted, outsourced or part-time employment on semi-formal contractual terms is becoming the preferred source of labour for many employers. This is resulting in a growing gap between the wages and benefits in the regulated and unregulated parts of the labour market. Where regulations raise the costs of job creation, employers turn to unregulated forms of employment' (Department of Finance 1996: 17).

The ameliorative potential of any policy intervention will have to be assessed in terms of whether or not it has adequately accounted for the twin challenges of a highly segmented labour market and one of the largest income inequalities in the world (Department of Labour 1996).

I have thus far devoted this paper to an analysis of the implications of fiscal policies on the discourses associated with, and likely outcomes of, lifelong learning. The fundamental assumption underpinning the economic and equity discourses on lifelong learning – the power of education, as a sole or major variable, to influence economic and social outcomes – has remained unproblematized. It is to this analysis that I will now turn.

Ever since Theodore Shultz (1961) delivered his seminal address to the American Economic Association on human capital theory, and Denison's

(1962) and Becker's (1964) highly publicized empirical investigation of the link between education and economic development, there have been cycles of optimism followed by periods of scepticism about the validity of these claims. The quantitative studies which underpin human capital theory and 'growth accounting' have been the subject of much controversy in intellectual and policy communities (Blaug 1976, Stronach 1990). Apart from the many challenges raised about the reliability of the data, the validity of the selection of variables and the accuracy of their assessment, the main claim that a 'residual' (that part of economic growth which cannot be attributable to factors of production such as capital, labour and land) is largely accounted for by increases in aggregate education has left many unconvinced (Stronach 1990). The decline of the residual after 1973 has challenged this assumption (Mincer 1984). Roderick and Stephens suggest that the propensity to isolate a single variable (such as education) across different contexts may be an over-simplification.

> 'The links between the education system and the rest of the social structure are peculiar to the society concerned. Separate analysis of the economy and education, therefore, if used to explain differential levels of economic performance, may lead to over-simplified accounts and optimistic hopes, through quick changes in educational policy, of rapid alleviation of malfunction, the roots of which lie in complex interrelationships between a wide range of social institutions whose characteristic quality may depend on the apparent vagaries of historical development' (1981, cited in Stronach 1990: 163).

Despite the many unresolved conceptual issues associated with the relationship between education and economic development, the policy discourse in South Africa has invested much faith in lifelong learning. A further assumption, on which much of this faith is nurtured, is the belief that moving from a 'low-skilled' labour force towards a 'high-skilled' labour force will be accompanied by a movement from a low wage economy toward a high waged one. This assumption is rooted in the following logic: high skills = higher productivity = greater economic growth – the very logic that lies at the heart of human capital theory. A common tendency in the discourse is the tendency to motivate strategies for a high-skilled labour force based on the view that many successful economies are increasingly being characterized by post-Fordist production (Edwards 1993, Avis 1996). In concluding that post-Fordism is an ideal goal on economic grounds, it is argued that an appropriate skills development strategy which responds to the needs of post-Fordism will encourage its emergence in the economy, lead to economic growth along a high-waged path with superior conditions for labour.

What is poorly understood, and remains largely untheorized, is an analysis of what factors would drive the transformation of the production process characterized by Fordism to one that is characterized by post-Fordism. The implicit assumption in the discourse that a transformation of the nature of skills development or training will constitute a sufficient catalyst for this transformation is asserted without convincing and contextually relevant empirical justification. Once again, this reflects how poorly we understand the forces that contribute to economic growth and, in this instance, the transformation of the dominant character of production. Surely there were primarily economic imperatives, rooted perhaps in the need to be competitive which drove the process in highly industrialized countries. It ignores the complex interplay of contextual variables, mediated by historical factors which must have shaped this process. There is no compelling empirical justification which warrant the power that has been invested in skills development which leads to the belief that post-Fordism can be the policy objective to be achieved almost exclusively through a high skill profile of the labour force. A further problem is that the thrust of the discourse on the relationship between education and economic development is firmly focused on only one factor of production: labour or, more precisely, the skills of labour. The other factors of production (such as capital and plant) are not, to a similar extent, catered for in policies for direct government intervention.

An equity-focused strategy involving poverty eradication and a reduction of income inequality will have to involve a co-ordinated approach, especially in respect of monetary, fiscal, trade, industrial, labour and education and training policies. The present discourses surrounding lifelong learning are narrowly focused on education and, even then, are severely constrained in scope by the present fiscal policies of government. What then is the attraction of these sets of conceptions? One very compelling attraction is that they represent an attractive conceptual shift which upholds the imperative of economic development along with more socially acceptable imperatives of equity and redistribution.

The strong support in the rhetoric for increased opportunities for learning, especially to those who were denied access in the past and who are also the most economically vulnerable, could result in a drastic increase in the demand for education and training. However a closer examination of the detail in emerging policies, coupled with the overall restrictions on government funding, suggests that the potential demand is only likely to result in actual demand in the formal employment sector. Although the proposed payroll levy to finance education and training outside formal schooling (Department of Labour 1997) may remove the possible disincentive for companies to invest in training because of the cost-of-training factor, there may still be a reluctance if employers believe that increased training would fuel worker expectations for higher salaries. The assumption of the government's education and training strategies is that increased training would result in higher levels of productivity, thus resulting in a win-win situation for employers and employees (and, indeed, for the whole of society). However, if productivity increases are not realized then the social return would be undermined.

I want to contend that a broader perspective on lifelong learning is required; one which inserts lifelong learning into a broader discourse on human development which accounts for the complex interplay of variables which mediate the outcomes of education and training. This expanded perspective would require that the role of government be assessed in respect to facilitating more active labour market policies, and targeting resources directly to the economically most vulnerable. This may include policies which facilitate economic development of poor communities by promoting access to wholesale credit and markets. Even on the assumption that government funds are made available, a focus on education and training for the low-income self-employed in the informal economy erroneously assumes skills development to be the major factor determining productivity and income in this sector.

In the context of South Africa's very wide income inequalities, class background becomes a very powerful variable in determining the capacity of parents and learners to supplement government spending on education and training. Consequently, the government's policy of reprioritizing the budgetary allocation to the formal schooling sector in favour of poor communities is unlikely to result in much equalizing of provision. I am not suggesting that there is an instrumental link between per capita expenditure on education and educational outcomes. However, a likely result may be that poor and rich communities move further apart in respect of access to cultural goods which mediate education outcomes. In this context an expanded perspective on lifelong learning needs to explore ways of developing the cultural *milieu* of communities which support educational success. This would mean addressing the drastic shortage of adequate institutions such as access to libraries, art, theatre, and adult learning all of which contribute to fostering a nurturing learning culture.

Perhaps the most compelling reason for a wider perspective on lifelong learning derives from the need to develop an expanded conceptualization of education and training and, particularly, its capacity to deliver on the range of social and economic outcomes entrusted to it. There needs to be a resistance of the propensity to have an all-embracing and comprehensive doctrine that delivers strategies for the many complex imperatives of transformation and development in South Africa. Instead, education and learning, or lifelong learning, comprises an empirical reality to be analyzed and reconstituted. It is precisely through this latter process that lifelong learning in South Africa could be reconceptualized to account for a major weakness of present policies: the insufficient attention given to theorizing and developing strategies for educational change and its dialectical relationship to socio-economic change. Bagnall (1990) has argued that lifelong learning is regressive because it could lead to the government abdicating its responsibility by shifting blame to people for their failure to contribute to their own socio-economic upliftment through education and training. In South Africa, unless a wider perspective is developed, lifelong learning as presently conceptualized could exacerbate social segmentation, where the rewards and smooth functioning of the emerging discourse only applies to a fraction of society who inhabit the privileged primary segment.

I have tried to argue that lifelong learning in South Africa is undergirded by a number of analytically distinct discourses. Their individual meanings and the way they intertwine at moments to shape education and training policies is strongly mediated by the overarching macroeconomic framework of the government. The present ideological climate has constricted possibilities for invoking strategies which depend on increased social spending by government and a progressive tax regime. Consequently, education and training is looked at as the politically most palatable government intervention in development and equity. It is precisely because of its conceptual malleability that lifelong learning has multiple utilities in the South African context. It may be meaningful or meaningless, it may be compatible with a progressive and even radical discourse while being fully consistent with a very functionalist view of the role of education in capitalist development. Consequently, it mirrors the dominant political agenda of reconciliation.

References

Avis, J (1996) 'The Myth of the Post-Fordist Society', in J Avis *et al.* (Eds) *Knowledge and Nationhood: Education, Politics and Work*, Cassell, London.

Bagnall, RG (1990) 'Lifelong Education: The Institutionalisation of an Illiberal and Regressive Ideology?' *Educational Philosophy and Theory*, 22, 1.

Becker, GS (1964) *Human Capital*, Princeton University Press, Princeton.

Blaug, M (1976) 'The Empirical Status of Human Capital Theory: A Slightly Jaundiced Survey', *Journal of Economic Literature*, September 1976, 827–856.

Christie, P (1996) 'Globalisation and the Curriculum: Proposals for the Integration of Education and Training in South Africa', *International Journal of Educational Development*, 16 (4).

Denison, EF (1962) *The Sources of Economic Growth in the U.S. and the Alternatives Before Us*, Committee for Economic Development

Department of Education (1994) *Draft White Paper on Education and Training*, Republic of South Africa Government Gazette.

Department of Education (1996) *Curriculum Framework for General and Further Education and Training*.

Department of Finance (1996) *Growth, Employment and Redistribution: A Macroeconomic Strategy*.
Department of Labour (1996) *Green Paper: Policy Proposals for a New Employment and Occupational Equity Statute*.
Department of Labour (1997) *Green Paper: Skills Development Strategy for Economic and Employment Growth in South Africa*.
Edwards, R (1993) 'The Inevitable Future?: Post-Fordism in work and learning', in R Edwards, S Sieminski and D Zeldin (Eds) *Adult Learners, Education and Training*, Open University, London.
Giere, U (1994) 'Lifelong Learners in the Literature: A Bibliographical Survey', *International Review of Education*, 40 (3-5).
Hofmeyr, J and Hall, G (undated) *The National Teacher Education Audit*, DANIDA.
Mincer, J (1984) 'Comment: Overeducation or Undereducation?', in E Dean (Ed.) *Education and Economic Productivity*, Ballinger, Cambridge, Mass.
National Institute for Economic Policy (NIEP) (1996) *From the RDP to GEAR: The Gradual Embracing of Neo-Liberalism in Economic Policy*. Unpublished.
Psacharopoulos, G and Woodhall, M (1985) *Education for Development: An Analysis of Investment Choices*, World Bank.
Shultz, TW (1961) 'Investment in Human Capital', *American Economic Review*, 51 (2).
Stronach, I (1990) 'Education, Vocationalism and Economic Recovery: The Case against Witchcraft', in G Esland (Ed.) *Education, Training and Employment, Volume 2*, The Open University, Milton Keynes.
Wain, K (1987) *Philosophy of Lifelong Education*, Croom Helm, London.

Chapter 10

Lifelong Learning: A Cure for Unemployment?
From *Betriebsakademien* to *Beschäftigungsgesellschaften* in Germany

Marion Spöring

Introduction

The unification of Germany and the following *Wende* (literally, 'turn') has led to a major 'restructuring' in all sectors of society. The impact of the political and economic changes has changed the lives of every citizen in the former German Democratic Republic, now referred to as *Neue Bundesländer*. (German terms used will be translated according to the terminology suggested by Nuissl(1994).) It has led to mass unemployment as the 'restructuring' occurred.

Vocational continuing education has been considered to be of vital importance in influencing the labour market and the general economic development of the *Neue Bundesländer* and Germany as a whole. This chapter outlines the development of vocational training measures, financed by the state with support from European grants. Provision in the Hanseatic city of Rostock provides an example of these developments.

Although the changes described occurred as the consequence of unique historical developments, which forced changes within a very short time span on to the population, it allows us to study clearly the impact of economic and political change. European measures to deal with mass unemployment and address regional problems are affecting many countries. Germany, with its well-established vocational training system (the so-called 'dual system') is often used as an example. An analysis of recent policies on education and training to lower unemployment in Germany may also inform the discussion elsewhere.

Pre-unification provision of vocational continuing education

Adult education was seen in the German Democratic Republic as one of four major sectors within the education system (primary, secondary, tertiary and adult). There was a strong emphasis on vocational continuing education (*Weiterbildung*, literally 'further education') and opportunities to acquire secondary school qualifications for adults. The latter could be gained in distance learning and evening courses, based in community education centres, company and village-based academies. Non-school-based education and training was done through a variety of organizations: lecture societies, cultural associations, Chambers of Technology, Urania/Society For the Promotion of Science, cultural adult education, houses of culture, libraries, Urania on television, church based education and so forth (Siebert 1994: 68).

The largest part of continuing vocational education, however, was delivered by *Betriebsakademien* ('company based training centres') attached to major industrial enterprises. These offered training leading to qualifications. This was in most instances available not only to their own employees, but also to 'outsiders', for retraining and the induction of pupils into work placements within the enterprise. Employees of other companies also attended training courses for specialists. In the Baltic seaport Rostock, for example, in 1988 there were 29 enterprise-based institutions out of a total of 53 institutions offering continuing vocational education (Rat der Stadt Rostock 1988: 7–13). (After unification, 83 institutions offered CE to the citizens of Rostock in 1996 (Hansestadt Rostock 1996: 6–7).)

The main task of the *Betriebsakademien* was to upgrade the skills of existing employees and provide qualifications which could lead to promotion within the company. Another important task was to provide retraining in response to structural adjustments within the economy. The centralized planning system allowed measures to be taken in advance to retrain workers for a new workplace to avoid unemployment.

The centralized character of the socialist planned economy led to a high degree of specialization in manufacturing within certain regions. Within the socialist system, with its established markets and infrastructure, this was appropriate and worked.

Post-unification provision of vocational continuing education

Unification, manifesting itself in the union of currency and the economic and social union of both states, led to the virtually entire replacement of GDR structures by West German structures. Restructuring the East German state led to mass unemployment, with social and economic consequences not previously experienced in East Germany. For the first six months the blow was cushioned by a period of euphoria and a spending spree for consumer goods, made possible by the transfer of GDR marks to German marks at an exchange rate of 1:1 and by the high rate of personal savings in the GDR.

However, the Western market economy system imposed on the previously centralized planned economy in the socialist sector led to disastrous consequences in the aftermath of unification, when traditional East European markets collapsed. Rostock's industrial base, for instance, had centred on shipbuilding, fishing and supporting industries. The workforce was highly specialized and skilled in these areas. When the key industries were being privatized through the *Treuhand*, an organization with the remit of privatization of all state-owned companies (VEB/*volkseigener Betrieb*, literally, 'owned by the people'), this created a major rise in unemployment. For example, 40 per cent of men and 30 per cent of women lost their jobs between January 1991 and January 1992 in Rostock (IAB Werkstattbericht 1992: 4). Over the period 1989–93 a sharp fall in the number of the employed in Rostock can be observed (see Table 10.1).

Table 10.1 *Employment in Rostock 1989–1993*

Date	Number employed
September 1989	158,250
January 1990	107,639
January 1991	98,424
July 1991	80,536
January 1992	67,916
December 1992	55,820
December 1993	55,123

Source: IAB Werkstattbericht, 8/1992, I, 15.

The year 1991 saw a marked increase in job losses, with redundancies, enterprise closures and bankruptcies. Some found re-employment in *Ausgliederungen* (parts of formerly large, diverse state owned enterprises established as independent companies). For example, the main shipyards in Rostock themselves produced up to 80 per cent of all components and supplies they needed. They also owned nurseries and hospitals. Many of these units became part of *Ausgliederungen*.

Large enterprises (*Kombinate*), especially the shipyards which dominated Rostock, were heavily affected by job losses, but smaller and medium-sized companies were able to increase their workforces. These smaller companies are mainly situated within the service sector, which had not been highly developed in the GDR. However, these small companies were unable to make up for the large scale job losses (compare IAB Werkstattbericht 1992: I: 19).

Although redundancies from former large *Kombinate* were high, this did not necessarily lead to unemployment. Measures were taken to transfer parts of the former workforces to a *Beschäftigungsgesellschaft* ('employment company') (IAB Werkstattbericht 1992: I: 22). This was achieved by government measures through the German Employment Agency, and made possible by funds allocated through the 'Work Promotion Funding Law' (*Arbeitsförderungsgesetz*/AFG). These drew largely on increased taxation (*Aufschwung Ost*/'upturn East programme') and European funding. These measures were also made available to *Kurzarbeiter* (workers on an enforced shorter working week).

Among the job losses, 39.2 per cent were lost due to redundancies, 26.1 per cent to transfer to an *Ausgliederung* company, 13 per cent to cancellation of the employment contract (without statutory rights with mutual agreement), 11.1 per cent to early retirement, 6.7 per cent to other redundancies, 2.4 per cent to other reasons and 1.5 per cent to retirement. (IAB Werkstattbericht 1992, I: 22). Many employees opted also for early retirement, established their own small businesses, or moved to the *Alte Bundesländer* in the West to find work. The number doing this last was, however, estimated at only 5 per cent, although the proportions varied as between the service industry and traditional industries (from 3 to 14 per cent) (I: 25).

Beschäftigungsgesellschaften

Beschäftigungsgesellschaften ('employment companies') had existed in West Germany before they were introduced in the East as a tool to influence the labour market. There are, however, some notable differences. Initially, they were introduced in the west, funded by the work promotion law (AFG) to target specifically disadvantaged groups in the labour market: women returners, the long term unemployed, the disabled and older workers, school leavers seeking work experience or vocational training, and so on. Projects like this usually had a preparation phase of two or three years.

In the East, however, *Beschäftigungsgesellschaften* were introduced to address an entirely different situation. In the former GDR the state faced a highly skilled and qualified workforce, never previously confronted by unemployment. To defuse a social and economic time bomb a specific form of Beschäftigungsgesellschaften was introduced.

The time-scale for the setting up projects was much shorter (about three months on average) and solutions had to be found to retrain an existing, highly skilled workforce. Very quickly it was recognized that schemes aimed at gaining new qualifications are not a substitute for creating jobs. It was claimed, however, that individuals' 'employability' had to be increased by creating an infrastructure which would attract employers to the region. This process was hampered by the very unpredictability of investments, which led to difficulties in structuring further vocational training according to regional training needs. Legal and other difficulties also made it difficult to forecast which industries would remain in the region and what new branches of industry could be attracted to the area.

In July 1991 a special form of employment company was introduced in the *Neue Bundesländer* to complement the provision of vocational training, which had been introduced after the *Wende* – the *ABS Gesellschaften*. The *Gesellschaften zur Arbeitsförderung, Beschäftigung und Strukturentwicklung* ('companies for labour promotion, employment and structural development') were given the task of 'bridging the gap to structural development' (IAB Werkstattbericht 1997a: 23). A network of some 400 such employment companies in the East has helped to 'soften the unemployment rates'. The main targets of these companies were areas with 'structural relevance' for the regions where they are based. They dealt mainly with areas of construction, manufacturing industry and leisure industry, working in fields like the re-claiming and re-cultivation work of industrial sites, measures for the improvement of transport and tourism (IAB Werkstattbericht 1997a: 24). Employment in these companies was combined with training programmes. In contrast to *Beschäftigungsgesellschaften* in the West these organizations had a different target group, ie generally well-qualified employees across the age range with unbroken employment records. (*Beschäftigungsgesellschaften* in the West aimed at people with little chances in the labour market, such as the long-term unemployed, unskilled workers and people with learning difficulties.)

As the new structures were being built up, projects had to be developed in a short period of time. *ABS Gesellschaften* thus had to undertake tasks without the administrative systems which existed in their Western counterparts. This was partially funded by wage supplements through the Labour Promotion (Funding) Law, other funding from the European Social Fund or special measures from the Department of Employment. In analysing the situation, however, research conducted by the German Department of Employment and Labour Research stresses that:

> 'the development in the new federal states highlights the fact that continuing vocational education policy has to pursue different objectives from those of funding of employment creation measures. Employment creation measures are focused mainly on short term employment and whereas therefore the funding of continuing vocational education in future still has to contribute to the current quantifiable stabilization of the labour market; the funding of continuing vocational education has primarily to focus on qualitative, structural targets. Therefore, the funding of vocational training and re-training has to lose it's role of a purely quantitative *Entlastungsfunktion* ('easing of pressure on the labour market', MS) which it partially had to play post-unification' (IAB Werkstattbericht 5/1997b: 26).

The authors of the report stress that 'the promotion of continuing vocational education is not an instrument of economic and labour market policy and the creation of jobs as a rule is not the consequence, but a pre-condition.' The authors therefore argue that the 'education market' (*Bildungsmarkt*) must be supported and shaped by the state to enable Germany to improve its competitiveness on international markets (IAB Werkstattbericht 5/1997b: 26).

Despite assurances, this remains an interpretation of continuing vocational education as the main basis for ensuring the competitiveness of individual employees in a market situation. It supports an individualistic view of individual personal responsibility in the labour market. Education and training is seen as a market commodity, despite assurances that the creation of jobs must be a pre-condition. It highlights the danger of reducing education, combined with employment measures, to a tool to influence the labour market, albeit in the economic interest of the individuals concerned, and fails to take account of the value of creating change both for the development of the individual and for society.

This is supported by another, university-based, researcher Siebert (1994: 77), who argues that one of the losses of the *Wende* was a *Kulturverfall* ('cultural decay'), because it led to the neglect of other educational initiatives, such as political education, which is now less well supported financially because of policy shifts and not seen as instrumental in gaining qualifications and employment. Less funding is now available for programmes of political education which would enable participants to question changes and analyse the changes in society as a whole and their impact on individuals. There is also less demand for them. According to Opelt (1993: 217) only 1 per cent of CE students in the *Alte* and *Neue Bundesländer* opted for courses under the heading of political education. A detailed analysis of the reasons for this has still to be conducted.

Questions must also be asked about the supposedly beneficial impact of employment companies. Deeke *et al.*, who have looked at the outcome of European Social Fund-financed projects, refer to the fact that the impact of continuing vocational education measures on the labour market can only be evaluated by analysing whether there are *Substitutionseffekte*, *Verdrängungseffekte* and *Mitnahmeeffekte* ('substitution', 'displacement' and 'carry-over' effects) (1996: 172) on the labour market. A 'carry-over' effect occurs when a company might have employed a person anyway even without an incentive. A 'displacement' effect occurs when an unemployed person undergoing a training programme reduces the chances of another unemployed person without this training from getting a job. A 'substitution' effect occurs when a company no longer conducts training itself but relies on workers who have received their training through government-funded schemes. These factors must be taken into account when examining the effectiveness of policy measures.

However, employment companies in the East have achieved 'a better provision of citizens with products and services' and have also contributed to 'improvements of social infrastructure, for example, the re-cultivation of industrial wasteland or the provision of social services' (IAB Werkstattbericht 1.4/1997a: 18). This has led to the creation of new jobs and shows a higher success rate in the East than in the West (3 per cent in comparison to 0.5 per cent (2/1997a: 16)). In the East, a highly qualified workforce has transferred to these companies, whereas in the West employment companies target specific groups of unemployed who are unlikely to be able to reach the objective of self-sufficiency for their companies. This success, however, remains minute in comparison to the overall figures.

Conclusion

Education and training measures should not be seen as a panacea. On their own, they are not even a strong measure for job creation. Used as instruments of labour market policies in pursuit of short-term political aims, continuing vocational education has not managed to solve the much larger-scale problem of restructuring. In a situation where acute social and economic pressure has led to major problems, continuing vocational education can – supported by extra funding – soften the blow of 'restructuring' (the euphemism chosen by government). The German example shows that social unrest, manifested in increased racially motivated attacks (East and West), increased crime rates and so forth, cannot be avoided, unless a long-term commitment to solving the underlying problems is made. This would require the establishment of industries which guarantee long-term employment prospects.

The danger of individualizing the problem is also a serious issue. If gaining qualifications, reskilling and retraining of workers are seen as problems for the individual alone, and individuals then find no employment, this has consequences for individuals' self-esteem and may lead to blaming themselves for failure or seeking for scapegoats. Understanding the economic and political context must form the basis from which people analyse their situation. In the light of the German experience, a number of lessons should be considered when making policy. Educational measures are not satisfactory tools for labour market manipulation. Education should be seen as a long-term investment without direct or measurable short-term outcomes for job creation. Education within a learning society or learning community is of intrinsic, and not just instrumental, value. It should not need to lead to a qualification or measurable outcome. Emphasis should be placed on the community rather than the individual. As long as governments are unwilling to tackle the roots causes of unemployment, individual frustrations about it will express themselves in many ways harmful both to society and the individual. This needs to be addressed on a larger scale, and on a political basis: education and training measures are not in themselves sufficient.

Acknowledgement

The author wishes to thank the Carnegie Trust for financial support for her research in this field.

References

Deeke, A, Hülser, O and Wolfinger, C (1996) *Begleitforschung zu den Maßnahmen des Bundes, die aus Mitteln des Europäischen Sozialfonds (ESF) mitfinanziert werden. Erster Zwischenbericht*, in: IAB projektbericht, Nürnberg, Institut für Arbeitsmarkt und Berufsforschung der Bundesanstalt für Arbeit.

Hansestadt Rostock (1996) *Weiterbildungsinformation und Beratung, Bildungsträger in der Region*, Amt für Pressearbeit und Stadtmarketing, Rostock.

Nuissl, E (1994) *Adult Education in Germany*, Deutsches Institut für Erwachsenenbildung.

IAB Werkstattbericht (1992) *Fallstudien zur Regionalentwicklung und Implementation arbeitsmarktpolitischer Maßnahmen*, Nürnberg, Institut für Arbeitsmarkt- und Berufsforschung der Bundesanstalt für Arbeit, Nr. 8.

IAB Werkstattbericht (1997a) *Beschäftigungsinitiativen in Deutschland*, Nürnberg Institut für Arbeitsmarkt – und Berufsforschung der Bundesanstalt für Arbeit, Nr. 2.

IAB Werkstattbericht (1997b) *Arbeitsmarktentwicklung und aktive Arbeitsmarktpolitik im ostdeutschen Transformationsprozeß 1990–1996*, Nürnberg Institut für Arbeitsmarkt- und Berufsforschung der Bundesanstalt für Arbeit Nr. 5.

Opelt, K (1993) 'Die Weiterbildungsmotivation in den neuen Bundesländern', in *Hessische Blätter für Volksbildung*, 3, 213–218.

Rat der Stadt Rostock (1988) *Information zur Erwachsenenbildung in der Stadt Rostock*, Rostock.

Siebert, H (1994) 'Erwachsenenbildung in der Bundesrepublik Deutschland – Alte Bundesländer und neue Bundesländer', 52–79 in, R Tippelt (Ed.) (1994) *Handbuch Erwachsenenbildung/Weiterbildung*, Opladen.

Chapter 11

Schools Run by Social Forces:
The Development of the Private Sector for Lifelong Learning in China

Xiao Fang

During the last two decades, China has developed a huge educational system for lifelong learning, which covers not only the public but also the private sector. The private sector, which disappeared between the 1960s and the 1970s, emerged and developed in the context of economic reform.

The socio-economic context

Education can never be developed in isolation. It always reflects and is influenced by politics, economies and other factors (Fang 1988). Lifelong learning, which covers all the educational aspects, also reflects and is influenced by other factors of the socio-economic context.

China has changed dramatically since the late 1970s. Politically, the downfall of the Gang of Four in October 1976 marked the end of the Cultural Revolution in which the whole Chinese educational system had been destroyed. Deng Xiaoping paid great attention to education and brought new leadership, starting a new revolution: the open policy and economic reform. Under the new policy, the private sector of the economy, excised as capitalism during the Cultural Revolution, has been developed in line with the development of the socialist market economy. Meanwhile, people's living standards have risen somewhat with economic growth and the development of new technology. Lifestyles and systems of values have also changed. There have been great demands for education from people of all ages. The 'one child' family-planning policy has led to a greater demand for better pre-school and regular education for children and young people. At the same time, socio-economic development has led to strong demand for education and training of adults. The entire educational system for lifelong learning, which provides education and training for the young and for adults, has been developed rapidly to meet great demands. This forms the socio-economic context in which the private sector of lifelong learning has developed in China.

The educational system for lifelong learning in China

In China, there is a saying *huo dao lao, xue dao lao*, which means 'learning throughout life'. This traditional concept of lifelong learning goes back thousands of years. Traditionally, Chinese people mainly fulfilled lifelong learning through self-study.

The concept of lifelong education, promoted by UNESCO in the 1960s and the 1970s, recognized education as a lifelong process. In the *Draft Recommendation on the Development of Adult Education*, the term 'lifelong education and learning' was introduced as the following.

> 'The term "lifelong education and learning", for its part, denotes an overall scheme aimed both at restructuring the existing education system and at developing the entire educational potential outside the education system ... education and learning, far from being limited to the period of attendance at school, should extend throughout life ... the educational and learning processes in which children, young people and adults of all ages are involved in the course of their lives, in whatever form, should be considered as a whole' (UNESCO 1976: 160–161).

Such a contemporary understanding of lifelong education and learning was not introduced into China until the 1980s. The terminology 'lifelong education' and 'the system of lifelong learning' was introduced by *A Dictionary of Adult Education* in 1989 (Guan Shixiong 1989). The book *Lifelong Education for Adults: An International Handbook*, edited by Colin J Titmus, was translated and published in Chinese in 1990. In the Preface to the translation of the *Handbook*, Cheng Fangping noticed that, in China, the conception of lifelong education for adults was far from widespread. He argued, 'however, the people started to recognize that the regular formal education, which still dominates the whole education system, has become limited and has difficulties in meeting the needs of the rapid social, political, economic, cultural, scientific and technological development'. He continued, 'in terms of future education, lifelong process will become the basic characteristic of education, that is, education will be a process throughout the life of everyone' (Cheng 1990: 2, translated by the writer).

In practice, however, the needs of socio-economic development have meant that education has covered the whole system of lifelong learning and has been rapidly developed in China since the late 1970s (see Figure 11.1). Within the system of lifelong learning, apart from the parallel formal educational systems for children, young people and adults, there are various forms of training and social, cultural and leisure education, as well as self-study activities. The system covers both the public sector and the recently developed private sector.

A brief history of the private sector

The tradition of Chinese private education goes back over two thousand years, to Confucius' private school (Fang 1991). In the early 1950s, some private schools set up before 1949 still existed. During this period, the government policy of 'maintaining vigorously, reforming gradually and subsidizing focally' encouraged the combination of public and private education. By 1956, when the private sector of the economy was reformed, the government had taken over the whole educational system. During the Cultural Revolution, while the educational system was destroyed, the remaining private vocational schools disappeared. At the end of the Cultural Revolution, no private sector of the economy remained.[1]

Schools run by social forces: the private sector for lifelong learning

The economic reform started in the late 1970s led to the re-emergence of a private sector of the economy. Meanwhile, the restoration of national unified entrance examinations for higher education brought great hope for the young. Children in schools studied hard for better careers. Millions of young people deprived of education during the Cultural Revolution returned to study with great enthusiasm. A big campaign of 'double complementary courses' – remedial education and vocational training for young and middle-aged employees – was launched. There was a great demand for all aspects of education, but the existing public sector was too weak to meet it. Various social forces were therefore encouraged to run forms of education, in particular for adults. Some private schools, were restored. In April 1981, the People's Government of Beijing City issued the *Provisional Management Measures on Schools Run by Private Individuals in Beijing City*. This was the first governmental document in China to encourage the development of the private sector of education after the Cultural Revolution.[2] In May 1982, the fifth National People's Congress passed a new Constitution, Article 19 of which stated:

> 'The state encourages collective economic organizations, state enterprises, undertakings and other social forces to run various types of educational undertakings according to laws and regulations' (PRC 1982: 116, translated by the writer).

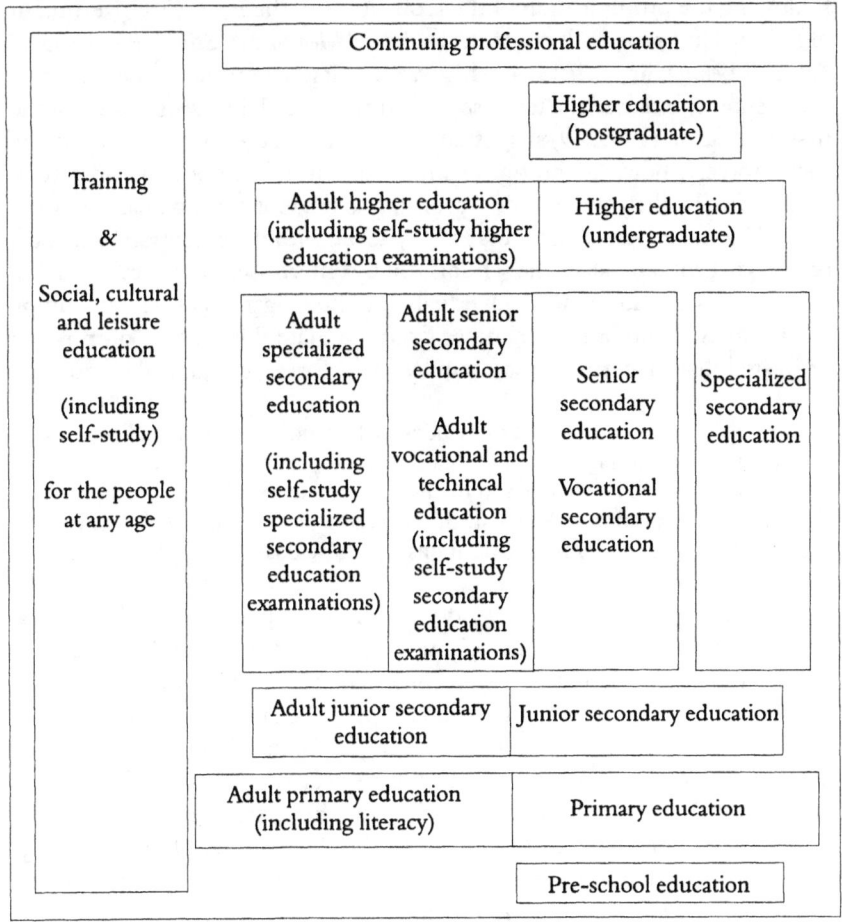

Figure 11.1 *The educational system for lifelong learning in China since the 1980s*

The Constitution formed the legal basis on which schools run by social forces developed in the 1980s. In his report on the draft revision of the Constitution, Peng Zhen, the then President of the National People's Congress, defined 'social forces' as follows.

> 'The state must invest enough resources to run educational undertakings. At the same time it should arouse various social forces, including collective economic organizations, organizations of the state enterprises and undertakings, other social organizations and those who run private schools with the permission from the state to run educational undertakings in various forms, relying on the support from the masses' (cited in Zou 1989: 59, translated by the writer).

Following the promulgation of the Constitution, the People's Government of Beijing City issued a document, *Provisional Measures on Schools Run by Social Forces in Beijing*, in April 1984. This was the first government document on such schools, and used the term 'schools run by social forces' officially for the first time.[3] Zou (1989: 49) suggested that, normally, the term 'schools run by social forces' indicated non-governmental private schools, in contrast to schools run by the government. According to the Constitution passed by the fifth National People's Congress in May 1982, with the exception of schools run by government, all of the schools run by enterprises, democratic parties, academic organizations and individuals could be regarded as schools run by social forces. A senior staff member from the State Education Commission suggested that the term 'schools run by social forces' could be defined as:

> 'the organizations and activities of non-qualification education and training run by state organizations, armies, state-run schools and state enterprises and undertakings, which are open to the public and are self-financed, mainly by fees; and qualification and non-qualification education run by social organizations, collective economic organizations and individual citizens.'[4]

This definition actually includes two component parts: the first could be regarded as non-governmental private courses within the public sector; the second as an independent non-governmental private sector. Schools run by social forces, which provide education for people of all ages, can therefore be seen as the private sector of lifelong learning in China. They reflect the needs of socio-economic development. There have been four phases in their evolution since 1978: first, from 1978 to 1982, a launching stage; second, from 1982 to 1986, a developing stage; third, from 1986 to 1991, a stage of setting up regulations, strengthening administration and readjustment; fourth, starting from 1992, a stage of new development.[5]

Emergence

During the first period, alongside the development of public educational system, the private sector for lifelong learning emerged due to the great demand from people of all ages for knowledge. During this period, provision by the private sector was chiefly short courses in remedial education for adults, including preparation courses for the higher education entrance and self-study examinations, and basic education and vocational training for young and middle-aged workers. At the same time, a few private vocational schools were also restored.[6]

Development

During the second period, the demand for remedial education decreased, due to the achievements of the 'double complementary courses' and of the educational reform in the early 1980s. Meanwhile, some private vocational courses for adults were developed to meet the needs of economic development.[7] Furthermore, as Professor You Qingquan pointed out, when students became rich, they sought opportunities for higher education for self-development. Most of the young people who graduated from secondary schools during the Cultural Revolution, however, were unable to enter a normal higher educational institution. From 1980 onwards, these mainly recruited fresh graduates from secondary schools under twenty-five years of age.[8] Demand for adult higher education was high: there were millions of young or middle-aged people seeking higher education, while number of providers of was limited. As a result, both public and private sectors of adult higher education developed rapidly. Private adult higher education institutions, running long-term courses at higher education level, emerged and developed to meet increasing demand. In Beijing, for instance, the Chinese Social University, the first private adult higher education institution, was established by some famous intellectuals in March 1982.[9] In the following year, four private institutions were set up.[10] By 1985, the number of private higher education institutions in Beijing reached about forty, including sixteen institutions offering face-to-face courses with total enrolments of 10,000, and twenty-four correspondence institutions which recruited students across the whole country, with a total enrolment of about 1,280,000 (Wei 1994). According to the available statistics, the total number of private higher education institutions across the country reached over 200 by 1985.[11]

These institutions mainly recruited graduates from secondary schools. They introduced a principle of 'self-governance: self-financing, self-responsibility for profits or losses, self-organizing, self-managing, self-development, paying one's own fees and hunting for one's own job'.[12] Their management was market-oriented. Unlike state institutions, they would have been unable to exist without markets and the market economy.

A senior staff member from the State Education Commission confirmed that the background of this period was a combination of the planned economy and the market economy, and that schools run by social forces were strongly supported by some major leaders of the Chinese Government.[13]

Readjustment

During the third period, the Party's general economic policy of 'readjustment' led to a policy of 'readjustment' in education.[14] A senior staff member of the State Education Commission (SEC) confirmed that schools run by social forces were the main targets to be readjusted.[15] In July 1987, the SEC issued *Certain Provisional Regulations on Schools Run by Social Forces*, which stated that education authorities at provincial level should enhance the leadership and administration for schools run by social forces and that schools run by social forces should be regularized. According to the *Provisional Regulations*, schools run by social forces were not allowed to be established or to advertise without the approval of the relevant education authorities. Schools run by social forces which were not approved for issuing qualifications recognized by the state were not allowed to issue certificates of graduation. They were only allowed to issue certificates to validate the courses taken by students and their transcripts. Students would have to take Self-Study Examinations for Higher Education if they wanted to have qualifications recognized by the state.

With the economic policy of 'readjustment' in the background, government policies on schools run by social forces during this period were strict rather than relaxed, controlling rather than encouraging.

Speeding up reform

During the fourth period, 1992 was a turning point of the reforms. The establishment of a socialist market economy became the target of China (Jiang 1992). The general policy of the Government changed from 'readjustment' to 'speeding up reforms'. Educational reforms also speeded up.

In August 1992, a National Conference on Adult Higher Education was held in Beijing. The first national conference on adult higher education in China, it marked a turning point for the reform of lifelong learning and for schools run by social forces. At the 1992 Conference, the government's attitude became more supportive. In his report, Zhu Kaixuan, a deputy director of the State Education Commission, confirmed that in accord with the Constitution schools run by social forces had emerged and developed since 1978 to meet the requirement of economic reforms and the open policy. He stated:

> 'Schools run by social forces form a necessary complement for the schools run by the state. Their development benefits both the state and the people. We should continue to implement the policy of 'supporting vigorously, supporting strongly, guiding correctly and strengthening administration' (Zhu 1992: 22, translated by the writer).

In his closing speech to the Conference, Li Tieying, a member of the Political Bureau of the Central Committee of Chinese Communist Party and of the State Council, and the then Director of the State Education Commission, stated that the requirements of running schools and learning symbolized the awakening and civilization of a nation. Seeking opportunities to study was the basic right of a citizen, and 'running schools had made contributions to the society'. He confirmed that adult higher education and schools run by social forces were an important part of the educational cause in China, and that they would develop more rapidly in the near future (Li 1992).

New recognition by the government

During this period, there was a new recognition of the role of schools run by social forces that used to be regarded as a complement to the public sector. Their role was redefined by policy makers.[16] In his speech at the Fourteenth Congress of Chinese Communist Party in October 1992, Jiang Zemin, the General Secretary of the Central Committee of Chinese Communist Party, stated that the Government should encourage a variety of social collective funding and non-governmental bodies to run schools in various ways. He emphasized that Government should no longer run the whole educational system. From then on schools run by social forces were no longer 'a complement' but 'an important component part of education cause'.

Furthermore, to meet the needs of the developing socialist economic system and of social progress in all aspects, the government encouraged various social forces to run schools in adult continuing education. In February 1992, the State Council issued the *Development Outline of Chinese Education Reform*, an important guiding document for development and reform in Chinese education at the turn of the century. It stated:

'The system of providing education should be reformed. The situation whereby the government used to run the whole education system should change. We should establish a system, in which, with the government as the main body to provide education, various social groups are encouraged to run schools jointly. At present, in terms of general education, local government is the main body providing education. In terms of higher education, with both the central government and local government as main bodies to run schools, various social groups run schools together. In terms of vocational education and adult education, we should mainly rely on professional trades, enterprises and undertakings, together with various social groups, to provide education' (SEC 1993, translated by the writer).

At the National Conference on Education held by the Communist Party and the State Council in June 1994, Li Peng, the then prime minister, made a speech introducing the *Development Outline of Chinese Education Reform* issued by the State Council. He confirmed that a new system of organizing schools should be set up step by step: the government should be the main body providing education, but various social groups should collect funds to run schools. He claimed that, under the administration of the government, schools of vocational education and adult education should mostly be run by professional trades, enterprises, undertakings and social organizations, or jointly by the social groups and individual citizens with some support from the Government (see *Zhongguo Jiaoyu Bao* 15 June 1994: 1).

Expansion

During the fourth period, the private sector of lifelong learning marched into a new stage of development. With government encouragement, schools run by social forces, first launched in adult remedial education, now spread to the whole system of lifelong learning: from pre-school to primary and secondary education; from vocational education to work training; from tutorial courses for self-study to higher education; and from continuing professional education to social, cultural and leisure education. According to Mr Dong Mingchuang, the Head of the Department of Adult Education of the State Education Commission, in 1994 the total number of schools run by social forces, as the independent non-governmental private sector, reached over 60,000. This figure included 18,284 kindergartens, 1,078 primary schools, 888 secondary schools, 392 vocational secondary schools, over 100 specialized secondary schools, over 800 institutions offering non-qualification higher education courses, eighteen private higher educational institutions offering qualifications recognized by the state and over 35,000 schools providing short training courses in non-higher education and social cultural studies.[17] Among them, about 5,000 institutions were 'Elderly People Universities', similar to the University of the Third Age. Thus, alongside the development of the market economy, a huge system of the private sector of lifelong learning has grown to contribute to the Chinese educational cause.

Conclusion and further discussion

Since the late 1970s, alongside economic reforms and the development of the market economy, a private sector of lifelong learning has emerged and developed to contribute to the cause of education in China.

Everything has both negative and positive aspects. While public resources are limited, the private sector provides more opportunity for people to invest in lifelong learning. However, under the market system, people have to pay for organized programmes of lifelong learning. The precondition is that people can afford to purchase them. The question emerges, therefore, of how far lifelong learning should be driven towards a market orientation? If lifelong learning is driven further toward a market orientation, what will be the effect on those who cannot afford it? Will people be excluded by high fees? If so, the consequence would be less education and training for poorer individuals, resulting in worse employment prospects still. Thus, the gaps between different social groups and different areas might become wider and wider. These potential social consequences of the market orientation need to be considered.

Notes

This chapter is based on a part of author's recent doctoral thesis *Going Into The Sea: The Relationship of Socio-Economic Developments and Changes to the Developments and Changes in the Education and Training of Adults in China and the UK, with Comparative Aspects in Hong Kong (1978–1996)*, under the supervision of Emeritus Professor William A Hampton, Division of Adult Continuing Education, University of Sheffield.

1. An interview with Chen Jixia, the Director of the Office of Schools Run by Social Forces of the Beijing Adult Education Bureau, on 9 April 1994.
2. *Ibid.*
3. *Ibid.*
4. An interview with an anonymous staff member of the State Education Commission in China, on 8 April 1994.
5. *Ibid.*

6. An interview with Chen Jixia, the Director of the Office of Schools Run by Social Forces of the Beijing Adult Education Bureau, on 9 April 1994.
7. An interview with Professor You Qingquan, the Principal of Hubei Correspondence University, on 13 December 1993.
8. *Ibid.*
9. An interview with an anonymous staff member of the State Education Commission in China, on 8 April 1994.
10. An interview with Yu Luling, the Principal of the Chinese Social University, on 13 April 1994.
11. An interview with Chen Jixia, the Director of the Office of Schools Run by Social Forces of the Beijing Adult Education Bureau, on 9 April 1994.
12. An Interview with Jiang Shuyun, Principal, University of Science and Technology Management of China, on 14 April 1994.
13. An interview with Qu Yandong, Head of Division of 'Ganwei' Training, and Assistant to the Head of the Department of Adult Education of the State Education Commission in China, on 14 April 1994.
14. An interview with an anonymous staff member of the State Education Commission in China, on 8 April 1994.
15. *Ibid.*
16. *Ibid.*
17. A telephone interview with Dong Mingchuang, the Head of the Department of Adult Education of the State Education Commission in China, on 27 March 1996.

References

Publications in Chinese are marked (C).

Central Committee of the Chinese Communist Party and State Council (1981, C8) 'Decisions on Strengthening the Work of Education for Workers by the CCCCP and the SC', in SEC (1991) *Comprehensive Collection on Educational Laws and Regulations of the PRC (1949–1989)*:356–60, People's Education Press, Beijing, (C).

Cheng Fangping (1990) 'The Preface of the Translation', in Colin J Titmus (Ed., Chinese translation 1990) *Lifelong Education for Adults: An International Handbook*: 1–5, Worker Education Press, Beijing, (C).

Deng Xiaoping (1977) 'Respect Knowledge, Respect Trained Personnel', in Deng Xiaoping (1984) *Selected Works of Deng Xiaoping (1975–1982)*: 53–54, Foreign Languages Press, Beijing.

Deng Xiaoping (1984) *Selected Works of Deng Xiaoping (1975–1982)*, Foreign Languages Press, Beijing.

Department of Laws and Regulations of State Education Commission (1992) *Selected Important Educational Documents since the Third Plenary Session of the Eleventh CCCCP*, Educational Science Press, Beijing, (C).

Fang, Xiao (1988) *Trends of Educational Development in China (1977–1986)*. Unpublished MEd thesis, Department of Education, University College, Cardiff, University of Wales.

Fang, Xiao (1991) 'Exploration on the Legislation of Private Adult Higher Education', in *Heiliongjiang Higher Education Research*, 4, 1991, Harbin, and Wei, Yitong (Ed. 1991), *Research on Private Higher Education*: 28–32, Xiamen University Press, Xiamen, (C).

Guan Shixiong (1989) *A Dictionary of Adult Education*, Worker Education Press, Beijing (C).

Jarvis, Peter (2nd edition 1995), *Adult and Continuing Education: Theory and Practice*, Routledge, London.

Jiang Zemin (1992) 'Speed up Reform, Opening-Door and Modernisation Construction to Achieve Bigger Victory of Socialist Cause with the Chinese Character: Speech on the Fourteenth National Congress of the CCP', in CCP (1992), *Collection of Documents of the Fourteenth National Congress of the CCP*: 1–55, Beijing: People Press, (C).

Li Tieying (1992) 'Speech on the Closing Ceremony of the National Conference on Adult Higher Education', in Dong, Mingchuan (Ed., 1993) *Selected Documents of the National Conference on Adult Higher EducatRudolfion*: 3–11, Liaoning People Press, Shenyang, (C).

PGBC (People's Government of Beijing City) (1984, BG63), 'Provisional Measures on Schools Run by Social Forces in Beijing', in SESBAEB (Ed., 1989) *Introduction to Schools Run by Social Forces in Beijing*: 5–14, Educational Science Press, Beijing, (C).

PRC (1982) 'Constitutions of the PRC (Digest)', in Department of Laws and Regulations of State Education Commission (1992), in *Selected Important Educational Documents since the Third Plenary Session of the Eleventh CCCCP*: 116–117, Educational Science Press, Beijing, (C).

SEC (State Education Commission) (1987, EHT014) 'The SEC Circular on Issuing Certain Provisional Regulations on Schools Run by Social Forces', in SESBAEB (Ed., 1989) *Introduction to Schools Run by Social Forces in Beijing*: 14–20, Educational Science Press, Beijing, (C).

SEC (1993, EP129), *Circular on Issuing 'Provisional Regulations on Minban Higher Education Institutions'*, internal document, (C).

SESBAEB (Social Education Section of the Beijing Adult Education Bureau) (Ed., 1989) *Introduction to Schools Run by Social Forces in Beijing*, Educational Science Press, Beijing (C).

Titmus, Colin J (Ed., 1989) *Lifelong Education for Adults: An International Handbook*, Pergamon, Oxford.

Titmus, Colin J (Ed., Chinese translation 1990) *Lifelong Education for Adults: An International Handbook*, Worker Education Press, Beijing, (C).

UNESCO (1976) 'Development of Adult Education', reprinted by permission of UNESCO in EK Townsend Coles (1977 2nd Ed.) *Adult Education in Developing Countries*, Pergamon, Oxford.

Wei Yitong (1994) *Early Research on Legislation of Private Higher Education*, a thesis for PhD degree, Institution for Higher Education Science, Xiamen University, (C).

Zhongguo Jiaoyu Bao, 15 June 1994, (C).

Zou Tianxing (1989), 'On Schools Run by Social Forces', in SESBAEB (Ed., 1989), *Introduction to Schools Run by Social Forces in Beijing*: 49–69, Educational Science Press, Beijing, (C).

Zhu Kaixuan (1992) 'Emancipate the Mind, Speed up Reform and Develop the New Environment of Adult Higher Education: Report at the National Conference on Adult Higher Education', in Dong, Mingchuan (Ed., 1993) *Selected Documents of the National Conference on Adult Higher Education*: 12–25, Liaoning People Press, Shenyang, (C).

Chapter 12

'Through-Life' Perspectives and Continuing Education in Hong Kong:
Policy Review and Policy Unformation

John Holford

Western enthusiasm for lifelong learning is underpinned by assertions that increasing globalization of markets threatens national economic performance, even survival. A 'culture of lifetime learning is crucial to sustaining ... international competitiveness' asserts a British report; papers in this volume show similar sentiments pervading in Australia, New Zealand, Europe and North America. Even in an era of impersonal and 'natural' market forces, the threat has been geographically – and arguably culturally – located: in the Pacific Rim and the Asian 'tigers'. It is, therefore, a little ironic that, Japan aside (Okamoto 1994), even the most economically advanced of the Asian 'tigers' have lagged behind the west in developing policies for lifelong learning. Singapore, for instance, has moved to formulate a policy only in the last year or so.

Hong Kong began to review its policies in the mid-1990s. While there had previously been no shortage of post-compulsory education and training provision (Chan and Holford 1994, Holford *et al.* 1995, Lee and Lam 1994), development had been piecemeal and rarely policy-driven. Policy has recently been (or is currently being) reviewed in four main ways. Changing needs in vocational training were examined in a major consultants' review of the Vocational Training Council (Segal Quince Wickteed (Asia) Ltd 1996). The Employees Retraining Scheme introduced limited retraining opportunities for unemployed workers (Holford forthcoming). Controls on foreign professional and higher education programmes delivered in Hong Kong were introduced (the Non-Local Higher and Professional Education Regulation Ordinance 1996). Finally, the role of continuing education (CE) as provided through higher education institutions has been examined, and recommendations made, by the University Grants Committee.

This chapter provides a critical account of the policy-making process in the last of these, the UGC's review of CE. The policy-making process, it is argued, has been badly co-ordinated, limited and flawed. This has been due in part to ideological and political constraints on the policy community. The result leaves Hong Kong with structures and systems which, apart from being politically neutered (which some may regard as a virtue in the context of the territory's delicate political transition) are divorced both from contemporary international experience and from developments in initial education in Hong Kong. They seem unlikely to provide a coherent framework for co-ordinated development of lifelong learning.

Hong Kong

Hong Kong, a British colony from 1841, reverted to Chinese sovereignty on 1 July 1997, becoming a Special Administrative Region of the People's Republic. Though tiny in area, its population (6.2 million in 1996) makes it roughly twice the size of New Zealand, Ireland, Singapore or British Columbia and significantly larger than Denmark, Finland, Norway or Israel. Developing into a major manufacturing centre during the 1950s and 1960s, it has undergone a further massive transformation since the mid 1980s, becoming a primarily financial and service-based economy. Hong Kong's manufacturing workers numbered 905,000 (41.7 per cent of the active labour force) in 1984; by 1995 there were only 386,000 of them (15.3 per cent of the workforce) (Berger and Lester 1997: 9). A *per capita* GDP of US$24,500 (1996) makes it one of the world's richest societies, now far outstripping the UK – though its affluence is by no means evenly spread.

Educational provision has been an important element in Hong Kong's economic and social development. In 1971 primary education became compulsory for all (and free except for those who preferred to pay); three years of junior secondary education became compulsory (and free) in 1978. Higher education – confined to an élite 3 per cent until the mid 1980s, but now to admit over 18 per cent of the age cohort to first degree programmes – is overseen by a 'buffer' institution, the University Grants Committee. Created in 1965 and modelled on its then British equivalent, the UGC is charged to keep higher education facilities, plans, and finance 'under review', and to 'advise government' – effectively to decide – on the allocation of funding between institutions (UGC 1996: 200). (Retitled 'University and Polytechnic Grants Committee' (UPGC) in 1972, it reverted to UGC in November 1994 when the polytechnics were 'upgraded'.) Two institutions initially fell under the UGC's aegis; there are now eight. (They do not include the Open University of Hong Kong, formerly the Open Learning Institute, which is funded directly by the government.) Supported by a secretariat, the Committee itself consists of about eighteen members.

Adult education and training in Hong Kong has been provided by a range of chiefly public and 'voluntary' sector bodies, although the role of the private sector has increased during the last decade or so. Higher education institutions' continuing education (formerly extramural) departments form the major element of public sector provision. However, for its first quarter-century, the UGC paid scant attention to them.

'Through-life' education

A major UPGC report in November 1993 reviewed progress on changes to higher education introduced since the late 1980s: chiefly the enormous expansion of full-time undergraduate education announced in 1989 after the 4 June 'incident' (as current usage has it) in Beijing. The report looked 'beyond the conclusion of those changes ... up to and beyond 2001', 'ask[ed] questions', and described and made proposals (UPGC 1993: 1). A section on 'higher education after 1995', included three paragraphs on '"through-life" education' (the first occasion on which 'lifelong'-type terminology was used). These posed the 'very important question ... [of] the balance between initial higher education and the updating and reorientation of knowledge which may be required throughout an individual's working life'.

The emphasis in the UPGC's previous work, it correctly asserted, had previously been on first degrees. Internationally, however, there had recently been 'an upsurge in the demand for continuing professional education' (CPE). Similar demand, from employers looking for a 'better or more appropriately skilled workforce', from individuals 'hoping to enhance their career prospects', and from customers, was likely to develop in Hong Kong. The UPGC would therefore undertake a study of continuing education and report in due course. Three issues were raised to set an agenda for this study.

The first related to providers and possible modes of delivery: CPE might be offered through universities' 'extramural or CPE departments', by the Open Learning Institute or 'by industry itself'; and within institutions, at the workplace or by distance learning (UPGC 1993: 6). Second, the UPGC argued that as well as CPE for the enhancement of employment skills, 'in an increasingly affluent and sophisticated society' there would also be growing demand for '"leisure" skills and for courses in the arts and the more accessible popular sciences' (UPGC 1993: 6). The third issue was how 'through-life' education was to be resourced. Both UPGC-funded and other institutions would face additional workloads, and the UPGC wanted 'to be sure that that load is supported by separate and adequate financial provision and not by diverting ... funds intended for other purposes' (UPGC 1993: 7). This funding, however, should in the main not come from government:

> 'Much of the cost of CPE or "leisure" courses should be met by the employer or the student, but there may still be a need for a Government input, particularly in providing for development into new areas' (UPGC 1993: 7).

This far from radical or imaginative agenda proved broad indeed when compared with the conclusions which emerged three years later. In relation to CE the major report, *Higher Education in Hong Kong* (UGC 1996), is both complacent and unimaginative. Four overwhelmingly descriptive chapters pay extensive lip-service to the importance of 'continuing and professional education' to the changing economy and society, but contain no new ideas or proposals. Even the term 'through-life education' has been dropped. The core conclusion sums up the attitude:

> 'The current system works well and is responsive to the needs of both the market and the individual. ... [However,] we believe that expanding CPE is important to the future economic and social well-being of Hong Kong, that this will proceed better if given some small financial encouragement by government, and that this support should be limited to certain specific objectives' (UGC 1996: 92).

Subsequent paragraphs explain (a little). Part-time courses leading to initial higher education qualifications could be supported (as previously), but otherwise public subsidy for CPE in the UGC sector should be limited to 'courses whose primary purpose is social benefit (such as the upgrading of teachers and social workers)' (UGC 1996: 92). The costs of all CPE courses should be recovered in full from fees. Infrastructural costs of units 'engaged in CPE' should as far as possible be supported 'from sources other than the block grant'. However, institutions themselves could if they wished help with the 'launching costs' of courses which 'it is in the public interest to establish' (UGC 1996: 176).

For Hong Kong's adult educators, then, this UGC report was Janus-faced. While CE was given significant attention in a public policy report for the first time since the 1950s, and its importance asserted, the rhetoric promised far more than it delivered. Indeed, while the 1993 report had asserted the aim and importance of ensuring adequate funding, the result of the review was that less funding was to be available. Gone, moreover, were two of the three issues apparently placed on the agenda in 1993: modes of delivery and the likely rise in demand for 'leisure' courses.

And if the review had a limited vision, neither were there structures or systems to provide strategic direction for development. There was no coverage of curriculum, organizational or management issues. This seems odd. It is not as though models and issues were unavailable. Hong Kong's schools sector, for instance, was undergoing major curriculum innovation. A system of 'targets and target-related assessment', introduced in 1990, had evolved by 1993 into a 'target-oriented curriculum', similar in many ways to reforms around the world which, for instance, 'focus on key competencies and national profiles (Australia), core skills (UK), benchmarks (Canada) and attainment targets (Netherlands)' (Morris et al. 1996: 39). Such approaches have underpinned recent lifelong learning policy thinking in many countries, including (for instance) the UK and Singapore. Issues such as quality assurance and credit accumulation and transfer were raised for discussion when UGC met representatives of university CE departments in December 1994 (UPGC 1994c), but ignored in the 1996 report.

The review process and Hong Kong's continuing education

How are we to account for the lack of vision in the 1996 report? This question can be addressed at a number of levels.

The conduct of the review

The review which eventually produced the CPE chapters of the 1996 UGC report was conducted during 1994 and the early part of 1995. Hong Kong economists tend to be strongly committed to 'the rational choice approach and methodological individualism' (Wong 1988: 93); such views were certainly strongly reflected in the process and outcome of the review. UPGC commissioned a single piece of research: a major study on the economics of CE. The terms of reference for the research were:

1. to identify the characteristics and dimensions of the market for continuing education
2. to identify factors that condition the supply and demand for continuing education, delineating the relationships as precisely as possible, so that implications of changes will become apparent
3. to identify possible market failures in continuing education, and possible roles for the Government, in particular the UPGC, to correct these failures, if any, presenting a list of proposed policy actions for the Government to consider (UPGC 1994a).

The report was commissioned from three researchers at the Chinese University of Hong Kong. Academic links between the researchers and a key member of the UPGC were close.[1] Their orientation and approach was inevitably reflected in the research findings and recommendations. This made the outcome relatively predictable. It was particularly unfortunate and short-sighted that no research was commissioned with a broader, educational, remit.

The research report (Chung *et al.* 1994), submitted in August 1994, was forwarded to the heads of UPGC institutions in late October (UPGC 1994b). It asserted the importance of CE in the light of changes in labour market structure and accelerating skill obsolescence. Census data recorded a contraction of enrolment in part-time courses during the 1980s, while the growth rate of CE enrolment in higher education institutions was slowing. There was 'market saturation' (for 'generic' CE in particular) 'brought on by a massive entry of new providers both locally and from overseas ... within a short period of time, competing for a pool of potential students that is no longer expanding' (UPGC 1994b: 122–3). An expanding niche market still existed, however, for specific, typically professional, courses. Concerns that quality might be compromised in pursuit of income or market share were unfounded: CE students are 'rather demanding in getting their money's worth'. 'Intense market competition for students,' indeed, far from being a threat to quality, 'provides the bottom line for quality control in continuing education' (UPGC 1994b: 124).

The kernel of the conclusions, however, lay in recommendations about public subsidy for CE. These very much followed the assumptions of a group of free-market economists. The case for public subsidy of CE 'based on externality arising from market failure and equity considerations' was 'much weaker' than the case for initial education (UPGC 1994b: 127), and there did not appear to be a case for intervention in any substantial way.

Although Chung, Ho and Liu drew fire from Hong Kong's adult educators (Holford 1994b), the report formed the major element basis for UGC consultations in December 1994 with representatives of the various university CE providers. Its line of thinking underpins the CE sections of the UGC's final report (UGC 1996).

The continuing education community in Hong Kong

If the UGC's agenda was narrow, and narrowed further during a flawed policy-making process, the CE community conspicuously failed to establish an alternative. This was not, in one sense, for want of trying. Several of the university CE units met or made submissions to the UGC (or both), as did the newly-formed Federation of Continuing Education in Tertiary Institutions (UGC 1996: 201–02). But their response was shaped by their history and role, by their perception of the UGC's agenda and by institutional priorities.

Hong Kong's system of CE effectively originated in the mid 1950s. Early attempts to create a system of university provision using the British extramural model proved only partially effective (Holford 1994a). With vast unmet demand, it was easy – and in many respects legitimate – to perceive market demand as a good indicator of need. This had three profound long-term effects. First, the university extramural departments saw themselves as competitors in a market. While this mattered little in the 1960s and 1970s, by the late 1980s more and more providers were entering the field. Competition tends to limit collaboration: communication and exchange in certain areas becomes circumscribed. This affected approaches to curriculum development, new planned areas or modes of provision, reasons for programme success or failure and the effectiveness of approaches to maintaining standards.

Second, defining need in market terms meant there was little call for debate about the curriculum. With relatively few exceptions, CE programmes were demand-led: CE units provided a marketing and administrative mechanism by which mainstream university staff could be matched with identified areas of potential or actual demand. Programme development was reduced, at best, to a technical level: where courses should be held, how long they should be, the organization of assessment, setting course fees and so forth. Indeed, the notion of curriculum has been almost entirely absent from Hong Kong's CE discourse.

Third, success came to be measured largely in financial terms: programmes 'succeeded' to the extent that they made money. A few courses might prove their worth in terms of social need but even they had to cover their costs in some non-trivial sense. Some departments and programmes achieved remarkable financial success, especially in the late 1980s and early 1990s. This contributed to a perception that CE units could manage without public subsidy. Some major figures in the field agreed: they could perform well in the market-place; this was success; it was well if others knew about it.

A fourth feature, hardly the result of the market orientation but certainly contributing to the weakness of CE discourse, was the formation of a 'provider culture'. Hong Kong's university CE culture differed from Britain's in many ways, but they shared an extramural model by which CE staff were specialists in academic disciplines and rarely had any wish to develop academic expertise in CE as such. One consequence was a very weak research base. Indeed, in the early 1990s, the number of active CE researchers was very small (three or four in the territory as a whole, and most also heavily involved in programme development and administration); output was small and its quality very variable. This certainly contributed to the ease with which the UGC could come to perceive CE solely in terms of 'market failure', as well as to the inability of the professional CE community to formulate a sophisticated or fully coherent alternative agenda.

Hong Kong politics and the policy community

Compared with many countries, Hong Kong's mainstream adult education has been remarkably free from political debate about its purpose and social role. Boshier (1997) and Holford (1994a) discuss this in terms of models and development of adult education, but it reflects too a characteristic of Hong Kong society as a whole.

Lau Siu-kai (1982: 157) characterized the three 'principal structural features' of Hong Kong as an 'autonomous bureaucratic polity, an atomistic Chinese society and weak links between them'. In this 'minimally-integrated social-political system' the 'bureaucratic polity' – a civil service and decision-making structure led by expatriate British or members of the Chinese élite reliant on the government for their preferment and subject to no democratic controls – had an effective monopoly on policy-making. 'The bureaucratic polity and the political arena are almost coterminous ... Consequently, if political power is to be procured, it has to be done *through* the bureaucracy, rather than *outside* of it' (Lau 1982: 158).

The Chinese society, chiefly refugees from rural China seeking stability and quick material gain, had to rely on their kin for material support and advance. What Lau terms 'utilitarianistic familism' developed: an adaptation of traditional Chinese familism to a new urban setting (Lau 1982: 72–85). This centring on the family meant that government and Chinese society co-existed in largely separate spheres. The Chinese society of Hong Kong saw its 'territory' in social and cultural terms: 'customs, mode of thinking, habits, mores, lifestyles and patterns of social organization' (Lau 1982: 158). For the bureaucrats, the essential rationale for Hong Kong's existence was economic activity. Their sphere was government: reshaping Hong Kong's Chinese society in a western image was not on their agenda.

Politics in Hong Kong were therefore 'boundary politics'. These could result in 'some modifications of public policies or some redistribution of resources between the two parties' (Lau 1982: 167), but no serious redefinition of the relationship between the parties, no restructuring of the fundamental parameters of the socio-political system, would be involved. Both parties were essentially content with this accommodation. However, as Lau noted, it was underpinned by structural and historical conditions which were contingent. These included China's endorsement of the Hong Kong *status quo*, the fact that Hong Kong was largely a society of immigrants from China, and rapid and sustained economic growth making competition an 'expanding-sum game' with 'seemingly endless chances for economic mobility' (Lau 1982: 174).

It was this political and social environment which originally set the mould of Hong Kong's adult education. The 'bureaucratic polity' had little time for the democratic aims of adult educators who arrived in the colony from Africa and Britain, while the 'Chinese society' was equally unresponsive to programmes which did not meet straightforward and practical economic or vocational needs. This environment set the scene for the market approach to programme development, for the absence of political debate, and for the absence of a discourse about curriculum. It established a narrow policy community unused to listening to external voices, except when they were raised to fever pitch. This would provide a strong explanation for the character of the UGC's policy-making in its review of continuing education.

But is it legitimate to apply Lau's approach to policy-making in the mid 1990s? Many aspects of Hong Kong society had changed in the fifteen or so years after Lau first outlined his theory. Among the most important were (politically) the introduction of limited forms of representative and democratic government, the emergence of now maturing political parties and the new relationship with China; (economically) the decline in manufacturing employment and the 'traditional' working class, the emergence of a new and affluent middle class, and increased economic integration with China; and (socially) the reduction in the proportion of the population born in China, the extension of welfare, the emergence of a Hong Kong culture or identity and the marked extension of educational opportunities and attainment.

However, as Lau among others has argued, there is evidence that in key respects not only did Hong Kong remain a minimally integrated social and political system in the mid 1990s, but that broadly speaking the people were content with – or at least prepared to acquiesce in – this position. Lau (1982: 160) argues that 'to the Hong Kong Chinese, 'political freedom' does not mean freedom to participate in political decision-making, but freedom *from* political oppression, and studies of emerging political attitudes are particularly salient here. For example, Lau (1992: 134–135) found that the most common conception of 'democracy' was a system where 'those in power would consult public opinion before making decisions': 39.5 per cent of his respondents accepted this definition, while only 27.9 per cent opted for a 'government that is elected by the people'. He discovered that 'in terms of public trust, institutions and groups which are elected do not differ significantly from the non-elected ones', testifying to 'the non-paramountcy of election as a source of political legitimacy in Hong Kong' (Lau 1992: 144).

On the basis of a later survey, conducted in the wake of the 'Patten reforms', Leung (1995) argued that while general attitudes to party formation have become more favourable, many people still hold ambivalent or suspicious views about 'settling political disputes and hammering out public policies through a genuine party system' (Leung 1995: 281). The findings led him to 'doubt whether political parties matter in Hong Kong people's daily life' (Leung 1995: 283). As a democratic political culture, therefore – and leaving aside the constitutional position – Hong Kong remains deeply compromised.

The prospects for lifelong learning

While these findings suggest that, pragmatically, Hong Kong's policy community need have few anxieties about the legitimacy of proceeding on the basis of highly constrained consultation, questions remain. Two will be posed here. There is, first, the issue of effectiveness: whether the UGC's review will have a positive impact on the development of lifelong learning in Hong Kong. If the market is the most effective mechanism for developing educational and training strategies, we may take a sanguine view. If the development of lifelong learning is best achieved by minimizing public expenditure on the part-time education, we may be similarly enthusiastic. Certainly one view is that a prime UGC aim in its review of CE was to kill any possibility that the principle of public funding, having crept inexorably from primary to tertiary education, should extend into the post-initial sphere.

Yet if the state does have a role – and this is accepted, albeit half-heartedly, in the notion of market failure – this needs substantially more elaboration than it received from the UGC. Public provision which does no more than ape the behaviour of private entrepreneurs in the market is indeed hard to justify. The role of public educators should be to shape provision. Such shaping can come at several levels. It might involve the elaboration of qualification or assessment frameworks – perhaps through articulation with the school-level Target Oriented Curriculum or with the vocational training sector. It might involve provision of a research and development base for lifelong learning. The weakness of research on curriculum, on programme development, on access and participation, on modes of learning, and so forth in the Hong Kong context is glaring; it is unlikely to improve significantly on a purely market basis. The public sector could seek to establish mechanisms of quality assurance: ironically, while the Hong Kong government now legislates for quality assurance for overseas programmes offered in the Hong Kong market, Hong Kong-based organizations are subject only to the quality control 'bottom line'.

Apart from whether the policy process has worked to good technical effect, there is a second broader issue. This was touched on by one of the questions the UGC put on its agenda in 1993 but did not seek to answer (the prospects for 'leisure' courses), though it is in fact both wider and deeper. Should Hong Kong's lifelong learning structures have a cultural, social and political dimension, as well as an economic and vocational one? Although the prime mover of recent lifelong learning policies internationally has been economic, cultural, social and political dimensions can also be significant. For the European Commission (1995), for instance, governance in a multinational, multilingual and multicultural context is key: aims include 'successful integration ... through the sharing of common values' and 'combating exclusion'.

Other chapters in this volume criticise the EU's vision of lifelong learning as economistic. This only underlines the myopic character of the UGC's vision of CE. Hong Kong's problems are very different from the EU's but lifelong learning is no less vital element in addressing the issues it confronts. They include the nature of Hong Kong culture and identity, the Region's relationship to and role in China, how to provide economic and cultural opportunities for the excluded and addressing the challenge of an ageing population. A further imperative lies in the anticipated influx from China, linked in part to family reunifications: as many as two million additional residents, many of them already adult, are forecast to arrive by 2011 (*Territory Development Strategy Review* 1996: 15, cited Berger and Lester 1997: 172–173).

The 'Great Hong Kong Success Story' centres on the role of free markets and unregulated entrepreneurship. The reality is that government has played an active strategic role in providing a framework for market-led economic development. Among the key elements of the government's strategy has been the provision of a skilled, and relatively cheap, labour force. Wage levels have been kept in check partly by intervening in the labour market – for example to discourage the emergence of effective collective bargaining – and partly by vast provision of subsidized public housing. Educational advances have been of central importance in establishing and maintaining a skills base. One issue which now faces Hong Kong – and which the UGC signally failed to address – is how a strategy for lifelong learning can be established for the society as a whole.

At the time of writing, Hong Kong's new SAR government is still less than a year old; nevertheless, it is hard to find signs of any radical shift toward a lifelong perspective in its educational policy discourse. Following the pattern set by his British predecessors, the Chief Executive, Tung Chee-hwa, unveiled his plans in a Policy Address to the Legislative Assembly on 8 October 1997. To be sure, a radical review of educational policy and some important innovations were central to his programme. But early indications are that Primary, Secondary and Tertiary structures continue to constrain the SAR political and policy mind-set.[2] When outlining his vision for education, the Chief Executive made no mention of any 'through-life' dimension.

> 'Education is the key to the future of Hong Kong. It provides a level playing-field for all and the human resources for further economic development. Our education system must be firmly rooted in the needs of Hong Kong; it must enable us to contribute to the development of our country; it must give us an international outlook. It should be diverse, drawing on the strengths of East and West. It must inspire commitment to excellence' (Tung 1997).

The plans Mr Tung set out for achieving these aims bear out the 'initial' and 'formal' nature of current thinking. He concentrated almost exclusively on schooling and the full-time undergraduate sector at university level. Even here, there was no reference to the need to develop skills and attitudes for 'lifelong learning'. The educational value of information technology was voiced only to support schools and universities.

The Chief Executive's sole specific reference to post-compulsory education tends to bear this out. He announced a $50 million (approx. US$6.4 million) grant to the Open University of Hong Kong 'to develop adult distance learning courses in both English and Chinese, to serve Hong Kong and mainland students' and 'to turn the Open University into a centre of excellence in adult and distance learning' (Tung 1997). Though welcome in itself, this reflects a rather traditional approach. Since its formation in 1989, a recurring theme in Hong Kong government educational thinking has been that the Open University (until 1996 the Open Learning Institute) was the vehicle for continuing education. This was always a somewhat bizarre assumption, considering the diversity of provision and the strength of other institutions in Hong Kong. From a 'lifelong learning' or 'through-life' perspective, it verges on the dangerous. Hong Kong's urgent need, given the challenges it now faces – economic, social, political and cultural – is to build a lifelong or though-life approach into all sectors of education and learning (and indeed elsewhere).

There is more than one risk involved. In locating adult and distance learning, even conceptually, in a single institution – and an institution which remains outside the UGC sector – the government may be sending a clear but damaging policy message to other educational institutions. For the UGC-funded sector, continuing education is seen as a distinct enterprise and must stand on its own financial feet. Any initiatives are to come from the Open University. This will hardly encourage the UGC institutions to review their curricula and structures to make them more supportive of lifelong learning. A centre of excellence is very much to be encouraged, but only if it is a vehicle for reform throughout *lifelong* learning. Hong Kong has a strongly 'executive-led' political culture: Hong Kong's educational managers are adept at reading policy signals; and they tend to act accordingly.

Where then does Hong Kong stand in the world-wide rush to 'lifelong learning'? The energy of its people, and their enthusiastic embrace of learning opportunities, give the SAR marked advantages. But policy lags behind the people. The UGC has made, at best, a faltering start. Hong Kong's educational policy framework is, of course, skewed. As elsewhere, structures inherited from the past constrain the policy options. So does Hong Kong's unique political mix. In this context, the UGC deserves some credit for raising the lifelong learning issue. The policy-making process, however, has suffered from many flaws. Within the UGC, confidence in market solutions for continuing education has been unbridled; alternatives have hardly been considered. Financial parameters, and in particular the desire to strengthen initial undergraduate education, seem to have played a major part. The UGC has developed its policies in effective isolation from other sectors of education and vocational training.

As a result, Hong Kong continues to lack a co-ordinated policy framework for lifelong learning. Lifelong learning suffers the worst of several worlds. Conceived still largely as 'adult learning' or 'continuing education', it is seen as separate from, and subsidiary to, other sectors. Yet responsibility for it is dispersed: the UGC, the Vocational Training Council, the Employees Retraining Board, the government's Educational and Manpower Bureau and its Education Department all have major roles in shaping policy. On the evidence of the fate of lifelong learning in the UGC review, little productive communication takes place between these separate policy worlds. This does not bode well for the future. Hong Kong needs mechanisms which will underpin effective and co-ordinated policy-making for lifelong learning across both private and public sectors, as well as across the entire life span. Unless such mechanisms and structures are introduced, the SAR seems unlikely to keep abreast of contemporary international developments in *lifelong* learning.

Notes

1. The UPGC member concerned, a very capable Chicago-trained economist, Richard Wong Yue-chim, had worked in the Chinese University's Economics Department until September 1992; two of the three commissioned researchers were staff of that department. He had co-authored a paper (Liu and Wong 1992) with at least one of them, and co-edited a book (Chung and Wong 1992) with the third.
2. In the 'Better Business Environment' section of his address, the Chief Executive also referred to the need to 'ensure that opportunity for training and retraining is open to every member of the workforce to maintain their prospects of finding work, as well as to improve the quality and productivity of businesses'. However, this appears to refer solely to the work of the Vocational Training Council and the Employees Retraining Scheme, and was not referred to in the 'Education' section of the speech.

References

Berger, S and Lester, RK (Eds) (1997) *Made by Hong Kong*, Oxford University Press, Hong Kong.

Boshier, R (1997) 'Futuristic Metropolis or Second-rate Port? Adult Education in Hong Kong Before and After 1997', *Comparative Education*, 33(2), 265–275.

Chan, FT and Holford, J (1994) 'The Hong Kong Adult Learner: A Profile', in Lee and Lam (1994): 71–84.

Chung Yue-ping, Ho Lok-sang and Liu Pak-wai (1994) *An Economic Analysis of Continuing Education: Costs, Benefits, Trends and Issues. A Final Report Submitted to UPGC*, Unpublished report, Hong Kong: UPGC.

Chung Yue-ping and Wong, Richard Yue-chim (Eds) (1992) *The Economics and Financing of Hong Kong Education*, Chinese University Press, Hong Kong.

European Commission (1995) *Teaching and Learning: Toward the Learning Society*, Commission of the European Union, Luxembourg.

Holford, J (1994a) 'Adult Education without a Soul? Colonialism, Economic Progress and Democratic Underdevelopment in Hong Kong', in *Proceedings of the 35th Adult Education Research Conference*, University of Tennessee, Knoxville.

Holford, J (1994b) *Report of a Workshop* (on Chung, Ho and Liu 1994). Unpublished Submission to UGC by University of Hong Kong School of Professional & Continuing Education.

Holford, J (forthcoming) 'The Employees Retraining Scheme', in A Lam and N Lee (Eds) *Professional and Vocational Training in Hong Kong*.

Holford, J, Gardner, D and Ng, JGH (1995) *The Hong Kong Adult Education Handbook*, Longman, Hong Kong.

Lau Siu-kai (1982) *Society and Politics in Hong Kong*, Chinese University Press, Hong Kong.

Lau Siu-kai (1992) 'Political Attitudes', In Lau *et al.* (1992).
Lau Siu-kai, Lee Ming-kwan, Wan Po-san and Wong Siu-lun (Eds) (1992) *Indicators of Social Development: Hong Kong 1990*, Chinese University Institute of Asia-Pacific Studies, Hong Kong.
Lau Siu-kai, Lee Ming-kwan, Wan Po-san and Wong Siu-lun (Eds) (1995) *Indicators of Social Development: Hong Kong 1993*, Chinese University Institute of Asia-Pacific Studies, Hong Kong.
Lee, N and Lam, A (1994) *Professional and Continuing Education in Hong Kong: Issues and Perspectives*, Hong Kong University Press, Hong Kong.
Leung Sai-wing (1995) 'Attitudes Towards Party Politics', in Lau *et al.* (1995).
Liu Pak-Wai and Wong Richard Yue-Chim 'Human Capital, Occupation Choice and Earnings', in Chung and Wong 1992: 113–140.
Morris, P *et al.* (1996) *Target Oriented Curriculum Evaluation Project: Interim Report*, University of Hong Kong In-Service Teacher Education Programme, Hong Kong.
Okamoto, K (1994) *Lifelong Learning Movement in Japan*, Ministry of Education, Science and Culture, Tokyo.
Segal Quince Wicksteed (Asia) Ltd (1996) *Strategic and Organizational Review of the Vocational Training Council: A Final Report to the Secretary for Education and Manpower.* 2 vols, unpublished report.
Tung Chee-hwa (1997) *1997 Policy Address by the Chief Executive (8 October)*, http://www.info.gov.hk/pa97/english/patext.htm.
UGC (1996) *Higher Education in Hong Kong*, University Grants Committee, Hong Kong.
UPGC (1993) *Higher Education 1991–2001: An Interim Report*, University & Polytechnic Grants Committee, Hong Kong.
UPGC (1994a) letter, A Wong, Acting Secretary-General, to J Cribbin, University of Hong Kong; ref. UPGC/GEN/254/93; 9 February.
UPGC (1994b) letter, A Leung, Chairman, to Vice Chancellor, University of Hong Kong; ref. UPGC/GEN/254/93 II; 20 October.
UPGC (1994c) letter, N French, Secretary-General, to N Lee, University of Hong Kong; ref. UPGC/GEN/268/94; 17 November.
Wong, Yue-chim (1988) 'The Economics of Organised Labour, With Some Reference To Hong Kong', in YC Jao, DA Levin, SH Ng and E Sinn (Eds) (1988) *Labour Movement in a Changing Society*, University of Hong Kong Centre of Asian Studies, Hong Kong.

PART IV

LEARNING, MARKETS AND CHANGE IN WELFARE STATES

Chapter 13

Demands and Possibilities for Lifelong Learning in a Market-oriented Society:
A Finnish Perspective on Public Policy and Reality

Jukka Tuomisto

Demands for lifelong learning

The point of departure for lifelong learning may be, on the one hand, the demands placed on the individual by social change and, on the other hand, the individual's own needs for growth and development. The social demands for lifelong learning are based on the democratization of society and the development of production. In addition, the natural environment forms a general framework and starting point for all learning.

The most central developmental area that covers the individual's whole life cycle is his or her development as a person and a cultural being. This always occurs in some historical and social context. In a democratic society, citizenship with its rights and responsibilities is part of each individual's life from youth to old age. The role of worker or employee is for most people the central life area of adulthood (Tuomisto 1997: 9). Arguments for lifelong learning have varied in the course of history. Sometimes its significance in building a citizens' society has been emphasized, while at other times its role in the development of production or the development of the individual's personality has been stressed. From the viewpoint of lifelong and versatile human development, all these developmental areas should be taken into account equally.

Lifelong education emerged into public discussion in Finland in the late 1960s as a result of a UNESCO report. All the education committees set up in the 1970s emphasized the significance of lifelong learning, but the principle itself did not actually guide practice (Alanen 1982: 39). An extensive report of the Continuing Education Committee (Kom. miet. 1983: 62) came out in the 1980s.

The government set up a committee in 1996 to design a national strategy for lifelong learning. The committee published its report *Oppimisen ilo* ('The joy of learning') in the autumn of 1997. According to the committee, the content goal of learning is to support an individual's personality development; to strengthen democratic values; to maintain active communities and social unity; to work for internationalism; and to enhance innovations, productivity and national competitiveness. In its strategy, the committee regarded increasing the choices and incentives as essential. Those citizens in particular need support whose experiences and scope of life limit their opportunities to see learning as something useful in their own case (Kom. miet. 1997: 14, 2).

Market-oriented educational policy

According to some political theorists, economic systems function most efficiently when controlled by the competition of free markets. The rise of neo-liberalism has increased market control in the public sector too. Market thinking is characterized both by the freedom of an individual to make choices and by free competition in the supply of goods. Supply of goods is achieved through private enterprise, so the state is left only with the role of distributing justice and protecting citizens from violence. The idea of 'perfect competition' is pivotal in market thinking. In such a situation there are several sellers and buyers for a single article or commodity, and none can alone influence the price. Manufacturers and consumers are not allowed to co-operate, buyers know where to acquire goods at the cheapest price, the enterprise knows the markets and new enterprises are able to enter the market freely. (Varmola 1995: 58, Jarvis 1993: 41–42) In practice, 'perfect competition' is very difficult to realize but different levels of competition can be used in developing services (such as education).

In 1980s Finland, as elsewhere, people began to demand that services provided by the public sector should be made private, or at least their volume should be reduced radically. The reason for this was that public expenditure and bureaucracy grew at the same time as economic recession set in. The old inflexible centralized administration was unable to make the necessary reforms, so a new model based on market ideology was introduced to the public sector in 1987–95. The reform of the school system was part of a wider reform by which the focus of educational planning was moved away from the Ministry of Education and its agencies to the municipal and school level. At the same time centralized administration was reduced and reformed; activity was controlled using management by results and continuous evaluation of productivity and efficiency. Detailed laws on different fields of education are being replaced by general legal frameworks.

Market-oriented educational policy has influenced all levels of education, but perhaps most significantly adult education. Traditionally this has been partly market-driven (staff development) and/or has functioned according to demand (liberal adult education). It has often been noted that the major part of adults' learning happens outside adult education, namely at work, at home, in connection with hobbies, etc (informal and incidental learning). Despite this, systematic studies in adult education institutions continue to be of great importance; on these courses, adults acquire the knowledge base and structures, orientations and instruments which help them to screen and deal with their perceptions and which guide their 'everyday learning' elsewhere. It is for this reason that adult education has a focal position in all societies that aim at promoting lifelong learning.

The Adult Education Committee set up in 1971 examined Finnish adult education in general and as part of the whole educational system, and produced a plan for an overall development of adult education. This marked the beginning of a policy phase of centralized planning in adult education (1970–1985). The idea was to promote educational equality in society. Advancing vocational education – at the time quite undeveloped – was also emphasized. Transition to the period of market-based adult education policy (from 1985) did not happen overnight but only gradually, as a result of a number of reforms. However, in the 1990s the adult education policy of the state has emphasized the role of market forces (Alanen 1993: 13–18).

Tuijnman (1992: 210–19) lists, among others, the following features as characteristic of the 'market model' in adult education: trust in the economic usefulness of education; increased emphasis on vocational education; education costs in the public sector can no longer be increased; the state now has a weaker role in decision-making related to education; focus on meeting the educational needs of individuals; calculating the effectiveness of all education should be possible; and all decision-making related to education happens more and more as a joint effort of corporations, the most important decision-makers being local authorities, employers, trades unions and individual adults themselves. All the above features are to be found in Finland, at least to some degree. Is it possible to implement the strategy of lifelong learning in a situation in which the prevailing adult education policy is market-oriented?

My aim is to threefold: to consider how far educational equality has advanced in adult education during the period of centralized and market-oriented planning; to examine the effects of the market-oriented planning model on certain sectors of adult education (employer education, open university, labour market training, adult education centres); and to evaluate the applicability of market-oriented planning in promoting lifelong learning.

Lifelong learning: a basic right of the citizen

Today lifelong learning is a basic right for all citizens in Finland. It is recorded in Article 13 of the Constitution, amended in 1995 (969/95) as follows.

> 'Public authorities must secure all people an equal right to other education than basic education, according to their skills and special needs, as well as the right to develop themselves without being prevented from this by lack of means.'

The idea of 'lifelong learning for all' has thus been 'officially' approved in Finland. How far has this become a reality? In other words, how have adult citizens been able to participate in adult education? On the basis of surveys made by the Adult Education Committee and Statistics, Finland, it is now possible to examine changes in participation over a longer period of time when different planning strategies have been used. The stage of centralized planning lasted until about 1990, which marked the beginning of market-oriented planning.

Table 13.1 *Participation in adult education in 1972, 1980, 1990 and 1995 by basic education (population aged 18–64)*

	1972	1980	1990	1995	Change 1972/95
Comprehensive school	17	23	31	33	+16
Secondary education	35	39	53	50	+15
Higher education	44	53	78	75	+31
All	20	32	47	48	+28

Source: Blomqvist and Simpanen (1996)

Overall, participation in adult education increased in the 1970s and 1980s, while in the 1990s the growth seems to have stopped. The differences in participation between the groups according to prior levels of education, always great, have actually grown. In the 1990s, this development has halted and somewhat more equal participation can be observed. However, the change is only slight and hardly significant. The development of adult education has consequently resulted in educational polarization.

In terms of areas of study, the proportion of vocational studies is today clearly bigger than that of independent, leisure time studies by adults. The proportion of vocational studies has continued to increase, while that of leisure time studies has not.

Table 13.2 *Participation in work-related education and other training in 1980, 1990 and 1995 (percentage of employed population aged 18–64)*

	1980	1990	1995	Change 1980–95
• in work-related education	24	45	50	+26
• in other education (social studies, leisure time studies)	17	18	18	+1

Source: Blomqvist and Simpanen 1996, Blomqvist *et al.* 1997: 94.

In vocational adult education, the differences between people with different levels of education are very clear: the well-educated participate in studies clearly more than those with less education. In independent studies, the differences were significantly smaller. Polarization seems to be a problem of the labour market and vocational adult education, in particular. This tells something about a deepening division of society into successful experts (core labour force) and marginalized, uneducated workers who no longer belong to the active work force (peripheral labour force) (Tuomisto 1997: 10–11).

Employers as education providers: study opportunities for the select only

This year Finnish industrial employers published a report entitled *Oppia ikä kaikki* ('Learning – a process for a lifetime. Industry's vision of lifelong learning'). Lifelong learning is defended by many arguments such as international competitiveness and the organization's economic success. It is also said to ensure an individual's professional growth. Although companies continuously emphasize the importance of human capital, in practice they are not too eager to provide education for all their staff.

Table 13.3 *Participation in staff education in 1980, 1990 and 1995 by socio-economic group (wage-earners aged 18–64)*

	1980	1990	1995	Change 1980–95
Executives	41	72	69	+28
Clerical workers	32	57	58	+26
Workers	10	26	33	+23
All	22	47	52	+30

Source: Blomqvist and Simpanen 1996.

In the past, in-service education was traditionally directed at executives and clerical workers. Although there has been more equality between groups in the 1990s, the differences between blue-collar and white-collar workers continue to be great. Education provided by employers is very selective. The possibilities for lifelong learning in working life are not the same for all.

There is a clear difference between public and private employers as far as in-service education is concerned. In Finland in 1990, private employers provided education for about 43 per cent of their staff, municipalities for about 54 per cent and the state for about 63 per cent. In 1995, the number of participants in in-service training provided by private employers remained the same (43 per cent); in the municipal sector the number had increased clearly (63 per cent) while in the state sector it had decreased slightly (60 per cent) (Blomqvist *et al.* 1997: 89–90). In general, we can say that private employers provide considerably less education for their staff compared with the public sector. This is common in other countries, too (OECD 1996: 151).

Staff development and training can be regarded as at present more or less obligatory for any company that wants to keep up with increasingly keen competition. For companies, 'continuing learning' is only an instrument, however, and not a value in itself – as it should be according to the humanistic concept of man and the best traditions of adult education. 'Learning organizations' and their lifelong learning strategies are necessarily organization-centred and do not take sufficiently into consideration the developmental needs of individual employees.

Openness of Open University?

When an Open University started functioning in Finland in the 1970s, one of its essential goals was to promote educational and cultural equality. For this reason, no educational or other requirements were set for student admission. It was taken for granted that education should be free for all. Consequently, Open University courses were first filled with young school-leavers who had taken their matriculation examination and were planning to continue their studies at university. In 1975, an age limit was set at 25 years and the students were also expected to have work experience. The situation has since then changed completely. There is no longer any guidance or control by society, and the students are mainly young school-leavers with a matriculation examination or persons in a fairly good position. In 1972 the proportion of students without a matriculation examination was 50 per cent, but in 1995 it had dropped to only 10 per cent (Parjanen 1997: 21).

This trend results from a number of factors. In the 1990s the general unemployment rate in Finland has been 15–20 per cent, while youth unemployment has been even higher (about 30 per cent). Because of this, the government removed the Open University age limit of 25 years in 1993 and has in many other ways encouraged young people to participate in education. The age limit is now set at 18 years. Since age and work experience are no longer criteria for selection, Open University students are now accepted in order of registration. This system favours those young people who are not working. In the early 1980s, tuition in Open Universities was free. Today students must pay a moderate fee. The unemployed have criticized this system, saying even such moderate fees are too high for them. The proportion of students in the whole population with matriculation has increased. This is clearly visible in the younger age groups, about half of whom now take this examination (some 30,000–35,000 young people each year). However, only about half of these can get into universities. In this situation it is only natural that they are very keen to choose the Open University.

The openness of the Open University is today a misnomer. The course fees alone may prevent many individuals from attending the courses. The students are selected on the basis of employment policy rather than educational policy which aims at cultural equality.

There is an abundance of Open University courses available to students in the 20 universities of Finland. However, education in a particular field is generally only provided by some two to five universities, not more.

Consequently, there is no real competition. Distance learning is increasing, however, and it may change the situation both nationally and internationally (see Jarvis 1996), because education provided by different universities will then be more openly in competition with each other.

Vocational education under the pressure of labour markets – competition for the sake of appearances

Vocational adult education centres used to be solely responsible for providing employment training. In the late 1980s, these institutions were made to compete with other vocational schools. The aim was to develop the educational provision and competitiveness of the centres by expanding their activity beyond employment training and into the private sector. The centres, however, did not succeed in expanding their services to free markets. The proportion of employment training still accounts for 80–90 per cent of their educational provision. Another negative result was that the gap between the centres and other vocational schools remained wide. Since the system is based on mutual competition, there are few possibilities for truly rewarding co-operation (Varmola 1995: 62).

Vocational adult education centres have two buyers in the state administration: the National Board of Education and the Ministry of Labour. The former orders mainly courses in self-motivated vocational studies, the latter primarily employment training. The state and municipalities subsidize self-motivated vocational studies; the state pays for all employment training. The market situation is thus not genuine in either case. Employment districts and provincial governments buy labour market training, and they can buy such education from either vocational adult education centres or other vocational institutions. In practice, however, just a few authorities (of the Ministry of Labour) have the expert power to direct hundreds of millions of adult education money, in accordance with the buyer-provider model. A genuine market situation was only reached in places where there was strong demand and supply, mainly in large population centres (Varmola 1996: 134–142). The centres have been able to increase the number of their activities, as well as their share of the total vocational adult education provision. They have also become more aware of prices. The change has most clearly influenced the teachers, their price-awareness and their way of teaching. The effect of the change on the quality of teaching remains unclear, however (Varmola 1995: 62).

In the past employment training aimed chiefly at finding jobs for people. Today it is more openly used for 'storing' the unemployed. This is of great importance for the present government, which has promised to reduce

Finland's present high rate of unemployment by half. For this reason training continues to be arranged even though it is common knowledge that many in training will not find jobs. The government recently decided that young people under the age of 25 with no vocational education will no longer receive labour market benefits but will be directed to vocational studies or work practice. This decision, in force since the beginning of 1997, in practice means that compulsory education of young people with no jobs will be extended to that age.

Adult education centres in a process of change

Traditions of liberal adult education are kept alive by adult education centres which focus on leisure time and voluntary studies. These centres have by law been entitled to a state subsidy since the 1920s. They have functioned quite independently for a long time. Sihvonen (1996) has studied changes in the adult education centres in the 1990s. He notes a change in their value basis, in that quantitative objectives and economic efficiency are now key factors in their development. The traditional goal of promoting equality is now pushed to the background, since the centres must produce results and compete in the educational market. Their function as institutions providing general and cultural education to adults does not exist any more. Today they may arrange virtually any kind of training and education from vocational to physical education and from interest-based studies to staff development. The minimum age limit of 16 years has also been removed, so students' ages vary greatly. Yet another change concerns the funding of the centres: since the beginning of 1993, the system of state subsidy has been arranged so that municipalities get a lump sum of money for all their educational provision. Elected municipal trustees have a free hand to determine how the subsidy is divided among different users. Adult education centres must now compete in two fronts: firstly, with the other educational and cultural organizations of the municipality for resources, and secondly with the other adult education institutions for students. As public financing has decreased, the centres have had to raise their fees (in the past the courses were free), and they have also started arranging different kinds of commissioned courses (Sihvonen 1996).

Market thinking in adult education centres is still not the most important aspect in their work, because they continue to receive considerable subsidies from the state. Having noticed this, some private trainers and instructors have demanded that subsidies to adult education centres should be abolished completely, because this way the centres are given a significant advantage in the competition. On the positive side, the quality of teaching has improved and fewer students now drop out of courses. On the negative side, the number of alternative courses has decreased and less wealthy students have dropped out.

Advantages and disadvantages of the market model

Though Finland has gradually shifted towards market-oriented educational policies, this has not proved as divisive as in many other countries. School institutions have not been privatized; the reform has rather been concerned with making public services more efficient and competitive by means of market methods (Varmola 1995). It is apparent that market-oriented adult education policy involves certain disadvantages, such as the following.

- Education is seen one-sidedly as an instrument for increasing efficiency and productivity. In other words, it is now a market commodity, and the same methods used to sell any product are used in 'selling' education. The 'client/consumer' is also inclined to perceive education only from the viewpoint of the 'benefit/gain' that it brings.
- The needs of labour markets have controlled the development of all adult education and the significance of vocational adult education is over-emphasized.
- State subsidies to liberal adult education have decreased and the share of independent studying by adults has declined.
- The costs of all education (course fees) have grown, but the number applying for further study places is no longer growing. Students now form a very select group.
- Equality as the goal of education has been virtually abandoned. Educational polarization between different groups of population is already obvious, and adult education reinforces this trend.
- Education is used more and more for 'storing' the labour force.
- Because of mutual competition, fruitful co-operation between different educational organizations has become difficult.

The advantages of the new educational policy include the following.

- Students are now more goal-oriented.
- Drop out has decreased, especially in independent studying; the reason for this, at least in part, is that course fees have grown.
- The quality of teaching has improved (at least in certain fields where there is genuine competition). More attention is now given to quality and evaluation.

- Teachers have become more aware of the price of education and really try to see to the quality of their work.
- Students demand more; there are even demands for consumer protection in educational matters. For the higher fees people expect better teaching.
- Educational institutions have redefined their own task and profile in order to be able to compete in the educational market, even if the competition is not always genuine.
- Schools have managed to decrease excessive administration and heavy bureaucracy.

The above shows that the use of the market model involves many serious problems. Consequently, if we really want to promote lifelong learning in society, we cannot resort to this model alone in educational planning. Society, particularly if based on a market economy, will always have groups who risk marginalization from normal social life. The process of polarization is real in most indusrialized countries. How far is this process allowed to go before something is done to prevent its harmful effects?

Should we be satisfied if adult education only serves the needs of economic life and employment policy? Where are the basic values of adult education, such as the promotion of democracy and equality? Adult education has always involved tasks related to civic education, individual growth and emancipation, and it has struggled to perform these task well. With a market-oriented model of planning there is no room for such goals. The emphasis should be shifted from specialized vocational education for experts to more general education for larger groups of citizens, enhancing their skills and preparedness to manage their own lives.

At present it seems that the principle of lifelong learning has been harnessed to serve the ideology of continuing growth and consumption. This is especially enforced by industry and trade, in other words, by the representatives of market forces. Adult educators must be able to bring forth alternative ways of thinking which rely on sustainable ecological ideas and a profound human concept.

Conclusions

Since the market model is not able to promote the demands placed on the individual, citizen and employee, we must initiate a more detailed discussion of its limitations. We need a new approach which goes beyond 'private' and 'public', competition and co-operation. The new model should balance the goals of efficiency and equality. It should combine the tradition of humanistic educational thinking and the dynamics of the market. This is no easy task, it may even be impossible. Some people, however, already see such alternatives developing (Martin 1994: 252–270, Jarvis 1996: 17). A conscious development of such alternatives is extremely important just now; otherwise lifelong learning will remain the right of just a few.

References

Alanen, A (1982) 'Lifelong Education – Permanent Education – Recurrent Education', *Adult Education in Finland*, 19, 2, 3–41.

Alanen, A (1993) *Aikuiskasvatuksen organisaatiomuodot (Forms of organizations in Adult Education)*, University of Tampere, Department of Education, Report B 7, Tampere.

Blomqvist, I and Simpanen, M (1996) *Aikuiskoulutustutkimus 1995 (Participation in Adult Education 1995)*, Ennakkotietoja, Tilastokeskus, Koulutus 1996: 6, Helsinki.

Blomqvist, I et al. (1997) Aikuisopiskelu Suomessa, Aikuiskoulutustutkimus 1995, Tilastokeskus, Koulutus 1997/4, Yliopistopaino, Helsinki.

Jarvis, P (1993) *Adult Education and the State*, Routledge, London.

Jarvis, P (1996) 'Oppimisen markkinat', ('Learning and marketing'), *Aikuiskasvatus* 16, 1, 12–18.

Komiteanmietintö (1983: 62) *Jatkuvan koulutuksen toimikunnan mietintö*, Valtion painatuskeskus, Helsinki.

Komiteanmietintö (1997: 14) *Oppimisen ilo. Kansallinen elinikäisen oppimisen strategia* Edita Oy, Helsinki.

Martin, B (1994) *Kenen etu? Yksityistämisen ja julkisen sektorin uudistaminen (In the Public Interests? Privatisation and Public Sector Reform)*, Vastapaino, Tampere.

Oppia Ikä Kaikki (1996) *Teollisuuden visio elinikäisestä oppimisesta*, Teollisuuden ja Työnantajien Keskusliitto TT, Helsinki.

OECD (1996) *Lifelong Learning For All*, OECD, Paris.

Parjanen, L (Ed.) (1997) *Avoin yliopisto Suomessa, (Open university in Finland)* Opetusministeriö, Edita, Helsinki.

Sihvonen, J (1996) 'Sivistystä kaikille vai valituille? Kansalaisopistotoiminnan kehitys vapaasta kansanvalistustyöstä maksupalveluun' ('Education for all or a chosen few? – The development of adult education centres from liberal adult education to tailored training without State subsidies'), *Acta Universitatis Tamperensis*, ser A vol. 519, Tampere.

Tuijnman, AC (1992) 'Paradigm Shifts in Adult Education', in AC Tuijnman (Ed.) *Learning Across the Lifespan. Theories, Research, Policies*, Pergamon Press, Oxford.

Tuomisto, J (1997) *Elinikäisen oppimisen teoreettiset ja historialliset lähtökohdat. Julkaisussa Elinikäisen oppimisen komitean mietinnön (1997:14) liite*, Opetusministeriö Edita Oy, Helsinki.

Varmola, T (1995) 'Adult education, Privatization and the Market', in Kauppi, Kontiainen, Nurmi, Tuomisto and Vaherva (Eds), *Adult Learning in Cultural Context*, Tammer-Paino, Tampere.

Varmola, T (1996) 'Markkinasuuntautuneen koulutuksen aikakauteen?' ('Market Orientation: Entering a new Educational Era? Instances and Interpreations of Vocational Adult Education'), *Acta Universitatis Tamperensis*, ser A vol. 524. Tampere.

Chapter 14

Market-oriented Policies and the Learning Society:
The Case of New Zealand

Michael Law

Introduction and purpose

New Zealand has gained something of a worldwide reputation for the enthusiasm with which successive Labour and National (conservative) Governments have embraced neo-liberal ('New Right') ideology and practices since the mid 1980s. In education, economic and social restructuring has resulted in radical changes to both schooling and 'post-compulsory education'.

The purpose of this chapter is to analyse critically the impact of those changes from a labour studies perspective that emphasizes the concerns of working people. The central theme of the chapter is that this ideologically driven push for a consumer oriented, market approach to lifelong learning challenges fundamentally the democratic assumptions that have characterized thinking and practice in adult education for much of this century.

Adult education's democratic impulse: an historical and theoretical note

Adult education, in the broad sense, contributed to the shaping of a democratic culture in New Zealand. Inspired originally by Owenism and Chartism, this mainly reformist impulse absorbed a mix of American and British influences, including Fabianism, in the late 1800s and eventually matured into a practical ideology that found its political expression in the Labour Party and the welfare state. At key moments, reformism was challenged by an articulate minority, often with a strong foothold in adult education, that advocated more radical utopias (Beilharz 1992). But that pressure was blunted ideologically by the achievements of reformism. It was also contained as a political movement by the peculiarities of an industrial relations system that fostered moderate unionism and compelled conciliation and arbitration, and by the vigour with which governments suppressed militant unionism.

The welfare state was a compromise: those who worked for wages and salaries accepted private ownership of production while the owners of capital accepted a political system that provided for a measure of income redistribution (Przeworski 1986). In New Zealand, the idea that a measure of public education, a basic public health system and the provision of minimum welfare payments were 'social rights' (King 1987) had been accepted and acted upon politically long before the election of a Labour Government in the mid 1930s. The establishment and expansion of public education saw reformist policies and practices attempt to reconcile the tension between two views of the purposes of education: the democratic impulse that was often associated with the more radical sections of the labour movement and the industrial pressures from employers to train and retrain an expanding workforce. One important consequence of that democratic pressure was the making of a constituency for a much richer vision of public education, including adult education, than industrial capitalism required and would have willingly conceded. Thus for much of this century, public policies and practices in education at any particular time can be viewed, both historically and theoretically, as a 'settlement' within a broader class compromise.

However, in recent decades three challenges to New Zealand's reformist tradition have influenced public policy with respect to lifelong learning. The first, grounded in left critiques of the 1970s, focuses on outcomes; that is, the poor achievement of identifiable groups: low income; Maori (indigenous); Pacific Islanders; and women. The second asserts the rights of Maori, both as citizens and as *tangata whenua* ('people of the land'). Rooted in the long history of Maori (indigenous) resistance, regrouping and cultural renaissance in response to 150 years of colonization and subjugation, it has crystallized into a powerful political force since the early 1970s (Walker 1990). The third is neo-liberalism. In general terms, the radical and Maori critiques share the liberal-reformist assumption that public education is a social right. Their common complaint is that public education does not deliver adequately on its promises. However the Maori critique also presses for *tino rangatiratanga* ('sovereignty'). During the 1970s and 1980s, these two critiques resulted in a greater emphasis on the need for more socially equitable educational outcomes. Quite cleverly, neo-liberalism too purports to be concerned at the poor achievement of particular groups. But both its analysis and its approach are at odds with the foundations of welfare state compromise on two counts: first, neo-liberalism's denies the very idea of social rights; second, it advocates a minimalist state. Indeed, neo-liberalism claims that the cause of inequity lies in the welfare state's inherent suppression of individual choice and opportunity. The answer, it argues, is the market model.

Lifelong learning and the welfare state

Tripartism was a cornerstone of the welfare state compromise. Governments worked with employers and unions, as social partners, in formulating and implementing economic and social policies designed to achieve the central goals of welfare capitalism: economic growth, full employment, a steady rise in the standard of living and the moderate reformation of work in order to humanize, within limits, production. In education, these goals implied policies that:

- integrated working people as citizens in the modern state
- satisfied their educational expectations for themselves and their children
- accommodated employers' desire to have the state bear the cost of training and retraining the workforce.

In the 1960s, New Zealand strengthened technical education, enacted a Vocational Training Act that established a Vocational Training Council (VTC) and a network of industry training boards, and identified enhanced training as vital to economic and social development. Unions and employers were well represented on the VTC and its boards and on the governing bodies of technical institutes (Law 1993).

In the 1970s, the OECD's concept of 'recurrent education', which placed priority on economic growth, the rights of capital and managerial prerogative, framed much of the thinking in vocational education. UNESCO's democratic vision of 'lifelong learning' was well received but viewed as more appropriate for non-vocational adult education. This vision received a boost with the election of the third Labour Government (1972-75) which was committed to the extension of educational opportunities at all levels. During this decade, little account was taken of the ILO's concept of workers' education, which went well beyond vocational and industrial relations training and which strongly affirmed workers' right to paid educational leave (PEL). However, Labour made an effort to breathe new life into workers' education. It increased resources for the Workers' Educational Association (WEA) and, in 1974, established a Trade Union Training Board (TUTB) under the auspices of the VTC. Although poorly resourced and greeted with suspicion by many left unions who distrusted the politics of industrial training, the TUTB successfully survived a change of government in late 1975. By 1980 it was approving more than 250 seminars a year attended by over 4000 officials, 95 per cent of whom were honorary (Law 1996).

Ambiguous restructuring: the Labour era, 1984-1990

Re-elected in 1984, Labour tried to reconcile social democratic beliefs and values with rapidly globalizing market economies. The welfare state was already in crisis. In adult education, the non-vocational/community sector had been hit by budget cutbacks in the early 1980s, while high school, polytechnic and university provision was under stress. The new Minister of Education, Russell Marshall, had a long-standing interest in lifelong learning. He moved quickly to implement Labour's comprehensive policy on trade union education. The 1986 Union Representatives Educational Leave Act (UREL), which established a Trade Union Education Authority (TUEA) and provided unionists with a measure of PEL, was a bold attempt to realize both UNESCO and the ILO's democratic visions (Law 1997). Marshall also encouraged attempts to produce a comprehensive policy for the rest of adult education. This was achieved by late 1985, but was immediately undermined by those who dissented from it. Marshall decided that the statutory National Council of Adult Education (NCAE) was ineffective, put it into recess and established an advisory committee that recommended the establishment of a non-statutory body, the Committee for Learning Aotearoa/New Zealand (CLANZ). The NCAE was abolished by statute in 1990 (Dakin 1996).

Meanwhile, the international labour market debates and New Right thinking were catching up with education and training in New Zealand. The labour market debates revolved around changes in workplace relations and work organization that implied a move from confrontational industrial relations and collectivism towards a more participatory approach. Workers needed to be more 'flexible', it was argued, and this required an upgrading of skills (Littler 1991). As international concern about a 'skills gap' became more urgent, greater stress was placed on the relationship between education and the economy and on the need for the private sector to 'assume primary responsibility for the provision of training and retraining opportunities' (OECD 1990: 64). These ideas intersected with two related strands of neo-liberal thinking:

1. a philosophical focus on 'individual freedom' which advocates an individually based, contractual employment relations system
2. an emphasis on the economic which argues 'that liberal institutions of free markets and limited government will maximize' best the aims of prosperity and liberty (Barry 1987: 26).

In most countries, the social partners staked out different positions. Governments focused on deregulating the labour market in order to reduce rigidities, including pay rigidities, and encourage greater overall flexibility. Employers focused on job flexibility, multiskilling and on increasing their ability to hire and fire. Unions and parties of the Left tried to emphasize the value of employee involvement, the need to develop career paths and to link skill recognition with bargaining, and the desirability of retaining the outline of a tripartite industrial relations framework while accommodating pressures for more flexible bargaining (Wood 1989). From the mid 1980s, much the same pattern of positioning occurred in New Zealand.

In 1987, Labour introduced a Labour Relations Act 1987 (LRA) that confirmed its earlier (late 1984) removal of compulsory arbitration and which made union coverage contestable. But the LRA retained the essence of the tripartite, welfare-state industrial relations framework. This failure to move substantially in the direction dictated by New Right ideology earned the condemnation of employers and the New Zealand Business Round Table which, by the late 1980s, concluded that Labour lacked the will to deregulate the labour market in line with the logic of the rest of its economic restructuring programme. Labour accepted the emphasis placed internationally on the centrality of education and training, as a unified concept, in economic strategies. It facilitated a tripartite study of developments in Australia and enacted legislation to establish a national qualifications framework (NQF) and an associated qualifications authority (NZQA).

However, while conceived within a neo-liberal context and indebted to British initiatives, Labour's model retained residual social democratic values and elements. In part this reflected an assimilation of the corporatist logic of the Australian 'Accords': a series of negotiated agreements between that country's Labour Government and its Council of Trade Unions (Alexander and Lewer 1996). Labour's approach also recognized the importance of a general education for all, placed some emphasis on equity consideration and, in response to growing political pressure, afforded recognition of Maori language, culture and knowledge. Also significant was the intention to structure the NQF and its associated NZQA along corporatist lines: tripartism; an emphasis on the training needs of industries, rather than enterprises; an assumption of industry based, nationally co-ordinated, development strategies; and a skills regime that was implicitly linked to wages.

From the outset, the NQF received strong union endorsement (NZCTU 1995). Unions welcomed the opportunities it offered working people, especially women, Maori and Pacific Islanders, to break through traditional qualification barriers. The NQF enabled them to gain portable, recognized qualifications that had the potential to be linked to better wages. It also recognized prior learning. Not surprisingly, many Maori welcomed two other possibilities:

1. the formal recognition of language and culture-linked skills
2. the accreditation of independent *iwi* ('tribe') based education providers.

The triumph of ideology

From the mid 1980s, a determined element within the National Party began to advocate a 'consumer-driven education' based on 'the philosophy of economics and liberty'. This view, which regarded all post-compulsory education, including adult education, as essentially a 'private good', was also in tune with the advice Treasury was giving the Labour government. Simon Upton (1987: 99–100), a shadow minister, argued for removing the distinctions between providers and for limiting state support to giving school leavers a 'three years' entitlement to education or training assistance with the educator or training of his or her choosing. This, he claimed, would provide 'consumer-driven flexibility' and would 'open the way to private education'.

National was determined to complete the transition from welfare capitalism to a neo-liberal market economy by restructuring the labour market. Its permissive approach was 'deceptively clean of overly harsh and oppressive measures' (Harris 1993: 6). It purported to allow employers and workers to do what they like. It assumed the primacy of individual property rights ('labour services' are a property right) and that employers, as the owners of jobs, should have full control of workplaces. It rejected tripartism and eschewed any substantial role for government, other than that of facilitating the employment relationship. The cornerstone of National's labour market policies was its 1991 Employment Contracts Act (ECA). The ECA purports to offer two basic 'freedoms': freedom to associate and freedom to contract.

However, workers' ability to exercise these freedom is limited in practice by the difficulties experienced by unions. The Act treats unions as third parties or bargaining agents, places no obligation on employers to bargain in good faith, provides no recourse to arbitration and, by omission, makes it difficult for unions to organize.

The new training regime

While National retained Labour's qualifications and training regime, it also redefined that regime along lines that were much more consistent with neo-liberal ideology. National's approach had much in common with trends in Britain:

- the undermining of apprenticeships
- individual and labour market disincentives
- enhancing the market and the employers
- minimizing government interventions (King 1993).

The main features of this approach reflect the British influence (Keep and Rainbird, 1995): permissive rather than prescriptive legislation; a rejection of tripartism; an emphasis on employer-led standard setting and co-ordination; a market model of provision; an accompanying encouragement of private training agencies; and minimal state funding.

National's permissive 1992 Industry Training Act (ITA) was consistent with the ECA and with other labour market legislation. Its underlying premise was the view that training must be 'industry-led' through narrow, self-defined Industry Training Organizations (ITOs) that set skills standards, organize the delivery of training and arrange for the monitoring of training and the assessment of trainees. The legislation effectively abandoned the tripartite approach to training. Membership of ITOs is not prescribed, although there is a vague requirement for the Education and Training Support Agency (ETSA) to ensure employee involvement. The ITA provides for some government funding, but assumes that the owners of an ITO (employers) will substantially fund its programmes. Initially the government contemplated making provision for training levies but under pressure from the employers' organization it retreated to a voluntary approach, whereby members of an industry contribute to the cost of the training if they value it. These policies spawned a plethora of ITOs, in excess of 50, although economic pressure is now resulting in some voluntary rationalization.

Workers' education in a new environment

In the late 1980s, New Zealand unions saw themselves as key players in a workers' education and training regime that promised positive economic, industrial, and social outcomes. Major unions and the New Zealand Council of Trade Unions (NZCTU) accepted much of the labour market debates. They supported a 'high skills/high wage strategy', endorsed the view that manufacturing operated in a global market and that this meant that manufacturers, services and workers were required to produce to equivalent standards of quality, flexibility, speed of response, variety and cost as the best producers in the world. The Engineers' Union's Mike Smith (1991: 4–5) suggested that there were four elements to manufacturing for a global market: new technology, upskilling, new work design and changed industrial relations. These imply, he argued, 'co-operative procedures, consultative committees, professional negotiation and dispute resolution all work to maximize production and minimize disruption to the mutual benefit of workers and employers'. Education and training, he held, 'provides the common core to all these developments. Training is not only required for upskilling, but a good base education will be required to make the best use of new technology'. From this perspective, the NZCTU (1995) developed a well-thought-through, integrated education and training strategy that supported workplace reform, advocated a 'quality future' through a co-operative growth strategy, stressed the need for a quality public education system from early childhood through to tertiary and promoted industry training plans that emphasize the development of skills.

However even before the NZCTU's strategy was finalized, National's labour market policies had already reduced organized labour's capacity to influence the direction of education and training. The NZCTU approach assumed organizational strength, including high levels of union membership, the continuation of TUEA and access to PEL, the retention of a tripartite framework and a continuing commitment by the government to general education. National's removal of compulsory union membership and access to collective bargaining structures quickly undermined unions' membership base. Union density had dropped from around 60 per cent of the labour force in the 1980s to around 20 per cent by the end of 1997. TUEA too was an early casualty of the new order and was abolished with effect from August 1992. National and its allies regarded TUEA and statutory PEL as ideologically and structurally inconsistent with employment relationships based on a libertarian philosophy of individual rights, a facilitative legislative environment, and the primacy of contractual arrangements (Law 1997). For unionized workers, this led to a major reduction in educational opportunities.

Despite the above, unions are represented on about 40 per cent of ITOs. However, in a voluntarist, non-tripartite environment, that participation is dependent on employers. In industries where unions and employers have long co-operated, employers recognize that unions have established expertise, can facilitate worker confidence in training programmes and may even be willing to contribute financially. In the manufacturing sector, for example, the Engineers' Union continues to be very influential. However in the dairy industry, following the enactment of the ITA, employers abandoned an established national training committee on which the union was represented and quickly constituted an ITO comprising employers only. The Dairy Workers Union objected vigorously and made strong submissions to ETSA, but ministerial pressure saw ETSA recognize the new ITO without worker representation (Law 1996).

Traditional adult education

Traditional adult education has fared badly under National. The 1991 and 1992 budgets and associated measures moved in the same direction as education and training: non-legislative, permissive, voluntarist, user-pays. Direct and indirect funding was reduced substantially or eliminated; CLANZ lost its advisory role and most of its funding. Tertiary funding, including that for tertiary provided community education, was restructured on a market model. Adults taking formal courses were hit hard by more 'user-pays' fees and the removal of a needs-based fee rebate. Fees also rose substantially for tertiary institution and high school-provided community education.

But the overall picture under the market model is more complex than a litany of cuts may suggest. The government still funds tertiary institution-provided community education at a cost of just over NZ $12.5 million per year (personal communication, Ministry of Education, 28 July 1998). High school night classes are still funded through an allocation of 'hours'. Some specified groups still receive direct funding, eg adult literacy. And there is a whole new world of adult education developing in the *iwi* (Maori) and the private sectors that may well be funded in tune with labour market demands but which cannot be dismissed simply as labour market training. For example, under its 'Skills New Zealand' programme the Government is purchasing a wide range of labour market training for those, especially young people, on unemployment and other welfare benefits. Much of this is targeted training provided by Maori or other private agencies that incorporate into their programmes cultural and social education. What is important here is that most of the young adults in these programmes are drawn from sections of the population that historically have not participated in adult education. All of this is blurring the boundaries between traditional adult and workers' education, Maori adult education, post-compulsory formal education and skills development and training.

Towards 2001: some concluding observations

From a human capital perspective, the new education and training regime is in trouble. In mid 1997 the government released a Green Paper which acknowledged the strong criticism of the NQF and NZQA but which also foreshadowed an even more hands-off, voluntaristic approach. Meanwhile, the country faces a serious skills crisis that is now the subject of widespread employer concern (Wailes and Haworth 1995). It was not until mid 1997 that the raw numbers in training contracts of one year or more reached the level of apprenticeships and traineeships achieved before the restructuring of the 1980s (ETSA 1997). Moreover, it is widely believed that the training now offered is much less comprehensive than previously. Employers who train are increasingly frustrated by the 'freeloaders': those who contribute nothing and then poach trained staff. The number of ITOs and the overlap between them is making life very difficult for industries and employers who are committed to training. In short, what is happening in New Zealand accords with British research that suggests that voluntarist frameworks do not deliver either the quantity or quality of training required (Keep and Rainbird 1995).

It is not at all certain that the learning society in New Zealand, as we have traditionally understood it, will be able to withstand the neo-liberal revolution. Throughout this chapter I have argued that the realization of a democratic vision of lifelong learning cannot be separated from the fortunes of reformist politics. Historically, such politics have required the institutional support provided by a vibrant labour movement. But six years after the enactment of the ECA, only a limited number of weakened unions have survived. Proposed amendments to the ECA may thin their ranks even further. This institutional weakness is compounded by the ways in which current policies are reconstituting traditional (liberal) adult education in line with the market model. Increasingly agencies and adult educators are viewing themselves as 'entrepreneurs' providing 'customers' with a 'product'.

However, despite the triumph of neo-liberalism, there are signs that the reformist sentiment has not been exorcised completely from New Zealand's political culture. One recent indicator has been the growing ground swell of popular opposition to cutbacks in public education and public health. The challenge of the late 1990s for those who believe that lifelong learning has a social purpose is to find ways to foster a practical utopian vision that not only can be linked to viable political alternatives but also can accommodate the

Maori quest for social justice, as citizens and for *tino rangatiratanga* as *tangata whenua* (Rameka with Law 1997).

References

Alexander, R and Lewer, J (1996) *Understanding Australian Industrial Relations* (4th Ed), Harcourt Brace, Sydney.
Barry, NP (1987) *The New Right*, Croom Helm, London.
Beilharz, P (1992) *Labour's Utopias*, Routledge, London.
Dakin, J (1996) 'Looking Back', in J Benseman, B Findsen and M Scott (Eds), *The Fourth Sector*: 2137, The Dunmore Press, Palmerston North.
Education and Training Support Agency (1997) *Skill New Zealand: A Stocktake*, Author, Wellington.
Harris, P (1993) *Labour Market Deregulation in New Zealand*. Unpublished background paper prepared for Swedish trade unionists, New Zealand Council of Trade Unions.
Keep, E and Rainbird, H (1995) 'Training', in P Edwards (Ed.) *Industrial Relations: Theory and Practice in Britain*: 515–542, Blackwell, Oxford.
King, DS (1987) *The New Right: Politics, Markets and Citizenship*, Macmillan, London.
King, DS (1993) 'The Conservatives and Training Policy 1979–1992: From a Tripartite to a Neo-liberal Regime', *Political Studies*, XLI, 2, 214–235.
Law, MG (1993) 'The Changing World of Worker Education: An Historical Perspective', *New Zealand Journal of Adult Learning*, 21 1, 7–33.
Law, MG (1996) 'Workers' Education and Training in a Voluntarist Environment: What Role for Unions?', in J Benseman, B Findsen, and M Scott (Eds) *The Fourth Sector*: 159–176, The Dunmore Press, Palmerston North.
Law, MG (1997) 'The TUEA Experiment: Trade Union Education in New Zealand 1986–1992', in P Armstrong, N Miller and M Zukas (Eds) *Crossing Borders, Breaking Boundaries: Research in the education of adults*: 275–279, Birkbeck College, London.
Littler, C (1991) *Technology and the Organisation of Work*, Deakin University Press, Geelong.
New Zealand Council of Trade Unions (1995) *Building Better Skills: Unions and Skill New Zealand*, Author, Wellington.
Organisation for Economic Co-operation and Development (OECD) (1990) *Labour Market Policies for the 1990s*, OECD, Paris.
Przeworski, A (1986) *Capital and Social Democracy*, Cambridge University Press, Cambridge.
Rameka, N with Law, MG (1997) 'Tiaki nga taonga o nga tupuna: Valuing the Treasures: Towards a Global Adult Education Framework for Indigenous People', in L King (Ed.) *Reflecting Visions: New Perspectives on Adult Education for Indigenous Peoples*: 161–170, UNESCO Institute for Education, Hamburg.
Smith, M (1991) Manufacturing Skills for the Global Economy, in *Curriculum-core or Corset? Community and Business Views*: 3–7, New Zealand Planning Council, Wellington.

Upton, S (1987) *The Withering of the State*, Allen & Unwin/Port Nicholson Press, Wellington.

Wailes, N and Haworth, N (1995) *Skill Shortage: Training and Recruitment: A Report on a Recent Survey of Enterprises in the Auckland Region*. Unpublished report prepared by the Auckland Business Development Board.

Walker, R (1990) *Ka whawhai tonu matou: Struggle Without End*, Penguin, Auckland.

Wood, S (1989) The Transformation of Work? Skill, Flexibility and the Labour Process, Unwin Hyman, London.

Chapter 15

An Analysis of Lifelong Learning Policy in Japan

Hiromi Sasai

The development of social education in Japan

Until the concept of lifelong learning was introduced to Japan, the approach generally adopted was known as social education. Social education was based on the Social Education Act of 1949. This Act divided education into school education and social education. Social education was defined as all education other than school education. Social education began with the aim of 'giving a learning opportunity to the younger generation who were unable to go to high school': few students could attend high school in those days. In social education institutions in each locality, various classes for the younger generation were introduced. In these circumstances, a Law for the Promotion of Youth Classes and a Law for the Promotion of Women's Classes were established. In this sense, social education (non-formal education for adults and youth) took the role of supplementing school education.

At that time, therefore, institutions known as 'public halls' were established in each city and town, to form the basis of education for this younger generation and for women. A large budget was required for this. The national government therefore introduced a policy of subsidizing such an institution in each town. Establishing 'public halls' also permitted communities to provide education and learning opportunities independently of the centralized education system which had prevailed before the Second World War. Japan is a country with a centralized legal structure, and the Social Education Act was significant in establishing a basis for 'decentralization'.

This role continued until the proportion of junior high school students who went on to senior high school exceeded 90 per cent. When this was achieved – from the end of the 1950s – most social education became leisure-oriented.

In 'public halls', therefore, social education programmes typically cover literature, the fine arts, music and dance. In 1995 there were some 18,000 public halls in Japan. Experts are employed to identify communities' learning needs and plan and teach lectures and courses. This approach is characteristic of the Japanese education system. In almost every case, the content of lectures and courses is cultural rather than vocational, in order to appeal to the inhabitants as a whole. The image (and practice) of social education has become separated from vocational education.

The policies adopted by the national government to encourage social education can be summarized as follows:

- subsidies for capital infrastructure, such as the construction of 'public halls'
- funding for provision of lectures and courses within 'public halls'
- training of social education experts.

A new concept: lifelong learning

The need for 'Integrated Lifelong Education' was emphasized in UNESCO's Adult Education Promotion Conference as early as 1965. From that time, a lifelong learning approach spread internationally. In Japan, lifelong learning had a virtually identical meaning as lifelong education, because learning and education form a single concept.

Japan's National Council on Educational Reform proposed policies designed to 'move towards the lifelong learning system' in 1987. After that, the term and idea of 'lifelong learning' came to be generally accepted. The structure of the Ministry of Education, Science, Sports and Culture (MESSC) was altered, and a Bureau of Lifelong Learning established within it. This introduced a national administrative system for regulating lifelong learning.

Lifelong learning, however, emerged against several backgrounds. The context of the UNESCO proposal included the perception that education or learning through life is necessary if a person is to respond to changes in the world. On the other hand, in discussions around the National Council on

Educational Reform, the limitations of school education in Japan were a major background factor.

The view that education means schooling is even now very common in Japan. Many believe that school education is wholly sufficient, and view social education is merely an optional supplement. Schools perform roles which could be left to educators outside school, such as dealing with serious problems arising from the home, and addressing illegal behaviour by pupils. They also of course provide guidance on learning, educational progress and employment. There is also some anxiety that Japanese society gives too much weight to academic performance and grades achieved in formal schooling. Lifelong learning arose in response to such concerns and considerations. The concept reduces the emphasis on school education and strengthens the educational functions of social institutions such as the home, corporations, learning groups and so on.

A further element in the decision to move to a lifelong learning approach was pointed out by the National Council on Educational Reform: 'for economic and social change'. In other words, in order to deal with economic and social change, we must recognize the value of education and learning. The changes include the onset of an information-oriented society, and the prospect of an ageing society in the twenty-first century. In this respect, the thinking behind the proposal clearly resembles the considerations which led to lifelong learning in Europe.

Therefore, lifelong learning is understood as a general idea encompassing school education, education at home, social education, co-operative education and so on. It refers to 'continuous learning extending over a life', the 'master concept' which contains all the general ideas about education and learning from which it developed. This is illustrated in Figure 15.1.

Policies to promote lifelong learning

To deal with this situation and to promote lifelong learning with the ultimate goal of building a 'lifelong learning society', national and local public organizations are adopting a wide range of measures. The measures taken by MESSC include: developing promotional mechanisms for lifelong learning; enacting a 'Lifelong Learning Promotion Law'; establishing a 'Lifelong Learning Council'; and setting up departments and councils responsible for lifelong learning in local government.

At the same time, social education plays a strong role in promoting lifelong learning. Social education activities are diverse, responding to people's voluntary and spontaneous desire for learning. The efforts of national and local government focus on the training and recruitment of social education experts, the encouragement of social educational programmes and the improvement of physical facilities for social education like 'public halls'.

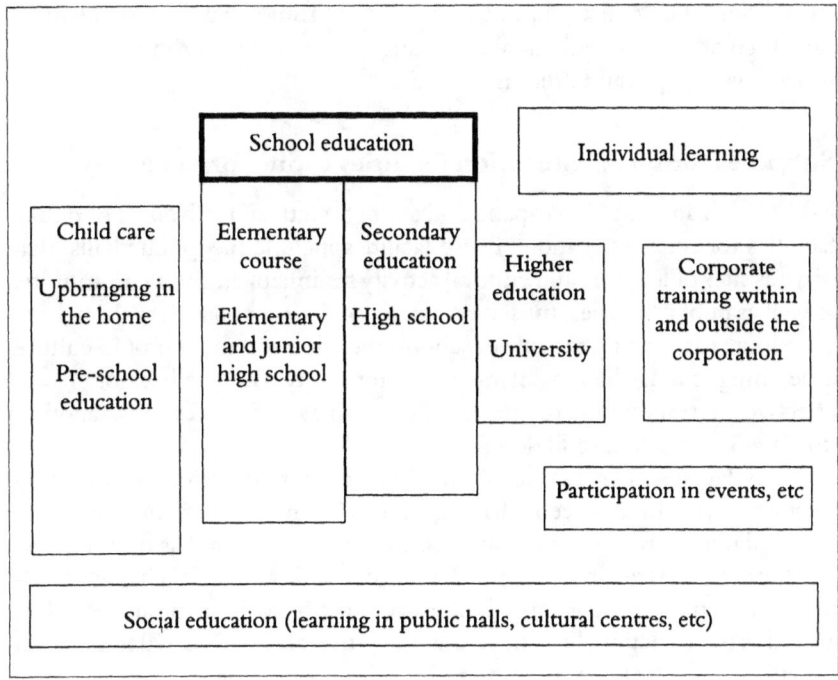

Figure 15.1 *The lifelong learning system in Japan*

Training of social education experts

Social education experts include social education officers appointed by the local boards of education, officers working in 'public halls', librarians, public museum curators and leaders of social education organizations, such as parent-teacher associations and youth organizations. In order to ensure the training and recruitment of adequate numbers of experts, as well as to improve their quality, national government encourages and assists in-service training and self-development activities for these experts at national, regional and prefecture levels.

Budget subsidies for lectures and courses in 'public halls'

The MESSC has facilitated the provision of a range of learning opportunities about contemporary topics for young people and adults. It has also provided financial assistance to various community development programmes and volunteer services, as well as to family education programmes and programmes designed to encourage community participation by the elderly. In addition, the Ministry has made efforts to promote audio-visual educational activities intended to make learning more effective through the use of movies, videotapes and other new media.

Subsidies for social education facilities capital projects

MESSC has attempted to expand and strengthen the effectiveness of public facilities for social education. These facilities include the 'public halls' that serve as sites of learning and cultural activity for inhabitants in a community, as well as public libraries, museums and so on. These policies are thought to contribute to reducing the role of school education and to promote a culture of learning among the inhabitants in a community. But it is has not proved effective in responding to the learning demand of professions, another important dimension of lifelong learning.

Many Japanese corporations have played an important role in educating their workers. This has been a driving force in Japan's economic advance, and is a symbolic characteristic of Japanese corporations. But it has been limited to educating workers in how to deal with economic and social changes relating to the corporation concerned. International competition in various fields, as well as trade friction, have intensified, and the rate of industrial innovation is marked. In this area, universities play an important role.

Making universities more open to society

In the context of current economic and social changes and the expected shift to a 'lifelong learning society', it is very important for universities to invigorate their own educational and research activities, while developing their own individual characteristics. This enables them to transform themselves to become institutions more open to the outside world. In this way, universities can respond to a wide range of demands from society, especially from professions.

There is, however, an important difference from other areas of policy. Decisions on whether universities open themselves to the community are taken by universities themselves, rather than by national or local government. Making universities more open to society is a major issue in promoting lifelong learning, because university extension is almost unknown in Japan, yet the demand for professional education is expected to increase in the near future. Policies to promote university extension will be a priority.

References

Amano, Ikuo(1996) *Educational System in Japan,* Tokyo: Tokyo University Press.
Aso, Makoto (1987) *The Meaning of Lifelong Learning System, Social Education,* Tokyo All Japan Association for Social Education.
Okamoto, Kaneji (1985a) *Lifelong Education System of Municipal Governments,* Tokyo, Gyosei.
Okamoto, Kaneji (1985b) *Lifelong Education System of Prefecture Governments,* Tokyo, Gyosei.
Okamoto, Kaoru (1994) *Lifelong Learning Movement in Japan,* Tokyo, All Japan Association for Social Education.
Sato, Mamoru (1986) *Promotional System for Lifelong Education. Annual Report of The Japan Society for The Study of Lifelong Education,* 7, 89–98.
The Japan Society for the Study of Adult Education (1986) *Lifelong Education Policy and Social Education,* Tokyo, Toyokan.
Ministry of Education, Science, Sports and Culture (MESSC) (1994–1996) *Annual Report of Educational Policies in Japan, Tokyo, Japanese Government Publishing Service.*
Research Group in MESSC for Social Education(1986–88) *The Book for Administration of Social Education,* Tokyo, Daiichihoki.

Reports concerning 'Lifelong Learning Policy' submitted by Japanese National Councils:
'Social Education in a Rapidly Changing Society' submitted by the Social Education Council (1971).
'Basic Plan for Comprehensive Improvement and Preparation of School Education' submitted by the Central Council for Education (1971).
'Lifelong Education' submitted by the Central Council for Education (1981)
the National Council on Educational Reform: The First Report on Educational Reform; The Fourth Report on Educational Reform (1985 –1987).
'Development of an Infrastructure for Lifelong Learning' submitted by the Central Council for Education (1990).
'Reforms of Educational Systems to Deal with a New Era' submitted by the Central Council for Education (1991).
'Improvement of University Education' and 'Improvement of Junior College Education' submitted by the University (1991).
'Measures for Promoting Lifelong Learning Corresponding to Future Social Trends' submitted by the Lifelong Learning Council (1992).

Chapter 16

Can User Choice Contribute to Lifelong Learning?
Implications of the Australian Experience

Fran Ferrier

During 1996, ministers of education and training from the Australian state, territory and federal governments adopted a policy initiative for the Vocational Education and Training (VET) system referred to as 'User Choice'. This paper outlines the context in which this initiative arose, its meaning and aims, and the findings of an evaluation of the projects that have piloted the User Choice concept. It then considers whether, and in what ways, 'User Choice' can make a contribution to the advancement of 'lifelong learning'.

The context: VET reform

Reform of the VET system has been under way in Australia since the late 1980s. This reform is justified on both social and economic grounds.

Economic justifications derive from a view that the nation will improve its economic performance and international competitiveness by developing 'a diverse and dynamic national skill pool'. Within this framework individuals are regarded as an economic resource, and there is concern that 'many Australian (have) potential skills and abilities that are not being utilized' (ANTA

1996). Social justifications centre on 'the capacity of education and training to change people's life chances, to enable people to development to their full potential and to have security and satisfaction in work and in life' (ANTA 1996).

Much of the reform effort is being concentrated on the creation of a 'training market' – a concept that envisages competition between different 'providers[1]' of VET for students, and for public and private funding. This approach is based on a view that competition will increase efficiency – optimizing value for money, and will force providers to be more responsive to the needs of students and employers, who are redefined as the 'clients' or 'users' of the VET system (ACG 1994, Anderson 1996, 1997).

What is User Choice?

One of the major complaints that spurred reform of the VET system was that too many education and training decisions were made at the point of supply, rather than demand. Reformers sought a way to turn this around – giving 'users' more influence over who would provide the education and training, what would be provided and how.

A major report commissioned by the Australian National Training Authority (ANTA) (ACG 1994) suggested that responsiveness could be improved through a 'user buys' approach in which funding, and the capacity to make choices, would be given to 'users' – similar to a voucher scheme. The report argued that this would strengthen the demand side influence by injecting more market signals into mainstream arrangements and would increase responsiveness as the needs of users would be more clearly articulated.

Following this report ANTA developed a modified approach that it referred to as 'User Choice'. The difference between 'user buys' and 'User Choice' lay in the treatment of funding. User Choice gave the same capacity to make choices to users, as 'user buys', but did not directly give them funding or vouchers. Public funding would remain with the public authority until the user had indicated the direction of their choice. It would then flow directly to the selected provider. This change reflected ANTA's view that it was not necessary for funds to flow to the user for the choice to be exercised and that to give funds directly to employers might involve them in unnecessary contractual and audit requirements.[2]

ANTA subsequently provided funding to the state and territory training authorities for a set of pilot projects that would test the User Choice concept and indicate how it might work in practice. ANTA indicated that these pilots should 'primarily be directed to enhancing client focused arrangements between providers, employers and employees/students' and further should 'be primarily targeted at decisions made by firms and their employees'. They were thus to be concentrated on apprenticeship and traineeship arrangements (contracts of training) and would be characterized by an 'increase in the ownership of the training program by the firm and workers and (would) allow for negotiation at a local level of delivery arrangements and greater customization of training' (ANTA 1994).[3]

The pilots were to include firms of varying sizes, including small businesses, and group training companies. They were also to be established in a range of fields of study and industry areas so that they would include the full range of providers and areas where competition in the training market was 'thickest', such as hospitality, business or computing studies (ANTA 1994).

In addition, ANTA indicated that it was important to 'test the impact' of User Choice on the 'broadest range of clients possible'. This meant that some pilots could involve clients not engaged in contracts of training. For instance, it was suggested that pilots could involve communities that did not have access to contracts of training, such as rural and remote Aboriginal and Torres Strait Islander communities (ANTA 1994).

The criteria to be applied in selecting suitable projects included that clients were to have relevant information on which to base choices; they should be given a choice of provider; and clients, or their broker would be able to negotiate and customize the training. The level of funding for each project would be based on standard unit costs determined by the relevant state or territory authority (ANTA 1995).

Fifty projects were subsequently funded around the country. Forty involved students who were apprentices or trainees with enterprises, employer groups, or group training companies, in a range of industries. The remaining ten were designated 'Aboriginal and Torres Strait Islander (ATSI) initiatives' and involved Indigenous students, most of whom were not in employment, and did not have contracts of training. These ten projects were focused on the achievement of economic outcomes including employment, self-employment and/or small business opportunities.

While they shared common features there was a great diversity in the projects. In some cases the enterprise was also the VET provider, or there was a broker mediating between employer and provider. The participating students had diverse learning and training needs. They were from varied backgrounds, of different ages, lived and worked in many different locations, were part of many different communities, had a variety of previous experiences in education and training, and varied levels of skills. Given the small number of pilots, this diversity underlined the many dimensions of the VET system as a whole.

From the outset of the projects, ANTA appointed consultants to evaluate them and provide advice on the wider implementation of User Choice. Some state and territory training authorities also appointed consultants to evaluate User Choice projects within their jurisdiction – particularly some additional projects which they funded separately.

Evaluation of User Choice

The evaluation team engaged by ANTA undertook the task in two stages.[4] Stage One, consisting of a telephone survey and consultations with participating employers, concentrated on aspects of the initiation of the pilot projects. An additional activity comprised consultations on key policy issues in the implementation of User Choice. These entailed discussions with many groups and individuals including state and territory training authorities, employer organizations, industry training boards, and VET providers.

Stage Two, undertaken some months later, consisted of a further survey and case studies of selected projects. Its objective was to improve the level of understanding of the operation of User Choice at the project level, indicating what might happen in VET if User Choice were introduced more generally. Ten case studies were undertaken – three ATSI initiative projects and seven of the larger group of projects involving contracts of training.

The evaluation produced several different reports and papers. In addition to separate reports to ANTA by the consultants on Stage One (Selby Smith *et al.* 1996a, 1996b), and on Stage Two (Selby Smith *et al.* 1997), a paper by the author (Ferrier 1997) focuses on the equity aspects of User Choice and draws particularly on the case studies and consultations in connection with the projects involving Aboriginal and Torres Strait Islander communities.

The Stage Two report presented five key findings of the evaluation:

- Users involved in the projects were all strongly committed to the User Choice concept. Compared with their previous experience of the VET system they preferred the User Choice approach. Support for User Choice was unequivocal and existed even where some difficulties were experienced at the local level. Having a greater say had made users more active participants in the system; and User Choice had brought some new users into the system.

'Definitely a good idea, prospect of competition, my having choice keeps all the providers on their toes.'

'Now [have] a faith in the system; will take on more trainees.'

- User Choice had potential to improve access and equity by encouraging responsiveness by VET providers to the needs of groups and individuals disadvantaged in the VET system. The User Choice pilot projects facilitated the development of a positive and supportive environment in which disadvantaged users had opportunities to express their needs and greater confidence that these would be met.

'I feel I can ring up the provider at any time and I appreciate the regular meetings.'

'The customer is always right... if we're not happy we have the right to change.'

- User Choice is valued by enterprises because it allows them to exercise greater flexibility when integrating training activities within their business objectives overall. All of the enterprises involved in the projects were operating in an increasingly competitive commercial environment. Many view training and other forms of learning as elements in their business strategy. They were paying increasing attention to the necessity to upgrade the workforce skills of those already in paid employment, new entrants and the unemployed. User Choice gave them training that better suited their needs and the organization of their work.

'The training suits our needs better; it's specific training for our needs and it's better-suited to the organization of our work.'

- Many employers expressed concerns about the commitment of training authorities to the effective and sustainable implementation of User Choice. They also were aware of constraints on these authorities that impacted on their capacity to respond appropriately. These constraints included industrial relations conditions.

'My only fear is how we will continue...'

'IR considerations limited the speed with which the local TAFE could respond to our changing needs...'

- Enterprises and organizations operating on a national basis were frustrated by the diverse training arrangements and requirements operating within different states and territories. As most public VET providers operate only in the state of their location it is not always possible for these enterprises and organizations to gain access to the education and training that best meets their needs.

'There has to be the possibility for a national organization to have a single national point of contact rather than having to deal separately with each individual State.'

In addition to these five key findings, the report included substantial material on the operation of User Choice at the local, project level. This covered outcomes of the training; the training process and the ease or difficulty of negotiating. Due to space limitations these will not be reported here, but will be referred to in the general discussion below concerning the links between User Choice and lifelong learning.

User Choice and lifelong learning

Can User Choice contribute to lifelong learning? Can it create the sort of conditions that will encourage students to 'continue learning throughout their lives, not only in ... formal contexts ... but at home, at work and in the community?' Will it assist in development of the characteristics of a 'lifelong learner': an inquiring mind; helicopter vision; information literacy; a sense of personal agency; and a repertoire of learning skills? (Candy et al. 1994).

The pilot project experience suggests that it might in VET, in three main ways: by encouraging more positive attitudes to VET; by increasing the self-confidence and self-knowledge of participants; and by providing additional and more appropriate opportunities for participation in VET for students with limited or poor previous education or training experience, or with little or no other access to publicly funded training.

User Choice encouraged VET providers to negotiate with participants and to create programmes that more directly met their needs. A consequence was the encouragement of more positive attitudes to VET among both the students involved and their employers. An indication of this change was that some employers became more willing to support participation in programmes by their employees. Some with little or no prior experience with VET came to appreciate its value; become advocates for it, and went on to provide more opportunities for participation to other employees:

'The fellow next door was pretty sceptical (when I started) but now he wants to be involved.'[5]

Employers and workplace supervisors, as well as students, indicated that they had learnt from their involvement.

> 'An advantage of doing the training on the farm, while we are working, is that it is more of a learning experience for me as well; heaps of discussion, it's great.'

> 'The traineeship has been a joint learning experience for the trainee and the supervisor.'

In negotiating with clients and customizing programs staff of the VET providers involved had been given opportunities to deepen their understanding of the needs and aspirations of particular students and improve their skills in designing and delivering appropriate modules.

> '...[the project has] opened our eyes to workplace training and workplace assessment and what we can contribute.'

Enthusiasm for their participation was often evident.

> 'I'm quite enthused for User Choice ... it's real world stuff. It's vibrant and exciting...'

A pronounced change in the self-confidence and esteem of many students occurred as the user/client focus affirmed the value and importance of their particular needs and empowered them to express and assert these needs. As the projects progressed, the participants exhibited more of the characteristics of a lifelong learner. They showed 'a sense of personal agency', with 'a positive concept of (themselves) as capable and autonomous'.

> 'Students feel important. It (User Choice) sets up a challenge for them ... putting something into their mind ... they become more confident and demanding.'

> 'It's given them confidence; they are showing a great deal more interest in work; they'll soon be in a position to tread on the toes of more senior staff.'

> 'The students have gone ahead, they're more confident and willing to take responsibility.'

They demonstrated a 'repertoire of learning skills' including 'knowledge of [their] own strengths, weaknesses and preferred learning styles' and an 'inquiring mind'.

> 'One of my employees has gone from lost soul to knowing where he wants to go.'

> 'Since I've started this course I've noted other things both at work and in general life.'

A challenge faced by lifelong learning is to provide opportunities for those who have 'missed the first boat' (Eliasson 1996). Many of the pilot projects provided second chance opportunities for participation in VET to students from remote and rural areas, with poor literacy, numeracy and language skills, prisoners and students with disabilities.

> 'Unemployment is very high around here; and the training has provided me with an opportunity that I probably would not have had.'

Moreover, through customization, the special needs of these students were addressed.

> 'We gave every student special tutorial support so that they were not set up for failure. Some had not passed Year 7.'

Some positive outcomes were achieved. In a correctional centre:

> 'Involvement in the course has encouraged [the prisoners] to share their knowledge. Trust and communication is not usual in a jail culture.'

In a workshop for people with disabilities:

> 'Many people are more capable and are able to be left to do their own work. Everyone is now capable of handling a more difficult product.'

In an Aboriginal organization:

> 'We're no longer pigeonholed ... we're multiskilled!'

Nevertheless, in relation to the contribution of User Choice to lifelong learning, two possible major problems are apparent. Firstly, User Choice emphasizes enterprise needs over individual student needs, favouring the economic objectives of VET over other broader objectives, including lifelong learning. Secondly, through its possible impact on the allocation of public funding for VET, User Choice could contribute indirectly to a reduction in the broad range of opportunities and options available for students in VET, thereby inhibiting the ability of students to 'continue learning throughout their lives, not only in ... formal contexts ... but at home, at work and in the community?' (Candy *et al.* 1994).

The report which proposed the original 'user buys' concept (ACG 1994) justified the prioritization of the needs of enterprises on the grounds that the needs of individuals and enterprises are converging. It argued that this convergence was most obvious in the area of apprenticeships and traineeships (ACG 1994). More recently ANTA (1996) has argued that because enterprises are the end users of skills acquired through training, compete nationally and internationally and create jobs for individuals, VET providers should respond directly to their needs rather than those of individual students (Anderson 1997).

The dominance of enterprise needs is apparent in the allocation of funding for the User Choice pilots primarily to projects involving contracts of training. However, it fails to reflect the reality of VET for most students. Only one in ten VET students enrolled in vocational programs are indentured apprentices and trainees. Moreover, individual students appear to undertake VET courses for a variety of reasons not all of which relate to employment outcomes (Anderson 1997).

The concern with work, employment and economic objectives that it suggests is echoed in some recent literature on lifelong learning. Butler, for instance (1998) argues that the language that has been used to 'sell' lifelong learning privileges the economic and includes the social: that the desired attributes of citizenship now mirror those of 'model workers ... flexible, adaptable, ready and willing to engage in continual (self) improvement/learning for the benefit of the nation' (1998: 63). Boshier (1998) notes that recent enquiries into lifelong learning have been fuelled by concern about the global economy, the workplace and individual learning. Kallen (1996) finds that the economic climate of the 1990s does not favour the 'somewhat utopian, idealistic philosophy of the earlier lifelong learning paradigms', but is 'propitious for plainly work and employment related lifelong training programmes' (1996: 21). The emphasis on enterprise needs and economic objectives in User Choice suggest that it is more likely to support and promote this lifelong training for work and employment, than the sort of lifelong learning to which Candy *et al.* (1994) refer.

An additional factor that may exacerbate this tendency is the failure of the User Choice arrangements to acknowledge that there are power differences in the relationship between employer and employee and that the restrictions on customization may prevent the degree of flexibility required to meet special needs. The power imbalance may make it difficult for individual employees to articulate needs that differ from those specified by their employer, particularly if they are unable to get access to the information they need in order to make informed choices. This is likely to be worse for those with poorer language, literacy or language skills, or in rural or remote areas. The problem of inflexibility was apparent in several pilot projects, but particularly those involving Aboriginal students:

> '[The provider] is no different to any other mainstream organization that has to meet industry standards. Sometimes this doesn't sit together with the needs of the Aboriginal community.'

There are several ways in which User Choice might impact on the allocation of public funding, and public resources and contribute to a narrowing of options and opportunities in VET. User Choice might contribute to a shift in the costs of VET from the private to the public purse. If enterprises that have done their own training in the past can get public funding for customized programmes will they continue to provide their own training, at their own expense? Without an increase in the overall level of public funding for VET this could mean a reduction in funding available for other programmes.

In a User Choice system private VET providers might seek to use public resources, where, for instance, they are chosen by a 'client' to deliver a programme, but do not have the required resources and equipment. If this access is granted (and there is a question about terms and conditions) there may be an impact on other 'users' of these resources.

Finally, in a VET system based on a User Choice approach, public and private VET providers may not compete on equal terms. It is likely that public VET providers would be expected to take primary responsibility for the provision of the more expensive programs that take access and equity concerns into consideration. This might strengthen and improve these providers, or it might lower their status, and create ghettos of disadvantage. In either case, if funding is based on unit costs that do not include access and equity considerations, the provider might incur financial difficulties that would ultimately affect its ability to provide a broad range of programs.

Notes

1. VET providers are now referred to as 'registered training organizations'. They include Technical and Further Education (TAFE) colleges or institutes, adult and community education organizations and private training organizations.
2. This is taken from internal briefing notes supplied to the User Choice evaluation team.
3. ANTA indicated that 'customization' meant the capacity to vary curriculum within the accredited framework to meet the particular needs of different students and could include variation of content,

within allowable limits, and use of learning resources or modes of delivery to suit local enterprise requirements (ANTA 1994).
4. The consultant organization was Joy Selby Smith Pty Ltd. The evaluation team consisted of Joy Selby Smith, Chris Selby Smith and the author. I am grateful to Joy and Chris for allowing me to draw on the evaluation material for this paper. However, the views I express are my own.
5. All quotes in this section are from the User Choice evaluation Stage Two report.

References

Allen Consulting Group (ACG) (1994) *Successful Reform: Competitive Skills for Australians and Australian Enterprises*, Australian National Training Authority, Brisbane.

Anderson, D (1996) *Reading the Market: A Review of the Literature on the Vocational Education and Training Market in Australia*, Monash University-ACER Centre for the Economics of Education and Training, Melbourne.

Anderson, D (1997) 'Students as Clients: Refocusing Training Market Reform', *The Market for VET, Papers and Proceedings from the NCVER Conference*, Adelaide Hilton Hotel, Adelaide, 28–30 July.

Australian National Training Authority (ANTA) (1994) 'User Choice: Discussion paper', 28 December, mimeo.

ANTA (1995) 'Administrative Arrangements for User Choice Pilot Projects', 14 December, mimeo.

ANTA (1996) *Equity 2001: Strategies to achieve access and equity in vocational education and training for the new millenium*, ANTA, Brisbane.

ANTA (1997) *Report to MINCO on the Implementation of User Choice*, ANTA, Brisbane.

Boshier, R (1997) 'Edgar Faure after 25 years: Down but not out'. (Chapter 1).

Butler, E (1997) 'Persuasive Discourses: Learning and the Production of Working Subjects in a Post-Industrial Era'. (Chapter 6).

Candy, P, Crebert, G and O'Leary, J (1994) *Developing Lifelong Learners Through Undergraduate Education*, National Board of Employment, Education and Training, Australian Government Publishing Service, Canberra.

Eliasson, G (1996) 'The Case of Life Long Learning', in *Vocational Training European Journal*, 8/9, May–December, 1–4.

Ferrier, F (1997) 'The Good, the Bad and the Unknown: Equity and User Choice', in F Ferrier and D Anderson (Eds) *Different Drums, One Beat? Economic and Social Goals in Education and Training*, Monash University-ACER Centre for the Economics of Education and Training, Melbourne.

Kallen, D (1996) 'Lifelong Learning in Retrospect', in *Vocational Training European Journal*, 8/9, May–December, 16–22.

Selby Smith J, Selby Smith C and Ferrier F (1996a) *Implementing User Choice: Policy Issues*, a report to ANTA, August 1996.

Selby Smith J, Selby Smith C and Ferrier F (1996b) *Survey of Users in 1996 User Choice Pilot Projects, Working Paper No. 7*, Monash University-ACER Centre for the Economics of Education and Training.

Selby Smith J, Selby Smith C and Ferrier F (1997) *National Evaluation of the 1996 User Choice Pilot Projects: Stage 2*, a report to ANTA.

Chapter 17

A Market for Lifelong Learning?
The Voucher Experience in the City of London

Peter Jarvis, John Holford and Colin Griffin

Learning in policy debates

Since the mid 1980s, the notion of learning has become increasingly important to policy debate the world over. This has been true at virtually all levels of policy-making. At the supranational level, the European Union declared 1996 to be 'European Year of Lifelong Learning' and issued a major White Paper entitled *Teaching and Learning: Towards the Learning Society*. The United Kingdom government issued its own *Lifetime Learning – A Consultation Document* at much the same time. In the commercial and business sector, management literature has given increasing emphasis to the importance of learning (eg Senge 1990). For example, much of the literature on total quality management, including that associated with ISO 9000 (BS5750), emphasizes feedback systems and 'organizational learning'.

Underpinning much of this literature has been the pace of technological and industrial change through the 1980s, the globalization of economies, the declining confidence in economic and industrial planning, and the relatively short-term timeframes within which policy debates can now be situated. The EU's view has been that these challenges call for a broad knowledge base, to avoid the 'risk of a rift between those that can interpret; those that can only use; and those who are pushed out of mainstream society and rely on social support: in other words, between those who know and those who do not know' (EU 1995: 9).

This calls, according to the EU, for an acquired body of fundamental and technical knowledge allied to social skills; and it argues for the creation of systems of competence-based accreditation networks, allied to the delivery of education and training within 'networks' which may be institutional ('education and training establishments co-operating with families or firms') or informal networks of knowledge ('adult education establishments, education co-operatives, etc.').

The EU has stressed the importance of policies to this end at the local, national and European level, and co-operation between the EU and its member states. Its case consists of several strands. Educational and training establishments must be strengthened and actively participate in setting up co-operation networks involving others concerned, particularly business and the social partners. Enterprises must have an increasing role in training and must help to disseminate any new skills developed from their experience, through closer collaboration with other agencies and social partners. 'Social exclusion' of vulnerable groups must be 'combated', for instance by second chance programmes and voluntary service. Individuals must also be able to enjoy permanent access to a whole range of better-targeted and more clearly identifiable education and training provision which complements general knowledge and can be acquired outside formal systems. A central target should be universal proficiency in three EU languages.

The former UK Conservative government argued along similar lines. 'Creating a culture of lifetime learning is crucial to sustaining and maintaining our international competitiveness ... It is also crucial to our national culture and quality of life.' It placed greater stress on individuals' responsibility for their own lifetime learning: 'our personal competitiveness will have a major effect on our prosperity'. At a local level, although stressing co-ordination and support, the government's chief concern was to encourage 'local strategies to encourage greater individual responsibility for lifetime learning', such as the Department for Education and Employment's initiative 'to encourage TECs and their local partners to support integrated strategies for individual learners'. The government also sponsored a programme of research on 'Individual Commitment to Learning' (Park 1994).

The Labour government brought new thinking, but at the level of technique and rhetoric rather than vision. Within three weeks of coming to power in May 1997, one of the key education and employment ministers, Baroness Blackstone, announced that their 'new approach to Lifelong Learning' would mean 'a society in which learning is valued and practised as part of everyday life – not just by the few but by the many'. This would mean making 'high-quality information about learning more easily accessible', recognizing 'the diverse needs of learners' and making 'learning opportunities available to them', and ensuring high quality. Specifically she mentioned two new initiatives: a University for Industry would 'open up access to learning through local opportunities in communities and companies; in colleges or clubs; in libraries or living rooms', and 'offer small firms realistic means of developing the most important part of any business – its people'. At the same time, new 'Individual Learning Accounts' would 'help people *take responsibility* for their own learning, to invest in their own future, to invest in their own skills and their own future' (DfEE 1997; emphasis added). Despite nearly a year of frenetic consultation, the Green Paper *The Learning Age: A Renaissance for a New Britain* (Cm 3790 1998) added little but detail to this statement.

There is a large gap, however, between this global rhetoric and national and supranational strategies, and the formation and implementation of public policies at a regional and local level. Notions of lifelong learning and the learning society are linked to perceptions of consumer sovereignty. Can leadership by public authorities be reconciled with free choice? It was this issue with which the Corporation of London grappled in the early 1990s.

The City of London

The Corporation of London had taken over responsibility for Education within the City of London (London's financial district, commonly known as the 'Square Mile') in April 1990 on the abolition of the Inner London Education Authority. It was, and remains, a most unusual education authority. The residential population is around 7,000. There are two highly prestigious private schools, but only a single (primary) school under Local Education Authority (LEA) control. There are no further education colleges, but there are two universities (though these are not controlled by the LEA). The bulk of the City's residents live in a very few estates, but while some of these are high-status private developments, others are public housing. In contrast, by day the City's population is swelled by some 250,000 men and women who work in one of the world's premier financial centres.

It was soon apparent that the unique character of the City demanded new modes of operation from its education authority. The scale of the Corporation's provision would be trivially small. The sole exception would be in the education of adults: and even then only if the Corporation was prepared to move beyond the statutory requirement to provide for its residents.

The Corporation sought a strategy for public provision that would encourage more of its citizens to take part in educational opportunities, as well as being innovative and high-profile. Largely composed of leading financiers, its ethos was very much a free-market one. After considering consultants' reports, the solution it found was in the concept of education vouchers. In developing voucher schemes, the Corporation made explicit reference to the aim of establishing London as a lifelong learning community. This aim must be judged in part against the background of the EU and UK policies which seek to operationalize the rather fuzzy concept of 'learning community' in terms of the creation of formal and informal learning networks and strategies.

Voucher schemes and education

The use of voucher schemes to fund education at the national and local level was an important tenet of the former Conservative government's policy. It was developed particularly in relation to the early years of schooling. The new Labour government abandoned these projects and has avoided use of the term 'voucher'. However, such schemes continue to be the subject of political and educational debate, and in particular Individual Learning Accounts are clearly 'a euphemism for education vouchers' (Jarvis *et al.* 1998). These approaches may have considerable implications for access to and provision for lifelong learning opportunities: this study was designed in part to contribute to the growing body of research into voucher-type schemes in general.

Political and economic arguments for the use of vouchers to fund education have been rehearsed over the last twenty years or so (Blaug 1972, Maynard 1975, Crew and Young 1977) and there have also been local education authority studies (Kent Education Department 1978). Vouchers remain an option of funding policy for higher education (McNair 1995) as well as basic skills training (Taggart 1993) and they have also been conceived as a means of access to education for adults in lower income groups who may well have had relatively few earlier educational opportunities. They were featured in the Further Education Funding Council's Further Education funding policy and, in this context, vouchers have also been incorporated into the provision of educational guidance (Salveson *et al.* 1994). Most recently, they have been advocated to offer computer training for all adults (*the Guardian*, 28 December 1996: 3), although it is in the school system that such schemes attract the greatest controversy and opposition (*The Times*, 13 January 1997: 4).

A number of arguments have been put forward in favour of vouchers, across a range of educational provision such as schooling, youth education and training, and further, higher and adult education. The arguments are: they provide the advantages of a market-based educational economy, giving greater scope to the private sector and allowing an element of competition to reduce what is seen to be the excessive role of the state in the provision of education; they offer a greater degree of consumer choice and influence over the nature of provision, whether the consumers are parents, employers or learners themselves; they increase opportunities and incentives for participation, with a consequent growth of the system of educational provision; and, finally, higher standards result from competition, diversity, accountability and incentives to greater efficiency on the part of the providers.

Voucher schemes have played a part in recent policy debates over the funding and structure of the post-compulsory sectors of education (McNay 1992). In particular, the role of the Training and Enterprise Councils (TECs) in relation to the LEAs has been highlighted by the introduction in 1991 of the Training Credits scheme, sometimes referred to as the FE 'voucher'. According to this, school leavers would be 'credited' to buy part-time training in employment, and thus it was envisaged that some kind of voucher scheme would form the basis of the funding of the post-compulsory education and training system. This would thus approximate to patterns of funding in countries such as France and Germany, where the voucher element is established in the relationship between governments, employers and trainees.

Voucher schemes do not necessarily function to deliver a public subsidy. Some major British companies, such as Rover and Unipart, have developed education and training programmes for their employees with analogous features. The best known of these is the Employee Development and Assistance Programme (EDAP) of the Ford Motor Company. This scheme was developed in 1988 in conjunction with Ruskin College Oxford, and involves an EDAP Budget into which the Company pays per annum per employee. Employees are entitled to apply for up to £200 per annum to pay the fees of the course of their choice. The only limitations on the choice of course are that it should not replicate the Company's own vocational and training provision, and that it should not be wholly 'recreational' (Moore 1994).

The EDAP scheme can be seen to have some characteristics in common with other voucher schemes, at least as far as the funding principle is concerned. It has been the subject of evaluation research by Ruskin College, with a recent focus upon non-participants. The outcomes of this research are primarily workplace related, and no conclusions could be drawn for other voucher schemes: EDAP is strictly speaking a 'study entitlement' scheme. Nevertheless, evaluation of the scheme does suggest that it is successful in encouraging participation in lifelong learning programmes, especially amongst 'non-traditional' learners.

More relevant to this chapter is evaluation research conducted by the Further Education Unit (FEU) into the Training Credits scheme, introduced in 1991 and briefly referred to above as the FE 'voucher'. The effects on Colleges involved in the initial pilots were investigated (FEU 1993), and subsequent research on broader aspects of the scheme's impact has also been published (FEDA 1995).

The Training Credits scheme incorporates several national initiatives all reflecting education vouchers as a funding principle, sometimes described as 'following the learner': Gateways to Learning, Skill Choice, Adult Training Credits, Open Learning Credits, etc. These initiatives, based in the FE sector and funded by way of the TECs, are directed towards the education and training needs of young people and adults, and incorporate a wide range of provision, including that for assessment, guidance and Assessment of Prior Learning (APL) services, and for 'target' skills and groups, such as the unemployed. Evaluation of the guidance element in all of this has already been noted (Salveson *et al.*).

The research project reported by FEDA took place in 1994 and involved 22 colleges and 3 TECs. Its main focus was the impact of voucher schemes upon the curriculum, and its conclusions are particularly relevant for the Corporation of London's scheme in that they tend to stress the beneficial effects for adult learners rather than for young people: 'Where credit schemes have pump-primed new provision, particularly for adults, the benefits are more apparent' (FEDA 1995: 12). It was evident that such schemes as these were attracting more adult learners to colleges.

Vouchers in the City of London

Thinking such as this led the Corporation to introduce two voucher schemes for adult learners: an Adult Education Voucher Scheme for City of London residents (introduced in 1993) and a City Workers' Study Voucher Scheme, for people who work in the City of London (in 1996).

The Adult Education Voucher Scheme (referred to in this chapter as 'the residents' scheme') provided a voucher which paid for 'all or part of the fees for any Adult Education course' offered by the 'major institutions' in and around the City. The value of the vouchers in 1996/97 varied between £40 (basic) and £275; they could be redeemed against the cost of any educational course. The basic resident's voucher was available to any person aged 18 or who lived at an address within the 'Square Mile'. Additional vouchers were available to residents who were also: aged over 60; unemployed; receiving income support, family credit or housing benefit; receiving invalidity benefit or severe disablement allowance; or taking up a course in basic skills (eg, literacy or numeracy). The maximum amount payable per person was £275.

The City Workers' Study Voucher Scheme (referred to in this chapter as 'the workers' scheme') provided a voucher worth one-third of the fee for an educational course, up to a maximum of £200, for any person whose 'workplace is based within the Square Mile'. The course of study had to be approved by the worker's employer, and the employer had to be willing to contribute an equivalent sum toward the course fee (the simple rule was that employer, employee and Corporation each contribute one-third).

Two elements of the Corporation's voucher policy were critical: that provision should encompass both residents and workers; and that the Corporation should secure provision by other agencies, rather than seeking to become itself a provider. In the latter respect, of course, it benefited from its contiguity with several major inner London LEAs which themselves make substantial provision, and from the proximity of major institutions such as universities and the City Literary Institute, as well as from the very diverse range of private sector education and training providers based in London. A key underlying theme with the voucher schemes was to integrate these public and private sector providers, guided by the principle that the LEA facilitated, encouraged and financed, but did not provide.

Various limitations and arguments against voucher schemes have been identified in the literature. In political terms, it has been argued that vouchers represent a misuse of taxpayers' money. Voucher schemes are said to be bureaucratic and costly in terms of administration, and competition may actually drive educational standards down. There is said to be no incentive for increased participation, since the introduction of vouchers does not in itself reduce the costs of education or increase motivation to learn. Finally, the introduction of such schemes may distort the system of provision by, for example, creating competition between state and private sectors.

The FEDA research found that it was also the case that the small scale of such schemes so far has meant that costs could be absorbed, and as a mechanism, credit funding is 'relatively high-risk and unreliable year on year'. Such consumer-led schemes are inherently unstable and ongoing market research is needed to track fluctuations in demand. Not all of the FEDA research project could be replicated in the present research into the Corporation's own scheme, since the educational sector in question was different in crucial respects. Nevertheless, there are implications for the evaluation process itself, not least in the context of quality control: 'Evaluation of schemes and performance of the providers should involve reference to measures of satisfaction of the client group during the learning process' (FEDA 1995: 14).

The City of London's exercise provides an opportunity to investigate how far vouchers can support the development of lifelong learning or a learning community. Documentary research was therefore conducted on the origins and development of the two schemes. Questionnaires were sent to a 25 per cent random sample of all voucher holders on the residents' scheme, and to all the workers' scheme voucher holders. In addition, semi-structured interviews were conducted with officials of the Corporation's Education

Department; and (chiefly by telephone) with 33 voucher holders, 50 City of London employers and 22 providers of educational programmes from the private and public sectors.

The participants

Broadly speaking, participants in both schemes tended to reflect demographic and socio-economic profiles of adult education participants in general. On the whole, the similarities between the two groups tended to reinforce that body of research which had established a strong connection between earlier education experience and qualification and the likelihood of continuing to learn later in life. There was, however, a substantial minority (about one-quarter) in both schemes who claimed never to have attended a part-time education or training course before receiving a voucher.

There were important differences between the participants in the two schemes. As the nature of employment continues to change and, 'worker' is a much looser category than 'resident'. For example, we encountered several people who worked in the City, but were not employed by City employers. They appeared to be part of a significant stratum of self-employed workers, such as consultants in information technology, who worked on extended contracts with City companies (often extending over several months or even years) and who, in some cases at least, did virtually all their work in the City. However, since they were self-employed and their business addresses were technically their homes outside the City, they appeared to 'fall though the net' in terms of eligibility for the workers' scheme. In addition, eligibility for the workers' scheme is mediated by an employer's idea about workers' learning needs.

Residents' scheme

Residents chose on the whole to follow recreative and expressive courses, at a lower level than the workers. Residents were, on the whole, older and their participation was influenced by family and domestic circumstances. Over one third of respondent resident voucher holders were retired.

There was little evidence of community learning activity: the residents' scheme remained an individual exercise on the part of participants. On the basis of our research, there seemed little likelihood of a 'learning community' emerging from this voucher scheme. It served the interests of those individuals who had some educational background and confidence, and in many instances made learning possible which they otherwise might not have been able to afford. However, the data about participants did not suggest that the residents' voucher scheme had significantly extended the social base of adult learning.

Workers' scheme

Responses from all companies and organizations, regardless of whether or not they had actually sponsored employees, suggested some goodwill towards the voucher scheme and an appreciation of its potential benefit to company and employees alike. However, a range of factors stood in the way of translating this goodwill into practice. One of the most important of these concerned lines of communication and information within and between organizations: in situations of rapid change and development, such as characterize City businesses, these can prove fragile systems. Frequently, the appropriate person or department for establishing and maintaining contact was either not properly identified or had changed.

One major source of diversity amongst employers surveyed, apart from factors of size and complexity, was their training and education policies. These policies influenced the perceived relevance of the scheme to company training and development needs: for most employers, the concept of lifelong learning was a rather remote (albeit desirable) matter, located in the world of education, rather than of direct business concern. The culture and policy of organizations and companies largely determined the kinds of study courses which were regarded as desirable and appropriate: language learning seemed to be the only universally agreed category of relevance to most employment. Another important factor in determining participation was therefore constituted by the workforce and types of work represented: companies with a wider range of occupational skills were more likely to see the benefits of the scheme, whereas highly specialized professional firms, such as those in law or accounting, saw little scope for in effect adding to the demands already placed upon their employees to seek professional qualifications.

Providers

Without exception, the providers felt that the schemes were positive for students and broadly in their own interests as providers of adult education. In view of criticism of earlier voucher schemes, the Corporation had sought to establish the schemes with as little bureaucracy as possible. However, this may have been taken too far. The Corporation had no mechanisms in place to ensure quality assurance, apart from the free play of market forces. Although the range and diversity of providers was considerable, and the great majority no doubt provided an acceptable standard of education, it also seemed likely that a few providers were of lower quality. No formal mechanism existed for approval of participating institutions: indeed, the Corporation argued that establishing such an 'approved list' would have contradicted the principle of consumer choice.

City vouchers and Labour ILAs

As a broad generalization, approaches to lifelong learning policy in Europe fall between two poles: at one end, the EU stresses the importance of government initiative to ensure a coherent policy which will meet a number of aims, including economic growth and overcoming social exclusion. At the other pole, the former British Conservative government argued that lifetime learning should be a matter guided by individual choice in a market context. The Corporation of London sought to introduce government initiative but with minimum direction and bureaucracy. The rationale for this lay partly in the unique character of the City of London (which, in contrast to every other British local education authority, has virtually no school system to administer). However, the political character of the Corporation also underpinned its perception of feasible policy options: the ideology behind vouchers was attractive.

With the Labour government's advocacy of Individual Learning Accounts, partnerships and the 'University for Industry', the Corporation of London's voucher scheme seems both prescient and highly topical. ILAs promise to be a high-tech form of voucher. The amount of money which is contemplated as the government contribution to each of the experimental accounts (£150 on average) is uncannily similar to London's £200. The emphasis on using ILAs to encourage employers, the state and individuals into partnership mirrors the Corporation's approach in its workers' scheme. In this light, issues raised by the London schemes may well have wider implications. Does making 'learning money' available mean that people will spend it? Who will define what is acceptable (or 'good-quality') learning? How good must educational guidance be? Will employers really be interested? And, if only some are, whose interests will be served?

On the basis of our research, it is difficult to conclude that a voucher or ILA-type approach (or a free choice one) can provide a viable framework for a coherent lifelong learning policy. This accords with much international experience (Jarvis *et al.* 1997: 47–48). The opportunities available for study were essentially those which already existed. The City of London is fortunate in being surrounded by a rich diversity of inner-city provision established through public expense by former local education authorities. When the demographic peculiarities of the City are set aside, the profile of the residents' scheme participants did not differ significantly from that of participants in adult education elsewhere. The workers' scheme aimed to introduce a learning culture into the City, but left unclear the structural lines of responsibility for planning and provision of learning opportunities in the workplace.

References

Blaug, M (1972) *An Introduction to the Economics of Education*, Penguin, Harmondsworth.
Crew, M and Young, A (1977) *Paying by Degrees: A Study of the Financing of Higher Education Students by Grants, Loans and Vouchers*, Institute of Economic Affairs, London.
CM 3790 (1998) *The Learning Age: A Renaissance for a New Britain*, The Stationery Office Ltd, London.
Department for Education and Employment (DfEE) (1996) *Lifetime Learning – A Consultation Document*, London.
Department for Education and Employment (1997) 'Barriers to Adult Learning How We Intend to Break Through – Blackstone', DfEE Press Release 107/97 (20 May).
European Union (EU) (1995) *Teaching and Learning: Towards the Learning Society*, White Paper on Education and Training, European Commission, Brussels.
Further Education Development Agency (FEDA) (1995) *The Impact of Voucher Schemes on the FE Curriculum*, FEDA, London.
Further Education Unit (FEU) (1993) *Training Credits: The Implications for Colleges*, FEU, London.
Guardian, the (1996) 'Tories Aim to Offer Training in Computers for All Adults', 28 December: 3.
Jarvis, P, Holford, J, Griffin, C and Dubelaar, J (1997) *Towards the Learning City. An Evaluation of the Corporation of London's Adult Education Voucher Schemes*, Corporation of London Education Department, London.
Jarvis, P, Griffin, C, Holford, J, Merricks, L and Tosey, P (1998) 'Why Lifelong Learning Is Not a Policy', *The Times Higher Education Supplement* (16 January).
Kent Education Department (1978) *Education Vouchers in Kent: A Feasibility Study*, Kent County Council, Maidstone.
McNair, S (1995) 'Paying for an Adult Higher Education', *Adults Learning*, 6, 9, 278–279.
McNay, I (Ed.) (1992) *Visions of Post-Compulsory Education*, SRHE and Open University Press, Buckingham.
Maynard, A (1975) *Experiment with Choice in Education*, Institute of Economic Affairs, London.
Moore, R (1994) 'Ford EDAP: Breaking Through the Barriers', *Adults Learning*, 5, 9, 225–226.
Park, A (1994) *Individual Commitment to Learning: Individuals' Attitudes*, Employment Department, London.
Salveson, P et al. (1994) *Gateway to Learning: Empowering Individuals?*, University of Leeds, Leeds.
Senge, PM (1990) *The Fifth Discipline: The Art and Practice of the Learning Organization*, Doubleday, New York.

Taggart, R (1993) 'An Ecumenical Approach', *Workforce*, 2, 2, 17–21.
Times, The (1997) 'Union Tells Teachers to Inform on Parents using Vouchers', 13 January: 4.

PART V

LEARNING AND CHANGE IN EDUCATIONAL STRUCTURE

Chapter 18

How Can University Work-based Courses Contribute to Lifelong Learning?

David Boud

A new form of provision for lifelong learning has emerged in the past ten years. Work-based learning takes a radical approach to the notion of a university education, as students undertake study for a degree or diploma through activities conducted primarily in their workplace and in topic areas in which there may be no immediate equivalence with university subjects. The learning opportunities found in work-based learning programmes are not contrived for study purposes but arise from normal work. The role of the university is to equip 'unqualified' people already in employment to develop lifelong learning skills, not through engagement with existing disciplines or bodies of knowledge and a programme defined by university teachers, but through a curriculum which is unique for each person. What is significant in these new approaches to work-based learning is that work is not a discrete and limited element of study, as is familiar in sandwich courses and co-operative education. Neither are issues arising from problems encountered in work used merely as subjects of assignments, as is common in many forms of flexible provision which use learning contracts. In work-based learning degrees, work is the foundation of the curriculum.

There now exist a number of major examples of this radical kind of work-based learning course. While there is a different emphasis in each institution, and arrangements for the management of learning vary, all permit the completion of a Bachelors or Masters degree primarily through work-based study. Moves to work-based learning are being prompted by the need for rapid diversification of university funding, as well as by the educational needs of members of the workforce and employers who have not benefited sufficiently from the older, front-end loaded models of higher education.

The aim of this chapter is to focus on work-based learning as an example of a major development, which highlights a new approach to lifelong education. A focus on this innovation moves discussion about lifelong learning beyond consideration of principles and ideals to the pragmatics of translating its goals into practice. While is not the purpose of this chapter to undertake a broader critique of work-based learning in the context of globalization and changing socio-economic roles of higher education, such an analysis can easily be undertaken drawing upon the resources of other chapters in this volume. Of greater interest to the author is an exploration of dilemmas which innovations of this kind pose. After a description of common features of current emerging practice, the chapter examines issues to be addressed if courses of this kind are to be credible as a normal part of the spectrum of university education and contribute to goals of lifelong learning.

Work-based learning: some examples

While there are many approaches which link work and study, the following are brief scenarios from universities which emphasize a particular approach which places work as central. work-based learning. These are drawn from the UK, mainly because it is there where this approach originated (notably at the University of Portsmouth) and where the most substantial examples can be seen.

- The University of Leeds is a civic university which has begun to institutionalize a scheme whereby any degree (Bachelors, Masters, etc) can be completed in full or in part through work-based learning. This typically involves a three-way partnership between the university, the employer and the student. Links are formed with enterprises which involve local support for study and a negotiated and registered programme. This can involve any mix of existing university courses, independent study and learning at work which is judged to met the criteria for a given award.
- Middlesex University established the National Centre for Work-Based Learning Partnerships as a quasi-faculty that accredits components of any

HOW CAN UNIVERSITY WORK-BASED COURSES CONTRIBUTE? 215

course which involves work-based learning and offers subjects to develop skills in work-based learning for students. It is possible to study through work-based learning for anything from a single module in a conventional course to an entire degree programme from pre-university to doctoral level.
- Developments at Anglia Polytechnic University have focused on extensive relationships with two major employers (Winter and Maisch 1996). Work-based learning is based on a specific competency framework in each area (automotive engineering and social work) combined with a general conception of intellectual development and professional responsibilities which crosses both.

Programmes such as these are designed for students who would not otherwise benefit from a university education: those working full-time who wish to focus their study on the work which they are doing, rather than traditional school leavers. The support of employers is gained through the curriculum acknowledging and developing the knowledge and skills required in particular workplaces and involving employers as active agents in developing courses and negotiating programmes with university staff and students.

Typical features of these programmes can be summarized as follows:

Role of industry/employers

- Employers appreciate and financially support work-based learning because employees (students) are typically engaging in study which directly advances the enterprise.
- Enterprises involved may be private, public or community organizations.

Role of the university

- The university determines what is ultimately acceptable for any given qualification.
- The content of courses and curriculum are not predetermined. The university is rarely offering an existing course in a new mode.

Learning processes

- Students take a more active role in negotiating their learning than in conventional courses. Negotiation usually involves three parties: student, university staff member and workplace supervisor.
- Specific guidance on learning-how-to-learn and work-based learning skills is provided.

Assessment

- Courses may be entered at any level according to the prior qualifications and experience of students and exited depending on what level of learning has been demonstrated. Learning outcomes are performance not time-related.
- The development of an explicit framework for assessment and determination of what constitutes a given level of achievement, including generic learning outcomes, is necessary across courses.

The examples of programmes from different universities vary greatly. However, they share the feature that learning which is considered as part of an award has to involve specific learning outcomes. These outcomes are assessed by the university through their own staff, or by work-based tutors who have completed an accredited university assessor training course.

While these courses are quite different in character from traditional full-time university study, they are the consequence of a trend which has been apparent for many years. The division between full-time study while students are engaged in part-time employment unrelated to their course and part-time study alongside full-time work, is rapidly breaking down. In Australia, for example, there is now no funding distinction between part-time and full-time modes and students are increasingly enrolling in a variety of fractions of full-time equivalent study in order to accommodate the demands of the rest of their lives. When students are involved in demanding and sophisticated work they are becoming increasingly intolerant of part-time courses which require them to complete what they see to be assessment tasks unrelated or even alien to the challenges of their job.

Dilemmas of work-based learning

The place of work-based learning within universities, and indeed as part of lifelong learning, is highly problematic. While it appears to be meeting previously unmet needs, it presents an unparalleled challenge to conceptions of what a university education is and how it contributes to lifelong learning. How flexible can a degree be before it can no longer be regarded as a degree? It is well-established that it need not be completed by learners who devote all of their time to being students (part-time study), nor undertaken at the site of the university (distance education), nor devoted to a single discipline or group of disciplines (modular courses), nor planned and assessed in ways exclusively determined by academic staff (negotiated, or contract, learning). Does it need to include subjects or units of study which are otherwise taught in the university? To what extent does it need to meet the same requirements as other degree courses? Radical answers are being proposed to questions of this kind.

The remainder of this chapter is devoted to the identification and elaboration of three key questions, the answers to which I believe will either enable work-based learning to take its place as another well-accepted mode of university study and lifelong learning, or will confine it to the margins as an innovation which was found wanting. These questions are: What is the curriculum in work-based learning? Can work-based learning address the general requirements of a university education? and How can barriers to using work as an education be overcome?

What is the curriculum in work-based learning?

Candy *et al.* (1994), in an influential Australian study of how undergraduate education can contribute to lifelong learning, identified five basic characteristics of successful courses.

1. They provide a systematic introduction to the field of study.
2. They offer a comparative or contextual framework for viewing the field of study.
3. They seek to broaden the student and provide generic skills.
4. They offer some freedom of choice and flexibility of structure.
5. They provide for the incremental development of self-directed learning (1994: xii).

They also pointed to characteristics of teaching methods that encourage graduates to become lifelong learners.

1. They make use of peer-assisted and self-directed learning.
2. They include experiential and real-world learning.
3. They make use of resource-based and problem-based teaching.
4. They encourage the development of reflective practice and critical self-awareness.
5. As appropriate, they make use of open learning and alternative delivery mechanisms (1994: xii).

In setting these features alongside those of work-based learning courses, it is possible to discern areas of compatibility and areas of potential tension, depending on how particular courses are designed. While many of these features can more readily be build into work-based courses than university-based courses, there are some aspects where it is not obvious what might meet these requirements.

In the first of Candy's lists, reference is made to 'a systematic introduction to the field of study' and to 'a comparative or contextual framework for viewing the field of study'. What is the field of study in the workplace? While there are many examples in which this is not problematic – work falls within the boundaries of existing disciplines or professions (eg manufacturing, engineering, marketing and legal studies) – there are far more examples of work which either crosses many boundaries and draws upon a variety of disciplinary knowledge (eg many mid-career tasks in large organizations or running small enterprises) or, indeed, is so limited in conception that it is hard to imagine it as the subject of university study (eg low-level technical occupations). It is relatively easy to exclude the latter on the basis that they provide insufficient opportunities for breadth of study, but the complex and diverse jobs which modern industry provides cannot easily be seen as a field of study in the commonly accepted sense as the boundaries are blurred and continually changing.

A challenge for work-based learning is to find ways of representing its 'field of study'. This is a demanding task, in that it:

- varies from student to student, as the curriculum cannot be the same for all even within a single enterprise
- is not documented in any form which can be scrutinized and critiqued in advance of students' engagement with it
- is changing as work changes and students move within or across workplaces.

Similarly, it is by no means apparent which 'comparative or contextual frameworks' might be used for viewing the field of study. Each one of us, depending on our personal history and disciplinary background, might offer a range of such frameworks according to whether the goal was to understand, critique or improve the 'field'. At present there are no academic specialists in the curriculum of work and it is not obvious that it would be desirable to create a new university discipline to go with this field. Indeed, it might be necessary to establish as many disciplines to cover the complexities of work as already exist for other purposes within the academy. Existing university disciplines represent past ways of organizing knowledge and occupations and they do not map onto the structure of modern work.

Can work-based learning address the general requirements of a university education?

A second feature of Candy's analysis of the role of university courses in lifelong education which provides a challenge to work-based learning is his emphasis on 'broadening the student and providing generic skills'. In recent years there has been a growth of interest throughout the higher education sector on the generic or non-subject-specific outcomes expected of graduates. While there appears to be consensus that there are such things as generic skills and attributes 'which should be acquired by all graduates regardless of their discipline or field of study' (Higher Education Council 1992: 20), there is considerable dispute about what they are, whether they can reasonably be expected to be developed through taught courses and how it is possible to determine whether or not a course has been successful in developing them.

Echoing a number of other writers, Clanchy and Ballard (1995) raise the question of what can a university commit itself to deliver in respect of all its graduates. They argue that there are a limited number of attributes and values which are generic to university education and which can reasonably be expected of all graduates. They give two examples. These are 'a critical approach to knowledge, ideas and argument' and 'a respect for the source of and ownership of knowledge' (1995: 159). These, they argue, can be reasonably and legitimately required, as they are 'integral to the processes of teaching and learning' universities employ, whereas those commonly listed are not.

Reasoning along these lines provides some encouragement for thinking that work-based learning can meet the needs of providing generic skills, so long as the generic skills to be developed are no more extensive than those which can realistically be developed by any university course. Whether it can also address the goal of 'broadening the student' is a function of the kinds of programme which are accepted by universities and the nature of the workplaces which form the context of learning.

How can barriers to using work as education be overcome?

The issue of context prompts the third question. Barriers to using the workplace for learning are many. They include, for example, the following.

- Learning has not traditionally been seen as the *raison d'être* of the workplace in the same way as it is in educational institutions. There is much rhetoric about the 'learning organization' in modern enterprises, but evidence that this notion has become well-embedded is hard to find.

- Learning on the job is often regarded as intrinsic to that particular form of employment and its application to other contexts is not as necessary a part of the process as it would be in an educational institution. However, more recent notions of multiskilling and self-managed teams challenge the extent of the task-specific nature of work.
- Time is not provided to enable learning to be drawn from action. This is a serious issue when organizations become particularly 'lean' and when there is a culture of performativity in the workplace which makes a cult of action and discourages reflection.
- Oppressive forces (such as the tyranny of productivity, hierarchy or exclusive groups) may interrupt and undermine learning. These forces are becoming increasingly apparent; but change in structure, key personnel and commitment is needed to address them and the prompt for doing so is more likely to come from pressing business needs than the needs of learning.

It requires fundamental change in attitudes to work and the role of learning in work to be made if workplaces are to become more than places of learning for immediate job-related tasks. While there are signs that some organizations are moving in this direction, thus permitting the idea of work-based university learning to be seriously contemplated now, it cannot be assumed that all workplaces provide a fruitful environment. Each of the needs above will have to be explicitly addressed if work-based learning is to deliver its promise.

The greatest challenge which work-based learning provides is to force us to take seriously the context of learning. Most contemporary analyses of vocational and professional education share a concern about the powerful influence of context on learning.

Transferability
Simple notions about the transferability of learning from one context of learning, or one domain of knowledge, to another have been rejected by researchers from diverse theoretical perspectives. What is learnt in one situation, whether it be classroom or workplace, is not necessarily transferred to another. Clanchy and Ballard (1995: 164), for example, suggest that while skills such as thinking, research and communication must be learnt in the context of a 'specific discipline and body of knowledge' they do not, once learnt, have to be learnt totally anew in each new context of learning. These 'generic' skills acquired at university can be expressed in ways that employers recognize as 'literate' or 'effective'. If this is true of skills learnt from campus-based courses, then if skills such as these can also be learnt in the context of the body of knowledge of work, it is possible for them to transfer at least as well from there. The question which this problem poses, though is: what are

of the initiative an idea which is both fundamental to lifelong learning and is even more radical than the move of education to the workplace. It is that the learner himself or herself has to tackle issues of context within his or her own situation. Learners have to create their own curriculum (guided, but not taught, by others) which is unique to their circumstances and opportunities. Developing the curriculum is no longer the responsibility of the university, but of the learner. This curriculum must meet the needs of the organization and the university as well as themselves. It is hard to imagine a more complete and challenging lifelong learning task.

The nature of the task is such that substantial credit must be given for planning, organizing and evaluating the learning programme, as it is this which provides for the development of the generic skills which have been mentioned earlier. It is a major form of independent study involving analysis, planning, accessing resources, critical reflection, communication, team-work and self-assessment. There will of course be other learning activities which are identified in this process and which may take on a more conventional form. However, it is the initiating and carrying out of a sophisticated programme of development which marks a university education, not the completion of a defined syllabus. When work-based learning is conceptualized in this manner, it can be seen that it is central to debates on teaching and learning, not just a new mode of study.

While it is easy to critique work-based learning as driven by market demands, focus on this would avoid the critique which the adoption of this approach makes of conventional university practice in promoting lifelong learning. All the issues identified in this chapter are equally applicable to other 'normal' university courses: to what extent do they address the broad range of requirements of a university education, to what extent do they critique their own practices and the institutions in which they are located, to what extent do they promote transferability from the abstracted world of academe, and so on? Work-based learning degrees are too recent a feature of the higher education scene for them to have made much of an impact, but the questions they provoke are central to all questions of the role of educational institutions in lifelong learning.

References

Boud, D and Miller, N (Eds)(1996) *Working with Experience: Animating Learning*, Routledge, London.
Boud, D and Walker, D (accepted for publication) 'Promoting Reflection in Professional Courses: the Challenge of Context', *Studies in Higher Education*.

of the initiative an idea which is both fundamental to lifelong learning and is even more radical than the move of education to the workplace. It is that the learner himself or herself has to tackle issues of context within his or her own situation. Learners have to create their own curriculum (guided, but not taught, by others) which is unique to their circumstances and opportunities. Developing the curriculum is no longer the responsibility of the university, but of the learner. This curriculum must meet the needs of the organization and the university as well as themselves. It is hard to imagine a more complete and challenging lifelong learning task.

The nature of the task is such that substantial credit must be given for planning, organizing and evaluating the learning programme, as it is this which provides for the development of the generic skills which have been mentioned earlier. It is a major form of independent study involving analysis, planning, accessing resources, critical reflection, communication, team-work and self-assessment. There will of course be other learning activities which are identified in this process and which may take on a more conventional form. However, it is the initiating and carrying out of a sophisticated programme of development which marks a university education, not the completion of a defined syllabus. When work-based learning is conceptualized in this manner, it can be seen that it is central to debates on teaching and learning, not just a new mode of study.

While it is easy to critique work-based learning as driven by market demands, focus on this would avoid the critique which the adoption of this approach makes of conventional university practice in promoting lifelong learning. All the issues identified in this chapter are equally applicable to other 'normal' university courses: to what extent do they address the broad range of requirements of a university education, to what extent do they critique their own practices and the institutions in which they are located, to what extent do they promote transferability from the abstracted world of academe, and so on? Work-based learning degrees are too recent a feature of the higher education scene for them to have made much of an impact, but the questions they provoke are central to all questions of the role of educational institutions in lifelong learning.

References

Boud, D and Miller, N (Eds)(1996) *Working with Experience: Animating Learning*, Routledge, London.
Boud, D and Walker, D (accepted for publication) 'Promoting Reflection in Professional Courses: the Challenge of Context', *Studies in Higher Education*.

Candy, P, Crebert, G and O'Leary, J (1994) *Developing Lifelong Learners through Undergraduate Education*. Commissioned Report No. 28, National Board of Employment, Education and Training, Australian Government Publishing Service, Canberra.

Clanchy, J and Ballard, B (1995) 'Generic Skills in the Context of Higher Education', *Higher Education Research and Development*, 14, 2, 155–166.

Higher Education Council (1992) *Higher Education: Achieving Quality*, Australian Government Publishing Service, Canberra.

Winter, R and Maisch, M (1996) *Professional Competence and Higher Education: The ASSET Programme*, Falmer Press, London.

Chapter 19

What Would Lifelong Education Look Like in a Workplace Setting?

Paul Hager and David Beckett

What is workplace learning?

Australia has joined the international enthusiasm for lifelong learning. One example is the Candy Report (Candy *et al.* 1994) aimed at the reform of undergraduate education so that graduates will be equipped to become effective lifelong learners. If graduates are to be as Candy recommends, much of their future learning will occur at work. This chapter concentrates on the workplace as a site for lifelong learning, as against the more formal and structured learning that occurs in classrooms and training settings. In doing so, we confront the traditional model of vocational preparation.

This assumes the transfer and application to the workplace of prior success in acquiring both a systematic theoretical education and some general adult learning strategies. We are not alone in regarding this as a fairly hit-and-miss affair. The extent of transferability and application seems to depend on the cognate proximity of the workplace to the intellectual core of the formal learning which preceded workplace entry. Sometimes that proximity is ideally regarded as the closer the better, such that better work in banking is underpinned by a Bachelor of Commerce preparation rather than a Bachelor of Arts degree with philosophy honours; sometimes the opposite is regarded as ideal, such as in the diplomatic corps or even in the public service.

Thus there is, traditionally, a spectrum of beliefs about the best model of transfer and application. We are concerned with the dissolution of that spectrum, since we believe lifelong learning moves the focus of vocational preparation from the 'front-end' model (which generates the spectrum, by definition) to the 'contiguous/continual' model, where learning and work are intertwined in various formal and informal admixtures. Our interest therefore is on site-specific locations for formal and informal learning. But our present focus is even tighter. We acknowledge that 'workplace learning' can refer to formal on-the-job training as distinct from off-the-job training in, eg vocational education institutions. However, in this chapter we want to restrict the term 'workplace learning' to informal learning that occurs as people perform their work and to its role in lifelong education. In the remainder of this chapter this kind of informal learning in the workplace is what we mean by the term 'workplace learning'. We use the term 'on-the-job training' for formal workplace learning.

Differences between workplace learning and formal learning

A major obstacle to workplace learning being taken seriously as part of someone's education is its difference on many criteria from traditional 'educational' activities. This is most obvious in the vast differences between workplace learning and typical learning in educational institutions, but workplace learning is also very different from on-the-job training. Nine differences stand out.

1. Teachers/trainers are in control in both formal learning in educational institutions and in on-the-job training, whereas the learner is in control (if anyone is) in workplace learning. That is, formal learning is intentional, but workplace learning is often unintentional.
2. Learning in formal education and in on-the-job training is prescribed by formal curriculum, competency standards, learning outcomes, etc. Workplace learning has no formal curriculum or prescribed outcomes.
3. In both educational institutions and on-the-job training, learning outcomes are largely predictable. Workplace learning outcomes are much less predictable.
4. In both educational institutions and on-the-job training, learning is largely explicit (the learner is expected to be able to articulate what has been learnt, eg in a written examination or in answer to teacher

questioning; trainees are required to perform appropriate activities as a result of their training). Workplace learning is often implicit or tacit (learners are commonly unaware of the extent of their learning).
5. In formal classrooms and on-the-job training the emphasis is on teaching/training and on the content and structure of what is taught/trained (largely as a consequence of points 1–4). In workplace learning, the emphasis is on the experiences of the learner-as-worker: not a concept to be taken lightly, given the power of self-directed learning in making sense of one's workplace, as well as one's own life at work.
6. Formal classroom learning and on-the-job training usually focus on individual learning. Workplace learning is more often collaborative and/or collegial, despite the current policy and rhetorical emphasis on self-direction and individual experience noted in point 5. This sociality occurs because workplaces are by definition socio-culturally located, and their consequently shared and site-specific experiences are collectively available for educative purposes. Thus workers invest much of their personal identities in work, and find these defined and re-defined by the local work culture – by 'the way we do things here'.
7. Learning in formal classrooms is uncontextualized, ie it emphasizes general principles rather than their specific applications. While on-the-job training is typically somewhat contextualized, even here the general is emphasized, eg training for general industry standards. But workplace learning is by its nature highly contextualized, as outlined in point 6, and must include emotive, cognitive and social dimensions of workers' experiences in advancing their learning.
8. Learning in formal education and in on-the-job training is seen typically in terms of theory (or knowledge) and practice (application of theory and knowledge). Workplace learning, though, seems to be appropriately viewed as seamless know how, in the Aristotelian sense of *phronesis* or practical wisdom.
9. In educational institutions and on-the-job training, learning knowledge typically is viewed as more difficult than learning skills (thus, eg more teaching effort is invested usually in the first as against the second). Workplace learning, as the development of competence or capability via a suitably structured sequence of experience, does not operate with the knowledge/skills distinction.

The educational significance of these differences

Given the differences outlined above, it is hardly surprising that formal learning/education is valued much more than informal learning (including workplace learning). Workplace learning is a paradigm case of informal education which is undervalued particularly by all levels in the formal education system. Historically, training has been viewed as the antithesis of education. Training as mindless, mechanical, routine activity has been contrasted with education as development of mind via completion of intellectually challenging tasks (Winch 1995).

Despite this 'chalk and cheese' conception of education and training, the differences outlined (1–9 above) show that they have more in common with one another than either has with workplace learning. No wonder, then, that for many involved in education the idea of workplace learning as genuine education is beyond the pale. Before we confront the re-conceptualization of education, via the strengths of workplace learning, we must deal with the standard rejection of lifelong education itself.

The debate over lifelong education

To repeat, our contention is that workplace learning is a vital but hitherto neglected component of lifelong education. In arguing for this thesis we need to confront not only the devaluation of workplace learning by educationalists generally (as discussed above) but also the rejection of lifelong education by many of these same educationalists. Critics have seen lifelong education as a threat to cherished and traditional educational values. Probably the main argument advanced against the notion of lifelong education by these traditionalist critics hinges on the charge that it uses the terms 'lifelong education' and 'lifelong learning' interchangeably, thereby confusing education and learning. Lawson (1982) presented the argument as follows. The lifelong education movement confuses learning with education. But education is much narrower than learning. Hence 'lifelong education' debases education.

Another important conceptual argument advanced against the notion of lifelong education was presented by Bagnall (1990). This is a variant on the Lawson argument and proceeds as follows. If all learning counts as education, governments may close down/reduce formal and non-formal education provision, as people can learn informally for free.

Wain (1987, 1993) has strongly defended lifelong education against both these arguments. For a start, he denies that proponents of lifelong education have conflated education with learning. He distinguishes the normative definition of education from its technical definition. Then, drawing on the work of Lakatos, Wain argues that the normative definition belongs in the ideological core of an educational research program; the technical definition belongs in the operational belt. (See Wain 1987: 47; Wain 1993: 65). Following Lakatos, the normative definition is inviolate, but the technical definition can be altered as the operational belt evolves in order to advance the ideological core of the research program. According to Wain, by their commitment to a narrow understanding of 'education', both Lawson and Bagnall read 'education' normatively whenever it occurs in the lifelong education literature. This leads them to conclude erroneously that proponents of lifelong education conflate all learning with education.

Wain maintains, further, that it is clear that lifelong education is related to lifelong learning as process is to product. By aligning lifelong education with process (Wain 1987: 50; 1993: 66), he means that the focus here is on all the kinds of learning that can affect the process of individual growth, ie formal, non-formal and informal learning. This does not mean that all instances of any of these are always educational – only that all three are relevant to education. For Wain, the interest is in how to enhance the education of learners. Non-intentional learning is seen as being very relevant to this interest. By aligning lifelong learning with product, on the other hand, Wain draws attention to the wide scope of learnt products. If, however, education rather than learning is viewed as a product, the focus shifts to what content should be taught, to teachers and to teaching, with informal learning being ignored. Thus the typical assumption by critics of lifelong education that for learning to be educational, it must be intentional. However, by distinguishing between process and product in this way, Wain evades the charge that he conflates learning with education. Both the Lawson and Bagnall arguments therefore fail as critiques of the concept of lifelong education because in both cases their first premise is false. How convincing is Wain's defence of lifelong education as a process? While it does accord with the views of many other proponents of lifelong education, we question later in the chapter the ultimacy of the process/product distinction.

But it is not only the traditionalists who reject the notion of lifelong education. Some writers on the educational left have seen lifelong education as an ideology primarily designed to manipulate workers into being more productive. The argument goes that, having expelled the adversarial workplace at the front door, what has intruded through the back door is a subtle form of surveillance, inducing strategies of compliance, such as the 'discourses of competence and management', in the new 'flatter', more ostensibly democratic, workplace (Usher and Edwards 1994: Ch. 5, drawing on Foucault). While rightly pointing to potential dangers, they tend to overlook the possibility that the workplace provides a point of cohesion for many people: it has an integrative function for many individuals' sense of identity, and many changes at work can have a potential for growth. It also needs to be remembered that many who engage in significant workplace learning are self-employed, eg professionals of various kinds, or are increasingly engaged on contractual and consultancy bases which generate and require the exercise of considerable discretion over what, when and how the work will be undertaken. Whilst we, like the left, share a scepticism of the appropriation of humanist adult education values by the workplace, and, accordingly, do not see workplace reforms as necessarily 'empowering', we nevertheless regard the workplace as a fascinating and fruitful arena for many of the traditional characteristics of education to be displayed. The following shows how this can be so.

The way ahead

The differences between workplace learning and more formal education/training were discussed earlier. As a consideration of these differences shows, both process and product characteristics are involved. Differences 1, 5, 6 and 9 emphasize process, while differences 2, 3, 4, 5, 7 and 8 mainly concern product. But we believe that, in arguing for the importance of workplace learning in lifelong education, it will be necessary to regard these characteristics as coalescent. That is, if we take the site-specific nature of workplace learning seriously, what will be most important will be the particular blending and melding of several characteristics, of which processes and products are two. The rest of this chapter discusses these characteristics and seeks to show how the old dichotomies, which relegated much informal learning and skill acquisition to a lowly status, can be dissolved. In attempting this, we are confronting the prevalence of what we call 'binary logic' in educational thinking and arguing for a more 'organic' logic. Organic logic does not concern itself with the demarcation of concepts by exclusion, so much as by inclusion. There is an integrative purpose in the application of organic logic in lifelong education – not so that anything can be claimed at whim, as 'lifelong' grist to the mill, but so that specific sites of learning, and all the judgements and decision-making that can occur at these sites, can be shown to generate powerful education, albeit under-recognized until the late twentieth century.

Put more concisely, research into the phenomenal spectrum of daily workplace experience – how decision-making and judgements go to make up a certain practical wisdom (or, in Aristotle's term, *phronesis*) – is showing a basis for a new and integrative epistemology of practice. We believe that the more these sorts of evidence are investigated, the more they can contribute to the structured mapping of learning beyond the mere undergoing of experience. Thus we argue that lifelong learning in the workplace, structured by mapped experience, is more accurately regarded as lifelong education in the workplace. An approach based in organic logic, seeking integrative analysis, will be interested in research which maps site-specific experience and thus shows workplace education emerging from the following:

- the contingent (rather than exclusively formal, sustained, and systematic studies)
- the practical (rather than the exclusively theoretical)
- the process (rather than exclusively the assimilation of content)
- the particular (rather than the exclusively universal and *a priori* as the 'context')
- the affective and the social domains (rather than exclusively the cognitive domain).

In these ways, we can show that lifelong learning (itself marked by these five characteristics, which actually accommodate their traditional 'binary' opposites) give a fairer, more organic perspective on learning in the workplace. To the extent that such learning can be structured, it can be regarded as lifelong education, albeit an educational experience rather different from that which was hitherto and traditionally the exclusive preserve of formal schooling (including universities) and traditional on-the-job training. The details of this new integrative approach to lifelong education are as follows.

The contingent (rather than exclusively formal, sustained, and systematic studies)

Daily, minute-by-minute activity at work is typically marked by rapid judgements, even when such judgements involve a high degree of routine. We find ourselves caught up in the daily flux of practical work which, *pace* Schön (1983), does not lend itself to reflection-in-action. This 'hot action', to borrow a term from Marshall McLuhan, is perhaps the core of the claim that workplaces can generate learning (Beckett 1996). Hot action has as its key feature an intense intentionality: we do what we find works! The action is hot because the demands of the work are shaped by the requirement to meet needs and solve problems as these present themselves contingently - that is, in the normal run of daily work life. For professionals like teachers, nurses, lawyers and surgeons, this means close attention to the requirements of particular situations, an ability to 'read' these situations for what they require and a keen sense of judgement about how to proceed. In all this, reflection-in-action is an inadequate model of what is happening. When the action is hot, we find ourselves caught up in thought and action, both intertwined in our 'trying something out'. The analogy that fits this close focus on the workplace is that of the artist before the canvas: there is no loss of conscious critical control of the brush; but in an integrative way, the canvas, the brush, the paint, the hand, the eye and the mind are all components of the next action, a 'trying' to see if the painting is improved in thus-and-so a way. Similarly, we can identify many components of workplace activity for, say, professionals' practice; but it is only when these are present altogether, in a single element of practice (a given time in a classroom, a surgery, a ward, a kitchen) that they have a cogency and therefore an impact as 'learning'. We intend to meet needs and solve problems; we learn that this is what we are doing when we actually find ourselves doing it.

Of course, such contingency, such tryings, are often shaped, and probably should be shaped, by knowledge acquired by sustained, systematic study. Organic logic includes the binary opposites which used to mark out the old high ground in education. This crucial, daily, phenomenal learning at work – the contingent – is a focus for all manner of prior learning; but its educational power lies in where it is heading: its efficacy. Hot action (or professionals' practice) is intelligent, outcome-oriented and situational. Formal learning may well have contributed substantially to that action.

The practical (rather than the exclusively theoretical)

The relation between education and the workplace has been conceptualized traditionally in terms of a supposed dichotomy between theory and practice. A satisfactory account of how to bring the two together when attempting to understand human action in the world has proved to be notoriously elusive. This has led various writers, including Schön (1983), to highlight the inadequacy of common assumptions about the preparation of professionals. Traditional approaches to professional education are based on what Schön calls 'technical rationality', ie the view that professionals must have command of disciplinary knowledge, mostly scientific, which they draw upon to analyse and solve the problems encountered in daily practice. Schön pointed out that this account, which hallows theory over practice, does not fit very well with what is known about the actual practice of professionals. For one thing, it is typical of real life practice that ready-made problems do not simply present themselves to the practitioner. A major role of professionals is to identify what the problems are in given circumstances.

The failure of theory/practice ways of conceptualizing the problem has generated a host of attempts in more recent work to think about these issues in a non-dichotomous way. These range from Schön's 'reflective practitioner' to problem-based learning. There is no scope in this chapter to detail these attempts (for an outline see Hager 1996). Though none of these non-dichotomous accounts of professional practice has so far gained majority assent over its rivals, this area continues to be a fruitful one for ongoing research. Amongst other things, this research has directed attention to the nature professional knowledge and its differences from disciplinary knowledge. What characterizes all of this later work is the replacement of the theory/practice binary by more unitary approaches to thinking about professional practice.

The process (rather than exclusively the assimilation of content)

As already noted, Wain and others view education as process and learning as product or content. However the convergence between these two becomes evident when we consider desirable attributes of lifelong learners. A 'Profile of the lifelong learner' proposed by Candy *et al.* (1994: 43–44) is as follows:

- An inquiring mind
    - a love of learning
    - a sense of curiosity and question asking
    - a critical spirit
    - comprehension monitoring and self-evaluation.

- Helicopter vision
    - a sense of the interconnectedness of fields
    - an awareness of how knowledge is created in at least one field of study, and an understanding of the methodological and substantive limitations of that field
    - breadth of vision.

- Information literacy
    - knowledge of major current sources available in at least one field of study
    - ability to frame researchable questions in at least one field of study
    - ability to locate, evaluate, manage, and use information in a range of contexts
    - ability to retrieve information using a variety of media
    - ability to decode information in a variety of forms: written, statistical, graphs, charts, diagrams and tables
    - critical evaluation of information.

- A sense of personal agency
    - a positive concept of oneself as capable and autonomous
    - self-organization skills (time management, goal-setting, etc).

- A repertoire of learning skills
    - knowledge of one's own strengths, weaknesses and preferred learning style
    - range of strategies for learning in whatever context one finds oneself
    - an understanding of the differences between surface and deep-level learning.

These proposed attributes of the lifelong learner suggest that even if education is process while learning is product, as suggested by Wain and others, the two are nonetheless related intimately. Many of these attributes are the kind of thing that can be learnt (or at least strengthened by learning). In that sense they are contents or products. But equally these attributes in turn enrich learning processes, whether formal, non-formal or informal. That is, these attributes make learning processes more likely to be educational. So process and content interact dialectically. Overall, then, it seems that the separation of process and content distorts as much as it illuminates.

The particular (rather than the exclusively universal and *a priori* as the 'context')

As was noted earlier, workplace learning is by its nature highly contextualized. It is thereby particular, local and contingent. By contrast, education traditionally focuses on the universal, the general and the necessary. Certainly, principles with these characteristics are preferred as subject content. If we think in these binary categories, such as particular vs universal, workplace learning and education remain disparate phenomena. However, universals as experienced are particularized, ie our judgements are always of particular cases which fall under various universal categories. Moreover, education as traditionally conceived is supposed to develop learners' capacity to make judgements (see, eg Anderson 1980). But our account of workplace learning as the development of *phronesis* is but another way of describing the development of a capacity to make the right judgements in the workplace. In support of our claim that both particular and universal are important in such workplace judgements, Burke (1994) demonstrates that Dewey's organic logic centred on judgements involving particular, generic and universal components.

The affective and the social domains (rather than exclusively the cognitive domain)

The Karpin Report (1995) advocates an integrationist managerial model of workplace learning, especially in the overt support given to the 'higher order social and cognitive competencies', which Karpin calls 'soft skills'. These are the interpersonal and communicative capabilities of strategic thinking, vision, flexibility and adaptability, self-management, team membership, problem-solving, decision-making and risk-taking. Obviously these capabilities are not adequately characterizable as merely cognitive, since they involve the social and affective. Indeed the tag 'soft skills' is a pejorative misnomer. It is quite difficult to educate for these capabilities, and even more so to have them count in corporate structures for productivity and promotion outcomes, Yet lifelong learning at its broadest is about acquiring these capabilities and exercising them in a sophisticated fashion.

Belatedly, interest in this acquisition has been accelerating. Goleman (1996) develops 'emotional intelligence' as a key concept for those who need to deal better with the opportunities and provocations of the workplace. Understanding the motivations, consequences and complications of people's feelings – and one's own – at work is now regarded as an essential aspect of the knowledgeable worker. As we have seen throughout this analysis, organic logic includes the hitherto oppositional or binary format of educational categories. Attention to the 'higher order' social and affective domains invites cognitive input. Clearly rational processes are essential at work, to advance learning as much as anything else, but it is equally important that personal and shared feelings (even of conflict) be identified and mobilized as powerful aspects of agency. In acting at work, we act as integrated persons, not just as minds or bodies, or as hearts or hands. The time for feelings to matter in workplace education is upon us! After all, such recognition of feelings is already central to lifelong learning across the life span.

Conclusion

We have tried to sketch a new philosophy of workplace education. We believe the focus for this is the specific workplace, where much informal learning goes on, largely invisibly. What is required is a new conceptualization of this learning that confronts the old 'binary' divide. This consisted of neat dichotomies between, on the one hand, learning that was formal, structured and systematic, and therefore high status, and, on the other, informal learning, seen as low status. To redress this, we have argued for the application of an 'organic' logic. This integrates the divide in two ways.

First, it enables the incorporation of the old binaries into a single concept, which is accessible through human phenomena experienced site-specifically, as detailed on pages 230–4.

Secondly, it actually makes more sense of those same human workplace phenomena that people undergo: judgements, actions and consequences are significant for workplace learning in this way.

Consider the emerging significance of this rich array of evidence of learning: portfolios, simulations, projects, case studies, coaching, mentoring, appraisals and the like, all of which can be more or less amenable to structuring. A new epistemology – an epistemology of practice rather than an epistemology of propositional knowledge – is what is required and now seems to be available. It is not that propositional knowledge is being devalued.

Rather there is a subsumption of propositional knowledge into judgement. In the process it is contextualized. To this extent, we are attracted to the 'postmodern turn' – its emphasis on the situational, its suspicion of the metanarrative, and its sensitivity to diversity and difference, are all helpful ways of unpacking what the 'context' might be like. We have referred to the context as the specific (workplace) site, opening the possibility of myriad versions of this new workplace education. We have argued that the workplace is educative. We also claim, more provocatively, that workplace learning is a chance to rethink what we mean by education in general.

References

Anderson, J (1980) *Education and Inquiry*, edited by DZ Phillips, Basil Blackwell, Oxford.
Bagnall, RG (1990) 'Lifelong Education: The Institutionalisation of an Illiberal and Regressive Ideology?', *Educational Philosophy and Theory*, 22, 1, 1–7.
Beckett, D (1996) 'Critical Judgment and Professional Practice', *Educational Theory*, 46, 2, 135–49.
Burke, T (1994) *Dewey's New Logic: A Reply to Russell*, University of Chicago Press, Chicago.
Candy, PC, Crebert, G and O'Leary, J (1994) *Developing Lifelong Learners Through Undergraduate Education*, National Board of Employment, Education and Training, Canberra.
Goleman, D (1996) *Emotional Intelligence: Why It Can Matter More Than IQ*, Bloomsbury, New York.
Hager, P (1996) 'Professional Practice in Education: Research and Issues', *Australian Journal of Education*, 40, 3, 235–47.
Karpin Report (1995) *Enterprising Nation* (Industry Task Force on Leadership and Management Skills), Australian Government Publishing Service, Canberra.
Lawson, K (1982) 'Lifelong Education: Concept or Policy?', *International Journal of Lifelong Education*, 1, 2, 97–108.
Schön, DA (1983) *The Reflective Practitioner*, Basic Books, New York.
Usher, R and Edwards, R (1994) *Postmodernism and Education*, Routledge, London.
Wain, K (1987) *Philosophy of Lifelong Education*, Croom Helm, London.
Wain, K (1993) 'Lifelong Education: Illiberal and Repressive?', *Educational Philosophy and Theory*, 25, 1, 58–70.
Winch, C (1995) 'Education Needs Training', *Oxford Review of Education*, 21, 3, 315–25.

Chapter 20

Towards the Learning Society:
an Italian Perspective

Aureliana Alberici

The 'learning society' calls for a reflection about educational policies as a whole. The 'life-course perspective' (Saraceno 1986: 20) opens up new opportunities for lifelong learning but it stresses at the same time the need for deep changes in the theory and practice of lifelong learning. We are no longer dealing with intervening in education for adults facing new needs – in the sense of a 'learning society' demanding education and vocational training – but, far more, with devising strategies to tackle crises and to help people project themselves towards the future.

Paradoxically, the future of lifelong education lies in a fundamental renewal of the role and function of 'formal' educational systems (Delors 1996: 115). There can be no role or development for lifelong learning unless the so-called 'formal educational systems' perform on a 'life-course' perspective. We are facing a transitional stage, even from the theoretical point of view. If lifelong learning means the possibility of learning all life long, moving from definitions to policies requires consideration of the extent of an individual's potential in the light of what may be feasible. One of the clearest aspects of modern society is the constant increase in the complexity, speed and variety of change: one cannot talk about the 'learning society' unless mid to long-term educational strategies are determined which have a built-in capacity to accommodate change.

There are two possibilities and two needs: short to medium-term strategies for dealing with crises here and now (unemployment, language and technological illiteracy, exclusion for social, gender or racial reasons, etc); and strategies for the longer-term future (how to prepare to train adults to be capable of facing changes and how to build a society of equal opportunities). These two paths are likely to co-exist but cannot be effective unless they operate in synergy. A new culture must be developed which acknowledges the strategic importance of medium to long-term training policies.

An Italian perspective

This chapter explains some aspects of Italian educational and vocational policies which have implications for the lifelong learning perspective. The Italian Ministry of Public Education approved a working document in January 1997 which was publicly discussed by interested parties and institutions over the following months. In June 1997 the government changed this working document into a bill which was adopted by the Council of Ministers. This framework bill redesigns and integrates the Italian school system with vocational training and university study. For the first time a national bill has included lifelong learning in the educational system and foreseen the possibility of developing specific adult education activities in line with the directives of the European Community through co-operation between school, institutional and social partners. When this bill is approved by Parliament, compulsory schooling will begin in Italy at the age of five (not six as now) and will continue to 15 (not 13).[1] Finally, it will introduce a 'right to education and vocational training', up to the age of 18, for all young people who leave school at the minimum leaving age, in order to increase their opportunity to achieve a certificated vocational qualification. This proposal was in line with the agreement, *Pact on Work* (September 1996) reached between the government and the trade unions, one part of which concerns continuing and adult education (*Accordo per il lavoro* 1997: 13–14), and which itself follows the European Commission's strategy. (This is set out in the EC White Papers *Growth, Competitiveness, Employment* (1994) and *The Learning Society* (1995).)

The reform of the educational system and the *Pact on Work* represent two different strategies aimed at the same medium to long-term goal: lifelong education. The proposal to rearrange the school cycle illustrates this. The intertwining of the school system with the life-course perspective shows the need for structural intervention if lifelong education is to be achieved as a right – like the right to citizenship – and not merely tied up with crisis and the ever present need for new 'training'.

The proposals to reorder the school cycle were presented whilst the Italian Parliament was voting on the law which regulates the functions of the Ministry of Public Education. This transferred to the Regions, local authorities and schools all responsibility for management and programming. Schools were given autonomy in administration, teaching, management, research and development.

For the first time, this law also gives schools responsibility for matters of continuing and adult education. This law is designed to promote collaboration between schools and local communities, partnerships between work and social partners and schools, and better relationships between education and vocational training, to raise 'formative' standards and develop lifelong learning (*Gazzetta Ufficiale* n.98 1997: 22–25).

Ambitiously, this project to reform the education and vocational training system also seeks to establish methods and aims that will measure up to change and to the future. Such methods and goals must have a cultural and political pulse that extends beyond the present, and must be effective in the medium and long term. In a complex and continually changing modern society, this is a most difficult issue to address. Historically, periods of education and training have always heralded the way for scientific, cultural and vocational growth. Today, the gap in respect of specialization, vocational competence, speed of innovation and scientific development is insuperable. Schools seem destined always to lag behind the requirements of modern states. On the other hand, as never before, development and growth are today structurally linked to, and even defined by, the production and consumption of knowledge. The European White Paper defined such modern societies as 'learning societies', and the agenda for the future of adult education as a 'knowledge explosion' (Confintea 1997: 3). Innovation rapidly renders everything, or almost everything, useless. Millions of men and women face change alone. Adults pass through these changes, very often with the tools and skills of another era. Young people face changes with neither old knowledge nor old work skills. (This point was made clearly by Tuijnman (OECD 1996: 26–27) in the presenting of the results of the First International Adult Literacy Survey (IALS).) Both young and adults are much at risk and need urgent help through education. It is, however, possible for them to make this critical transition.

How, then, can we advance along this 'narrow pass leading to modernization' (Censis 1996: 107)? How can we propose strategies for the medium to long term when faced with a crisis in human conditions – and while, at the same time, reducing public spending? Will there not be reluctance, for some years at least, to invest in areas where there are no immediate returns? Are conditions are suitable for investment? The Fifth General Objective proposed by the European Commission is: 'Treat capital investment and investment in training [and, I should prefer to add, education] on an equal basis.' But is it realistic to carry through this aim in the light of economic parameters established by Maastricht (EC 1995: 47)?

In Italy, many decisions made in the past – such as the increase in school numbers – can be seen as spontaneous, often contradictory. Decisions and actions, unguided by any overall strategy, have modified the role and function of institutions. Schools have been left stranded 'in mid-stream'. It is therefore now critical to establish a strategy for education and vocational training. The educational system, without adequate reform, has already experienced a sea-change – from a quantitative point of view. As so often when such changes are not guided and sustained by political wisdom, individuals have paid the price of the gamble over the value of instruction as a personal investment.

But the quantitative expansion of schooling already seems yesterday's vision. Statistically noticeable behaviour, albeit partial and limited to certain areas of the country, indicates a reversal of the rising trend of participation in schooling of the past twenty years (CENSIS 1996: 110). This is seen in the data on the admissions to, and drop-out from, secondary school, as well as in the higher proportions of adolescents in areas of socio-economic difficulty (such as the North-East and the Val d'Aosta) who fail to obtain school leaving certificates (CENSIS 1996: 118). There appears to be a new disaffection from schools and training – from education – as a result of economic development, the quality of life, and society's emphasis on wealth. The values of education and schools are seen as less and less relevant.

In the final analysis these data constitute a concrete example of the difficulties arising from a complex co-existence of needs. The need for an educational strategy for the medium to long term is undercut by immediate pressures. The latter call on individuals to look for specific, short-term solutions and not to invest in their longer-term prospects. From the lifelong learning and adult point of view, this close relationship between education and the needs, questions and motivations arising over the life-course and in different individual careers is real and calls for examination. But, for the younger generation, the close linkage of education with needs and motives is threatening: it appears to reduce everything to the present, with its scarce resources and dramatic and probable risk of failure (school drop-out, unemployment, discrimination and so on). The key is to face up to this historically new phase, to rediscover the importance of knowledge and culture in the life of individuals as something worthwhile in itself; worthwhile, in that it helps people to resolve the problems they face in life, to learn to choose, to have confidence in possible outcomes – especially when faced with lives in which individual choice and responsibility risk being reduced to 'virtual reality'.

At the level of theory, definitions of education, continuing education, lifelong education and learning and vocational education are also currently going through a transitional phase. Research and educational practices have drawn attention to the potential benefits of 'lifelong learning': we must look at the problems of school and learning through this same 'new lens'. This amounts to a real 'U-turn' because, up to now, educational systems have been based upon the hypothesis that a set, and substantially unrepeatable, period of time for education and study occurs in a person's life – corresponding with the years of schooling. In contrast to an individual's life, schooling has had a foreseeable end; it has implied that one could acquire all the knowledge one needed for life within predetermined time limits. This also implied a distinction between time for study and time for work, and that they have relatively little in common.

An adequate reform of education can only occur within a culture of lifelong learning and continuing education. This means eliminating from these notions the concept of an activity dedicated solely to adults – a 'subsequent' phase adding to the greater or lesser amount of formal education already received. It means, instead, thinking of educational needs and paths for individuals, using a logic of 'possible continuity' – putting real live people at the centre of educational plans and appreciating the multiplicity of time-patterns involved in growing up, maturing and developing (Boshier 1998). This leads to an awareness that the need for knowledge and competence, which is the substance of the learning society, cannot be met at times of crisis, nor can it be left to adulthood (Delors 1996: 99–100). On the contrary, it recreates a new and unusual role for formal education, and especially for school systems, in the lives of the widest possible number of individuals. From this perspective, the objective of quality in school and education generally becomes fundamental. Although it is difficult to argue for 'a lot of schools, but good ones!', this is the only possible strategy. The Italian school reform project attempts to realize this difficult objective by concentrating on quality.

We must avoid the hypothesis of 'culturally weak' schools. We should propose 'culturally strong' schools – that is, schools which produce individuals capable of coping with change, in a society ever more ready to favour equal opportunities – not just formal egalitarianism. From this is born the importance of specifying curricular and qualitative standards for every stage of the educational process. In view of ambitious and complex projects such as this, it seems more appropriate to think of raising the minimum school leaving age, not to 15 as proposed in the Italian bill, but to 16 at least. This would provide a wider range of choice and a longer period of schooling. The European trend today is toward 18. Finally, the reform bill proposes to reduce the length of the non-compulsory cycle of education, putting it on a par with other European countries. Secondary studies would therefore end with a 'School

Leaving Certificate' at 18 instead of 19. More flexible solutions are required. They should not necessarily address only the minimal need to avoid making young people waste time before starting university studies or jobs. In a system founded upon a 'life-course perspective' and lifelong learning, we should think about different exits, discriminate in the length of courses on the basis of effective individualized routes which use educational and vocational training credits and debits.

Lifelong learning: from school system to work

The future will call for a permanent state of lifelong learning by an ever-increasing number of people. This will be achieved by an effective recognition system which facilitates entry to and exit from educational and work situations. This flexibility may frighten some, but the integrating school and work can only increase the rate of participation in education and, from a lifelong learning perspective, renew its quality. We need to pay attention to actual educational needs. Still more, we need a serious and non-crisis-oriented assessment of the problems of work and employment to provide a basis for deciding what outcomes we seek from school systems and vocational training.

One cannot tackle the problems of an effective system of vocational training without defining the role of educational strategies as a whole, especially 'to give everyone access to a broad base of knowledge' (EC 1995: 9).

We should remind ourselves of the definitions and types of literacy, and of the what we have learned from the literature about the skills and competencies needed for the year 2000 and beyond: for example, from the EC White Paper or the First IALS (OCSE 1995). Schools in the most advanced countries must provide specifically defined knowledge and areas of cross-competence – the so called 'new alphabets'. What is required is a literacy which helps people to grow and face the complexities of life, in study and at work – rather than the reverse (CERI/OCSE 1996: 36–47).

This leads us to reflect on the relationship between schools and vocational training from the lifelong learning perspective. On this matter, the most important Italian goal consists of proposing a 'right to education and vocational training' (Camera dei Deputati 1997: 17) for those who take employment when their compulsory schooling ends. This is the main route to a real re-evaluation of vocational training. It suggests abandoning the view that basic vocational training is a surrogate for schooling, and developing training practices which connect more directly to work and 'training contracts' (Presidenza del Consiglio dei Ministri 1996: 25). 'Training contracts' refer to combining work with 'stage' contracts for young people, as well as to activities between school and work (in dual systems). These can work if educational and vocational training credits, taking account of job experience as well as on-the-job and vocational training, can be implemented. In the new educational reform bill, an 'educational and vocational booklet' (Camera dei Deputati 1997: 22) or 'personal knowledges and skills card' is introduced for all. This is designed to accompany the student through his or her educational career and to remain with the adult thereafter. Recalling the 'personal card' of the White Paper (EC 1995), the Italian personal booklet will also include information and certification about all studies carried out and about competencies and skills acquired.

To permit the introduction of the system of credit transfers, the teaching system will be founded on the 'unity of values' and on 'modular organization of disciplines'. The bill actually states:

> 'The positive attendance in any part of the secondary school cycle, for one year or for one part of the (modular teaching) programme will involve the acquisition of credit which can be used to re-enter studies which have been interrupted, to pass from one area or one type of study to another, or to enter vocational training. In the same way, vocational or on-the-job training can generate 'credits' which can be used to return to education or lifelong learning.'

This is not the place to explain all the Italian government's strategies for educational reform, vocational training and lifelong learning. In conclusion, however, some suggestions may be made about the priorities and the fundamental goals the life course perspective implies. Among the fundamental objectives, the following seem of particular interest.

First, a 'European convergence over new educational and vocational training goals' (CNEL 1997: 5–7) implies the following goals for Italy:

- ten years' compulsory schooling
- improving student retention and preventing 'drop-out'
- a right to education and training, and therefore to re-entry and progression through different aspects of the system
- development of further education, lifelong learning, adult education and dual systems
- adoption of a system of certification and recognition and transfer of educational and training credits
- adoption of a national quality assessment system for education.

Second, 'system integration' implies integration between school and other educational and vocational systems and between these and the world of work.

System integration also means integration between formal and informal settings.

Finally, these suggestions for the reform of educational and vocational training systems in the light of lifelong learning imply a new function for teachers and adult educators. A new University Faculty of Educational Science has been created, which should be an important testing ground for new school curricula and for the certification of adult competencies. It will also lead to a new educational and vocational curriculum for teachers, adult educators and educational programmers. As Jarvis (1997: 107) argues, curricula 'should be provided…to learn about the practical and also to begin to develop theoretical perspectives from it'.

Generally speaking, these reforms present the possibility of developing lifelong learning. They contribute to realizing a partnership between schools and vocational training and employment, and – for many – they also offer new opportunities for progress.

They are strategies for educational reform and for addressing the problems and opportunities presented of complex modern society. They also constitute an important attempt to advance a new approach to lifelong learning, the strategic goal of democratic rights and equal opportunities for the people and the nation.

Note

1. On 22 May 1998 the Italian Council of Ministers approved a new bill raising the school leaving age to 16 and fixing 16 as the age of entry to work for young people. This bill was being considered by Parliament as the present chapter went to press (May 1998).

References

Boshier, R (1998) 'Edgar Faure After 25 Years: Down But Not Out'. (Chapter 1).
Camera dei Deputati (1997) *Legge quadro in materia di riordino dei cicli scolastici*, Atti Parlamentari n.3952, Rome.
CENSIS (1996) *30° Rapporto sulla situazione sociale del paese*, Franco Angeli Editore, Milano.
CERI/OCSE (1996) *Uno sguardo sull'educazione. Analisi politica (1 vol). Gli indicatori internazionali dell'istruzione*, Armando Editore, Milan.
CNEL (1997) *Formazione: strategia del Patto per il lavoro e la sua declinazione operativa*, Conference Proceedings, CNEL, Rome.
Confintea-UNESCO (1997) *Agenda for the Future of Adult Education*, Hamburg.

Delors J (1996) *Learning: The Treasure Within*, UNESCO and Presse Universitaire de France, Vendôme.
European Commission (1994) *Growth, Competitiveness, Employment*. White Paper, Official Publications of EC, Luxemburg.
European Commission (1995) *Teaching and Learning. Toward the Learning Society*. White paper on Education and training, Official Publications of EC, Luxemburg.
Gazzetta Ufficiale (1997) *Deleghe per il conferimento di funzione e compiti alle regioni ed enti locali, per la riforma della pubblica amministrazione. Legge 15 marzo 1997, n.59.* (G.U. n.98) Istituto Poligrafico dello Stato, Rome.
Jarvis, P (1997) 'Adult Education at University', *Educazione Comparata*, 26/27, 101–110.
OCSE (1995) *Litératie, Economie et Societé*, OECD Publications Service, Paris.
OECD (1996) *Lifelong Learning for All*, OECD Publications Service, Paris.
Presidenza del Consiglio dei Ministri (1996) *Accordo per il lavoro sottoscritto da Governo e Sindacati*, Istituto Poligrafico dello Stato, Roma.
Saraceno, C (1986) *Età e corso della vita*, Il Mulino, Bologna.

Chapter 21

Sentencing Learners to Life:
Retrofitting the Academy for the Information Age

Cliff Falk

'We are clearly witnessing a change in the character of academic life. The question is, how is this change to be understood? This development could be read as just another phase in the long history of the university to adapt to the requirements coming its way from its host society. For most of its history, the university has been tolerated and indeed supported by crown, church or state on the condition it acted the part set for it. Other functions were allowed provided they did not affect the larger and dominant mission. The current realignment is merely that: simply an adjustment to a new level of requirements from the wider society...' (Barnett 1994).

Sentencing learners to life

When Plato in the *Republic* sentenced his Guardian class to a life of learning, his project concerned vocational training for the few who, because they would learn to identify and implement Good, would justly rule the many. Lifelong learning as a modern populist form of adult education worked towards the opposite, offering the many enhanced understandings that would disallow rule by the few (democracy). Of late this comforting academic binary has come undone. The great emancipatory project of modern education (Lyotard 1984), elitist or popular, has collapsed, the often willing victim of a transcendental <Market>.[1] Education's semi-autonomous formal and informal cultural spaces, which in part lived within Bourdieu's 'habitus' or Habermas' 'lifeworld', are being moved to a hypercolonized confine termed the Information Age. Lifelong learning, in its headlong pursuit of relevance as defined by Market, finds itself in the vanguard of this move, perhaps unwittingly championing an information age academic diaspora.

The radical late twentieth century systematic, structural, semiotic and discursive (Lowe 1995) rewrite popularly termed the Information Age has its inhabitants scurrying about, caught within the glare of a reductionist Market ethic – *Adapt or You're Toast* (Kroker and Weinstein 1994). With a new Information Age bourgeoisie ascendant, this new 'virtual class', as Kroker and Weinstein explain, is:

> 'projecting its class interests onto cyberspace from which vantage point it crushes any and all dissent to the prevailing orthodoxies of technotopia. For the virtual class, politics is about absolute control over intellectual property by means of strategies of communication, control and command... [And further:] Key to the success of the virtual class is its promotion of a radically diminished vision of human experience and of a disintegrated conception of the human good: for virtualizers, the good is ultimately that which disappears human subjectivity, substituting the war-machine of cyberspace for the data trash of experience' (http://www.ctheory.com/gal.4-theory_virtual.html).

This paper argues that lifelong learning is a central ideological and pedagogical apparatus (discursive device) for the promotion of this radically diminished vision of human experience and of a disintegrated conception of human good. It argues that 'disappearing (delimiting) subjectivities' is the unstated goal of lifelong learning. It posits that the womb-to-tomb state supported projects of instrumental learning that increasingly define lifelong learning (Boshier 1997), far from assuaging the demons loosed by global competition, will excite them even more, leaving its purported goals of fostering individual empowerment and personal and social security receding ever further into a bleak though high-tech future.

Locating the Information Age

Befitting a saga of renovated social Darwinism, the provenance of the age is located in the American military. The technology that spawned the age became visible *circa* 1970 with the Mohammed Ali/Joe Frasier boxing match titled the 'Thrilla in Manila' (not to be confused with the Mohammed Ali/George Foreman 'Rumble in the Jungle' in Kinshasa, staged later). This fight marked the first time the command, communications and control system developed during the war in Vietnam was put to large-scale civilian (commercial) use to capture a prime-time home audience with a live (real-time) feed of an entertainment event. A search for the source of the Internet, the defining information technology (IT) of the moment, locates it in that self-same military, because planners held that a diffuse decentralized electronic communications system built around many nodes (the Internet) would be difficult to destroy if the Cold War turned hot (Dizard 1997). The original system is being rebuilt according to the specifications of capital, and even more specifically to the capital of Bill Gates, who, along with forays into cable and cellular distribution, is working with Boeing to blanket the globe with 228 low-flying communications satellites. The 'microchip' finds itself in similar company, a product of publicly-funded research and development, which, like satellite communications, found itself internationally conscripted by the 'private' sector.

In itself the martial provenance and commercial reconstruction of these enabling technologies is unremarkable, except that unlike the Nuclear Age, Jet Age or Space Age, and like its more distant antecedent the Steam Age, the Information Age is discursively constructed as the issue of heroic rather than state capitalism. For example, Steve Jobs, working in his family's garage in California, comes up with the Apple, only to see its user interface 'modelled' by Bill Gates. The Titans battle and Gates' Microsoft wins; along the way Gates becomes about the richest man on earth and the popular icon of the era. This tale of down-home competition leading to untold power and wealth grounds a cultural imaginary that harkens back to a less complex era of less restrained (free-booting) capitalism. With Bill and Steve popularly constructed as 'info-neers' in much the same mould as their forebears, Alexander Graham Bell and Thomas Edison, viewers may concur that within a free-enterprise system genius will to the top. That the genius and enterprise is far from 'free' goes missing in this narrative of meritocratic hope and technological redemption. The hundreds of billions of dollars of publicly funded education, research and development that ground the age, and the opportunity costs that accompanied them, are written off (out), only to be derisively reintroduced (Usher and Edwards 1994) as deleterious to the workings of a transcendental 'invisible hand'.

Locating the Information Age in rejuvenated free enterprise and individual opportunity instead of, for example, in social intelligence and wealth ties it neatly to the 'ideology of competitive individualism'. A seamless fit between the political and economic (neo-liberalism, social Darwinism) and the economic and technological (instrumental rationalism, functionalism, scientism) moments grounds a hegemonic narrative of the reduction of life possibilities for the many, those included in what JK Galbraith terms the (dys)Functional Underclass. Unlike the beginnings of the industrial age in

Britain, which saw the Luddites fighting negative aspects of its imposition so well, today's Luddites seem lacking in moral authority. Without a neo-Luddite 'General Ludd' to lead, resistance to the Information Age remains muted, though thousands of intense rearguard actions, often led by public sector unions, continue to be fought. Yet the ability of Murdoch, Gates and Turner, Fairchild, Sony, Matsui, Samsung, Disney, Phillips, Siemens, Time/Warner (or whatever the latest polyglot mega-conglomerate may be) to define Information Age production/consumption in terms of their making remains intact. Eliding existing classes as well as physical and social geographies, this age, very like the industrial one before, forms new and often repressive geographies and classes within a hegemonic narrative of rekindled hope. Virtually overnight the gilding on the Information Age seems as permanently affixed as the gilding layered onto the age of steam a century ago.

Cold war to old war

A political economy of irony marks the Information Age. With the industrial revolution replayed as a virtual post-industrial revolution, 'symbolic-analytic service workers' replace the civil and mechanical engineers who wrote the first industrial revolution on to global land and mindscapes. The discursive constructions of these 'image-ineers' are the information age. With the rise of this 'virtual class' corresponding with a 'race to the bottom' for so many others (the functional underclass), constructing a reason (an ideology) for this popular impoverishment and justifying the privilege of the 'digeratti' and their hosts has kept thousands of symbolic-analytic service workers on the job for years. Their work, for one thing, leads to the imbrication of 'globalization' which means, simply, world trade, and signifies the hegemonic valuation of Market (Jameson 1994) with 'information' (for example see the work of Bell, Toffler, Gilder, Drucker, Naisbitt) to construct the contemporary information age. As Kumar (1995: 34) states:

> 'To call the information society an ideology, and to relate that ideology to the contemporary needs of capitalism, is to begin, not to end, the analysis. Capitalism has had many ideologies over the past two hundred years – laissez-faire, managerialism, welfarism, even, arguably, varieties of fascism and communism... What kind of ideology is the ideology of the information society, and what are its particular contradictions?... 'The Information Society' may be a partial and one-sided way of expressing social reality, but for many people in the industrial world it is an escapable part of that reality.'

With intra-capitalist competition of the Information Age replacing extra-capitalist competition of the Cold War era, 'global competition' displaces 'missile gaps' and the 'race in space' as the prime threat to individual and social security in nations in the 'West'. With that, educational strategies, though the challenge of Sputnik is nostalgia now, remain central to national security (Baldwin 1996). Education joins with nation, both falling victim to a highly sophisticated postmodern semiotic shell game that promiscuously usurps and recodes signifiers by deliberately changing the signification historically associated with them. In the post-industrial 'West' one enemy (global competition) stands in for another (communism). This rhetorical displacement constructs a post-national info-age 'nationalism' that occludes 'nation' by harkening back to and redistributing the now polysemous signifiers that defined it originally. Words like individualism, freedom, competition, co-operation and democracy are redeployed on the quickly shifting terrain of post-industrial consumption/production. In the process, the meanings attached to the signifier nation, like the signifier education (and lifelong learning), have been inverted, used now to institute, justify and maintain a globalized (or regionalized) economic system deliberately designed since WWII to facilitate extra-national capital and technological flows (Bretton Woods, GATT, NAFTA, European Union, ASEAN, etc) that cannot but undermine the 'nation' and 'self' hood that the signifiers purport to renew.

David Cook in his 1994 review article of the work of the three leading liberal economists in the US (Thurow, Galbraith and Reich) titled 'Farewells to American Culture, Work and Competition' addresses these 'post-national' social and geographic formations:

> 'what is left [in today's global economy] are transnational global knowledge webs (that is no longer property based corporations per se) and large holding areas of labour identified with nation states or trading areas. These labour encampments contain in turn "workers" in three classes: "routine production services, in person services, and symbolic-analytic services". Of these categories the first is completely fungible (clonal) with any other labour source and hence is consigned to permanent "poverty", the second being more site specific is marginally better off but going nowhere (homeostasis), leaving only the third as the skilled technical class created by the rich but whose future Reich sees in terms of the universal, transnational economy' (1994: 174)

Cook comments further on Reich's work, saying that for middle and Eastern Europeans, 'basic attitudes about fairness will have to change' (1994: 97), and acknowledging the projected growth in inequalities and the unstated creation of an underclass governed by technological demands.

In Canada, 'clonal' workers who in large comprise this fast-emerging underclass are provided lifelong learning 'opportunities' through sometimes compulsory short-term on-the-job training, frequently in fast food outlets, often combined with equally short-term institutionally based training.

Second-level 'on-site' (ie relatively immobile) workers are offered technical and business training, retraining and upgrading. These 'opportunities' are usually funded by the workers themselves through the federally administered 'employment insurance' program. An array of continuing education courses and programmes are offered to this group by distance (now called distributed) learning or on site in schools, colleges and universities in every corner of the country. The cost of this 'CE' is most often borne by the individual directly rather than through an employer or government. Finally, postgraduate university programs, short-term learning experiences such as those offered at the Banff School and management training courses sponsored by experts like Peter Senge exemplify lifelong learning for the third class.

Colonizing management studies that incorporate techniques such as Total Quality Management (TQM), though beyond the purvey of this paper, are lifelong learning exercises absolutely central to the dissemination of the ideology of the Information Age. The (tautological) interior logic of this managerial discourse (eg Senge 1990) grounds a recolonization of labour, a 'de-' and 're-' skilling that emphasizes attitudinal (affective attributes) rather than technical or knowledge based 'competence' (see for example British Columbia's Employability Skills website at http://www.est.gov.bc.ca/btp/welcome.htm). Again strategies of rhetorical redeployment of terms like worker empowerment, which have been stripped of their previous meaning, legitimize the realties of the info-age workplace (exile in cyberspace?). This new managerial ideology provides the foundation for the 'learning organization' and the 'learning society', which is the inverse of the utopian model for lifelong education envisioned, for one, by Faure in 1972 (see below). Lifelong learning, it seems, is somewhat dismissive of class, sentencing all but the wealthy to it.

Lifelong learning: a recuperative moment in the information age

In *Lifelong Education: A Psychological Analysis*, A. J. Cropley (1977: 20) writes:

> 'The conceptualization of education as a tool for developing individuals who will learn throughout life and thus become more valuable to society is to be found in the writings of both Matthew Arnold (see, for example Johnson 1972), and Comenius (see Kyrasek and Polisensky 1968), as well as educational writers in antiquity. Dewey (1916: 90–91) expressed the view that education and learning are lifelong processes over 60 years ago. A report to the British Government at the end of the first world war (Ministry of Reconstruction of

Adult Education Committee 1919) specifically recommended that education should be 'lifelong', as a matter of national importance. However, it is apparent that in the 60 years or so since Dewey's recommendations for the US and the Ministry of Reconstruction's recommendations for the UK, truly lifelong-oriented educational systems have not been developed.'

Since 1977 truly lifelong-oriented educational systems – as a tool for developing individuals who will learn throughout life and thus become more valuable to society – have been developed in the nations of the 'West', though these systems invert the utopian systems envisioned in the 1960s. Lifelong learning today is largely a project of economic, social and epistemological recuperation dedicated to delimiting rather than expanding the subjectivities of learners exposed to it (see below). Boshier (1997) addresses this changed trajectory in lifelong learning:

> 'Many educators thought the 1970s and 1980s would be a linear extension of the 1960s and reform along the anticipated lines would not be a problem. But after the OPEC oil crisis of 1973 the mood changed and the utopian vision anticipated by Faure (*Learning To Be*, the UNESCO report of 1972 authored by Faure) was significantly cooled by new right discourses. But despite these developments there were significant theoretical elaborations of lifelong education in the 1970s (Kallen 1979), important reforms were made and in several UNESCO member states, some of Faure's ideas were implemented. But now, 25 years after Faure, educators are struggling with cutbacks and restructuring and some of the liberatory developments anticipated by Faure (such as distance education) have been hijacked by architects of the new right.'

Today's lifelong learning differs in appearance and kind from recent constructions of adult, or indeed childhood, education. Much of it is predicated upon breaking down the binary between adult/child and valorizing learning in both formal and informal environments that stretch from the cradle to the grave. As Clinton's home-school-work 'educational initiatives' demonstrate, learners are indeed being sentenced to life. While there is undoubtedly a liberating moment attached to the removal of such binaries and to extravagant extensions of education, especially the learning experiences dedicated to the 'new middle class' (Usher and Edwards 1994: 190-191), which provides a description of service-analytic workers in repose, nonetheless lifelong learning designed for the many remains a discourse of instrumentalism concerned with constructing subjectivity (human capital) according to the specifications of the current Information Age regime of virtual production/consumption.

This competency-based discourse redesigned for the Information Age came late to British Columbia. Like its imperial precursors in the UK and the US, it is being implemented by attaching 'advisory committees' to ensure the programmes are relevant to info-age 'industry needs', by state funded curricular initiatives, for example the compulsory Career and Personal Planning curriculum for grade school students that teaches the 'value' of lifelong learning, by private-sector curricular initiatives like the Conference Board of Canada's (the country' largest 'think tank') Employability Skills Profile which emphasizes the market value of lifelong learning, and by Ministry funded initiatives to de-emphasize 'content-based' academic education and emphasize competency-based education aimed at the development of 'process skills'. The new strategic plan for the province's colleges and institutes warns that if institutions do not take on these voluntarily the government will do it for them (British Columbia Ministry of Education, Skills and Training 1996: 28–29), though the report also states that the 'Ministry, however, favours an approach of revitalized partnerships. BC [British Columbia] will work to create a revitalized public system that can act as a 'hub' for new approaches to lifelong learning.'

A document produced by the state-funded Centre for Curriculum and Professional Development in British Columbia captures the trajectory of this contemporary project in which lifelong learning is a component of a larger discourse of competency-based education dedicated to Market:

> 'Strategically presented and tactically supported over time, these actions [prior learning assessment] can help create the 'seamless learning system' BC needs: one that will value, recognize and credit the skills, knowledge and abilities of British Columbian citizens, regardless of how, when or where they were achieved and provide flexible learning options adults require as part of their growing commitment to lifelong learning' (Centre for Curriculum and Professional Development 1995: 39).

An adaptable workforce that is constantly being re(under)developed to compensate for the skills, knowledge and attitudinal obsolescence built into the Information Age provides the specifications to which British Columbia's colleges and institutes are being retrofitted. This economic 'downloading' on to the worker/learner, as so many stories about the 'new' poor attest, cannot but have deleterious effects, especially for those relegated to 'clonal' status. By consciously designing learning for everyone to limit the production of consciousness not dedicated to Market, and by limiting the production of 'officially sanctioned' surplus consciousness once again to the few (élite universities), lifelong learning, in aspects, relegates mass education to the disciplinary role used to justify its implementation during the steam age.

Lifelong learning, in an inverse of its original intent to make learning more attractive by removing associations with 'schooling' (Boshier 1997), has made 'education' more intrusive. 'Dropping out' at age 15 or 50 has become much more difficult, for drop-outs don't just leave school; they leave already reduced life possibilities. The learners that do continue their 'schooling', and various compulsory educational schemes for adults see to it that more and more do, engage a highly-scripted scenario that increasingly finds them sentenced to an unending search for the Holy Grail of 'value-added' learning, a grail that is proving more ephemeral in this era of post-Fordist labour displacement and outsourcing than the one pursued by Galahad some time ago. Lifelong learning 'for tomorrow', in practice, has become mandatory if one is to participate in the redundant and highly-stylized performance piece referred to as labour today.

Learning 'to be' *on demand* and *just-in-time*

By most accounts the Information Age has arrived, and its varied and disputed effects are being academically mapped and analysed. Marc Poster, addressing postmodern society specifically, states:

> 'Telephone, radio, film, television, the computer and now integration as "multimedia" reconfigure words, sounds and images so as to cultivate new configurations of individuality. If modern society may be said to foster an individual who is rational, autonomous, centred, and stable (the "reasonable man" of the law, the educated citizen of representative democracy, the calculating "economic man" of capitalism, the grade-defined student of public education), then perhaps a postmodern society is emerging which nurtures forms of identity different from, even opposite to, those of modernity' (Poster, 1995: 24).

Forms of identity, it appears, can develop variously and do not necessarily hypostatize as 'modem' subjectivity supposedly did. When this technologically determined subjective fluidity is combined with the (post)philosophic challenges (poststructuralism, etc) to a unitary subjectivity from within an academy that was until the mid 60s unilaterally humanist, the changed social, economic and technological conditions termed the Information Age (the rise of the underclass, the 'digeratti', globalization, mediated communication) speak of a new space within which 'subjectivity' is itself being rewritten.

As Donald Lowe (1995: 88) explains:

> '...we have in late capitalism the valorization of social reproduction, gender, and sexuality, and even psychic make-up. In other words, the regime of accumulation in late capitalism can no longer rely on a relatively stable, relatively autonomous mode of regulation, but needs to underdevelop and thus destabilize it.'

Education has been a bulwark of the relatively autonomous, relatively stable mode of regulation (social reproduction) that Poster equated with modernity. Underdeveloping it is precisely what the social reproduction activity termed lifelong learning does. Like advertising, lifelong learning roots out stable competency and constant identity, for which it substitutes lack and desire (underdevelopment). This harmonizes 'education' with the current regime of production/consumption, for example the micro-credential required each time a new software program is purchased. Recurrent (re)learning is a necessity if the education system is to continue to produce the malleable but disciplined consumer/producer/citizen that the Information Age is built upon.

The power that has recently accrued to lifelong learning is massive and suggests possibilities not included within current parameters of design. As the private-sector initiatives outlined above demonstrate, in British Columbia, Market is, in effect, reaping the rewards of a system designed to its specifications without incurring the costs. When lifelong learning is viewed as a deliberate and refined process designed to construct subjectivity in accord with info-age specifications, as a vehicle for selling commodities, and as a profitable commodity itself, it occludes many pedagogical possibilities. Examining all the 'opportunity costs' attached to its implementation might cause celebrationists pause, dampening some of their enthusiasms, at least in terms of the long run.

Note

1. Following Jameson <Market> denotes the discursive concept, that is the simultaneous conjuring of current ideological and material aspects of the Market into consciousness, as opposed to the word /market/ within its etymological origins, more originary significations, etc. The term is used in the expanded sense throughout.

References

Baldwin, D (1996) 'Security Studies and the End of the Cold War', *World Politics*, 48, 1, 117–41.
Barnett, R (1994) *The Limits to Competence: Knowledge, Higher Education and Society*, Society for Research into Higher Education and Open University Press, Buckingham.
Boshier, R. (1997) 'How Lifelong Learning Was Mugged On The Road To The 21st Century'. Paper presented to the Conference of the Comparative and International Education Society, Mexico City.

British Columbia, Ministry of Education, Skills and Training (1996) *Charting A New Course: A Strategic Plan For The Future of British Columbia's College, Institute and Agency System.*

Centre for Curriculum and Professional Development and British Columbia Council on Admission and Transfer (1995) *Prior Learning Assessment and Educational Reform.*

Cook, D (1994) 'Farewells to American Culture, Work and Competition', *Canadian Journal of Political and Social Theory*, 17, 1–2.

Cropley, A (1977) *Lifelong Education A Psychological Analysis*, Pergamon, Oxford.

Dewey, J (1916) *Democracy and Education: An Introduction to the Philosophy of Education*, MacMillan, New York.

Dizard, W (Jr) (1997) *Old Media, New Media: Mass Communications In The Information Age*, Longman, New York.

Faure, E et al. (1972) *Learning To Be*, UNESCO, Paris

Jameson, F (1994) 'Postmodernism and the Market', in S Sisek (Ed.) *Mapping Ideology*, Verso, London.

Johnson, L (1972) 'Matthew Arnolds' Concept of Culture and its Significance for RS Peter's Analysis of Education, Australian Journal of Education, 165–74

Kallen, D (1979) 'Recurrent Education and Lifelong Learning: Definitions and Distinctions', in T Schuller and J Megarry (Eds) *Recurrent Education and Lifelong Learning*: 45–54, Kogan Page, London.

Kroker, A and Weinstein, M (1994) *Data Trash: the Theory of the Leisure Class*, New World Perspectives, Montreal.

Kumar, K (1995) *From Post-Industrial to Post-Modern Society: New Theories of the Contemporary World*, Blackwell, Oxford.

Kyrasek, J and Polisensky, JV (1968) 'Comenius and All-embracing Education', *Convergence*, 1, 4, 80–6.

Lowe, D (1995). *The Body In Late-Capitalist Society*, Duke University Press, Durham.

Lyotard, JF (1984) *The Postmodern Condition*, The University of Minnesota Press, Minneapolis.

Ministry of Reconstruction (1919) *Final Report of the Adult Education Committee*, His Majesty's Stationery Office, London.

Poster, M (1995) *The Second Media Age*, Polity Press, Cambridge.

Senge, P (1990) *The Fifth Discipline*, Century Business, Random Century, London.

UNESCO (1972) *Learning to be* (The Faure Report), UNESCO, Paris.

Usher, R and Edwards, R (1994) *Postmodernism and Education*, Routledge, London.

Chapter 22

The Role of the Public Library in Lifelong Learning:
Can Cinderella Go to the Ball?

Matthew J Williamson and Margaret K Wallis

The public library is one of very few centrally funded services which is available to all, free at the point of service. The right of the ordinary person in the street to have free access to information and learning is enshrined in legislation the world over. As can be seen from Sumsion *et al.* (1996) public libraries are a heavily used resource, with over four hundred and fifty million items issued in England in 1994–95 and with 330 million visits by the public in the same year. Add to these figures the fact that research at the University of Brighton shows that over 87 per cent of library authorities in England and Wales provide open learning centres for their users and the potential for the public library as a lifelong learning resource is staggering. Yet the role of the public library in this field is in some doubt. The British government accepts, in its White Paper *People, Jobs and Opportunity* (Department of Employment 1992), that the siting of learning centres in public libraries was to be encouraged. Despite this, its own agencies, notably the Employment Service[1], seem to be reluctant to agree. This paper is based, in part, on Department for Education and Employment sponsored research which is being carried out at the University of Brighton. This research is entitled *Redefining the role of the public library in information service provision to jobseekers in England and Wales* and is an attempt to identify how jobseekers use public libraries, how the libraries view their jobseeking clients and how other agencies, most notably governmental, see the library's role.

This chapter then is an attempt to redefine the role of the library. Firstly, it will look at the historical role which the public library service in England has fulfilled with particular regard to its educational function. Secondly, it will then draw upon current research at the University of Brighton, highlighting the conflicts which exist between government agencies and public libraries. Thirdly, it will reconceptualize the present and future roles of the public library in providing lifelong learning opportunities to the public.

Since the reign of Queen Victoria, the public library has been seen, primarily, as a centre for learning, particularly for the working classes (Kelly 1965, Minto 1932). This was not a new idea, but a reworking of a 'fifteenth century idea that promoted literacy and independent education through "common-profit libraries"' (ASLIB 1995: 2/1). The background to William Ewart's Public Libraries Bill of 1850 was an increasing call for opportunities to be made freely available for the working classes. In some part this was already being provided by the Mechanics' Institutes, the first of which opened in 1823 in Glasgow (Minto 1932). Although an advance in terms of access to information, the libraries in the Mechanics' Institutes were only free to those actually undertaking a course at the institute. Charges and membership for those not undertaking a course varied from institute to institute, with the Glasgow Institute offering access to the library for life to all those who had completed five courses at the Institute 'on payment of half a crown annually' (Minto 1932: 42). Free access to information for all was yet to come.

The bill, which was first to enshrine the notion of the public library in British law was, as has already been mentioned, introduced by William Ewart, MP for Liverpool. One of the main reasons for the bill was the establishment of similar institutions in other European countries, notably Belgium. Ewart was, in part, worried that England would lag behind Europe in the skills of its workers. Ewart's bill became law in 1850 and enabled councils to add up to one penny in the pound per year to the rates in order to pay for the establishment of public libraries. Thus, those who paid more rates (and who therefore were wealthier) paid for the education and enlightenment of their poorer brothers (Kelly 1977a). This led a working-class leader in Liverpool to say:

> 'Our leisure hours, instead of being spent in the tap-room, the singing room and the dancing room, must be given to study, to thought, to perseverance and to industry' (Kelly 1977a: 81).

The passing of the Act did not, however, lead to the immediate appearance of public libraries in every town and city. In fact, many boroughs resisted introducing the new charge on the rates for some time, because rate-payers resented it. It was also resisted by the very people for whom it was intended, with the working classes swayed by pressure from publicans that the public library was a retrograde step. This led to a famous cartoon by J Williams Benn entitled 'The Rivals', which compared the Red Lion public house to the Free Library. In some areas, the new charge on the rates was not implemented until the early years of the twentieth century (Kelly 1977a). Once the new rate-aided free libraries had been established across the country the man in the street had more access to books and information than ever before. This freedom of access meant more than it perhaps sounds at first. Compulsory state-aided education was not introduced into law until the first Education Act was passed in 1870 (Kelly 1977b). For those who had not attended parish or other voluntary schools, the public library offered the chance to better themselves. It could be said, perhaps, that the public library system was the originator of lifelong learning, even before the school system.

The nineteenth century saw the introduction of statutory free libraries and thus the possibility of learning for all for the first time in Britain. The twentieth century has seen the role of the public library change greatly, from being primarily a house of learning for the working classes to the multifarious services which public libraries today offer. Throughout the twentieth century diversification has been the watchword for public libraries, first in their extension from large libraries in the large towns to community libraries situated within smaller communities such as villages and new, generally post-war, housing estates. The old roles of education have not been forgotten, however, although for a time in the middle of the present century this idea became a sub-plot rather than the main thread of public library history. In recent years libraries have again awakened to their ideal location for the provision of adult learning with the establishment of open learning centres in many libraries.

These centres are the basis for lifelong learning in most public libraries and are part of the branch of public library services known as extension services (Murison 1988). These are services which are not part of the statutory requirement for library provision but are considered, by public librarians, to be important services to provide. As well as learning opportunities, other extension services are services to the blind, the housebound, prisoners and non-English speakers. As can be seen, most of these services are aimed at the disadvantaged and, as the Department of Education and Science[2] said in 1978, 'the socio-economically disadvantaged'. The aim of such centres is primarily to enable library users to update their skills for the workplace and to learn new ones. This is achieved by use of computers and software packages designed to train users in various skills (notably keyboard and computing skills, such as spreadsheets, word processing and database management). Centres often also house videotapes, audiocassettes and traditional hard-copy material. Our research shows that the centres are generally heavily used and highly regarded by their users. The formation of these centres reaffirms the public library's commitment to education. This reawakening has been part of a major reconceptualization of the role of the public library in time for the new millennium.

As has been shown, the basis for the formation of the public library service was a need for free education to be available for all and, for those lucky enough to have received formal education, an outlet through which they might better themselves. The situation in most public libraries, despite the changes in society and to the service, is much the same. Although accepted wisdom states that the public library is primarily a leisure service, the trend shows fiction borrowing falling and non-fiction borrowing rising over the last nine years (to 1995). This is illustrated in Figure 22.1.

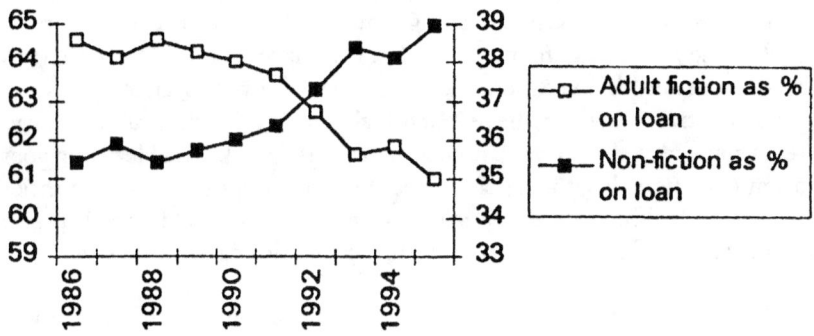

Source: Sumsion et al. (1996)

Figure 22.1 Books on loan 1986–1995

If these figures do not show how the learning role in libraries has re-emerged as being of prime importance, then the number of library authorities which offer open learning centres (or equivalent) confirms it. The research at the University of Brighton surveyed all 142 public library authorities in England and Wales (this does not include new unitary authorities which came on stream in April 1997). A completion rate of 81 per cent was achieved. Of those authorities which completed the questionnaire, only 11 per cent said that they did not, at the moment, offer open learning in any of their libraries.

Of this 11 per cent the overwhelming response, when asked why they did not offer open learning, was that they hoped to offer it in the future. One point which must be borne in mind when looking at these results is that a number of the authorities which said that they did not provide open learning centres were unitary authorities which came on stream in April 1996 and who may not yet have sufficient funds or space to house such centres. One of the drawbacks of open learning centres is that they take a great deal of space and resources and, in small authorities, provision such as this which lies outside statutory responsibilities is simply unaffordable.

It is not only open learning centres which libraries offer in the way of lifelong learning. Many authorities have developed special collections, of both books and other materials, with particular regard to retraining, career change, jobseeking and updating skills. These collections often travel around libraries in the authority, thus making specialist information available at even the smallest units.

So why, if all these resources are being provided by public libraries, is this chapter entitled 'Can Cinderella Go to the Ball'? The service is operated with a fair degree of success. Open learning initiatives are expensive to start up and run but the fact that so many public libraries have followed an accelerated trend and made this investment shows that they have been seen to be a worthwhile initiative. However, the title of this chapter implies that public libraries are, in some way, the poor relation, at least far as far as lifelong learning goes. In some quarters this does appear to be the case. Despite library authorities' attempts to highlight the services they offer in relation to lifelong learning, and despite the fact that in the White Paper mentioned earlier it says:

> 'People need easier access to relevant opportunities if training is to be practicable and sufficiently attractive... Too much training is built round the institution, not the individual. Too often training seems like "going back to school" – not an attractive prospect for many adults' (Department for Employment 1992: 30).

Government departments, particularly the Employment Service, do not recognize the role of the public library as a provider of learning-based opportunities.

The research at the University of Brighton shows that job centres[3], in their *Gateway* role[4], do not recommend their clients use public libraries for their learning needs, preferring their own agencies. In fact, it is not that they only do not recommend the public library to their clients, they do not even acknowledge the existence of the public library as a provider of lifelong learning opportunities. Also, library authorities, in answer to our survey, often highlighted the fact that they do not get co-operation from job centres on information provision, so that resources in libraries are often stretched in order to duplicate resources held in job centres. Jobseekers themselves are also ignorant about library provision. All those surveyed said that if the library provided resources which would be of use to them they would use these resources, yet many were unaware of the services that were offered. On numerous occasions jobseekers said that they wished the job centre would tell them about what happens at public libraries. Ironically, perhaps, 70 per cent of those surveyed used public libraries regularly.

It can be seen, then, that the provision for lifelong learning which is made by public libraries is not utilized to its full potential. This begs the question: what is the role of the public library in this arena? Should it confine itself to a back-up role, filling gaps left by other agencies, or should it attempt to provide as much as finances allow and, therefore, duplicate what is being provided elsewhere?

It is a generally accepted fact that the public library has a role to play in the delivery of lifelong learning services. The Public Library Review, carried out by ASLIB for the Department of National Heritage[5] in 1995, states:

> 'We recommend that the government should consider the role of libraries in the context of information providers for employment opportunities. Expenditure on new agencies might be better directed to services jointly developed with public libraries, which clearly have the trust and patronage of the unemployed who are trying to find work' (ASLIB 1995: 4/39).

It is also clear, from the research at the University of Brighton, that jobseekers feel that the public library has a role to play in this arena. When asked what was the most important role of the public library – to provide a cultural heritage, to provide leisure resources, to educate its users, or to provide high-quality information its users – 68 per cent said that the most important role was to provide high-quality information and 70 per cent ranked the public library's educational role as second in importance.

There are two crucial factors in determining the role of the public library in lifelong learning, particularly in regard to jobseekers. The first is the attitude of Government agencies such as the Employment Service. With the support and co-operation of this agency and others like it, the public library can justify allocating extra resources to open learning and other initiatives. The major problem which the public library faces in delivery of lifelong learning initiatives is financial. Because of the ethos which surrounds the public library of 'free information for all' it cannot charge the rates that private sector organizations can and, therefore, is not able to provide the wealth and range of resources that these private sector bodies can. Until the public library can prioritize the provision of learning opportunities it will never be able to compete on an even footing with the private sector. Unfortunately, present statutory requirements are such that an ever-reducing budget for library services has to be spent in certain areas first, before extension services can be provided.

The second crucial factor in determining the public library's role is their own advertisement. Our research shows that 88 per cent of jobseekers do not think that the public library advertises itself and its services well enough. The public library cannot maximize the potential of their open learning centres without increasing their clientele, and the only way that this can happen is if more people who at present do not use the learning opportunities the library provides begin to make use of it. This will only happen if libraries find some way of advertising their services. Some library authorities have tried to do this, notably Sheffield[6], who took advertising space in the city centre to advertise the European Year of Lifelong Learning. This is particularly important since the University of Brighton research has shown that 93 per cent of those surveyed said that they would use public library services if they were advertised so that they knew what was on offer. Again, this determining factor is reliant on financial resources. In an age when public library authorities are finding it hard to provide statutory services with the budgets that are set for them the money for advertising, which is not even an extension service, is increasingly hard to find. Those who control the budgets for public libraries – local councillors – do not, in general, see advertising as a relevant expense from the public purse.

What can be done, in that case, to rectify this situation? It seems that, although central government tends to back public libraries in learning provision, agencies of government do not agree. The only way in which this hurdle can be overcome is for dialogue to be established between library authorities and the Employment Service. Some library authorities have already set up such dialogue which has led to very positive results and we recommend that more authorities attempt this. Another possible solution is partnership with private sector organizations. One area, taken from one of the pilot case studies of the research, where this has been put into practice is the St. John's Centre in Margate[7], part of the East Area of Kent Arts and Libraries. This is an open learning centre set up and funded by the library authority, the local TEC[8], and a private computer company. Since the library has, arguably, more visitors than most other institutions in the community, it is an ideal location for partnerships of this kind. 330,040,000 visits were made to public libraries in England in 1994–95. Figures like this show just how well used the public library is and demonstrate how ideal it is for the siting of open learning centres and the provision of learning opportunities.

The public library started life as an educational resource for the working classes in order that they might better themselves and, thus, improve the economy of the country. The public library is still excellently placed to continue this work and, in co-operation with government and private enterprise could be the focus for high-quality, high-use and highly successful learning opportunities at low cost to the user. This is the role which the public library must adopt for the twenty-first century.

New Library: The People's Network (Library and Information Commission 1997), commissioned by the Department for Culture, Media and Sport, confirms this shift in attitude with its proposal for the establishment of the UK Public Library Network. The report acknowledges that:

> 'Public libraries complement formal educational provision by providing a resource base and a platform for people of all ages to participate in lifelong learning' (Library and Information Commission 1997: 6).

The report proposes that libraries will form an integral part of the National Grid for Learning:

> 'As part of a return to work plan, skills development or reskilling for a different job, the UK Public Library Network will provide information and learning resources for independent study in a supported environment. It will also provide information on training and job opportunities' (Library and Information Commission 1997: 9).

A major multi-million pound injection of funding is proposed to create this national infrastructure which will confirm the public library's role at the heart of lifelong learning.

Notes

1. The Employment Service is an agency of the British Government, part of the Department for Education and Employment which is responsible for the running of job centres (q.v.).
2. Now the Department for Education and Employment.
3. Job centres, previously known as labour exchanges, are the offices of the Employment Service which jobseekers attend. They have a selection of vacancies on offer and those claiming Jobseeker's Allowance (the benefit for those out of work) have to attend fortnightly to sign on to the Unemployment Register. Benefits Agency (the government agency which assesses claims for benefits) staff are also now based in job centres.
4. The *Gateway* role of the job centre is an acceptance that job centres cannot provide all the information that their clients may need. In this role

they attempt to act as a gateway for information, referring clients to other bodies where necessary.
5. The Department of National Heritage (now the Department of Culture, Media and Sport) was a new department created in 1992 and is responsible for government policy on the arts, broadcasting, museums and galleries, the press, sport and recreation, heritage, public libraries and tourism.
6. Sheffield is a metropolitan council in the north-east of England, within South Yorkshire. It is based on the city of Sheffield, and has a population of around 503,000.
7. Margate is one of three major towns on the Isle of Thanet (the others being Ramsgate and Broadstairs), the most north-easterly point of Kent. Thanet has a population of around 123,000 and traditionally has a high level of unemployment, with much of the local employment being based on tourism, the railway (Margate and Ramsgate are the termini for the two major rail services from London through Kent) and the Port of Ramsgate.
8. TECs (Training and Enterprise Councils) are 'local employer-led strategic bodies, working in partnership to achieve sustainable economic growth ensuring increases in employment, prosperity and quality of life' (*The Training and Enterprise Directory* 1997: 40). They are formed by local people working for their community. There are 81 TECs in England and Wales and 22 LECs (Local Enterprise Councils), the Scottish equivalent.

References

ASLIB (1995) *Department of National Heritage Review of the Public Library Service in England and Wales. Final Report*, ASLIB, London.

Department of Education and Science (DES) (1978) *Libraries Choice*, HMSO, London.

Department of Employment (1992) *People, Jobs, and Opportunity*, Cm 1810. HMSO, London.

Kelly, T (1966) *Early Public Libraries*, Library Association, London.

Kelly, T (1977a) *Books for the people*, Andre Deutsch, London.

Kelly, T (1977b) *A History of Public Libraries in Great Britain: 1845–1975*, Library Association, London.

Library and Information Commission (1997) *New Library: The People's Network*, HMSO, London.

Minto, J (1932) *A History of the Public Library Movement in Great Britain and Ireland*, Library Association, London.

Murison, WJ (1988) *The Public Library: Its Origins, Purpose, and Significance* (3rd Edn), Clive Bingley, London.

Sumsion, J et al. (1996) *LISU Annual Library Statistics 1996*, Library and Information Statistics Unit, Loughborough.

Training and Enterprise Directory (1997) Kogan Page in association with the TEC National Council, London.

PART VI

LEARNING AND CHANGE AT WORK

Chapter 23

Beyond the Threshold:
Organizational Learning at the Edge

Paul Tosey and John Nugent

Introduction

Increasingly, organizations are viewed as contexts for lifelong learning. The 'learning organization' theme has been prominent since the late 1980s. Within this theme there has been much interest in the relationship between individual learning and organizational learning and change.

In this chapter we reflect on consulting experience (John Nugent (JN) is the consultant) within one company, 'Country Produce'. We have used the work of Fisher and Torbert (Torbert 1991; Fisher and Torbert 1991, 1995) both in the consulting practice and in this chapter's reflections. Of particular relevance are their concept of 'action inquiry' and their model of stages of managerial development, which correspond closely to adult developmental stages identified by, for example, Loevinger (Loevinger and Wessler 1978). JN has an in-depth knowledge of Torbert's work, based on postgraduate study, and has several years' experience of its practical application. Both authors find Torbert's models illuminating, but with limitations.

Our principal aim is to draw out some themes and characteristics of learning during an effort to pursue personal development and organizational change in tandem. On the basis of reflections on the case discussed in this chapter, we suggest that there may be a threshold in the propensity for

270 INTERNATIONAL PERSPECTIVES ON LIFELONG LEARNING

companies to become 'learning organizations'. We argue that this may be linked to individuals' ability to shift from a problem-solving approach to one of 'inquiring', in the sense of integrating systematic research with personal development.

The 'Country Produce' story

'Country Produce' was founded 25 years ago. The company is based in the Midlands, has 80–90 employees and makes foodstuffs which they sell to retail outlets and wholesalers. The current family has been in control for four years and Alan, the current CEO, took over responsibility for the business when Peter, the chairman, moved to a non-executive role. The business was declining rapidly and the company had acquired a blame culture. Now 'Country Produce' are addressing the need to improve bottom line results, at the same time as thinking about going to another factory. They also have a high staff turnover, and so aim to create a culture to which people want to belong.

Here we concentrate on Alan's personal development since JN started the consultancy in June 1996, and we indicate connections with organizational and business issues. When talking with JN initially about the company's purpose, Alan said, 'Everyone can make bloody ****, there's loads of them all over the country, so what are we here to do, then? It must be something for the local community. Jobs for the local community are not the whole of it. There is the possibility of creating a small organization that helps to transform people's lives.'

This showed JN that Alan was open to seeing business issues within a wider context, including a higher purpose for the organization. Building on this, and informed by his own interests in Fisher and Torbert's work, JN introduced the idea that if Alan was serious about organizational change, he might need to undergo personal transformation too. In terms of Fisher and Torbert's model of stages of managerial development (see Figure 23.1), JN perceived Alan to be in the transition from Achiever to Strategist (JN's own test results report him to be at the Strategist stage of development).

According to Fisher and Torbert (1991), this is a critical stage of learning and constitutes transformation. The Achiever is goal-focused and identifies closely with the success of the organization. It is a heroic stance, the positive aspect of which is its inspiring and enthusing quality. The Strategist frame, by contrast, involves 'learn(ing) as he or she prompts others to learn. It is a form of leadership that generates individual and organizational learning concurrently' (Fisher and Torbert 1995: 77).

The Strategist frame requires an integration of personal and organizational quality improvement through action inquiry. This means 'behaviour that is simultaneously inquiring and productive…that simultaneously learns about the developing situation, accomplishes whatever task appears to have priority, and invites a redefining of the task if necessary' (1995: 13). They regard this 'close-up focus on the thought and behaviour of the manager' (1995: xiii) as a missing dimension in strategies for change – such as, for example, Total Quality Management (TQM).

Action inquiry involves a shift in consciousness that enables managers and leaders to call upon transforming power. This 'is a rare, little understood type of power that invites mutuality, seeks contradiction and requires heightened awareness of the present. If…the chief executive officer…favour(s) quality improvement, but they use power in unilateral or otherwise manipulative ways, they will in fact generate resistance…' (1995: xv).

Table 23.1 *Governing frames at six successive developmental stages*

Stage	Name	Governing frame	Focus of awareness
1	Opportunist	Needs and interests rule impulses	Outside world, effects
2	Diplomat	Expectations rule interests	Socially expected behaviour
3	Technician	Internal craft logic rules expectations	Internal logic, thought
4	Achiever	System success in environment rules craft logic	Interplay of plan, practice and effect
5	Strategist	Principle rules system	Synthetic theory of system-environment development over time
6	Magician	Process (interplay of principle/action) awareness rules principle	Interplay of awareness, thought, action and outside world in Eternal Now

Source: Fisher and Torbert 1995: 61

Having checked his perception of Alan's developmental stage over time, and gained Alan's commitment to engage in this learning, JN negotiated to assist and intervene on three levels:

- one-to-one work with Alan
- helping to create a new top management team

- introducing quality improvement groups involving all levels of employee.

During his work with Alan, JN has noticed various types of shift. We present these here in the form of excerpts from JN's story of the consultancy.

Inquiring

At first Alan was intense, anxious and rather formal. Now I see his mask dropping. He has shifted from seeing business issues as to do with quality, 'out there', to being open to looking at his personal and spiritual development as well. He had a confrontational approach. Now he is finding more creative, inquiring ways to resolve conflicts, rather than swinging about on a pendulum – which, to me, indicates an earlier level than the Strategist. He knew the value of questions, but had not realized just how valuable they were. His willingness to listen is increasing and he is asking questions where in the past he would have been advocating a solution.

Alan is gaining new perspectives, for example through talking more to his wife, an acupuncturist, about the company. He has realized how acupuncture could relate to the business. As another example, about three sessions into our work, Alan dragged me out to the canal. He said 'I've just started doing this, I've never been out of my office, I didn't realize all this was here.' We were out in the country and he said, 'I can't believe I've not been taking time to experience what is around me.'

Being and doing

An important influence on Alan was *The Tao of Leadership* (Heider 1986). He started to think about the difference between being and doing. Having been highly identified with what he did, he began to realize that there might be another way of leading – from being highly active to being more of himself. This is a dichotomy that I have had to work through myself. For me the shift occurred when I integrated the personal and professional. The essence of the difference was that my professional mask fell away; it was no longer applicable.

A split between the personal and the professional can be stressful. I remember a person in another company who would say 'I'm completely different at work to how I am at home. I have to be like this because I'm in a male-dominated organization, and to do this I have to become a male. I couldn't be like this at home.' This person experienced ill health and, at that time, was disliked intensely by her subordinates – this type of split increases the possibility for negative projection. She has since changed the focus of her work from 'carrying out the organization's strategy no matter what' to developing an ethical strategy. This has helped her.

The shadow side

There is a shadow side to Alan, as there is to anyone. The shadow side is important because it indicates incongruity between purpose, strategy, operations, and outcomes. Only by raising the shadow side do people start to appreciate how, unconsciously, they are out of alignment.

One aspect of Alan's shadow is wanting to over-control. The pressure to see results and quick change has been difficult for him. He wanted to lead one of the collaborative inquiry teams and discovered that he may be over-parenting the team. He was called out of the meeting by an urgent phone call saying his daughter was ill. I was there in a facilitation role, and when Alan left the room the energy changed. Everyone became more animated – before, they had been quite passive. That was new feedback for Alan. When he came back we included it in the review.

He has also begun to find his perceptions of people being confronted. For example, he was saying 'we're going to have difficulty with the idea of Rose (the administrator) running the IT team'. Alan thought she had no experience of leading teams, only to find out that in her home life she had been leading groups and teams in her local community.

Metaphor and language

Another difference is Alan's use of metaphor. Achievers' metaphors do not always make good sense; it is more difficult to relate to them and build on them. Someone operating at the Strategist level uses metaphor in a different, subtler and more holistic way. While looking at the top team's developmental needs I asked them to think of natural metaphors to describe how they saw themselves. Alan said, 'Well, I'm on a yacht, and I'm on it myself, but I don't know everything about how to do this, so I'm having to learn all the different aspects; having to learn how to be a navigator, and how to trim the sails, and having to learn all these different things, while the sea is rolling around me.'

Alan has also started to use mythological ideas and apply them to visioning. I suggested using a story-telling process, which I have experienced in my previous company, rather than creating a mission statement. Alan came back to me on the phone, saying excitedly, 'I've just realized that we could create a fairytale, a "Country Produce" fairytale. We could get everyone involved in telling their part of the fairytale and we could get them to illustrate it, and we would have the "Country Produce" story in a kind of book which combines both the vision, the past and the present.'

The management team and the organization

There are significant parallel processes complementing, and complemented by, Alan's personal transformation. The management team is operating in a collaborative, inquiring mode. This does not mean that everyone is at the Strategist stage, indeed Keith and Dave (the other members of the top team) appear to be at the Technician/Achiever transition. We all (including myself) have personal development or learning contracts with each other, and we work on our personal and spiritual development at the same time as on the business.

As an example of this, Dave's learning contract was to facilitate the development of a marketing strategy. He had not written it, was avoiding it and wanted to withdraw from the learning set. He told the group this, and also that he was feeling vulnerable. In response, Alan and Keith said how much they would miss him and asked what they could do to help him with the workload. This task was then reframed into something he already was doing, not something new. His pattern was to exclude himself, but his vulnerability elicited the first overt expression of love within the group and created the context for Dave to stay. Being confronted by the group with love brought Dave into conflict with his reactive strategy. If he had continued with his old perspective then his misalignment with the organizational purpose would have become wider, yet the alignment came through becoming more in touch with his personal vision than with the organizational.

We have introduced the same action learning approach through quality groups in the organization. These use both quantitative research and systematic qualitative inquiry. Alan's ability to inquire has been vital for the effectiveness of these teams. It is easy in the production environment to say 'when I've got all this work on, how can I justify spending time on my learning?' Alan emphasized that, for the work the team needed to do and for the time set aside, quality improvement was a higher priority than production. Whenever there is feedback that 'we haven't been able to do this because we haven't had time,' Alan inquires into what's stopping it. They then work on those issues. Alan is therefore modelling inquiry through his managerial actions.

Themes and issues

The intention of the work in 'Country Produce' is to introduce action inquiry into a production-oriented environment. This works through developing an interplay of purpose, process and task, such that learning is co-created rather than residing in individuals. The change process appears to have been relatively organic and non-programmed. There has been some intentional change, but it has not been recipe-driven. A wider or higher purpose has been defined, but not from any sense of obligation to produce a mission statement.

What themes of learning are apparent so far in JN's account of his work with Alan and 'Country Produce'? We believe the following are noteworthy.

From dichotomy to integration

The overriding theme is of a movement from dichotomy towards integration. This theme is recognized not only by Fisher and Torbert but, for example, by Charles Hampden-Turner (Hampden-Turner 1990) and Abraham Maslow (Frick 1971). In 'Country Produce' some important dimensions of integration seemed to be:

- *The personal and professional* Alan is more able to relate business to home life, to perceive similar patterns in his experience and to let go more of the 'professional mask' that JN experienced initially. Dave's experience of being vulnerable in the management team has enabled him to bring more of himself into the professional arena.
- *Being and doing* From a very active management style, Alan is seeing himself less as the cause than as an influence able to help others place themselves 'at cause'.
- *Learning and working* Alan has adopted an inquiring style in which he is curious about, and able to allow, others' different perspectives and abilities. He is modelling and supporting that style, especially with the message that learning is priority work.
- *The local and the general* Connections are appreciated between immediate, local task issues and wider, systemic and environmental concerns. The shop-floor quality group has shown a remarkable capacity for systemic awareness by inquiring into the source of problems, and not remaining fixated on solutions.
- *Conscious and unconscious* Alan now has greater access to his emotional, intuitive capabilities. In particular JN is helping Alan to attend to his 'shadow side' – the apparently negative, potent side of his style which, if it were to remain split or denied, could well prove destructive.

Conceptual implications

What are the implications of this consulting experience for our understanding of, and hypotheses about, learning and transformation? The usage of 'transformation' is wide and varied, and currently seems to be a buzzword. Organizational transformation, a term first coined by Adams (1984), is an increasingly common label. For example, the fourth edition of a classic book on organizational development has become entitled *Organizational Development and Transformation*, subtitled *Managing Effective Change* (French et al. 1994). French *et al.* do define what they mean by transformation. A critical survey of usage seems desirable, but there is insufficient space here.

We suggest that the transformation 'genre' at the moment is strongly Achiever-based, in Fisher and Torbert's terms. The consequence of an Achiever-based perspective on organizational learning is that the need for personal transformation is likely to be overlooked. Strategies for change are interpreted from, and mediated by, the developmental frame. If Fisher and Torbert's research into the distribution of stages of development amongst the managerial population is accepted, in most cases strategies for change are used from a Technician perspective. From a Technician frame, Total Quality Management (TQM) may become a box-ticking control system. TQM can be operated from Strategist's perspective, an Achiever perspective, or any other; but prior to the Strategist phase, implementers are unlikely to perceive the need to transform themselves.

Reflections on Fisher and Torbert's model

Fisher and Torbert exemplify Strategist behaviours (for example Fisher and Torbert 1991) but have not yet, to our knowledge, examined examples over time and in depth. Nor do they appear to have looked in detail at how the transition from Achiever to Strategist can happen. We agree broadly with Fisher and Torbert's distinctions between the Achiever and Strategist stages but we find them less clear on what is being integrated. It seems that they underemphasize, or over-rationalize, the emotional processes and the significance of the shadow side. We wonder, with reference to the example of Dave's learning contract, about the need for love to be more explicitly in the framework.

Fisher and Torbert (1995) argue that successful corporate transformation is likely to be possible only where sufficient numbers of senior managers have experienced an appropriate degree of personal transformation. There is some counter-evidence from 'Country Produce', where a quality improvement team seemed able to inquire through a Strategist frame. It does seem to us to be important for the consultant to be in a place of awareness, able to bring an alternative, inquiring paradigm to the client's attention and able to model action inquiry for them – as, in 'Country Produce', JN's own story was a guide for Alan.

We would argue for a distinction between stage of development (eg as measured by Loevinger's scale) and the characteristic awareness associated with stage. From this optimistic place, we hold the possibility that people measured at any stage of development can enact action inquiry, given the right context. The issue may be one of facilitation and support to create the right conditions, rather than one of 'personality'. Even so, we would caution against an Achiever-based usage of this possibility.

Critical reflection on this research

This chapter reflects on a single case study and utilizes principally the same conceptual framework that guided the consultancy. There are difficulties with relying on the practitioner's perspective for an account of a change intervention. The literature shows the tendency to produce 'success stories' (Mirvis and Berg 1977). We have challenged ourselves, for example, about the possibility of JN's projective identification with Alan, and the extent to which his account would be recognisable to the clients or consistent with their non-professional accounts. We have sought Alan's views and he (clearly with his own vested interests) endorses the essence and pattern of this presentation. However, the claims that Alan and 'Country Produce' are showing signs of integration undoubtedly merit challenge and further research that explores other participants' perspectives (which is in progress). Our main purpose here is to identify some characteristics of this type of learning, not to present a definitive analysis of the organizational change process in 'Country Produce'.

Conclusions

First, we support Fisher and Torbert's view that an Achiever-based perspective on learning is likely to be inadequate for the 'transformational' challenges perceived today. To the extent that models and programmes designed to promote 'organizational learning' are limited to that stage of development, we suggest that individuals and organizations are likely to experience a learning 'threshold'. Achiever-based learning does not address integration on dimensions such as those we have set out above, which therefore are likely to continue to be experienced as splits. The organizational paradigm seems unlikely to change if we do not change our learning paradigm (for example, Hawkins 1994).

Second, illustrations from 'Country Produce' indicate the type of learning needs raised at this threshold, and the type of learning that may be appropriate. Our tentative list of dimensions of integration seems largely consistent with Fisher and Torbert's work. Our contribution is to look in more detail at this learning, and to emphasize body-mind integration in the Strategist's development.

Third, we raise the hypothesis that action inquiry – as a mode of operating that enables such integration – is not confined to those who would be deemed to have reached the Strategist stage of development. We also emphasize that action inquiry, like every other strategy for organizational change, is mediated and altered by the frame from which it is used.

Fourth, we advocate greater discrimination in the use of the concept 'transformation', especially in the current climate of popularity. Fisher and Torbert's is not the only model available for this type of learning, and there is a need for a critical comparison of relevant sources and frameworks. Our bias is towards models that incorporate a transpersonal or spiritual perspective and we caution against transformation being seen as some necessarily benign process, just as spirituality can sometimes be perceived as wholly 'a good thing'. As indicated above, transformation is likely to involve turbulence for both individual and organization, inviting deep questioning of self, deeply ingrained assumptions, business goals and ethics, and more.

Finally, we suggest that this type of study has important implications for the theme of lifelong leaning. To highlight just two:

- We note that organizations have become a highly significant context for learning. There is much curiosity in this field about the relationship between individual and collective learning, and in methods for promoting collective learning. To the extent that lifelong learning is intended to yield direct benefits for organizations, communities and society as a whole (as opposed to incidental benefits arising from the sheer quantity of individual learning taking place), we suggest that organizations such as 'Country Produce' represent important sources of emergent ideas and research.
- The work of authors such as Fisher and Torbert not only addresses the individual and the collective aspects of learning but also encompasses spiritual development alongside (for example) skills acquisition. We believe this to be a legitimate and important focus within the field of lifelong learning.

Note

We thank Alan of 'Country Produce' for his co-operation and support in the writing of this chapter. The authors are wholly responsible for the views expressed.

References

Adams, J (Ed.) (1984) *Transforming Work*, Miles River Press, Virginia.

Dehler, GE and Welsh, M (1994) 'Spirituality and Organizational Transformation', in *Journal of Managerial Psychology*, 9, 6, 17–26.

Fisher, D and Torbert, WR (1991) 'Transforming Managerial Practice: Beyond the Achiever Stage', in RW Woodman and WA Pasmore (Eds) *Research in Organizational Change and Development (Volume 5)*: 143–173, JAI Press Inc, Greenwich CT.

Fisher, D and Torbert, WR (1995) *Personal and Organizational Transformation*, McGraw-Hill, London.

French, WL, Bell, CH and ZAWACKI, RA (Eds) (1994) *Organization Development and Transformation* (4th Edn), Irwin, Burr Ridge, Illinois.

Frick, WB (1971) *Humanistic Psychology: Interviews with Maslow, Murphy and Rogers*, Charles E. Merrill Publishing Company, Columbus, Ohio.

Hampden-Turner, C (1990) *Charting the Corporate Mind*, Blackwell, Oxford.

Hawkins, P (1994) 'The Changing View of Learning', in J Burgoyne, M Pedler and T Boydell (Eds) (1994) *Towards the Learning Company*, McGraw-Hill, London.

Heider, J (1986) *The Tao of Leadership*, Wildwood House, Aldershot.

Loevinger, J and Wessler, E (1978) *Measuring Ego Development, Vols 1 & 2*, Jossey-Bass, San Francisco.

Mirvis, P and Berg, D (1977) *Failures in Organization Development and Change: Cases and Essays for Learning*, John Wiley, New York.

Torbert, WR (1991) *The Power of Balance*, Sage, Newbury Park, California.

Chapter 24

Creating Contingency Workers:
A Critical Study of the Learning Organization

Fred M Schied, Sharon L Howell, Vicki K Carter and Judith A Preston

Proponents of the learning organization have argued that this concept was developed to help organizations meet the competitive demands of the global market-place and the new information age (Senge 1990, Watkins and Marsick 1993). Although this corporate rhetoric can be persuasive, it can also be problematic. Some troubling facets of the learning organization involve the unquestioned acceptance of the demands of a global economy, which equates productivity with model employees and 'smart' workers (Kincheloe 1995). As Butler asserts:

> [D]iscourses of learning, and especially learning for work, are colonized by the dominant discourse of globalization and its discursive practices associated with global competitiveness and late capitalism. Such a stance calls into question the discursive interconnections between globalization, the changing nature, organization, management and distribution of work (and workers) and the knowledge practices and pedagogies associated with learning/work' (1998: 70).

Butler (1998) also discusses how discourse affects worker subjectivity and the complicity of learning organization rhetoric in creating compliant, flexible workers. This chapter examines the relationship between adult education and the learning organization. It addresses issues of agency, briefly decodes some of the language of the learning organization and suggests that corporations typically cited in the literature as exemplary learning organizations have used this construct as means drastically to reduce labour costs.

The learning organization and adult education

In a recent paper, Fenwick asks: 'To what ends are professional pedagogues posturing as engineers of "learning organizations" ... What kinds of knowledge are valued ... and what kinds are ignored? ... Whose discourse predominates? What sorts of human selves are being moulded or repressed by organizational "learning" cultures' (1996: 119)? These are questions that often go unasked and unanswered in learning organization literature in the United States. The corporate discourse on the learning organization places great emphasis on the role of the individual in the learning process. With the turmoil and constant change experienced by organizations in the global market-place, learning purportedly supports incrementally improved performance and seeks to shape workers who are flexible and adaptable in response to uncertainty. A central assumption undergirding the conceptual basis of learning organizations includes viewing learning as a means to improve future organizational performance.

Another key assumption is seeing learning as a way to keep organizations in alignment with their environment as a mechanism for survival and growth. Thus from this perspective learning is directly connected to productivity. As Zuboff illustrates:

> 'Learning is no longer a separate activity that occurs either before one enters the workplace or in remote classroom settings. Nor is it an activity preserved for a managerial group. *The behaviours that define learning and the behaviours that define being productive are one and the same* [emphasis added]. Learning is not something that requires time out from being engaged in productive activity, learning is the heart of productive activity. To put it simply, learning is the new form of labour' (1988, 395).

Dilworth (1995) takes this one step further when he compares the learning organization to DNA. Much like a genetic code, learning is not an external activity but rather is embedded in everyday work activity through the internalized values and beliefs that govern team and individual behaviour.

These ideas mesh easily into adult education concepts of self-directed learning, continuous learning and lifelong learning. Lifelong learning has long been an important tenant in adult education. Similarly, concepts such as continuous learning for continuous improvement easily fit into the transformative learning model of the learning organization. The organization relies on individuals willingly taking charge of the process of learning and personal mastery for effective self-management. In return, the organization puts its trust in the learner and the value of the learning process (Aubrey and Cohen 1995). Watkins and Marsick, in two of their books on workplace learning (Marsick and Watkins 1990, 1993), write from the perspective of the adult educator, emphasizing management's role, especially upper-level management, as a key element in building a learning organization. Marsick and Watkins (1990) identify generic skills needed by managers, such as strategic thinking for visioning, goal-setting, identifying ideas of others, understanding the cascading effect of decisions and understanding factors that affect company planning. However, these notions co-opt the very idea of empowerment and learning because there is no consideration of power or different interests. The current concept of learning organizations fails to locate the organization within broader social and economic systems, instead suggesting that all would be for the best if only people co-operated in identifying common visions that are in accord with the views of management (Brown 1996). This chapter calls into question the claim that learning organizations empower workers and suggests that this concept serves to first construct and then sculpt a docile and flexible workforce.

Questions of boundaries and agency within learning organizations

Although the goals of a learning organization encompass building worker responsiveness and resiliency, many of its precepts are unclear. For example, Fenwick (1996) examines the workplace learning experiences of eighteen women over the course of their adult life. Learning, for the women in this study, is a reflective process, continually circling back and creating new understandings. While the learning organization literature places great emphasis on verbalized forms of reflection, dialogue and performance outcomes, the women in this study place learning within a more private reflection and self-dialogue that is not possible within the timed boundaries of the workplace. 'Systematic reflection through talking or articulating perspectives was viewed as laboriously slow, inadequate for understanding, and often structured meanings artificially' (1996: 117). As a result of her inquiry, Fenwick questions the role of adult educators within the corporate discourse of organizational learning and its use of critical reflection, problem-framing and error detection which perpetuate the focus on the deficit of the individual.

'What seems [to be] missing from the literature is an appreciation of how the circles of people's lives and learning cross between family, work, household duty, personal relationships, play and spirituality ... This orientation is not usually congruent with organizational visions, missions and continuous learning initiatives' (1996: 119).

Workplace learning focuses on systems thinking, culture and group learning from a global perspective, at the expense of how this affects the lived worlds of individuals. 'The individual is always striving (therefore always in deficit) to be more, better, faster' (Fenwick 1996: 119).

Brooks (1992) points out that the relationships between individual learning and organizational transformation are unknown. On the basis of a qualitative study, Brooks concludes that individuals, not teams, work to transform organizations. Similarly, the group Brooks identifies as active change agents are described by Hughes and Conner (1989) as opportunity-oriented, seeing positive response to change as an advantage and a way to exploit a situation. These opportunity-oriented people tend to be focused, pliable, self-assured and risk-taking, proactively delving into change and developing structures to manage ambiguity. These studies correlate with Butler's (1998) description of workers willing to enter into the discursive community of workplace learning as inscribed subjects.

Other questions about learning organizations involve how they are developed, how they are managed and how to measure them. For example, has the metamorphosis into a learning organization taken place once individuals at all levels have been transformed? Does learning among individuals, teams, processes and the total system occur concurrently? How does this learning occur? Is it based on experiential or adaptive learning or is it anticipatory and innovative? If the process is concurrent, how is work distinguished from learning – when does one end and the other begin? And how is learning measured? Is it measured by an increase in profit? Does a learning organization exist – is its learning valid? – if the whole organization has not mastered team learning, shared visions, mental models, personal mastery, and systems thinking.

Learning organization discontinuities: three brief corporate examples

Whirlpool, Motorola and General Electric are cited in human resource development literature as examples of learning and transformation within learning organization models (Marquardt 1996, Marquardt and Reynolds 1994, Watkins and Marsick 1993). In 1989, when Whirlpool first expanded outside the United States and Canada, CEO David Whitwam initiated annual Worldwide Leadership Conferences with the goal of developing a unifying corporate vision and enabling a culturally diverse group to learn together to produce and market home appliances in the most efficient way possible (Marquardt 1996, Watkins and Marsick 1993). This conference established the vision of global learning and a values statement that included a promise to '...pursue our business with honour, fairness and respect for both the individual and the public at large ... ever mindful that there is no right way to do a wrong thing...' and to '...serve responsibly as members of all communities in which we live and work, respecting cultural distinctions throughout the world. We will preserve the environment, prudently utilize natural resources and maintain all property we are privileged to use' (Marquardt 1996: 116). However, starting in the 1950s, as Whirlpool was growing first nationally and then globally, the corporation was moving their manufacturing operations first south and then overseas, in search of cheaper non-unionized labour. Today, Whirlpool has no manufacturing plants in Benton Harbor, Michigan, the location of its original plants and still the current location of its world headquarters and training centre. This pattern of production migration to lower labour-cost regions parallels Detroit, Chicago and numerous other large urban areas across the United States.

Motorola prominently identifies itself as a model of organizational responsiveness to cultural differences, with training delivered in several languages. According to the director of training and development: 'Motorola believes that sensitivity to cultural, religious, political and social differences of our worker population is of paramount interest' (Marquardt and Reynolds 1994: 219). However, underlying this move into more culturally diverse locations is the search for cheaper labour. Motorola hires primarily young single women for its assembly lines. According to the plant manager in Malaysia: 'We had to change the culture because the Malay home does not encourage women to speak out ... We use positive reinforcement, just like you would work with schoolchildren' (Greider 1997: 82–83). Yet, in contrast, many companies deliberately hire young women for 'the sense of discipline that women have acquired through subjection to patriarchal domination in the household' (1997: 98).

General Electric has cut its workforce by 25 per cent and closed 50 plants in the United States. Many of the lay-offs were among highly skilled, professional and white-collar workers, for example engineers and electricians. Yet at the same time the corporation strongly advocated increased government support for better education and more funding for job training programmes. According to a GE spokesperson: 'Our industrial economy ... is generating more jobs than we have people with skills to fill them' (Greider 1993: 344).

However, where, when and how these new high-skilled positions would occur is not specified.

Towards decoding the language of the learning organization

In the face of rapid technological change and increasing global competition, management literature of the 1980s and 1990s co-opts the language of critical theory. Specifically the learning organization literature includes references to intuition and the telling of stories, the need to understand connecting patterns and relationships as well as system archetypes, the involvement of employees at all levels as active producers of knowledge, the collective nature of thought, generative learning and creative tension, and critical reflection (Senge 1990, Watkins and Marsick 1993). While much of the language of the learning organization appears to embrace such concepts as empowerment, participation, trust, collaboration and teams, these concepts are often used by corporations and institutions to regain control of the workplace while taking advantage of increased input from workers. The single-minded focus of corporate management is on the organization's ability to survive and profit within the global market-place, while ignoring the increasing levels of poverty and suffering at the one extreme and the massive accumulation of wealth by the few at the other extreme. People become human resources, another economic commodity to be combined with other forms of capital to produce increased wealth for owners and shareholders. Social and ethical issues are rarely a part of the discourse; a commitment to social responsibility, freedom and human dignity is largely ignored.

Concepts such as quality, collaboration, teamwork and empowerment which frame the learning organization often come into direct conflict with the strategic initiatives of most organizations. Not only do these programmes conflict with traditional hierarchical and linear models of management, but they also clash with the economic model of firms seeking to maximize shareholder wealth, emphasizing individual self-interest, placing a high priority on individualism and accountability, and keeping power in the hands of the few at the top (Grant *et al.* 1994). Groups excluded by the organization at large also are excluded on teams. Moreover, failure of teams within organizations is blamed on skill deficits of individual team members. A focus on individual team members as problems assumes a fixed definition of success based on set standards (Schied *et al.* 1997). This deficit model places blame on the individual and fails to take into account alternate forms of knowledge. And so, there are conflicting messages within organizations: '…the discourses and organizational structures and policies about competitive individualism versus co-operation, short-term financial returns versus quality improvement, and control and accountability versus participation and risk-taking' (Brooks 1995: 43–44).

Moreover, learning organization literature is in part based on increased critical reflection by workers. For example, Marsick (1987) recommends a paradigm shift from the cause-effect relationships supported by logical-positivism to a paradigm which supports understanding multiple viewpoints and analysing taken for granted norms and rules within the organization.

> 'The organization provides a clear picture of its perception of desired outcomes, but training is not a lock-step process inculcating these predefined objectives. Individuals are encouraged to develop a habit of reflectivity in both formal and informal learning modes in which ... they continually probe their experience to determine why they are or are not effective and how they can learn to become so' (1987: 24).

Hart (1992) points out the paradigm shift proposed by Marsick is missing any ties to the larger social, economic and political issues. Like other learning organization proponents, Marsick uses the vocabulary of critical reflection, participation and empowerment which actually remains embedded in traditional forms of hierarchy. In the United States, economic growth and increased productivity remain the unquestioned norm for corporations, while economic decline is owned by the worker as an individual deficit. Individuals and teams are directed to learn why they are ineffective and take corrective action. According to Hart (1992), the ideal worker is a self-sufficient nomad, prepared for the instability of constant change, ever flexible with low expectations for pay, job security and working conditions. Workers in different locations within the United States and internationally are pitted against each other because the goal of the organization is to find the cheapest labour possible.

Using the advances in technology and communications, corporate leadership no longer needs multiple layers of intermediaries to pass information up and down the organizational structure. This levelling of the organization pushes responsibility and control lower in the organization, which in turn requires a particular kind of worker: one who learns and adapts quickly and communicates effectively. According to Gee *et al.* (1996) this leads to the paradox of needing empowered workers who '...will throw themselves heart and soul into the work of the company ... workers must be "eager to stay", but also "ready to leave" ... the new capitalism is now quite open about the need to socialize people into "communities of practice" that position people to be certain kinds of people' (1996: 19–21). Corporate discourse for the new worker involves making meanings from words which are very compelling but also carefully coded by the organization. Perfection becomes the standard and change is the normal way of life. Knowledge refers to '...the knowledge it takes to innovate, design, efficiently produce, market and transform products and services as symbols of identity and lifestyle in a high-risk world' (1996: 28). Empowerment, trust, collaboration, teams, self-directed learning and quality, among other words, are all used to mould workers to the desired form. This discourse builds a totalizing set of values and practices which blur the division between the public and private self. While purporting to place trust in workers, giving them real control over their work, rarely are workers allowed '...to assess and (re)frame the goals of the organization or to generate a more powerful role for themselves in decision-making processes...' for example in decisions relating to downsizing and moving production to another location (1996: 35). Job knowledge no longer becomes the central point of training, but rather the shaping of attitudes and beliefs to match the vision and goals of the organization.

> '...the fast-capitalist literature is quite open about the fact that worker participation and worker empowerment in the culture and values of a new-capitalist business are ultimately a business strategy for competitive success and, as such, constitute an overt form of hegemony in favour of the leaders and major stakeholders in the business ... the paradox ... is that this same literature claims that new-capitalist businesses need and want workers who are critical and who can think for themselves' (Gee et al. 1996: 102).

Participatory initiatives are powerful weapons in the hands of management but may also create a kind of paradox 'where loyalty, commitment and critical thinking, as well as allegiance to "core values", are at bottom economic strategies for the business's benefit' (Gee et al. 1996: 103). However, real learning cannot occur and workers cannot learn to use critical thinking skills without questioning and/or researching assumptions (Kincheloe 1995). Consequently, these initiatives may actually create possible sites of learning that can be turned in favour of workers. There is the opportunity to find new meanings for quality, empowered, committed, participation, trust, collaboration and teams. The ability of workers to increase their skills on the job builds confidence in their ability to take control of their lives and their work. In practice, however, workers too often underestimate the amount of control that is built into the formation of teams and the boundaries within which their work is done (Brooks 1994, Gee et al. 1996, Kincheloe 1995, Wells 1987).

Conclusions

Many organizations have undergone extensive restructuring in an attempt to remain competitive in the fast-changing global market. The result is organizations utilizing the cheapest labour available. Efficiency still means '...the maximum yield that could be produced in the shortest time, expending the least amount of energy, labour and capital...' (Rifkin 1995: 49). Multinational corporations, such as Whirlpool, General Electric and Motorola, are still reducing the number of full-time workers employed in the United States. 'Increasingly they are relying on cheaper ... leased or temporary – "even use and throwaway" – workers' (Rothwell and Kazanas 1994: 28). Yet, at the same time, workers are expected to take more responsibility for their own lives, careers and job changes. Two recent articles in *Newsweek* speak to the growing fear and insecurity created by the large number of lay-offs which are affecting workers at all levels of organizations (Samuelson 1996, Sloan 1996). Sloan negatively characterizes what he terms 'in-your face capitalism' as follows:

> 'There's something different in the air these days when it comes to people's jobs ... You lose your job, your ex-employer's stock price rises, the CEO gets a fat raise. Something is just plain wrong when stock prices keep rising on Wall Street while Main Street is littered with the bodies of workers discarded by big companies...' (1996: 44).

A close look at learning organization literature, with its rhetoric of trust and pledges of 'win-win', when contrasted with actions actually taken by many organizations defines a significant discontinuity between what is espoused and what really happens. Butler's study reveals the effect of '...managerial colonizing of learning, and restricting learning opportunities, that illustrates the illusory nature of depictions of shared loyalty, mutuality and trust between managers and workers...' implicating these practices in '...the production of capitulated corporate subjects' (1997: 67).

Efforts expended in learning, in being flexible, in taking on additional responsibility and self-management go unrewarded in a contemporary capitalist economy. Business and industry demands more of workers but compensates less. In the name of learning, companies create flexible workers by requiring them to be co-operative as well as responsible for quality, efficiency, teamwork, documentation of job processes and production of new knowledge. In some cases, workers give up hard-earned labour rights in exchange for hope and the expectation of keeping their jobs when often these very acts result in management acquiring worker expertise and worker diagnoses of work problems, closely followed by outsourcing, downsizing and plant closings. The learning organization's maxims of flexibility and trust fit in with management's promises and goals of organizational viability and profitability, but are seldom actualized as outcomes which ultimately optimize the well-being of workers.

References

Aubrey, R and Cohen, P (1995) *Working Wisdom: Timeless Skills and Vanguard Strategies for Learning Organizations*, Jossey-Bass, San Francisco.
Brooks, A (1992) 'Building Learning Organizations: The Individual-Culture Interaction', *Human Resource Development Quarterly*, 3, 4, 323–335.
Brooks, A (1994) 'Power and the Production of Knowledge: Collective Team Learning in Work Organizations', *Human Resource Development Quarterly*, 5, 3, 213–235.
Brooks, A (1995) 'The Myth of Self-Directed Work Teams and the Ineffectiveness of Team Effectiveness Training: An Argument with Special Reference to Teams that Produce Knowledge,' in *Proceedings of the 36th Annual Adult Education Research Conference*: 41–47, University of Alberta, Edmonton, Canada.
Brown, D (1996) 'The "Essences" of the Fifth Discipline: or Where does Senge Stand to View the World?', *Systems Research*, 13, 2, 91–107.
Butler, E (1998) 'Persuasive Discourses: Learning and the Production of Working Subjects in a Post Industrial Era,' in *Proceedings of the Lifelong Learning: Reality, Rhetoric & Public Policy Conference*: 63–69, University of Surrey, Guildford, England.
Dilworth, R (1995) 'The DNA of the Learning Organization', in S Chawla and J Renesch (Eds) *Learning Organizations: Developing Cultures for Tomorrow's Workplace*: 243–256, Productivity Press, Portland, OR.
Fenwick, T (1996) 'Women's Continuous Learning in the Workplace' in *Proceedings of the 37th Annual Adult Education Research Conference*: 114–120, University of South Florida, Tampa.
Gee, J, Hull, G and Lankshear, C (1996) *The New Work Order: Behind the Language of the New Capitalism*, Westview Press, Boulder, CO.
Grant, R, Shani, R and Krishnan, R (1994) 'TQM's Challenge to Management Theory and Practice', *Sloan Management Review*, 35, 2, 25–35.
Greider, W (1993) *Who Will Tell the People: The Betrayal of American Democracy*, Simon & Schuster, New York.
Greider, W (1997) *One World, Ready or Not: The Manic Logic of Global Capitalism*, Simon & Schuster, New York.
Hart, M (1992) *Working and Educating for Life: Feminist and International Perspectives on Adult Education*, Routledge, New York.
Hughes, K and Conner, D (Eds) (1989) *Managing Change in Higher Education, Preparing for the 21st Century*, College and University Personnel Association, Washington, DC.
Kincheloe, J (1995) *Toil and Trouble: Good Work, Smart Workers, and the Integration of Academic and Vocational Education*, Peter Lang, New York.
Marquardt, M (1996) *Building the Learning Organization: A Systems Approach to Quantum Improvement and Global Success*, McGraw Hill, New York.

Marquardt, M and Reynolds, A (1994) *The Global Learning Organization*, Irwin Professional Publishing, Burr Ridge, IL.

Marsick, V (1987) 'New Paradigms for Learning in the Workplace', in V Marsick (Ed.) *Learning in the Workplace*, Croom Helm, London.

Marsick, V and Watkins, K (1990) *Informal and Incidental Learning in the Workplace*, Routledge, New York.

Rifkin, J (1995) *The End of Work: the Decline of the Global Labor Force and the Dawn of the Post-Market Era*, G P Putnam's Sons, New York.

Rothwell, W and Kazanas, H (1994) *Improving On-the-job Training: How to Establish and Operate a Comprehensive OJT program*, Jossey-Bass, San Francisco.

Samuelson, R (1996) 'Are Workers Disposable?', *Newsweek*, CXXVII, 7, 47.

Schied, F, Carter, V, Preston, J and Howell, S (1997) 'Knowledge as Quality Non-Conformance: A Critical Case Study of ISO9000 and Adult Education in the Workplace', in *Proceedings of the 37th Annual Adult Education Research Conference*, Oklahoma State University, Stillwater, OK.

Senge, P (1990) *The Fifth Discipline: The Art and Practice of the Learning Organization*, Doubleday, New York.

Sloan, A (1996) 'The Hit Men', *Newsweek*, CXXVII, 9, 44–48.

Watkins, K and Marsick, V (1993) *Sculpting the Learning Organization: Lessons in the Art and Science of Systemic Change*, Jossey-Bass, San Francisco.

Wells, D (1987) *Empty Promises: Quality of Working Life Programs and the Labor Movement*, Monthly Review Press, New York.

Zuboff, S (1988) *In the Age of the Smart Machine: The Future of Work and Power*, Basic Books, New York.

Chapter 25

Consultative and Learning Approaches
In the Context of Organizational Process Innovations

Annikki Jarvinen

Introduction

In the future, a great part of an adult's lifelong learning during working life will take place within organizational work processes. Training will be integrated with the development of employees' qualifications and work and of the organization itself. We therefore prefer to speak of organizing learning inside the workplace. The nature of adult educators' work as facilitators of employees' lifelong learning and of organizational learning processes will also become more consultative.

In different countries around the world there is much discussion of successful enterprises' lines of development in relation to so-called 'global good practices'. This chapter assumes that these lines of development form the context for adult educators' activities. The approach is twofold: on the one hand, how new organizational forms shape the organization of learning; and, on the other hand, how the new approaches to lifelong adult learning shape changes in organizational processes.

Organizational science researchers working on enterprise 'good practice' tend to focus on such constructs as 'lean production' and 'business process re-engineering' (BPR). Both constructs have been debated, but in the recent years a generally accepted view has emerged. In the future, competitive enterprises will share the following features.

- The enterprise environment will change more rapidly.
- The functional division of labour will be replaced by multifunctional process teams, flexible units and production workshops.
- Typical enterprises will exchange knowledge with other firms and co-operate with them using information networks.
- The management and accumulation of knowledge and expertise will become central competitive factors.

This view has been criticized as mere rhetoric, because workplace reality is far from the ideal. Organizational changes will be necessary, but the EU Commission's *Green Paper on Innovation* (1995), for instance, points out that the scarcity of organizational innovation is a particular weakness of European innovation systems. In Finland, one sustainable solution for the structural problems in working life is to develop a national innovation system to utilize and develop staff know-how and innovative forces in workplaces. This is why the Finnish National Workplace Development Programme (1996; Alasoini 1996), proposed by a tripartite Ministry of Labour expert group, was launched in 1996. The focus is to change operational procedures in enterprises. Many different aspects are covered, for instance: learning new professional skills; learning new working methods and the use of new tools; establishing team and network activities; and reforming organizational cultures. How learning can be organized in these different aspects is of central significance.

In this chapter we first analyse two approaches considered fruitful for organizing learning during organizational innovations. The analysis is followed by a discussion of the qualifications required by adult educators and consultants in these new work processes. In conclusion, some preliminary findings of a case study are presented.

Two approaches for organizational learning

Nonaka (1994) claims that organizational knowledge is created through a continuous dialogue between tacit and explicit knowledge. While new knowledge is developed by individuals, organizations play a critical role in articulating and amplifying it. Boland and Tenkasi (1995) argue that producing the knowledge to create innovative products and processes in firms – which consist of multiple communities with specialized expertise – requires the ability to make strong perspectives within a community, as well as the ability to take account of others' perspectives. This section presents the main constructs of both Nonaka's and Boland and Tenkasi's approaches to organizational learning.

According to Nonaka, the dialogue between tacit and explicit knowledge postulates four different modes of knowledge conversion:

1. from tacit knowledge to tacit knowledge (socialization)
2. from explicit knowledge to explicit knowledge (combination)
3. from tacit knowledge to explicit knowledge (externalization)
4. from explicit knowledge to tacit knowledge (internalization).

Socialization as the mode of knowledge conversion enables individuals to acquire tacit knowledge through interaction. The key to acquiring tacit knowledge is experience. Without some form of shared experience, it is extremely difficult for people to share each others' thinking processes. The combination mode involves the use of social processes to combine the different bodies of explicit knowledge held by individuals. Individuals exchange and combine knowledge through such mechanisms as meetings and telephone conversations. The internalization mode, according to Nonaka, bears some similarity to the traditional notion of 'learning'. The externalization mode is triggered by successive rounds of meaningful dialogue within a team. The sophisticated use of metaphors enables team members to articulate their own perspectives and thereby reveal hidden tacit knowledge that is otherwise hard to communicate.

Boland and Tenkasi (1995) analysed knowledge-intensive firms with specialization and knowledge disciplines. They used the term 'community of knowing' of a group of specialized knowledge workers. The authors argue that producing knowledge requires the ability to make strong perspectives within a community, as well as the ability to take the perspectives of others into account. The knowledge work involved in perspective making and perspective taking requires individual cognition and group communication. They present two models of language, communication (language game and conduit) and cognition (narratives and information processing) for amplifying thinking.

The dominant way of understanding cognition today is to emphasize its paradigmatic mode, as reflected in information-processing models of cognition. This view of cognition emphasizes the rational analysis of data in a mental problem space and the construction of deductive arguments. It must, however, be supplemented by recognizing that humans also have a narrative cognitive capacity. We narrativize our experiences almost continually as we recognize unusual or unexpected events and construct stories which make sense of them.

One of the most important messages in Nonaka's four modes is externalization: conversion from tacit to explicit knowledge. It corresponds closely to narrativizing in Boland and Tenkasi. To demonstrate that this conversion really occurs, we refer to Barley's (1996) careful ethnographic study on technicians in the workplace. He shows that material and symbolic work cannot be completely segregated. When important symbols represent material phenomena, symbolic work will lack accuracy unless the symbolic and the material are linked. The core in the technicians' work was in creating these linkages between two complementary processes: transformation and care-taking. Technicians employed technologies, techniques and the knowledge at their disposal for transforming (externalizing or narrativizing) the material entities into signs, symbols, indices and representations. Care-taking almost always required that the technicians employed the representations they created in some ways.

Some critical comments may be made about these approaches. First, the preconditions for successful individual learning and teamwork are taken for granted, and their absence is not problematized. Second, they fail to analyse the importance of mapping organizational defensive routines (Argyris 1993). Third, the ability for critical reflection on actions and how they are justified is taken as a permanent capability of members of a work organization. The development of reflective practice at the individual level demands, however, opportunities for dialogue and shared reflection in the group (Jarvinen 1992). Is there a possibility of conflict between the employee's critical reflection and a collective group reflection? Nonaka and Takeuchi (1995: 278) refer only to collective reflection, not to individual reflection. Is it possible to plan individual career or development goals in these approaches of organizational learning? These are challenging questions for adult educators and organizational developers.

Learning becomes visible where individual and collective learning meet. In research on working life, individual learning and collective learning are often seen as quite similar. They are not. At the organizational level, learning requires communication and the creation of shared meanings. The approaches of Boland and Tenkasi (1995) and Nonaka (1994) represent this view.

Organizing learning in the work community

There are many strategies for organizing learning in work communities. One of them is *research-supported workplace development* (see the Finnish National Workplace Development Programme 1996), where the researcher-expert has a central role in development work. This means that he or she must have not only process-management skills and co-operative skills but also the necessary knowledge about business processes.

Another approach for organizing learning in workplaces is *external consulting*, although it must be said that the roles of researcher, developer and consultant are becoming blurred. The *European Handbook of Management Consultancy* (1995: Foreword) points out that if consultants play a central role in developing strategic innovation in small and medium-sized companies in the EU, the consultancy sector must demonstrate the professional competence to be able to perform that function. This means that consultants should not only address companies' immediate, short-term problems, but also help them to transform themselves into learning organizations. The consultative process can be organized as an experiential learning cycle, so it is possible to facilitate the learning skills needed during the organizational change processes (Cockman *et al.* 1992: 21).

The third approach is *a learning project*, which is an instrument to systematically organize informal, incidental, and formal learning activities conducted by a group of employees, around a central work-related problem (Poell *et al.* 1997)

The fourth approach is *internal training* (in-house training), which means using internal expert trainers. Their competence can be that of an adult educator, knowledge-expert or a combination of both. According to Nordhaug (1994: 153), internal training seems to be used more frequently than external training: larger firms prefer the use of in-house training to buying external training services.

Internal trainers and consultants must get more acquainted with the phases of the knowledge creation approach mentioned earlier (Nonaka 1994). They will need the following kinds of *new skills* to facilitate the knowledge creation process and perspective taking, and to create processes needed for organizational innovation:

- considering the preconditions of the organizational innovation process
- evaluating and analysing the phases of organizational learning and consultative processes
- mapping and evaluating organizational defensive routines
- developing and monitoring teamwork

- keeping up continuing reflective action at the organizational, team or individual level
- evaluating employees' skills for knowledge combination and externalization, reflective learning and teamwork.

New kinds of expert knowledge are also needed for these tasks:

- knowledge of business processes
- constructs based on organizational science for analysing organizational situation, culture, power relations, etc.
- knowledge of developing communication forums.

A case study of pilot projects

The Finnish National Workplace Development Programme mentioned above has the following aims:

- to support workplace-initiated projects
- to boost the use of research in developing process-innovations in work-life
- to create and maintain co-operation networks in order to disseminate and create knowledge and competence
- to increase international information exchange
- to speed up local initiatives.

In total, 37 pilot projects started within the programme during 1996. At the beginning of 1997, a new research project started. This is analysing what kinds of approaches and constructs are used by an expert/consultant who offers research-oriented support to innovative processes in an enterprise. At the first stage three cases were selected. The criteria for selecting the cases were:

- the case was successful to some degree
- the cases were at different stages of the consultative process (one was just finished, one about to finish and one in the middle of the process)
- the consultants had different educational backgrounds and orientations (engineering orientation, adult education orientation and business process orientation).

We present some preliminary findings about these piloting cases below.

The main research questions were: How do the above mentioned skills emerge and develop in the action approaches of consultants, developers and experts? How do they reflect on their own consultative practice during or after the project? The research method was a theme interview which lasted two hours. Other materials investigated were project plans and intermediary evaluation reports. The interview themes were as follows.

Monitoring and reflecting on the whole innovation project

- 'Describe the starting point of this project.'
- 'Describe and evaluate the phases of the innovation process, and your consultative process.'
- 'What were the critical points of the process?'
- 'How did you monitor and evaluate team work?'
- 'What kinds of tools did you have for evaluating the results of the whole process?'

Reflecting on own consultative practice:

- 'Describe yourself as a consultant.' (This included approach models, intervention styles, strengths and weaknesses, etc.)
- 'How do you change approaches and intervention styles during the consultative process?'
- Evaluation of own consultative skills.
- Description and evaluation of the tools and models of the own consultative practice.
- Facilitating own professional development.

Case I (completed January 1997): medium-sized metal industry enterprise

The goal of the project was to support re-engineered production process teams in co-operation with the teams of key clients and key deliverers. The development method was participatory planning where by the interaction and co-operation inside and between teams were facilitated. The expert-consultant was about 35 years old, a male graduate engineer (BSc) with many-sided expertise and practice in energy and metal industry and a good knowledge of industrial psychology and production economy. He had five years' experience in consultative work, a consultant firm of his own since 1992 and he also worked as a partner in another firm (since 1995).

Case II (completed June 1997): new large/medium-sized pulp and paper industry enterprise

The goal of the project was to develop models for group work in a process industry and tools for analysing the efficiency of group work. The consultant was a female graduate psychologist, aged about 50, with over 20 years' experience as an adult educator and an internal trainer in enterprises. Since 1990 she had owned her own consultancy firm.

Case III (completed autumn 1997): small-sized construction industry enterprise

The goal was to develop and change lines of action from a functional organization towards a process organization and to integrate a quality assurance system with it. The male consultant was over 40 years old, graduated with a Master of Science in Economics and had seven years' experience as a sales manager. He had had his own consultancy firm since 1988 and had been a graduate student in adult education since 1991.

In analysing the interviews, an attempt was made to evaluate which of the new kinds of skills emerged in the these consultants' 'good practice' during the particular consultative process. In addition, how they reflected on their own consultative practise in general was analysed.

Preliminary results

Monitoring and reflecting on the innovation project

The preconditions of the organizational innovation processes were carefully examined in all the cases, with regard to the different phases and approaches. In the first case this took place after the pilot team for the enterprise was planned. The consultant had to confront the client and point out that both a team organization and a new production control system were needed. He had to convince the client over many discussions and using very concrete examples. In the second case, the consultant had already worked for many years in the large enterprise, so this project was a natural consequence of a recent training project for employees in the new part the firm. The third consultant used organizational climate questionnaires, interviews and observations before he decided to start the project with this client.

In describing and evaluating of phases of the innovation process and the consultative process, the consultants differed from each other as to what kinds of concepts their used and in their ability or willingness to evaluate the innovation process. The first consultant's description was very modest and cursory. The second one described her own working processes carefully, but not the consultative process, and then changed just the description towards monitoring the team work-phases. The third consultant used special diagrams and schedules with which he had modelled the former organizational processes and the new planned business processes with the employees.

It was interesting to find out how the consultants mastered the whole complex system. In Case I, different consultants from the same consultancy firm were involved at the different phases of the process, forming a consultant network. In Case II, two key persons monitored the entire process. In Case III, a planning group of about 20 employees used the diagrammatic procedure mentioned above. It seemed to me that the three consultants are capable of developing a better system for monitoring and mastering of the whole process of change.

In evaluating and mapping resistance to change (organizational defensive routines), every consultant undertook a very careful analysis, although their findings were different. The first consultant met strong resistance from the management when he tried to indicate the real need for new product controls. Another critical conflict took place in a product department, where their old experiences about efficiency in production made them very suspicious of the new goals and methods of achieving them. The second consultant found a difficult situation when the whole process was suddenly interrupted because an already negotiated agreement (on how to organize on-the-job learning for new tasks) was drawn back into the negotiation process between employers and employees. The third consultant said that a manager's resistance to the new management culture formed a considerable difficulty at the outset of the project.

All three coped successfully with these defensive actions. But they also all identified the same permanent problem of resistance to change: middle management was opposed to these process innovations throughout the entire project. And the consultants' comments were similar: middle management lost power and their situation was most threatened.

All the consultants were skilled in monitoring teamwork but they intervened in different ways. The first consultant, as mentioned above, himself tried to initiate the developments that he saw as required. An insight was developed in the middle of the project, however, that foremen should train team coaches and give more responsibility in development to the teams. The second consultant sought to disengage from an active role as coach as soon as possible and became an observer, recording the team meetings on video. The third consultant saw himself as helping the employees to use the new action procedures without solving their problems, taking a role as active team consultant or coach as required.

In the first case, the employees had undertaken teamworking skills training on different courses outside the enterprise. In the second case, employees were trained inside the enterprise by the consultant before the team-work phases, while in Case III they were trained 'on-line' during the process.

The preliminary analysis shows that all the consultants succeeded quite well in keeping reflective action going at the upper management level and at the employee team level ('where we are going on'), but that the middle management level proved problematic.

All had good expert knowledge about business processes and they had many techniques and methods for organizational analysis (climate, power relations, etc). Most important, they had 'hard' data (numbers, etc) to provide evidence for successful results in production.

Analysing consultants' own practice and its development

When analysing their own practice, these consultants enable us to recognize phases in the consultant's 'life cycle'. The youngest regarded himself as a very competent and expert consultant; knowing the solutions, he saw his role as convincing others about them – a 'prophet' about the 'right way', especially at the beginning of the innovation process. The other two consultants had adopted a typical trainer approach, with some predetermined models of teaching and learning. But both described how they shifted toward a more flexible approach, listening and supporting their clients.

There were also some differences between them. In the second case, the consultant described herself as an analytical observer with a research-oriented approach. She liked to use many-sided study methods and tools for analysing the conditions and processes in the organization. She saw her strength as understanding and mastering large entities. In the third case the consultant spoke of himself as a 'therapeutic consultant', and in a lively and precise way described his role as like a sparring partner.

All of these consultants felt they used no overall or defined theoretical models in working with their clients. The first seemed quite anti-theoretical in his attitude to consultative and innovative processes. The others said they had several kinds of models 'in their tool kit', but that they planned a unique model and process for each and every firm.

They also had different approaches to facilitating their own professional development. The first consultant had teaching and research tasks at university level, and was writing about consulting (among other matters). The second consultant had collected a large amount of research material for a doctoral dissertation, which she intended to write that the next year. The third consultant was very enthusiastic about further study in the educational sciences. The last two each have a mentor of their own with whom they reflect on their work and any problematic situations.

Discussion

The consultative approach is an important way to facilitate organizational and team learning processes during process innovations. In this study, the successful consultants/adult educators already had many of the skills needed for such work. Their special strengths were their analytical skills, in acquiring information from the firms and reflecting on action during the team processes and conflict situations. Much of their personal skills in consulting and modelling the whole process, however, consisted of so-called tacit knowledge, which seems to be difficult to externalize. Communicating and exchanging knowledge was problematic in all these cases. A big challenge to process consulting is how to create new communication networks and forums for perspective making and taking.

While facilitating organizational innovations, the acquisition of new staff development skills is at a premium: the skills of high-level communication, team learning, network learning, knowledge conversion, perspective sharing and reflective practice. This is why it will be necessary in future for educators of adults to learn from the consultative approach and gain a deeper understanding of product and business processes. These can be seen as lifelong learning skills. They are valuable and applicable not only at workplaces, but in many fields of human life.

References

Alasoini, T (1996) *The Finnish National Workplace Development Programme. Background, starting premises and initial experiences*, Working Papers 3, Ministry of Labour, Helsinki.
Argyris, C (1993) 'Leading-Learning', *Organizational Dynamics*, 25, Winter, 5–17.
Barley, SR (1996) 'Technicians in the Workplace: Ethnographic Evidence for Bringing Work into Organization Studies', *Administrative Science Quarterly*, 41, 3, 404–441.
Boland, RJ and Tenkasi, RV (1995) 'Perspective Making and Perspective Taking in Communities of Knowing', *Organization Science*, 6, 4, 350–372.
Cockman, P, Evans, B and Reynolds, P (1992) *Client-Centred Consulting*, McGraw-Hill, London.
European Commission (1995) *Green Paper on Innovation*. Document drawn up on the basis of COM(95)688 final, Bulletin of the European Union, Supplement 5/95, Luxemburg, Brussels.

The European Handbook of Management Consultancy (1995) European Innovation Programme, Oak Tree Press, Dublin.

Finnish National Workplace Development Programme (1996) *A proposal of Tripartite Experts Group to the Ministry of Labour*, Ministry of Labour, Publication of Labour Administration: 122 e, Helsinki.

Jarvinen, A (1992) 'Development of Reflection during High-level Professional Education', in *Quality and Communication for Improvement. Proceedings. 12th European AIR Forum, Lyon 1990*: 93–109, Lemma, Utrecht.

Nonaka, I (1994) 'A Dynamic Theory of Organizational Knowledge Creation', *Organization Science*, 5, 2, 14–37.

Nonaka, I and Takeuchi, H (1995) *The Knowledge-Creating Company*, Oxford University Press, New York.

Nordhaug, O (1994) *Human Capital in Organizations. Competence, Training and Learning*, Scandinavian University Press, Oslo.

Poell, R, Tijmensen, L and van der Krogt, F (1997) 'Can Learning Projects Help to Develop a Learning Organization', *Lifelong Learning in Europe*, 2, 67–75.

Chapter 26

Promoting Learning Networks for Small Business:
How Can Group Learning Facilitate Change?

Sue Kilpatrick

Background

Australian agriculture is dominated by small business. Agriculture is a significant contributor to the Australian economy, producing 29 per cent of exports. Both industry leaders and government recognize that farm businesses must be flexible and adaptable in order to manage the risks of the Australian climate and changes in global markets, and for Australian agriculture to be internationally competitive. Farmers are being urged to acquire new skills in order to manage change.

> '...the skills required of farmers in the past in order to succeed in agriculture will in future need to be supplemented with additional skills in order to cope with the changes that have emerged over recent decades. Good technical skills in crop and livestock husbandry will need to be supported with skills in financial management ... and with skills in risk management' (National Farmers' Federation 1993: 75–76).
>
> 'Education and training were identified as key mechanisms by which enhanced productivity, initiative, financial self reliance and smooth

adjustment could be better achieved ... Farmers need to be able to identify challenges arising out of change and how best to deal with those challenges ... attitudinal change is a complex and long-term task which needs to be addressed through education...' (National Rural Finance Summit Activating Committee 1996: 1–2).

The future of Australia's agricultural sector is closely related to the ability and willingness of it's farmers to become lifelong learners, continually update their knowledge and skills learn across a broader range of areas. This is a new challenge for farmers who traditionally acquire a relatively narrow range of technical agricultural skills, mostly early in their farming careers. Skill acquisition has usually been by on-the-job learning. The narrow skill base and on-the-job learning have until recently been sufficient for a lifetime in farming. Now farmers, along with many other groups in the workforce, are being urged to change and become lifelong learners.

This chapter explores the ways in which training can assist farm businesses to become adaptable and responsive learning organizations. Lundvall (1992) proposes that change is a cumulative process which builds on existing knowledge and practices through interactive learning. Organizations which adapt and change as a result of interactive learning activities are learning organizations. Learning organizations are characterized by both intra-organizational learning and inter-organizational learning.

Individual farms have small workforces, with consequently limited opportunities for interactive learning within the 'organization'. This is reflected in the amount of change occurring in single and dual operator family farm businesses. These small businesses, which comprise 74 per cent of all Australian farm businesses, are less likely to make changes to farming practices than those with larger management teams, according to results of a survey of 2500 farm businesses presented in this chapter.

Learning in small business

Change, or adaptation, in organizational innovation is a social process involving interaction and collaboration between individuals within organizations and within networks of organizations (Lundvall 1992, Mathews 1994). Learning organizations occur because of:

> '...the vision of individuals, groups and organizational networks committed to and capable of continuous learning through information exchange, experimentation, dialogue, negotiation and consensus building' (Kochan and Useem 1992: 391).

Farmers network via farmer organizations, informal social contact with other farmers, government extension officers and rural educational institutions, in producer-purchaser arrangements with food processing companies and retailer-consumer relationships with input suppliers (Phillips 1987). These networks have features of learning organizations (Senge 1993); they enable the social, contextual learning to which farmers respond.

Kilpatrick (1996) found that the vast majority of farmers who made changes to their farm management practice were influenced to change by a number of sources. Further, most farmers used both 'expert' and 'social' sources of support (other farmers and family) in implementing changes to practice.

The literature on farmer decision-making often ignores that part of the process which occurs within the farm business, concentrating only on external information sources and communication channels. Phillips (1985) is one of the few studies which described a role for 'intimates', who he said acted as a checkpoint for information and decision-making, reflecting the importance of intimacy, trust and support in decision-making.

Support in implementing a change is vital if the change is to be successful. Social support is just as important as physical infrastructure in ensuring that, once implemented, a change is not discontinued (Rogers and Shoemaker 1971). The isolation experienced by many living and working in rural areas reduces the opportunity to build information and support networks. By developing 'learning networks', increasing participation in organized 'learning events' will improve the performance of businesses by promoting the ability to make appropriate change in their managers and providing support in the implementation of change (Kilpatrick 1996, 1997).

This chapter explores the role of interaction between participants, and with 'expert' facilitators, in learning process which leads to changes to management practices. That is, the chapter explores how interaction during and after training can foster lifelong learning.

Methodology

This chapter uses data from a large study of Australian farm businesses to describe the change process and the training in which their managers participate. These data are supplemented by data from interview surveys of participants in a number of types of training. The chapter uses data from three sources.

1. The Agricultural Financial Survey (AFS) is an annual survey of farm business units conducted by the Australian Bureau of Statistics. The

sample is a stratified one based on the value of operations by industry. The sample size in 1993/94 was approximately 2500, out of an estimated farm business population of 107,538. Respondents are interviewed face to face and legislation requires that all those selected in Australian Bureau of Statistics' surveys must participate. Australian Bureau of Statistics (1995: 54) describes the sampling method. Questions about changes to farming practice, educational qualifications held by the farm management team, formal and non-formal training attended in the past year and future training intentions were added to the financial questions in the 1993–94 survey.
2. An interview survey of 65 Tasmanian farmers, 45 of whom had completed one of three agricultural training courses (labelled 'Tasmanian survey').
3. Semi-structured interview surveys of approximately 100 farmers who had participated in one of four training programmes: a TAFE course, a non-formal course run by a Department of Primary Industries, a discussion group programme and a one-day training session on quality assurance.

Further information about the first two sources is found in Kilpatrick (1996); information about the third group of studies is found in Kilpatrick (1997) and Falk *et al.* (1997).

Results and discussion

Propensity to make changes to practice

The AFS asked farm managers whether they had made any change to their practices over the last three years which was intended to improve farm profitability or viability. Australian farm businesses with a single manager were least likely to have made a change to practice, and farms with two managers are less likely to make a change than those with larger management teams (see Table 26.1). This supports views that single and dual-manager businesses have limited opportunities to engage in interactive learning, and so are less likely to innovate or make changes within the business.

Table 26.1 *Size of management team and percentage making a change (AFS)*

Number in management team*	percentage of businesses making a change	percentage of all farm businesses
One	52	23
Two	63	51
Three	69	26
All farm businesses	62	

c2 probability for distribution of change/no change for 1 and 3 or more managers compared to 2 managers is less than 0.00001 per cent.
* The value of the assets owned by single and dual-farm businesses is not statistically significantly different. Multi-manager farms have a significantly higher asset value than the other groups. Large farm businesses by value of assets are more likely to make changes.

Triggers and support in implementing change

What factors trigger farm managers to make changes? Who supports them in implementing change? The AFS survey asked for the trigger for the most important change made by the business in the last three years and who provided the most support as the change was made. Other farmers and family or staff were particularly important in prompting changes for dual and multi-manager farm businesses (see Table 26.2). Single-manager businesses were most likely to be prompted by 'other' triggers. The majority of the 'other' triggers were specified as 'self', 'own idea' or 'no one'. External events such as drought, flood, hail and fire and reasons such as worn-out equipment make up the remainder of the 'other' category.

Family or staff provided the most support in implementing changes, providing support for 41 per cent of changes. Other farmers as well as family and staff are socially close to the decision maker. Table 26.2 indicates that those socially close to the decision maker are the most important source of support in implementing change, confirming the work of Phillips (1985). Experts, such as consultants and government extension officers, were the most important sources of support for only 26 per cent of all changes.

Training events were the trigger for 17 per cent of all changes. The next section addresses the question: does the impact of training on the likelihood of making changes vary with the size of the management team?

Table 26.2 *Triggers for change and sources of support in implementing change by size of management team (AFS)*

	One manager	Two managers	Three or more managers
Trigger for change			
Training event	19	14	21
Consultant or field officer	24	27	30
Family, staff, other farmer	25	39	37
Other trigger	31	20	12
Source of support in change			
Consultant or field officer	22	28	23
Family, other farmers	51	56	68
Other support	11	9	7
None	17	7	2

Training participation and farm business changes

Farm businesses with one, two and three or more managers are more likely to make changes to their practice if they attend any training than if they attend no training, although the difference is greater for larger management teams (see Table 26.3). Single-manager farm businesses that do train attend less training 'events' on average than those from dual and multi-manager farm businesses. Lower participation may be due to the resource constraints, for example lack of human resources to replace the manager while training occurs (Kilpatrick 1996).

Table 26.3 *Number in management team, training participation and changes (AFS)*

Number in team and training participation	Percentage of category making a change	Percentage of team size in category
One manager, no training	47	33
One manager, training	53	67
Two managers, no training	37	16
Two managers, training	63	84
Three or more managers, no training	28	14
Three or more managers, training	72	86

Probability from X^2 distribution that the proportion of 'changers' is the same for training and no training groups is less than 0.0001 per cent for each size of management team.

How does training influence the change process?

The role of training in fostering change is not limited to introducing new ideas. Almost two thirds of people who had completed one of three courses for farmers made some change influenced by their course, but the subsequent change was new to only 20 per cent (see Table 26.4). The table also shows that training influenced the decision to change, without being the critical factor or trigger for change, for 34 per cent of participants.

Table 26.4 *Influence of training on changes to practice (Tasmanian survey)*

Impact of training on change	Percentage of participants
Became aware of change during training	20
Training was trigger for change	27
Training influenced decision to change in some way	64

Even when people are already aware of possible practices covered in a course, the course can play a role in motivating them to actually implement new practices.

> 'After doing a Whole Farm Planning Course it certainly gives you a burst of enthusiasm and you go home and get stuck into a few of these issues that may

not have been tackled if you hadn't done the course. You may have been aware of it, but it is a motivation' (Non-formal course participant).

Learning from each other

Discussion between participants can be a learning experience in itself. Discussion allows participants to test ideas and possible actions against the values and norms of their peer group and to learn from others' experiences. The process of 'checking' possible new actions or strategies with peers facilitates changes to behaviour, by allowing people to examine their own attitudes and values toward a new practice. There is a considerable amount of research which holds that interaction with peers assists the adoption of new practices (see, for example Rogers 1995).

> '[The course] gave you confidence in the stuff that you picked up through papers and the media and bits and pieces. It put it into perspective, and some of that was by tuition and some of it was sharing it with the people' (Non-formal course participant).

> 'Probably [the most useful thing about the programme was] learning from others, the interaction between the growers which I felt was excellent ... there were growers who I thought were very efficient growers; seeing ideas that they were running off with, things that I hadn't thought of before, and *vice versa*' (Discussion group participant).

> 'There were some portions that confirmed the way I have been thinking, and that other people think the same way. That gives you confidence that others either agree with you or understand your point of view' (Non-formal course participant).

These quotes confirm that interactive learning is taking place in training situations. The following two quotes illustrate interaction within the management team as ideas are taken from training to the business. This woman was a partner in a dairy farm:

> 'I take it home and I tell the hubby, he has picked my brain. I think he has learnt as much as me. And sometimes there is a good idea there that we have been able to say we'll try that next year' (Formal course participant).

Attending training as a management team facilitates interaction within the team:

'My wife and I both went together because we both work the farm together and we found it better than if only one of us had gone. We talked to each other and we both understood what was going on' (Quality assurance training participant).

Support networks

One course was particularly successful in bringing about change. Over 90 per cent of participants had made a change influenced by their course. The course was also successful in establishing ongoing support networks amongst its participants, networks which were still functioning up to three years after the group had completed their course.

> 'You made friends that you still have through the network. Definitely our networks are still retained, some of those throughout the course and [the course] certainly generated others' (Non-formal course participant).

> 'That is one thing that I learnt, if you don't have the knowledge, where do you go and find it? ... Who the best contacts are ... you go out and find out who made the mistakes first and learn by them rather than your own' (Non-formal course participant).

In contrast, the quality assurance (QA) training programme examined by Falk *et al.* (1997) has not been successful in bringing about change. There are approximately 19,900 beef-producing properties in Australia. As at mid January 1997, only 55 were QA accredited, while 7,500 producers had attended QA training or awareness sessions over the previous 15 months. QA experts estimate it should take no more than six months to make any necessary changes to infrastructure and practices and become QA accredited. The relatively complex changes to practice required for the many farmers to fully implement QA requires an associated change in attitudes and values. The authors found that the QA training did not encourage interaction between participants, and that support groups were not formed following training. The authors recommended interactive training sessions, more sessions and facilitating formation of support groups to improve the rate of adoption of QA by providing 'social' support.

Conclusion

Managers from single-manager farm businesses attend less training events and are less likely to make changes to their practice than managers from businesses with larger management teams. The data presented here suggest that other farmers, family and staff have a major influence on farm business change. Single-manager businesses have limited opportunity for interaction within the businesses, compared with those with larger management teams, as no family member is identified as having a management role. Lower participation in training means less opportunity to learn from and with other farmers in learning networks.

The finding that farm managers who engage in training are more likely to make changes to their practice is consistent with the idea that learning which leads to change takes place within organizational and 'social' networks (Lundvall 1992) and the idea that farmers who engage in training have appropriate support for implementing new practices from networks of other farmers and experts. These networks are established or reinforced at training courses and sessions. Single managers' lower participation in training reduces their opportunity to participate in support networks and so reduces the likelihood of implementing change.

Participants learn from each other as well as from trainers or facilitators. Participant interaction during training programmes also assists learning by allowing participants to test their attitudes and values relating to the new knowledge and skills presented during the programme. Participant interaction fosters a change of attitudes toward new behaviours and practices and so increases the effectiveness of the training in changing behaviour and practices. Training which emphasizes opportunities for networking and interaction will be more effective in translating decisions to change into continuing changes to practice by providing support as change is undertaken.

Farmers and other small business managers must become lifelong learners if Australia is to become a flexible, responsive and adaptable learning society. They must continually update their knowledge and skills and extend their learning beyond a narrow range of technical skills to other areas, such as management and marketing, in order to manage ongoing change. Lifelong learning in farm businesses and other small business can be fostered by taking note of the findings presented here. Providing opportunities for interaction during training and encouraging the development of networks of small business managers will enhance their learning. Interaction and support networks are important for all organizations, but they are especially important for helping small businesses along the path of lifelong learning.

References

Australian Bureau of Statistics (1995) *Agricultural Industries Financial Statistics Australia, 1993–94*, Cat. No. 7507.0, Australian Government Publishing Service, Canberra.

Falk, I, Kilpatrick, S and Morgan, H (1997) *Quality Assurance in Agriculture: Promoting Access for Beef Producers*, Centre for Research and Learning, University of Tasmania, Launceston.

Kilpatrick, S (1996) *Change, Training and Farm Profitability: National Focus. A National Farmers' Federation Research Paper*, National Farmers Federation, Canberra.

Kilpatrick, S (1997) *The Effectiveness of Delivery Methodologies for Education & Training to Rural Australia*, Centre for Research and Learning, University of Tasmania, Launceston.

Kochan, T and Useem, M (1992) *Transforming Organizations*, Oxford University Press, New York.

Lundvall, B (1992) *National Systems of Innovation*, Pinter Publishers, London.

Mathews, J (1994) *Catching the Wave: Workplace Reform in Australia*, Allen and Unwin, Sydney.

National Farmers' Federation (1993) *New Horizons: A Strategy for Australia's Agrifood Industries*, National Farmers' Federation, Canberra.

National Rural Finance Summit Activating Committee (1996) *Beyond the Summit*, National Rural Finance Summit Activating Committee, Canberra.

Phillips, T (1985) *Development of Methodologies for the Determination and Facilitation of Learning for Dairy Farmers*, University of Melbourne, Melbourne.

Phillips, T (1987) 'Farmers' Perception of Extension – Learning Model Using Information Networks', in M Littmann (Ed.) *Rural Extension in an Era of Change*: 449–453, Australasian Agricultural Extension Conference Proceedings, Brisbane.

Rogers, E (1995) *Diffusion of Innovations* (4th Edn), The Free Press, New York.

Rogers, E and Shoemaker, F (1971) *Communication of Innovations*, The Free Press, New York.

Senge, P (1993) The *Fifth Discipline: The Art and Practice of the Learning Organization*, Random Century, London.

PART VII

AIMS, ETHICS AND SOCIAL PURPOSE IN LIFELONG LEARNING

Chapter 27

The Liberal Instrument

Evan Alderson and Mark Selman

Introduction

Those of us who work in universities are awash in a sea of voices lamenting the end of academic standards, disciplinary rigour and the general bankruptcy of the enterprise in which we are engaged. Central to this sense of despair and decline is the lament that the liberal arts have lost their pride of place as the centre or focal point of the university as a distinctive institutional form. In the same vein, a liberal education is no longer, apparently, the central mandate of institutions which are caught up in pursuing excellence in research, increased efficiency through the application of learning technologies and management practices aimed at heightened accountability. Lifelong learning, especially, though not only in its vocationalist forms, can be understood as yet another symptom of this crisis.

Many of the responses to this crisis tend to fall into one of three categories. One is to accept the displacement of the liberal arts and to plunge wholeheartedly a kind of institutional consumerism in which student numbers or tuition fees determine the fate and size of programmes of study. A second response is generally conservative and nostalgic and calls for a return to the eternal verities and classic texts which constitute a 'real' education. The third and most influential response is to reframe universities as institutions of excellence, institutions which stand for no particular sort of academic commitments or values – just a claim to be outstanding at whatever it is that universities do.

The authors of this chapter have been involved both as teachers and administrators in two university degree programmes which attempt to deal with this crisis differently from any of the responses outlined above. Both involve mature students in their thirties and up. Rather than give up on the centrality of liberal education or call for a return to a time when its place was unquestioned, we have chosen to try to rethink liberal education and its place in the institution and in students' lives, while recognizing that many of the foundational beliefs which once underpinned a liberal education can no longer carry that weight, if they exist at all. The project, therefore, becomes something like a research programme in the sense associated with Imre Lakatos (1970: 116–138). The hard (and, in this case, normative) core of the programme is a continued commitment to the centrality of the liberalizing function of university education, combined with a willingness to dispense with, or at least be ironic about, many of the core values and fundamental beliefs which have been held to underpin it. The programmes we are developing and the reflections we engage in chapters such as this one can be thought of as the experimental activity through which we explore the fecundity of the research programme. Given the early state of our programmes and reflections, even this way of putting it may be overstating the case, although it does capture our intention.

Our interest in thinking about the university in this way has been reinforced by encountering Bill Readings' book *The University in Ruins*, in which the purpose of the modern university is displayed not as an unwavering commitment to certain ideals but rather an evolving core which he summarizes as consisting of three main parts: 'the Kantian concept of reason, the Humboltian idea of culture and now the techno-bureaucratic notion of excellence' (1996: 14). Given what he takes to be the absolute emptiness of the notion of excellence as a guiding ideal (ie it can say nothing about what to try to be excellent at) and the battered and contested state of reason and culture (understood in those ways), there would appear to be every reason to try to develop alternatives.

This chapter is a preliminary attempt to think through alternatives, drawing on both our practical experience with programmes for adults which incorporate liberal studies and more theoretic or philosophical considerations, drawn mostly from Readings. The chapter proceeds by some analysis of the traditional ideology of liberal learning, a description of the educational programmes with which we are engaged and an attempt at rethinking some aspect of the central purposes of liberal education as instantiated in these programmes.

Ideology of liberal learning

The following three propositions, with corollaries, constitute what we take to be the inherited ideology of liberal learning.

1. Liberal education is primarily formative, or in the terms of German educational theory (from Readings) is the agent of *Bildung*. The predisposition here is that the person to be educated is to be formed, or by implication is a young person who during a particular sensitive and receptive period of maturation is brought into full adulthood through education of this type.
2. What is to be formed is the autonomous subject. This has been understood as a universalistic concept which has often masked class or other particularities: In the words of Cardinal Newman: 'It is common to speak of "liberal knowledge", of the "liberal arts and studies" and of a "liberal education" as the special characteristic or property of a university and a gentleman' (Readings 1996: 74). Despite such hidden particularisms, a close corollary is that the autonomous subject is the citizen leader, governance being idealized as the free consent of citizen-subjects, and leadership requiring the perspicacity that liberal education is particularly suite to engender. In this sense Antonio Gramsci, the Italian Marxist, could be as positive about the value of a liberal education for prospective leaders from the proletariat as Newman was for potential gentlemen.
3. Liberal education proceeds toward the formation of the autonomous subject both broadly and by indirection. 'Educated properly, the subject learns the rules of thought, not a content of positive knowledge, so that thought and knowledge acquisition become a freely autonomous activity, part of the subject' (Readings 1996: 67). The kinds of abilities it produces are understood to take time, the time of formation, to develop. Critical thinking, the ability to speak and write clearly and persuasively, disciplined freedom of mind, breadth of perspective and ethical sensitivity are all abilities to be honed through practice in one or another subject of study. These general abilities are to be contrasted, in RS Peters' words, to 'the mind being constricted to ... specialist training ... or one mode of thought' (1966: 44). Even more so, the socialization effects of liberal education, both the adaptation to social and intellectual behaviours among young students and the selective certification of a degree, are understood to happen over time.

These features of the inherited model have undergone some changes in response to contemporary pressures. In particular, scepticism about the presumption of a universal subject and the obvious indefensibility of any proposed common core of knowledge essential for citizenship or almost anything else have led to skirmishes pitting various nostalgic and relativistic gestures against each other, and to a number of constructivist 'solutions' emphasizing communicational process. The central role of the state and therefore the centrality of citizenship have undergone degrees of displacement under forces of globalization, the growth of institution-based (or disciplinary) power, and the spread of information technologies.

In the particular kinds of programmes with which we are concerned, programmes involving adults returning to university or coming for the first time after extensive experience as adults outside of educational institutions, the notion of *Bildung*, or formation, is also less apt. Clearly some rethinking of the assumptions embodied in liberal learning, the educative process involved and the objectives to be sought, is required. But before beginning such reflection, it is helpful to understand something more about the actual programmes in which initiated it.

Description of programmes

The two programmes are a Masters programme in Liberal Studies and a Bachelor of General Studies programme in Liberal and Business Studies. The former has existed for about six years and is similar to programmes at a number of American universities. It is open to adults, typically those who have at least a first degree, who wish to undertake advanced education outside of the constraints of a particular discipline. Most students are in their thirties to fifties with a few either younger or older. They come from an enormous range of walks of life and few see the degree as directly related to career advancement. Many enter with a strong feeling that they have missed something in their previous education and with enthusiasm for taking part in a community of learning.

Students typically take one course per semester. For the first two semesters, they study together as a group and then for the next two to four years pick and choose among a limited set of interdisciplinary seminars. The programme is quite selective, in that there are some 80–100 applicants for 20 student places each year, which results in a group of rather capable students, albeit one which lacks the shared base of knowledge one would expect in discipline-based graduate programmes. The content of the programme explores tensions in contemporary thinking ('Science and human values', 'Freedom and authority', 'Passion and reason') through classic and contemporary texts and discussion.

The other programme is newer and perhaps more unusual. It is a three-year programme of part-time study (covering the last two years of a full-time undergraduate degree programme), developed in conjunction with major employers. The employers, for the most part, pay the costs of the programme and provide their employees with some paid time in which to attend classes. Students tend to have specialized educational credentials, such as two-year diploma programmes from technical institutes and have somewhere between five and twenty-five years of experience with their organizations. The primary purposes behind the development of the programme are to give employee/students greater breadth of understanding and knowledge, so that they are not limited to particular niches within their companies, and a credential which will be recognized across the various sections of their companies or elsewhere.

Students take two courses per semester, three semesters per year. Classes are organized into three-day blocks of time, spaced about three weeks apart. All the courses are taken by almost all of the students together as a cohort, thus creating a rather intense experience of community. Student motivations vary somewhat, with some students being strongly oriented to degree acquisition (directly for career advancement or as a stepping-stone to graduate degrees) with others placing more emphasis on the acquisition of associated goods including increased confidence, improved ability to write and think clearly, or a broader understanding of identity, organizations and society. There is a presumption on the part of both employers and students that the knowledge and abilities developed in the programme will have a pay-off in a work setting.

Obviously, the traditional ideology of liberal learning does not fit these programmes, in part because the participants are already formed or at least cannot be presumed to be youthfully receptive. In neither case is there the time or requisite patience for disciplinary initiation as a precursor for critical engagement. Further, each of these programmes represents a characteristic 'danger' to the ideology of liberal learning. The Graduate Liberal Studies programme flirts with consumerism – the danger that education becomes primarily a form of entertainment, rather than an engagement capable of deeper transformation. The Bachelors programme is more prone to dangers associated with application – the demand that each text or idea be relatively directly applicable to one's work situation. How can we understand the values of a liberal education to survive in these environments, or what aspects of those values can be fairly understood to persist without the rationale of the autonomous subject-in-process? Part of our current response to this problem is embedded in the very structure of the programmes: the fact that the community of students forces attention towards the individuals themselves and their various interactions with the texts, rather than exclusively towards the texts themselves. Recognition of the significance of this shift in emphasis away from a universalist or disciplinary orientation and towards the relations and differences between individuals makes salient an alternative set of dispositions[1] to be cultivated.

The relative autonomy of singularities

A useful way to understand the position of both the students and the teachers as they enter the pedagogic situation in both these programmes is aligned with postmodern critiques of the subject: in Readings' vocabulary they are not subjects so much as singularities. 'Singularity provides a way of talking about individuals other than as subjects. It recognizes the radical heterogeneity of individuals, the sheer fact that as an agglomeration of matter, history, experience, whatever, you just are not someone else; there is nothing you can be presumed in advance to share with someone else' (Readings 1996: 115). The individual as singularity is not different from others in every respect, but is merely a unique combination of attributes shared with others. Commonalities with others are easily discovered and, indeed, easily exploited within consumer society. Sometimes, as Foucault notes, such commonalities are actively constructed by institutional practices in order to make possible documentation and comparison (1984: 200–204). But the points of commonality do not have the potential to add up to a common culture that satisfies any sensible criteria of balance, wholeness or centrality. Students and teachers alike within the graduate programme may have a nostalgic desire to be enfolded into culture by teaching and learning what is truly important, but the arbitrariness of the manoeuvre quite rapidly becomes manifest. Students in Liberal and Business Studies may share that nostalgia to some extent, but are more likely to use the test of application, which essentially reasserts their enclosure within the role of employee.

This understanding of contemporary subjectivity recognizes the permanent isolation of teachers and students alike from a centrally grounding culture, not because they are incapable of interpersonal relationships or moral seriousness – far from it – but because of the waning force and reach of any claims to cultural centrality. It is our view that within this understanding the sustainable values of a liberal education undergo a partial shift from formal knowledge to ethical practice. As Readings puts it is a different context: 'Teaching thus becomes answerable to the question of justice rather than to the criterion of truth' (1996: 154).

We want to discuss this shift as it reveals itself in the most satisfying modes of pedagogy within each programme and in each programme leads to the development of certain dispositions. These dispositions are not of the sort readily named within the vocationalist rhetoric of lifelong learning, but we believe them nonetheless to have subtle and powerful effects.

The first of these dispositions can be called the recognition of difference. Students entering these programmes typically manifest a striking mixture of self-confidence and trepidation. Because each programme is selective, students take some pride in having been admitted. They are almost all competent, mature and poised individuals with an established sense of personal identity. Yet they are entering a programme, with some sense of adventure, of a kind in which very few of them have recent evidence of success. While in general they do not manifest quite the anxiety of most young students first entering university, nor the ambitiousness of some, nor the innocent righteousness of a few, there is in each programme a significant atmosphere of personal risk in every entering class.

It is of course the job of teachers in each programme to assist the transition from anxiety to confidence. As in other programmes, allowing students to sense their provisional mastery of material plays a large role in this effort, but in these programmes there is an additional opportunity to build confidence out of respect for difference. Because the participants are more formed characters than they are characters-in-formation, their individual ethical attitudes, intellectual dispositions and habits of mind quickly assume a strong presence in the classroom. Subordination to a common subject-matter or a common discourse becomes much less the point than in applied studies or with youthful groups, because of the opportunities the classroom affords for the understanding and appreciation of difference.

Although it is seldom directly expressed, the central imperative of both programmes is the continuity of ethical obligation among teachers and students. The ability to actually hear difference requires commonality – mutual care, a will to lend respect and a common topic. The collectivities created by these cohort groups entering a course of study together are actually remarkable communities of difference.

These communities show both remarkably strong elements of bonding and many of the tensions of familiarity that develop in communities of other kinds. Like all communities, success depends upon mutual accommodation. In these communities, however, the social shifts toward accommodation of difference are at times accompanied by an observable intellectual shift. What sometimes emerges out of deeply held differences, even where these are insistently maintained, is not just routine opposition or polite indifference but a recognition of the continuity of character, ideas and values such that individualities are both visible and appreciated, knowledge is understood as always embodied and always social and a respect for persons becomes a principle of learning.

A second and corollary disposition is self-definition. Through recognition of difference, there is a gathering power to perceive and declare one's own values. The thoughtful encounter with other 'singularities' creates an ability to recognize and have confidence in one's own self-coherence even as one understands it as one among many. It is worth noting that in much of the writing of the Canadian philosopher Charles Taylor, the combination of these two attributes, self-understanding through the recognition of difference, forms the basis of democratic hope under the conditions of modernity (eg Taylor 1992).

The third and last disposition to be discussed here is that of irony. In a more conventional language of liberal education one might call this the ability to establish of critical distance, but irony suggest something more, which can be aptly summarized through Richard Rorty's definition of the ironist as fulfilling three conditions: '(1) She has radical and continuing doubts about the final vocabulary she currently uses, because she has been impressed by other vocabularies, vocabularies taken as final by people or books she has encountered; (2) she realizes that arguments phrased in her present vocabulary can neither underwrite nor resolve these doubts; (3) insofar as she philosophizes about her situation, she does not think that her vocabulary is closer to reality than others, that it is in touch with a power not herself' (1989: 73). For contemporary mature students the disposition to adopt this attitude of irony is perhaps the most appropriate corrective to the already well-honed tendencies towards gullibility and cynicism they bring to the table. Corporate employees can be observed asserting as convictions propositions that sound remarkably like their company's public relations manifesto, and at virtually the next moment savaging their employers for incompetence and cruelty. Liberal Studies students can be almost abject in their desire to receive the goods of culture and almost totally indifferent to the actual argument in a classic text which contradicts their own opinion.

Irony in this sense can be taken as a more resolved form of the tensions between uncertainty and self-confidence, self and other, through which at least some manage to take appropriate responsibility for their own judgements and actions while doing justice to encounters with others and their ideas. Further, an ironic attitude seems to be an apt response to many phenomena in a society in which contradictions and injustices once thought likely to be resolved (by revolution or by progress) have proved to be rather more intractable. Irony here does not imply resignation, which would be an evasion of one's obligations, but it does embody a kind of realism about the social and moral quandaries and the possibilities for action which exist. Our best efforts may be successful in the sense of alleviating an injustice or creating a new way of looking at things, but they are not going to provide solutions in an absolute sense.

As must be clear already, this chapter is not attempting to be a final word. It is an early attempt to wrestle with what the authors take to be a significant challenge – the ability to build, among what Readings names as the ruins of the modern idea of a university, some kind of coherent basis for judgement and action. This is in place of either cynical claims to excellence or vehement nostalgia for an impossible sense of certainty. Without some such basis, universities' efforts to play a role in lifelong learning are likely to appear as either opportunistic or irrelevant.

Note

1. This use of 'disposition' is taken from Ryle (1949: 112 *et passim*) and is used in preference to notions such as 'skill'. This preference is not meant to deny the role of practice or habituation in developing these complex character traits but rather to emphasize that repetitive practice cannot tell the whole story of their development.

References

Foucault, M (1984) 'The Means of Correct Training', in P Rabinow (Ed.) *The Foucault Reader*: 188–205, Pantheon, New York.
Lakatos, I (1970) 'Falsification and the Methodology of Research Programmes', in I Lakatos and A Musgrave (Eds)*Criticism and the Growth of Knowledge*: 91–195, Cambridge University Press, Cambridge.
Peters, RS (1966) *Ethics and Education*, Allen and Unwin, London.
Readings, B (1996) *The University in Ruins*, Harvard University Press, Cambridge, Mass.
Rorty, R (1989) *Contingency, Irony, and Solidarity*, Cambridge University Press, Cambridge.
Ryle, G (1949) *The Concept of Mind*, Penguin, Harmondsworth.
Taylor, C (1992) *The Malaise of Modernity*, Anansi, Concord, Ontario.

Chapter 28

Teaching/Learning and Decision-Making:
The Face-To-Face Versus the Interface, Some Implications for Ethical Practice

Del Loewenthal and Robert Snell

> 'The face is exposed, menaced, as if inviting us to an act of violence. At the same time, the face is what forbids us to kill' (Levinas 1985: 86).

Introduction

This chapter discusses the appropriate mix in professional development of the face-to-face versus computer technology, giving particular attention to ethical decision-making. Both the teaching/learning processes in the development of professionals and the way professionals subsequently practise are of interest. The discussion forms part of a larger study of the bases of decision-making in Freud's three 'impossible professions': management, therapy and education (Freud 1937: 247).

In our thinking about ethical decision-making we start from a Levinasian perspective of 'responsible relatedness' (Gans 1997) and justice rather than legal practices and ethical codes. Thus, in ethical decision-making, 'instead of being primarily concerned with systems of power and knowledge, we should be concerned with justice on a case by case basis, for real justice cannot be appropriated or territorialized, instead as with ones client's, one has to be just in the moment with another' (Loewenthal 1996). It will be argued here that the face-to-face is an essential aspect in preparing students and their teachers for such ethical decision-making.

The use of the Internet for teaching and learning is growing rapidly. However, there is very little research on the implications of the use of computer interfaces. Thus, whilst the 1996 'Contents pages in Education' has seen a dramatic increase to 72 references from previous years involving the Internet, only one (Brunt 1996) touches on the subject of this proposed research. In further research the implications of postmodernism with particular reference to Levinasian ethics will be examined for the research process, and such questions as the implications of being responsible for the others responsibility will be explored, with a view to developing a post-phenomenological research approach, in which it is assumed that both researcher and researched are not at the centre of their own phenomenological worlds.

It is intended that future research will further develop the argument presented in this chapter, particularly in the light of the implications of electronic communication for how we are with one another. When are electronic versus face-to-face approaches most appropriate for effectively carrying out professional decision-making and training in it? What are the implications for education in general? For Derrida, 'what is no longer archived in the same way is no longer lived in the same way' (Derrida 1996: 18); the way in which we record and learn effects how we experience our lives. For Derrida's mentor in philosophy, Emmanuel Levinas, our original (ethical) relation to one another 'takes place in the concrete situation of speech. In speaking or calling or listening to the other, I am not reflecting upon the other, but I am actively engaged in a non-comprehensive, non-subsumptive relation to alterity where I focus on the individual in front of me and forgo the mediation of the universal' (Peperzak et al. 1996: 1–2). What might be the relations of the 'virtual classroom' to 'the concrete situation of speech', and what might interactive learning on the net – in the absence of an embodied listener – imply for responsible relatedness?

The delusional lure of ideal intelligibility

> '...the face is not "seen" ... it is uncontainable, it leads you beyond. It is in this that the signification of the face makes it escape from being, as a correlate of a knowing' (Levinas 1985: 87).

It has been often reported how it is more difficult to kill someone looking at you (Levinas 1985: 86). In the UK *The Times Higher Education Supplement* (Utley 1997) has commented on how the advent of email has led to a new level of violence in internal communication in the workplace. One report has pointed to a 'flaming' epidemic in UK industry; among its findings is that one in seventy people annually leave their jobs as a direct result of electronic bullying, the more so it seems as email is used as a management tool (*PC Pro* 1997: 52). Does the use of the interface lead to a more potentially murderous culture?

We wish to show, primarily through the works of Levinas, how concern with 'being' leads to a focus on self-knowledge and knowing (through knowing myself I can come to know the Universe). 'The ontological identification of truth with an ideal intelligibility' (Peperzak 1992: 198) is the Western notion of making consciousness transparent: the contents of consciousness becomes identified with knowledge, and from this follows the idea that all can ultimately be known. Whilst the acquisition of such 'knowledge' may well be appropriately catered for through the interface, through the face-to-face a middle ground can be sought, as the face-to-face moves us to an infinity, the infinite unknowability of the other, which is beyond the tyranny of egocentricity. The latter leads through appropriation to a violence that leaves as our only choice totalitarianism or anarchy, to totalizing moves: it must claim a central position from which to know, a central position that can only be maintained by its claim to be the sole vantage point from which to know.

> 'Absolute knowledge, such as it has been sought, promised or recommended by philosophy, is a thought of the Equal. Being is embraced in the truth. Even if the truth is considered as never definitive, there is a promise of a more complete and adequate truth. Without doubt, the finite being that we are cannot in the final account complete the task of knowledge; but in the limit where this task is accomplished, it consists in making the other become the Same. On the other hand, the idea of the Infinite implies a thought of the Unequal' (Levinas, 1985: 91).

The post-Socratic Western emphasis on being founds our ideas about knowledge and intelligibility – by studying the products of our own consciousness we believe we come to know – and in the process the other is relegated to a bit player, more of the same and less than me. Yet the hope of the Western project is that one day we will know it all. I will become the possessor of knowledge and be in a known transparent world where nothing is hidden from me for everything will be intelligible. It is this delusion of ideal intelligibility that leads us to violence: what moves me is to make the world transparent to me and the face of the other is not there to stop me. Drug companies have been reported to be giving Aids sufferers in Third World countries life-saving drugs which, whether or not they work, will be withdrawn after two years (*Observer* 8.6.97). Perhaps those who make these decisions hope they will be far enough away not to have to face the consequences (as with the starving family on TV versus facing them at the next table: it appears a better decision for me not to see them at the next table, but is it a better decision for me?).

It is only through heteronomy as described below that a post modern learning can take place. For it is only through the face of the other that once can learn of the infinite.

'To be or not to be?' is the wrong question

For Hamlet, as for Heidegger and most of Western thought, the question has been 'To be or not to be?' Here primacy is given to the ontological and it is this question of being which has formed the unquestioned basis of most developmental theory, leading to an emphasis on autonomy, egocentricity, a bounded unitary self, etc (Loewenthal 1996). Levinas was also very interested in Hamlet (Levinas 1985: 22). He challenges the ontological by suggesting that ethical questions must always precede those of being and this, as we will attempt to show, is for Levinas a phenomenological rather than a moral necessity. For Levinas, as arguably for Shakespeare, Hamlet is asking the wrong question, the consequence of which is those he is closest to are killed off. This is because he puts himself rather than the other first. By asking the question 'To be or not to be?' Hamlet is concerned with himself before he is concerned with anyone else. It is as if he in his famous soliloquy is tapping the question into his terminal. For Levinas there was also a related important reading in that by asking this question it was as if Hamlet could be in charge of his own death: 'Hamlet is precisely a lengthy testimony to this impossibility of assuming death' (Levinas 1989: 42). The tragedy of Hamlet is that he tries to stay on top of that which he cannot.

Greek vs Hebraic: autonomy vs heteronomy

Levinas points out that 'Every philosophy seeks truth. Sciences too can be defined by this search...' (in Peperzak 1992: 47), as can teaching and learning. Our Western culture can be seen as having two major influences: Greek and Hebraic. However, it is the Greek notion of autonomy that has more often than not won the day over the notion of heteronomy.

Levinas describes the idea of truth in terms of heteronomy, in the following way.

> 'Truth implies experience. In the truth, a thinker maintains a relationship with a reality distinct from him, other than him – "absolutely other", ... for experience deserves its name only if it transports us beyond what constitutes our nature. Genuine experience must even lead us beyond the Nature that surrounds us, which is not jealous of the marvellous secrets it harbours, and, in complicity with men, submits to their reason and inventions; in it men also feel themselves to be at home. Truth would thus designate the outcome of a movement that leaves a world that is intimate and familiar, even if we have not yet explored it completely, and goes toward another region, toward a beyond ... Philosophy would be concerned with the absolutely other; it would be heteronomy itself ... Truth, the daughter of experience, has very lofty pretensions; it opens upon the very dimension of the ideal. In this way, philosophy means metaphysics, and metaphysics inquires about the divine' (Levinas in Peperzak 1992: 47).

In contrast to heteronomy, Levinas describes the Greek notion of autonomy as follows.

> 'But truth also means the free adherence to a proposition, the outcome of a free research. The freedom of the investigator, the thinker on whom no constraint weighs, is expressed in truth. What else is this freedom but the thinking being's refusal to be alienated in the adherence, the preserving of his nature, his identity, the feat of remaining the same despite the unknown lands into which thought seems to lead? Perceived in this way, philosophy would be engaged in reducing to the Same all that is opposed to it as other. It would be moving toward autonomy, a stage in which nothing irreducible would limit thought any longer, in which, consequently, thought, non-limited, would be free. Philosophy would thus be tantamount to the conquest of being by man over the course of history. Freedom, autonomy, the reduction of the Other to the Same, lead to this formula: the conquest of being by man over the course of history. This reduction does not represent some abstract schema; it is man's Ego' (Levinas in Peperzak 1992: 47–48).

We have deliberately quoted Levinas at relative length here as the above is key to our argument that Hamlet and much of teaching and learning have wrongly chosen autonomy over heteronomy, encompassing every Other in the Same. The other is not represented in the search for 'knowledge'; the other as represented by the interface becomes a bit player with at best a walk on part on our stage. There is, of course, always a danger that the student is a bit player on the lecturer's stage and through education everyone else becomes a bit player on the 'successful' student's stage, but without the face to face the ethical can be irreversibly lost.

To illustrate this last point: a teacher recently recounted a situation in which she was being appraised and a student, generally regarded as a 'problem kid', said he wasn't feeling well. This teacher replied 'Oh baby, feeling ill – better go and see the year teacher'. Soon after, this boy's friend and another 'problem kid' said quite typically 'I'm not in the mood to work today', to which the teacher replied 'Go and see your year teacher then'. At the end of the lesson this teacher's appraiser said 'no problems with that, it looks good to me.' Later it turned out that the first student had taken an overdose which the second student knew about. This teacher later recognized that she is under pressure to get as many of her students through the exams on as high a grade as possible and that she and the appraisal system combine in making her decision-making such that she is putting herself first in the name of putting the other first – but how would she ever have realized what was happening if the teaching had been done via a VDU?

In a conference workshop on distance learning it was notable how misgivings about the virtual classroom emerged – between the lines, as it were – and were brushed aside. There were nudging references to pornography, and there are, it was acknowledged by one enthusiast, students who do not flourish on the net, who have difficulty dealing with 'flaming'; the conclusion seemed to be that they needed better training. An institutional partnership with IBM was jocularly described as 'like selling one's soul to the devil'; the theological metaphor was striking, in the light of another contributor's opinion that the 'infinite' – he meant, all available knowledge – might be found on the Internet. It was an 'infinite' with seemingly little to do with otherness.

Values, ethics and ontology

As decision-makers and educators, what then are our values? We are assuming that as decision makers we will always be subjective – our values determining how we collect information and what we decide. That is insofar as we are able to say what our values are (for we are suffused with the values of our culture which we can only ever partly step outside) and subject to our unconscious (which may be two different ways of saying the same thing). So it is vital for decision making that we attempt to consider what we regard as essentially human: under what circumstances is the world an alive and meaningful place for us as decision makers and educators? Is it when we can assertively go after that which appears important to us (autonomy) or does it begin with putting the other first (heteronomy) in a way that recognizes the otherness of the other (their alterity)? In this way our values and ethics are linked. When speaking of ethics we do not mean codes of conduct. These in fact can be seen as unethical as they, however well intended in their systematization, are putting the code rather than the other first. Levinasian ethics is not therefore about my right to exist (Spinoza), it isn't even just about the other's right to exist, but can be seen as my responsibility for the other's responsibility to others. As Child *et al.* (1995) argue, ethics subsumed in the ontology of situatedness is problematic in education and could encourage a violence. Child quotes Levinas: ethics cannot be subsumed by ontology but rather precedes ontology. For the other always exists first, precedes our own being, whether or not we make the choice (in the words of John Wild in his preface to Levinas' *Totality and Infinity*) for 'generosity and communication' (Levinas 1969: 14). To choose 'autonomy' does not annihilate this prior claim of the other – though we can of course annihilate the other.

For Levinas '...my duty to respond to the other suspends my natural right to self-survival' (Levinas 1981: 189). This 'right to exist' is in the face of the other which asks us both 'do not do violence to me' and 'do not let me die alone ... as to do so were to become an accomplice in his death' (Levinas 1981: 189). 'In the relation to the face I am exposed as an usurper of the place of the other' (Levinas 1981: 189). Thus, for teaching and learning, if students were only to learn through the interface we would be irresponsible in letting them die alone.

So who was Levinas? Levinas was born in Lithuania in 1905 of Jewish parents, moved to the Ukraine where he was during the Russian Revolution, then went as a young man to France. He was to live most of the rest of his life in France, surviving a prisoner of war camp, dying in France in 1995. However, in 1928–29 he went to Freiburg where he attended Husserl's lectures and this was the decisive encounter with phenomenology and through this, with Heidegger. Whilst Levinas is now accredited with bringing phenomenology to France and greatly influencing Sartre and such postmodern thinkers as Derrida and Lyotard, it was not until he was 55 that he became a full professor. He gained his international reputation with the publication of *Totality and Infinity* in 1961. Besides his interest in philosophy he renewed in France his commitment to Talmudic studies and revived them as a university pursuit.

Education as an ethical practice

Besides Child *et al.* (1995), referred to above, Williams (1992) and Jarvis (1997) are the only other references found concerning Levinas and education. Williams argues using Levinas that through actually involving teachers face-to-face at various stages of professional development students are willing to change in response to the needs of others and are more likely to be involved in the research community in ways that benefit teaching and teacher education. Jarvis acknowledges this thinking and provides a summary of Levinas' ideas.

Of the few references concerning Levinas and psychotherapy (see Gondek 1995) we wish to focus on Gans (1997) as providing a useful reading of the implications of Levinas for counselling and psychotherapy. Which we are interested in as a form of teaching and learning.

Rather than considering the implications of Levinasian ethics for practice we would subscribe to the notion put forward by Gans (1997), in relation to psychotherapy, of education as an ethical practice.

Gans describes his 'Levinasian oriented ethical psychoanalysis' as an "endeavour to bring out the good of the Other by opening him/her to the between of responsible relatedness.' This responsible relatedness 'involves being able to enjoy, to dwell, to love intimately and to meet others face to face, and ultimately to realize that the face of the other is the aspect of divinity open to us.' Gans appears to be getting close to a religiosity in his language which interestingly may or may not reflect Levinas (see for example Levinas in Peperzak *et al.* 1996: 8).

In accordance with Levinas' *Totality and Infinity* Gans describes how the therapist can help the client/patient with the blocks that prevent them being able to fully enter 'the zones of relatedness'. The psychotherapist can help the patient to move from Levinas' 'there is'(the infinite void prior to experience, a continuous night of insomnia fearing annihilation) through his:

- 'living from' (we live from good soup through our embodied love of life without which we can never enter into the between of genuine relatedness)
- 'dwelling'(for this to occur there must be a surrender to embodiment and finitude so that we move from being only for oneself to dwelling where one can accept others and be touched by them)
- 'the face to face' (this is not reducing the other to the same, to a supporting role in one's own play as with Hamlet but instead recognizing and accepting the other's difference from the standpoint of difference rather than a comparison with oneself)
- 'eros' (this is the realm of intimacy where the erotic as intimate loving is only possible).

Aren't all the above points, albeit to varying extents, the job of the educator and manager as well as the psychotherapist? Furthermore isn't this process necessary for any ethical decision making? In which case isn't it the face-to-face rather than the interface which is the essential element?

Conclusion

Gans (1997) notes that eros 'takes us beyond ethical analysis to ethical life' and it is this type of value that we hope decision makers will find helpful in thinking what it is that determines what they find out and how they respond. There are criticisms of Levinas. Derrida (1995) argues that Levinas has been caught in a Christian conspiracy that developed the notion of ethics because they couldn't take life's rawness and Grosz (1996), following Derrida, has argued that Levinas has ignored gender. For others what has been presented may appear like a form of humanism. If so then it is a postmodern humanism as unlike Hamlet we as ethical practitioners try not to attempt to be at the centre of our World but are always subject to an ethical imperative.

The Enlightenment project which promises that one day science will know leads educational theories to be caught up with totalizing moves. We attempt to know rather than to accept who we are. This has enormous importance regarding how we educate our students (and for the authors for the way we examine the implications of the literature on phenomenology, existentialism, psychoanalysis and postmodernism for our students' practices). Levinas can be seen to deconstruct the modernist project. For Levinas we are always subject to the other who is always an infinite mystery. We may think as educators that we sometimes for example get some ideas about our students but we will never know them. This contrasts with the various attempts at scientific approaches to decision making (what we assume can be more appropriately learnt through electronic means). Freud, for example, was often caught up in this way: he periodically expressed a hope that physiology would one day vindicate his discoveries. As a consequence if we can't have this knowledge we can't for example systematize Levinas which we are in danger of attempting here, for to do so would prevent us making decisions justly in the moment with our clients and each other.

Through interfaces, which our economies are encouraging, rather than the face, there is a greater danger that we merely encourage self-consciousness, and re-write our experience in a way that helps us accumulate power. We can hope to select a future so we can dominate with our apparent survival strategy. Each of us can put each of us on a map and through our values select a path towards a goal and work against other species and our own, ostrich like preferring our own stories to what is around us.

This is similar to where there is trauma in our lives and there is restriction and we cannot learn. In trauma the world does not make sense to us. There is a war between ourselves and others rather than a rapport. For Freud we can only become ourselves in relation to the other. The other is otherwise seen as threatening locking us into an omnipotent grandeur which is empty. Bion (1967), extrapolating from Freud, also describes how no thinking is possible without a living link to the other. This has profound implications for our thinking about learning inhibitions and deficits: damaged links with an embodied other (or pseudo-links with a disembodied fantasy other) can and do, for Bion, produce damaged or non-links between thoughts. We engage in pseudo-knowledge while not wanting to know. One can refuse to accept the other whilst being caught up with a ideal of transparent intelligibility. The truth of the other is missed, and in the process we do not learn in way that enables us to make the right decisions (From the perspective developed above there are also questions for psychotherapy: did psychoanalytical theory become more violent because we couldn't see the face of the other except when they paid at the end of the session? Is Lacan (1988) in some ways modern, as he talks of the gap when we do not know what the other thinks of us, but is this still egocentric – not seeing the other as beyond me, and wondering at the resulting infinity? We can also ask whether it is possible for managers to be more infinitizers than totalizers.)

The whole dichotomy is that there is no mediation – as Winnicott (1971) would say no play space – where one can acknowledge the other and learn from each other recognizing the differences.

Levinas then emerges because he shows a way, through philosophy, in which it is possible to come together and appreciate the other's personal space and allow the other their otherness. As managers, educators, psychotherapists, perhaps we can only learn through the other if we see the other as someone we can serve and learn from.

References

Bion, WR (1967) *Second Thoughts*, Karnac, London.
Brunt, J (1996) 'Can You Put Your Arm Around A Student on the Internet?', *Adult Learning*, Jan 1996.
'Cumulative Subject Index' (1996) *Contents Pages in Education*, 10, 12.
Child, M et al. (1995) 'Autonomy or Heteronomy? Levinas's Challenge to Modernism and Postmodernism', *Educational Theory*, 45, 2, 167–189.
Derrida, J (1995), *The Gift of Death*, Chicago University Press, Chicago & London.
Derrida, J (1996), *Archive Fever*, Chicago University Press, Chicago & London.
Freud, S (1937) *Analysis Terminable and Interminable, The Standard Edition of the Complete Psychological Works of Sigmund Freud, vol. 23*, Hogarth Press and the Institute of Psycho-Analysis, London, 1953–1974.
Gans, S (1997) 'Lacan and Levinas: Towards an Ethical Psychoanalysis', *Journal of the British Society for Phenomenology*, 28, 1, January 1997.
Gondek, H (1995) 'Cogito and Separation. Lacan/Levinas', *Journal of European Psychoanalysis*, 2, Fall 1995–Winter 1996, 133–168.

Grosz, E (1996) *Space, Time and Perversion – Essays on the Politics of Bodies*, Routledge, London.
Jarvis, P (1997) *Ethics and Education for Adults in Late Modern Society*, NIACE, Leicester.
Lacan, J (1988) *The Seminars of Jaques Lacan, Books I & II* (Trans, J Forrester), Cambridge University Press, Cambridge.
Levinas, E (1961) (1969) *Totality and Infinity: An Essay on Exteriority* (Trans. A Lingis), Duquesne University Press, Pittsburgh.
Levinas, E (1969) *Totality and Infinity*, Dusquesne University Press, Pittsburgh.
Levinas, E (1981) 'Ethics of the Infinite', in Kearney, R *States of Mind Dialogues with Contemporary Thinkers on the European Mind*, Manchester University Press, Manchester.
Levinas, E (1985) *Ethics and Infinity. Conversations with Philippe Nemo* (Trans. R Cohen), Duquesne University Press, Pittsburgh.
Levinas E (1989) *The Levinas Reader* (Ed. S Hand), Blackwell, Oxford.
Loewenthal, D (1996) 'The Post-modern Counsellor: Some Implications for Practice, Theory, Research and Professionalism', *Counselling Psychology Quarterly*, 9, 4, 1996, 373–381.
PC Pro (1997) 34, August 1997, Dennis Publications.
Perperzak, A (1992) *To the Other: An Introduction to the Philosophy of Emmanuel Levinas*, Purdue University Press, Indiana.
Peperzak, A, Critchley, S and Bernasconi, R (1996), *Emmanuel Levinas. Basic Philosophical Writings*, Indiana University Press, Bloomington and Indianapolis.
Utley, A (1997) 'Abusive E-mails Ignite Work Fury', *The Times Higher Education Supplement*, 1282, 30 May 1997.
Williams, D (1992) *Preparing Teachers as Naturalistic Inquirers; Responding to the Face of the Other*. Paper presented at the Annual Meeting of the American Educational Research Association, San Francisco, CA, April 20–24.
Winnicott, D (1971) *Playing and Reality*, Tavistock, London.

Chapter 29

Lifelong Learning:
The Path to Lifelong Liabilities for Women?

Venitha Pillay

Now that the dust of celebrations has set, it has become imperative on the government and the people of South Africa to tackle the challenges of building a new ethos, in all aspects of life, that would remove the injustices of the past and simultaneously shape the future of the country. It is with this in mind that new education ideals are being discussed, debated and finally accepted as policy. One of the most significant changes in education policy is the merging of education and training as a singular educational concept. The development of a National Qualifications Framework (NQF) is seen as a key strategy in integrating education and training. A core and a welcome, element of the NQF is the recognition of prior learning (RPL). A closely related recognition is that learning can take place in multiple modes and at multiple sites. Hence, it is argued, the new education framework makes lifelong learning not simply a desirable objective but also a very real possibility. This means that, theoretically, those who in the past were unable to fulfil their educational ambitions may now have the opportunity to do so irrespective of where on the educational ladder they may currently find themselves. It also changes the education landscape of the future; it would be possible to plan one's educational path with much more flexibility; it allows one to build a career without sacrificing educational aspirations and it allows for the transportability of educational achievements and work experience into different areas of learning and into different work situations.

This paper seeks to address two main questions. The first is whether the new education model, in claiming to deal with the imbalances of the past, sufficiently recognizes and acts upon the gender inequities of the apartheid education system. The second is to examine whether the concept of lifelong learning, realized through the NQF, and which forms one of the central pillars of the new education model, is one that promotes gender equity or serves to create and/or maintain gender inequalities either implicitly or explicitly. It should be noted that the two issues are ultimately linked as the first will have an impact on the realization of the goals of lifelong learning.

One important variable that shapes the current conjuncture is that there does not appear to be any overt feminist theory that dominates the landscape of South African feminisms. Much of the development of feminist theory in this country is rooted in the discourse of the liberation struggle. While such an evolutionary path for feminisms in South Africa may seem almost 'natural', one of the main weaknesses of this approach has been the historical tendency to prioritize issues of race and class liberation over the liberation of women and men from gender oppression. Coupled with this was the reluctance among the liberatory women's movement, comprising a number of liberation-aligned women's organizations, to accept the idea of 'feminism', believing it to be a Western import that is foreign to Africa.

The price of this path for feminism and for the gender struggle in South Africa is becoming increasingly clear in the current political context. With the end of the liberation struggle and the focus now being on transformation, the nature of women's organizations in the country has changed. While the major political parties each have their own 'women's wing', there does not appear to be a significant broad-based cohesive women's movement comprising of women from civil society and being held together by similar goals. The Women's Coalition formed in the early 90s to draw up the Women's Charter has completed its main task and no longer has a notable political or social presence. The fight against gender oppression has been institutionalized into a variety of state machinery. Unfortunately there is, as yet, no strong voice in civil society to monitor and give strength to the struggle for gender liberation. Pat Horn describes the situation as follows.

> 'The women's movement, and feminism in South Africa, has lapsed into a state of disarray for the moment ...The task therefore is to regroup into the kinds of structures which are most appropriate for the tasks at hand in this historical conjuncture' (1995: 73).

The arguments in this paper are premised on the belief that the structure and arrangements of social institutions should not, either implicitly or explicitly, compromise the practice of equity and justice. In fact, I would argue that it is incumbent on government, especially one that in its discourse is committed to all forms of social and political equity, to ensure that the goal of equity is achievable for all. Education is one of the primary commodities provided by the government and it is imperative that the principles of equity are fully realizable through its development of policy. While acknowledging the numerous transformatory policies developed by the Ministry in its quest to provide better education for all, my concern is with what appears to be a 'undo apartheid' approach which underlie strategies for achieving equity. The question for me is, to what extent can gender inequities be addressed through this apparent circumscribed approach.

The latest draft White Paper on Higher Education ('the White Paper') (Ministry of Education 1997) clearly sets out the challenges confronting Higher Education. The two most significant and simultaneous challenges are firstly to:

> '...overcome an historically determined pattern of fragmentation, inequality and inefficiency, increase access for black students and for women, generate new models for learning to accommodate a larger and more diverse student population' (Ministry of Education 1997: 15).

The second challenge is that:

> 'successful policy must restructure the higher education system and its institutions to meet the needs of an increasingly technologically oriented economy' (Ministry of Education 1997: 15).

These are noble and necessary goals. While the White Paper does provide a level of strategic direction as to how some of these concerns may be addressed, it is silent on how to increase access to female students. In the first instance there is no recognition of the fact that female students often enjoy a numerical superiority, albeit a small one, at the school level. In African schools in particular, they comprise 55 per cent of the student population (Truscott 1994: 84). It is necessary therefore to interrogate why the situation changes at the tertiary level. This would be a crucial exercise in order to determine what structural or social forces act as obstacles to potential female students. In other words one cannot increase access without knowing what hinders access. It cannot be assumed that the same factors that prevented black students and financially disadvantaged students from entering university applies equally to female students. For example it is possible that teenage motherhood, which is widely documented as being very common in South Africa, could pose a problem to young mothers wishing to attend a tertiary institution. While they may have been able to arrange child care during the shorter school day and where they would have closer to home, the same may not be possible if they were to attend a tertiary institution. In the same vein there may be other factors that prevent females in particular from attending tertiary institutions.

It is also disconcerting to note that the Ministry speaks of 'equity' and 'equality of opportunity' in a gender-neutral way. I would venture to argue that in the main 'equity' and 'equality of opportunity' refer to equality between black and white students and an increased opportunity for financially disadvantaged students but not to gender equity. In fact, the paper goes as far as to say that to achieve the two main objectives identified earlier:

> 'there must be increased participation with an expansion of student enrolments, with students recruited from a broader distribution of *social groups and classes*' (Ministry of Education 1997: 11; emphasis added).

It is almost as if, having dispensed with the issues of gender in an opening statement, the matter can now be put to rest. The problem really is an approach that simply tacks on the word 'gender' at strategic points without any real interrogation of how it may be integrated into policy and what the gender implications of policy may be.

This 'tack on gender' approach has serious implications for the second objective that the Ministry prioritizes. What we seem to be heading for is a situation in which areas of study previously dominated by white males will now become dominated by black males. According to the 1990 annual report of the National Department of Education, of the 4,912 students enrolled for Engineering, 134 were females. Of these only two were black females. Similar disparities are to be found the Physical and Mathematical Sciences (Truscott 1994: 85). Although the Minister of Education repeatedly stresses the importance of the study of science and technology, the White Paper fails to address the problem of the absence of female students in this field in any significant way.

The belief that the study of science and technology is the path to a successful career and the means to building the South African economy immediately accords it a level of economic and social power that towers above any other area of study. If female students remain outside this area of study then they inevitably become excluded from some such power. The simplistic approach of increasing access to female students may in fact exacerbate an existing problem ; the 'feminization' and consequent ghettoization of typically 'female' areas of study.

McLennan makes a salient point that signals the dangers in the Ministry's equality of access approach.

> 'The distributive paradigm tends to depict justice as the allocation of material goods and social positions, at the expense of considering social relations of power and domination. This can be seen in the South African context where women have equal access to education but often lack access to suitable employment and positions of power' (1993/4: 54).

Even if women do register for any of the so called male domains of study the difficulties they face are extremely discouraging. McGivney, in examining the experience of female students in the United Kingdom, argues that:

> 'studies which have documented the experiences of girls who have attempted to cross gender boundaries ... graphically illustrate that the prospect of surviving or thriving is unlikely ... They provide a picture of a largely hostile male environment in which girls feel isolated, harassed and excluded by fellow male trainees...' (1993: 27).

The problem is compounded by a highly restrictive labour market that appears reluctant to employ women in male-dominated fields of work. Although the principle of lifelong learning is meant to open the doors of learning to all, some doors remain firmly closed to women. In short, educational equality is not simply a matter of equality of access but, more importantly, equality of outcomes.

Perhaps one of the weaknesses of the use of universalizing concepts like 'learners' and 'students' is that the gender differences between learners is obliterated. In this instance the gender differences between learners have become subsumed by their race and class differences. The danger herein is that in practice all learners are treated as male and it is assumed that the needs of female learners are the same as that of male learners. Such an approach immediately reduces the possible success rates of female students, as they have to function within a male-defined ethos. To extrapolate, the black, working-class female is inevitably set up for failure. Her frame of reference as a student is not how to pass but how not to fail. Dale Spender makes an analogous point in her article 'Educational Institutions: Where Co-operation is Called Cheating'.

> 'Men have assumed that the male is the norm ... and have imposed their view on women for whom this may be an alien understanding in terms of our own existence but one which we must internalize if we are to function in a male-defined society' (1980: 40).

Unless positive steps are taken to act upon this situation the gender inequities of the past will not only remain but will in all probability be unwittingly reinforced.

To sum up this first aspect of my discussion – that is, can the new education model address the gender inequities of the past – I believe that it has a number of shortcomings, not all of which are covered in this paper. For example the issue of the campus environment being antagonistic to female students has not been addressed at all. In particular, the instances of rape at tertiary institutions is known to be a problem. I believe that if the Ministry is serious about gender equity in education institutions then it is obliged to address these realities.

If the formal education system, at the tertiary level, fails to adequately incorporate the principle of gender equity, then it is questionable as to what extent the principle of lifelong learning becomes achievable, particularly by those who get the short end of the equity stick. The goal of lifelong learning cannot be achieved if the structural and economic factors that surround its functioning is not mediated by a gendered lens.

Perhaps the experience of the Gender Task Team, one of 20 Task Teams (TTs) constituted to draw up an implementation plan for the new education model, is a telling one. A report of the Gender Task Team says that they failed in their task of encouraging each task team to integrate an analysis of gender in their respective areas of work. They advocate two reasons for this failure. The first is that they assumed that the TTs were aware of the gender dimensions of their respective areas of work. It was evident that the understanding of TTs went little beyond the rhetoric of gender equality. The second reason was that:

> 'the generic terms in which the Policy Framework and Implementation Teams work, militates against approaches which seek to address substantive issues of gender ... such approaches by their very nature suppress consideration of real inequalities' (Gender Task Team 1994: 4).

I suggest that these two shortcomings apply to the Ministry's new education model as well. It is the second aspect, that is of the dangers inherent in the use of universalizing frameworks, that I want to look at in more detail in my discussion of the NQF and lifelong learning.

Earlier I pointed to the dangers inherent in the use of universalizing terms like 'learners' and 'students'. The argument applies also to the concept of learning which is presented in a gender neutral way in the documentation describing the NQF. The Ministry of Education stresses its commitment to RPL and says that this means an attempt to 'recognize all learning, irrespective of how it was achieved'. In the first instance what is missing here is the gendered perceptions of what constitutes knowledge and learning. Luttrell argues that women's classification of their knowledge is very different from that of men's.

> 'The women's classification of their knowledge as "affective" not "cognitive", as "intuitive" not learnt, or as feelings not thoughts all reflect an acceptance of dominant conceptions of Knowledge and ultimately diminish women's power' (1992: 183).

My experience as a teacher, borne out by similar experiences of colleagues, suggests that male students are far more willing to advance their own perceptions of the world as valid and authentic than female students, who tend to be more reluctant to do so. Females are also more eager to make allowances for the possibility of understandings other than their own than are males. I would venture to argue that females often do not perceive what they know to be a valid form of knowledge. Acker adds weight to this view. She argues that the:

> 'sociology of knowledge suggests that what is known is a product of the historical and socio-economic position of the knower ... women have been largely excluded from the work of producing the forms of thought and the images and symbols in which thought is expressed and ordered' (1994: 130).

If access to lifelong learning is dependent on RPL then women would be seriously disadvantaged if what they know is not seen as valid forms of knowledge. Hence it is imperative for the concept of RPL to hinge on the recognition that knowledge is gendered and that active steps need to be taken to understand and include women's ways of knowing. If the conceptualization of RPL is apparently gender neutral then the practice and application unfortunately becomes male-defined. There is little point in saying that women should speak out for themselves. In the first instance it is unlikely that they would. In the second instance they should not have to. There should be no need for them to struggle for acceptance, for recognition as authentic knowers. What is necessary is an integration of gender in defining and understanding knowledge. Unfortunately the new education model fails to do so.

A closely related and equally important point is that most women perform innumerable domestic duties. Looking after children and running a home is usually the responsibility of women. Of course this is unpaid work and is often regard as a labour of love rather than gainful employment. Whether it is a labour of love or not does not detract from the fact that it is hard work that requires a variety of skills and a particular knowledge base. A large number of women balance domestic work with paid employment as well. The skills acquired in running a home and bringing up children must fall within the ambit of prior learning. These skills need to be defined and evaluated. According to the government document *Getting to Grips with NQF*:

> 'learners who have gained skills and knowledge outside a formal learning environment will be able to receive credit towards unit standards and qualification, provided they are able to meet the requirements for assessment'

and

> 'learners will need to identify the specific unit standards in which they want to be assessed and then to have access to assessment' (Phillips 1996: 36).

This procedure raises a number of implications specific to women.

Although there is acceptance that learning and skilling can take place outside the formal learning and formal work environments, there needs to be an extension to this point to recognize that learning and skilling may take place outside both these conditions. Understandings of the term 'unemployed' may have very different implications for men as for women. Women who have spent all their adult lives in the domestic tasks of running a home may not be considered to have been formally employed, neither were they in informal employment and nor have they been unemployed.

For me significant areas of concern are the issues of who will perform assessments, what kind of training in gender awareness will these individuals have, who is going to set the criteria for assessment and how gender sensitive will these criteria be? None of these questions are answered by the Ministry; in fact there is little evidence of an awareness of such questions.

The NQF makes a strong point about the need for maintaining standards and for assessors applying their criteria for assessment equally to people in similar situations. Unfortunately, applying criteria equally to people in apparently similar situations does not necessarily result in fairness. For example a woman who has been running her home but has not been in formal or informal employment is not in the same position as a man who has not been in formal or informal employment. To coin a popular yet very relevant phrase, there is nothing as unfair as treating those who are unequal equally. I agree that standards need to be set, but in doing so one needs to be wary that certain sections of the population are not prejudiced by the standards set, nor are they particularly disadvantaged in the process of meeting the standards.

A point worth mentioning here is that the NQF speaks only of work-based assessors in describing the process of registration of assessors. Immediately the question of how people will who are outside the formal workplace have access to assessors? Budlender's report on the women's budget reveals that 75 per cent of African workers in the informal sector are women. Once again it seems that structural arrangements shove women outside the NQF's parameters of functioning. I am hoping that the promised forthcoming piece entitled *Getting to Grips with Assessment and Registered Assessors in the NQF* will throw some light on these questions.

Assuming that women do manage to get through the arduous and perhaps prejudicial process of being assessed and evaluated and may now be placed somewhere on the new education ladder, does not mean that the battle is over.

A Survey of Adult Basic Education in South Africa in the 1990s, edited by Harley et al., reveals that in many areas of the country more women than men attend adult education (AE) classes. However it is not clear what percentage of women needing AE actually attend AE classes. According to Budlender, 20 per cent of African women aged 20 and above have had no formal education, compared to 14 per cent of African men (1997: 27). It is heartening to note that the 1997 education budget accommodates a doubling of the 1996 budget for AE. However, Budlender makes a valid point that the figures take on a new perspective when one realizes that AE budget is a mere 1 per cent of the total education budget. The implications of these figures take on more alarming proportions when one examines government reliance, rightly so, on business to provide education and training in order to upgrade workers' skills. Invariably, the business sector is going to choose to allocate resources to those already in employment or those who have the potential to be employed. (The Department of Labour makes frequent reference to the 'young' and the 'unemployed'.) In other words the large number of women who work in the informal labour market will probably have to depend entirely on government provision of AE and to some extent NGO (non-governmental organizations) provision of AE. At this stage there does not seem to be much clarity on how the government intends to develop its provision of AE. However it must be noted that in the past, AE mainly focused on literacy (much of this was provided by NGOs) and as far as women in particular were concerned, AE classes provided tuition in typical 'women's work' like sewing classes, basket-making, etc. If this is the only option available to unemployed women and to those in the informal sector, then AE will serve to reinforce and perpetuate gender hierarchies in the labour force. In the long run the extent to which women may contribute to and benefit from economic growth is circumscribed and hampered by their gendered location in the labour market. Wolpe suggest that it is likely that:

> 'any training they [women] may receive will not provide them with access into an hierarchically structured labour force in which the semiskilled and skilled jobs are terrain of men' (1993/94: 140).

She also sounds a relevant note of warning that is worth noting.

> 'Having campaigned for so long to get access to skilled work, is it likely they [black men] will allow women into their ranks?' (1993/94: 141).

The scope of this paper does not allow for a more detailed discussion of the provision of AE. Suffice it to say at this stage that AE needs to undergo a process of restructuring and reconceptualizing if it is to provide any significant benefit for the majority of its users, that is, women. It is evident that the provision of AE is crucial to the 'success' of lifelong learning.

I believe it is necessary at this point to briefly examine the Ministry of Labour's Green Paper: *Skills Development Strategy for Economic and Employment Growth in South Africa*. In particular, I want to focus on areas where it may interface with the provision of education and training and contribute toward the realization of the objectives of lifelong learning.

In the main the document proposes a system of learnerships for skills development and economic growth. A learnership is:

> 'a mechanism to facilitate the linkage between structured learning and work experience in order to obtain a registered qualification which signifies work readiness' (Ministry of Labour 1997: 3).

Learnerships are designed to act as an interface between theoretical education and skills development. It goes on to explain that one of the factors proscribing learnerships is access to structured work experience. According to Budlender 50 per cent of employed African women are to be found in unskilled occupations like cleaning and farm work. If one reads this statistic together with the literacy figures quoted earlier, it becomes abundantly clear that not too many African women will be able to fulfil the requirements for access to learnerships. Even if they are able to meet these initial requirements it is uncertain as to what extent they may actually benefit from the system of learnerships. If history is anything to go by then the prospects look bleak. In 1991 the Department of Manpower (*sic*) spent R93m on 'mainly unemployed work seekers'. Most of this was spent on training in typically male jobs. Training for women centred on typically women's work like sewing classes (Wolpe 1993/94: 140).

It is heartening to note that the Ministry of Labour makes a commitment to attract women to areas of non-traditional work and that learnerships are 'designed for areas of so called "women's work"' (1997: 35). A further welcome recognition is that a 'multi-pronged approach is needed' to address the needs of women in rural areas and informal settlements (1997: 35). What is worrying however is that there is no indication of how this is to be done. If one reads this silence with the statement that 'learnerships directly address the "how" of the skills development strategy' then it seems that women have not been adequately incorporated into the strategy. I suggest that the recognition of gender in the development of an economic growth strategy is but a rhetoric one. Unless the gender implications of the system of learnerships is consciously interrogated it is very probable that women will be left out of the strategy for economic growth and skills development. The consequences of the lacunae in the proposal becomes worrying if one remembers that women are the poorest of the poor in South Africa. Sadly, the indications are that they will remain so for a long time to come.

Finally, I suggest that in the first instance, all education policy development should be premised on the recognition of 'gender' as a variable that can have significant outcomes in the education equation. For as long as policy makers 'solve' the 'gender problem' with the simplistic answer of 'more women', then the real issues of gender discrimination in education will remain unchallenged. I am aware that the suggestion is not a new one. That it is being repeatedly made points to firstly, its importance and secondly, the Ministry of Education's failure to heed these suggestions.

Secondly, the relationship between education provision and the labour market has specific and different impacts on men and women. The gendered fragmentation of the labour market has to be factored into the development of policy that is concerned with capacity building. The aim may not necessarily be to change the face of such fragmentation, but to ensure that gender does not adversely affect the potential for individual and national capacity building.

References

Acker, S (1994) *Gendered Education: Sociological Reflections on Women, Teaching and Feminism*, Open University Press, Buckingham.

Bagnall, RG (1990) 'Lifelong Education: The Institutionalisation of an Illiberal and Regressive Ideology?', *Educational Philosophy and Theory*, 22, 1, 1–7.

Budlender, D (1997) 'The Women's Budget', *Agenda*, 33, 37–42.

Budlender, D and Hirschowitz, R (1993/94) 'Adult Education, Gender and Access', *Perspectives*, 15, 1, 149–170.

Education Policy Unit, University of Natal (1996) *Understanding the NQF: A Guide to Lifelong Learning*, unpublished.

Enslin, P (1993/94) 'Education for Nation-building: A Feminist Critique', *Perspectives*, 15, 1, 13–25.

Finley, MK (1992) 'The Educational Contest for Middle- and Working-Class Women: The Reproduction of Inequality', in J Wrigley *Education and Gender Equality*, Falmer Press, London.

Gender Task Team (1994) *A Plan for Gender Equity in Education and Training: Implementation Plan for Education and Training* (IPET), unpublished.

Harley, A, Aitchison, J, Lyster, E and Land, S (1996) *A Survey of Adult Basic Education in South Africa in the 1990s*, Sached Books, South Africa.

Highet, G (1991) 'Gender and Education: A study of the ideology and practice of community based women's education', in S Westwood and JE Thomas (Eds) *The Politics of Adult Education*, NIACE, Leicester.

Horn, P (1995) 'Where is feminism now?', *Agenda*, 26, 71–74.

Klugman, B (1990) 'How are Women Incorporated into the Struggle? Ideas from Uganda', *Agenda*, 6, 62–66.

Luttrell, W (1992) 'Working-Class Women's Ways of Knowing: Effects of Gender, Race and Class', in Wrigley, J *Education and Gender Equality*, Falmer Press, London.

McGivney, V (1993) *Women, Education and Training: Barriers to Access, Informal Starting Points and Progression Routes*, NIACE, Hillcroft College.

McLennan, A '"And Women, Too, Will Play Their Part"; The Relevance of Gender to Equal Education in South Africa', *Perspectives*, 15, 1, 53–68.

Ministry of Labour (1997) *Green Paper on Skills Development Strategy for Economic and Employment Growth in South Africa*, Ministry of Labour, Pretoria.

Ministry of Education (1996) *White Paper on the Organisation, Governance and Funding of Schools*, Ministry of Education, Pretoria.

Ministry of Education (1997) *Draft White Paper on Higher Education*, Ministry of Education, Pretoria.

Ministry of Education (1996) *Schools Bill*, Ministry of Education, Pretoria.

Phillips, B (Ed.) (1996) *Getting to Grips with the National Qualifications Framework (NQF)*, Sigma Press, South Africa.

Replan (1991) *Women Learning: Ideas, Approaches and Practical Support*, NIACE, Leicester.

Scientech 97 (1997) *Women in Science and Technology*, Foundation for Research and Development, South Africa.

Spender, D (1980) 'Educational Institutions: Where Co-operation is Called Cheating', in D Spender and E Sarah (Eds) *Learning to Lose*, The Woman's Press, London.

Truscott, K (1994) *Gender in Education*, University of the Witwatersrand, Education Policy Unit.

Westwood, S and Thomas, JE (Eds) (1991) *The Politics of Adult Education*, NIACE, Leicester.

Wolpe, A (1993/94) 'Inserting Feminism into Adult Education', *Perspectives*, 15, 1, 131–147.

Wrigley, J (Ed.) (1992) *Education and Gender Equality*, The Falmer Press, London.

Chapter 30

Education of Employees and Business Social Responsibility:
The Question of Political Utilitarianism

Janko Berlogar

Adult education has always meant politics, and still does. The same applies to the education of employees and to business social responsibility. The education of employees is an important, internal but usually neglected part of business social responsibility. 'The only way to plan responsibly is to act politically' argue Cervero and Wilson (1994: 117). They refer, of course, to planning for adult education – planning through negotiating power and interests. Adult education is the field where '...we need to understand much more thoroughly the connection between education and the ideological, political and economic spheres of society' (Apple 1985: 8). The same author's still more radical claim is that 'we are witnessing a remarkable business offensive, one in which our educational system is slowly being more and more drawn into the ideological orbit of the corporation and its needs' (Apple 1985: viii). Perhaps some enthusiasts still believe that educational processes occur, and those who participate in them live, in 'splendid isolation' (Jarvis 1987: 11). If so, then this chapter is meant as an act of 'de-dreaming', to wake them up. The reality in which employees strive for their education is that of political utilitarianism.

Education of employees and lifelong learning in the learning society

My approach to the problem discussed is rather critical and my language sometimes political. Besides, the language is the language of adult education. How does discussion of employee education relate to lifelong learning and the learning society – the central concepts of this book? The relations and connections are clear, but need some explanation.

The beginning of this explanation is short and straightforward: education of employees is the missing link, the essential step to be made on the way to learning organizations and learning society. There is no lifelong learning and no learning society without education of employees. Lifelong learning is a concept, a vision; and the learning society, too. No doubt the vision will become reality some day – but till then it is reminiscent of the idea of democracy. Who does not wish to live in democracy? But then ask management about democracy and participation in their (business) organizations! Ask not about the vision, but about the actual decisions. I asked them (Berlogar 1995). Their response: ignorance at least, if not denial. Deetz and Kersten (1983: 54) stated clearly: societies cannot assert beliefs and values that are at the same time ignored or even denied by organizations within the societies.

Learning organizations, learning society and lifelong learning are also values. Their destiny is much the same as that of other values. They are acceptable – but they are not accepted. Ask managements again what are they willing to do in their organizations. I asked them that too (Berlogar 1997) and the answers were just what I had expected. They all agree that education is important, learning is important, too, but: excuses, excuses, and excuses again. We should be worried – not because of the excuses themselves, but because many of these excuses might be found acceptable.

We can agree with Marquardt's sixteen steps towards the learning organization (Marquardt 1996). We can enjoy reading Senge *et al.* (1995). But much of what is proposed simply does not work. Why? I quote Jarvis again (1987: 11): 'Learning is not just a psychological process that happens in splendid isolation from the world in which the learner lives, but is intimately related to that world and affected by it.' That is perhaps part of the answer. The part I dare to add is perhaps a little provocative. Learning organizations, learning society and lifelong learning remain more vision than reality. We all like visions. But education of employees is both obligation and responsibility. Usually we do not like too many obligations. If I use the language of adult education, it is to encourage us all to accept obligations and responsibility, and thus to enable the vision of lifelong learning to be realized.

Back to reality

Even if it is not true that the only task and responsibility of business is to make profit, in immediate and financial terms, the fact is that this function is basic to business organizations. Education of employees does not make money, at least not immediately, nor does it make 'as much as possible'. It is an input without measurable output. Nevertheless, many business organizations nowadays accept obligations beyond the purely economic. They accept social responsibilities and some even see economic, if longer-term, benefits in it. Education of employees is, no doubt, more a social and political than an economic function and responsibility of business. Social functions and responsibilities – not just employee education – are usually accepted not because organizations want them but because of pressure. But businesses learn soon enough that neither their environments nor their stakeholders behave responsibly. Neither will they guarantee the organizations survive while waiting for the long-term benefits of social responsibility to accrue.

So organizations 'make selections' in the fulfilment of their social tasks. The bases of these selections are power relations. They do not behave strictly economically, nor from social responsibility. They behave politically, and such behaviour can be called political utilitarianism. Business behaves according to what is possible, in the light of all kinds of demands and according to the expected consequences of its behaviour. In the end, it is persuaded neither by profit nor by social principles. It is persuaded by the power of various 'partners'.

Employees, although far from powerless, are the partners who 'give' management the opportunity to choose how to behave in contacts with them. Employees do not have enough power, and the state does offer little support and has no real interest in changing the situation. As a result, management does not need to behave differently. Recent empirical research reveals clearly the existence of politically utilitarianistic philosophy and behaviour (Berlogar 1995, 1997). The problem, perhaps, would not be so large if the education of employees were unnecessary. But the needs really exist. We must learn to adapt to change.

There is no doubting the educational needs, but are they met? Whose needs are met? The White Paper on Education in the Republic of Slovenia, which was meant to change the situation, frankly admits:

> 'The programmes for adults which prevail are those meant for already more educated people. These people can cover the costs of education themselves ... Programmes meant to give support and stimulate higher educational levels and make possible to acquire a higher level of general education are extremely rare' (White Paper 1995: 300).

The empirical data from the research (Mohorcic-Spolar 1996: 41) strongly supports this statement. Almost one-third of all Slovenia's employees have not been educated to a level required by their jobs. Even more indicative is the fact that only one per cent of employees who needed lower (basic, vocational) education actually participate in educational programmes. At the same time 27 per cent of those (usually in positions 'higher on the organizational chart') trying to get higher professional or even academic formal or non-formal education were given the opportunity and support required. The category of employees most in need of education get the least of it.

Can the reality of political utilitarianism, and the practices based upon it, be changed? Can more enlightened views be brought into force? If so, who will do so? Who has the power to do so? The employees on their own certainly do not. Society as a whole – the state, its institutions, individuals – do have it. But a society which neither behaves responsibly itself, nor gives support for employee education, can hardly demand social responsibility from business organizations. A new and clear social contract has to be 'signed'. Without it there is no chance that the education of employees will be accepted by business organizations.

What has already been said

Before analysing the possibilities of such a contract, let us examine what has already been said about the problem discussed above. The very fact that quite a lot has been said provides proof of the urgent need to act. Adult education is an extremely interdisciplinary field of study, and I am not the first to discover that politics, economics and other disciplines are incorporated within it. Even when following the goals of profit extremely closely, an enterprise is an open system which cannot (in its social functions) be isolated from its environment (Berlogar 1996: 29). Businesses' first and most important connection is with their employees. Employees cannot be expected to practise democracy outside work while suffering autocracy and hierarchy – with no chance of participation – inside the corporation.

Participation is a chance for self-realization even when 'great' decisions are excluded. Education of employees provides an opportunity for participation. And if realizing participation depends on its compatibility with the interests of business, we must consider again what the real interests of business are and redefine the concepts of productivity and efficiency and how they are measured. There really is no good reason to support the existing, educationally unfavourable, situation, nor to resist change. My own research (Berlogar 1995) clearly indicates that the need for knowledge and education is one of employees' strongest but least fulfilled needs. Critical rethinking about the problem may help us to understand the situation as it is, and to direct our search for ways to change it.

If our efforts are to succeed, we cannot stick to theory alone. We have to listen to even the most orthodox functionalists, economists and practitioners. Cervero and Wilson comment on the usefulness of theories about planning educational programmes for adults. These theories, they argue, have been written:

> 'as if the world in which they must plan were devoid of disagreeable people, nasty politics and concern about the economic bottom line. Thus planners feel they are walking through quicksand and are getting advice about characteristic land formations instead of a rope' (1994: xi).

It would also be wise to bear in mind that, long ago, Adam Smith wrote:

> 'The man whose life is spent in performing a few simple operations of which the effects too are, perhaps, always the same, has no occasion to exert his understanding or to exercise his invention in finding out expedients for removing difficulties which never occur. He naturally loses, therefore, the habit of such exertion and generally becomes as stupid and ignorant as it is possible for a human creature to become' (quoted by Rubenson and Schutze 1993: 2).

There are many who demand changes. But they do not show how these can be realized in practice. The education of adults is not only a question of pure science and theory. It is politics, it is economics, it is manipulation and dominance. The functionalists themselves admit that:

> 'A company's educational decisions are governed by considerations regarding productivity and profit. Goals like equity seldom enter the discussions. Education for broader skills and general knowledge, as distinct from company or product-oriented training, is rare and generally directed toward managers and other skilled white-collar groups' (Rubenson 1992: 27).

The problem exists and it is clearly 'international'. 'In Britain', Griffin argues (1991: 265), 'adult education has been largely transformed into a kind of welfare and employment policy'. The social and political processes connected with this transformation include increased government control over public spending, the ideological trend in favour of an unrestricted market economy, and powerful government intervention in favour of an educational system designed first and foremost to serve the needs of the economy.

So is the behaviour of business organizations difficult to understand? Are managers alone to be blamed? Are they irresponsible, immoral, unethical? I believe we are dealing with a kind of situational ethics, political utilitarianism which takes place in the environment willing to accept it. Business behaviour should be explained as a response to different kind of forces – market and non-market, economical and political. Managers do not seek profits alone; they seek power and security first. They conform to the values and norms of their societies because they fear the consequences if they do not do what is expected of them. It is difficult to convince them of the need for education of employees from the market point of view. Management can obviously regulate the political dimension as they desire. Changes, therefore, must be carefully planned and carried out. Is this possible?

What has to be said

The first question to be asked is: What and who must change in the policy and practice of employee education? Interests, measures, programmes, educators or managers? Organizational culture or the whole society? How can change be achieved? There are many questions, but few useful answers available.

The fact is that 'the self-made man gaining economic success without any educational qualifications is increasingly becoming a myth' (Hunt 1985: 67). The 'qualifications' required far exceed narrow professional, functional or vocational training and knowledge. I do not believe in some kind of educational revolution. But still less do I consider that society and its institutions are in a process of autonomous and deliberate 'self-purification' or that some new 'social contract' giving employee education, and education as the whole, their due importance is being written. No such process is taking place today.

Perhaps the only educational part of such a process which is occurring follows a 'work training model' (Elsey 1986: 15), in which commitment to social purpose is interpreted largely in terms of vocational preparation and work skills training for economic ends. Life skills and social awareness education are excluded. But it is not only a problem of content – the problem of adult education, and of employee education in particular, begins with its marginality. It has little political support, and those interested in change have still less political and economic power. Hence, for adult education professionals and adult education practice, pragmatism is more a value than a sin. Claiming that developing people makes good business sense is simply not enough.

According to Evans (1987), adult education provision is decided in the last resort by external circumstances which have little to do with adult learning theories, radical or otherwise. There has never been a shortage of social philosophical analyses of adult education, culminating in the radical utopianism of its guru figures. However, adult educators must act politically to be effective. A pressure group for the education of adults can have some impact if it emphasizes the relevance of adult and continuing education to increased productivity. That is why an education lobby and not a radical theory is needed.

The change mentioned above is concerned with education and educators. It is the right way to begin. A lobby, a single united pressure group would mean greater professional cohesion among adult educators (Evans 1987: 231). We can continue to work with others 'signers' of the new social contract. We have seen that corporate (business) educational policy does not change automatically. Social responsibility is not an act of good will. It is really a contract preceded by the negotiation of interests, and by power (Davidson 1995). When educators fail, what can other parties do? Despite constant fear and the need to keep their jobs, employees can be a strong pressure group. This is not a matter of trades unions alone. Managers may be dictators, leaders, democrats or humanists, but it is employees themselves who really create organizational culture. This is a long-term process. No change in organizations, even today, takes place overnight.

What about the state? It can and should have a major role, but its willingness to do anything at all may be doubted. It is often thought preferable for business to regulate some issues alone before the state steps in. Some such issues never are regulated -either by business or by the state. The education of employees may well be one of these problems, despite all the much-vaunted educational policies. What is more difficult to understand is whose interest are served by such a situation.

Society as a whole is the last party to the educational negotiation process. Is it really willing to bring about change in employee education? If not, why blame business for neglecting its social responsibility when the business environment is equally guilty? Social responsibility, business ethics and similar concepts sound beautiful. But however desirable, they all bring additional costs. Business must include 'social' costs within the price of their products. That is economics. Regrettably, neither society nor individuals are willing to pay. That is politics – and reality. We must start to look for new solutions.

Is there any other solution? Faced with the urgent need to pay the price, society may well lower the standards of acceptable social responsibility. The first step will, no doubt, be to reduce the costs of employee education. How will they then be met? Will employees themselves have to pay them alone? Who will then be able to negotiate, and whose interests will prevail? In what sense shall we then be able to speak of the post-industrial or informational age? Production and educational outcomes (Monk 1990: 322) will then be all that counts – not people, as Morgan (1994: 4) tries to persuade us.

Finally, let me repeat: in practice adult education has always meant politics. Today, changes are needed. Employees and their education and learning pose a most serious test for the concepts of learning society and lifelong learning. They can become reality, remain a vision or change into a myth.

References

Apple, W (1985) *Education and Power*, Ark Paperbacks, Routledge & Kegan, Boston, London and Henley.
Berlogar, J (1995) *Organisational Communication: From Dominance to Participation*, unpublished MSc paper, Faculty of Social Sciences, Ljubljana.
Berlogar, J (1996) 'Neizobrazevanje zaposlenih – izvirni greh managementa' ('Neglecting Education of Employees – Management's Original Sin'), in *Andragoska spoznanja*, 2/96, 29-32, Gospodarski vestnik, Ljubljana.
Berlogar, J (1997) *Political Utilitarianism or Critical Theory of Organisational Ethics*, unpublished ScD dissertation, Faculty of Social Sciences, Ljubljana.
Cervero, R and Wilson, AL (1994) *Planning Responsibly for Adult Education: A Guide to Negotiating Power and Interests*, Jossey-Bass, San Francisco.
Davidson, S (1995) 'Making Needs: Toward a Historical Sociology of Needs in Adult and Continuing Education', in *Adult Education Quarterly*, 4/1995, 183-196.
Deetz, A and Kersten, A (1983) 'Critical Models of Interpretive Research', in L Putnam and M Pacanovsky *Communication and Organizations*: 147-171, Sage Publications, Beverly Hills.
Elsey, B (1986) *Social Theory Perspectives on Adult Education*, Department of Adult Education, University of Nottingham.
Evans, B (1987) *Radical Adult Education: A Political Critique*, Croom Helm, London, New York, Sydney.
Green, S (1988) 'Strategy, Organizational Culture and Symbolism', in *Long Range Planning*, 21, 4, 121-129, Pergamon Press, Oxford.
Griffin, C (1991) 'A Critical Perspective on Sociology and Adult Education', in J Peters, P Jarvis and associates *Adult Education: Evolution and Achievements in a Developing Field of Study*: 259-277, Jossey-Bass Publishers, San Francisco, Oxford.
Jarvis, P (1987) *Adult Learning in the Social Context*, Croom Helm, London, New York, Sydney.
Marquardt, J (1996) *Building the Learning Organization: A Systems Approach to Quantum Improvement and Global Success*, McGraw-Hill, New York.
Mohorcic-Spolar, V (1996) 'Potrebe po izobrazevanju zaposlenih v podjetjih in drugih organizacijah' ('Educational Needs of Employees in Enterprises and Institutions'), in *Andragoska spoznanja*, 1/1996, 40-44, Gospodarski vestnik, Ljubljana.
Monk, H (1990) *Educational Finance: An Economic Approach*, McGraw-Hill, Inc., New York.
Morgan, G (1994) 'Empowering Human Resources', in *People & Potential, Reader*, 73-76: The Open University, Walton Hall, Milton Keynes.
Rubenson, K (1992) 'Human Resource Development: A Historical Perspective', in L Burton (Ed.), *Developing Resourceful Humans: Adult Education Within the Economic Context*: 3-29, Routledge, London, New York.
Rubenson, K and Schutze, H (1993) 'Learning At and Through the Workplace – A Review of Participation and Adult Learning Theory', in D Hirsch and D Wagner (Eds) *What Makes Workers Learn?*, Hampton Press, Cresskill, NJ.

Senge, M, Kleiner, A, Roberts, C, Ross, R and Smith, B (1995) *The Fifth Discipline Fieldbook, Strategies and Tools for Building a Learning Organisation*, Nicholas Brealey Publishing, London.

White Paper on Education in Republic of Slovenia (1995) *Bela knjiga o vzgoji in izobrazevanju v Republiki Sloveniji (White Paper on Education in Republic of Slovenia)*, Ministrstvo za solstvo in sport, Ljubljana.

Index

'Lifelong learning' occurs too frequently to be individually indexed.

aboriginal communities (Australia) 189
access, to education and learning 52, 65
Accomplishing Europe through Education and Training (EU) 33
Allen Consulting Group 187, 194
Acker, S 343
Adams, J 276
Adkins, L 75
Adult Education committee (Finland) 157, 158
adult education 16–17, 81–90, 92, 95–6, 97, 157–66, 176–7, 345–6, 349, 350, 353, 354, 355,
   for social responsibility 81–90
   in GDR 116
   in Hong Kong 139, 145
   liberal 163–4
adult learning projects 8–9
aesthetic communities 84–90
affective learning 233–4
Africa 52, *see also* South Africa
African National Congress (South Africa) 17, 107
agriculture 303–12
Alanen, A 156, 157
Alasoini, T 292
Alheit, P 40
Ali, M 246
Anderson, D 187, 194
Anderson, J 233
Anglia Polytechnic University (UK) 215
Angus, L 72
Antikainen, A 40

Aotearoa/New Zealand, *see* New Zealand
apartheid education 105
Apple, W 349
Archer 59
Argyris, C 294
Aristotle 22, 23, 24, 25, , 27, 28, 30, 229
Arnold, M 250
assessment of prior learning (APL) 10, 203, *see also* recognition of prior learning (RPL)
Aubrey, R 282
Australasia 17
Australia 69–80, 137, 141, 186–97, 303–13
Australian Council of Trade Unions (ACTU) 172
Australian National Training Authority (ANTA) 72, 188, 186, 187, 189, 194, 195
autonomy 329–31
Avis, J 110

Bagnall, RG 113, 227, 228
Bakhtin, M 69, 77
Baldwin, D 249
Ball, SJ 22–3, 25, 28, 30
Ballard, B 219, 220
Bangladesh 52
Barley, SR 294
Barnett, R 245
Barry, NP 172
Bawtree, V 5
Beck, U 34, 35, 36, 39, 62, 63, 66, 83

359

360 INDEX

Becker, G   110
Beckett, D   xi, 230
Beijing   127, 129, 130, 139
Beilharz, P   169
Belanger, P   45
Benn, J   258
Bensemann, J   14
Berg, D   277
Berger, P   36
Berger, S   138,147
Berlogar, J   xi, 350, 351
Beschäftigungsgesellschaften, see employment companies
Betriebsakademien   116
biography, biographical learning   40, 41
Bion, WR   334, 335
Bisovsky, G   35
Blackstone, T   199
Blaug, M   110, 201
Blomqvist, I   158, 159, 160
Blueprint for Survival   7
Boland, RJ   292, 293, 294
Boshier, R   ix, x, 8, 10, 12, 14, 17, 61, 144, 194, 246, 251, 252
Botkin   45
Boud, D   ix, 221
Bourdieu, P   34, 36, 39, 52
Bowles, S   52
Bramer, WL   38
British Columbia (Canada)   51, 138, 250, 251, 252, 254
Brooks, A   283, 286, 287
Brown, D   282
Brown, P   39
Brunt, WJ   327
Bryant, I   17
Budlender, D   346
Bureau of Lifelong Learning (Japan)   181
Burke, T   233
business process re-engineering   292
  business, social responsibility and   349–55
Butler, E   ix, 70, 72, 76, 77, 194, 280, 283

Campbell, C   63
Canada   12, 16, 141, 249–50
  Business Council of   12
Canadian Association for Adult Education   12

Candy Report   224, 232
Candy, P   21, 191, 193, 194, 217, 218, 219, 221,
Carnegie Trust   122
Carter, C   26
Casey, C   75, 76, 78
Censis   238, 239
Cervero, R   349, 353
Chambers, S   97
Chan, FT   137
Chartism   169
Chen, J   133,134
Cheng, F   125, 126
Child, M   332
China   124–36
Chinese Social University   129
Chinese society, in Hong Kong   144–6
Chinese University of Hong Kong   142
Christie, P   103
Chung, YP   142, 150
City Literary Institute (London)   204
Clanchy, J   219, 220
Clinton, WJ   251
Club of Rome   7
co–operation in learning   341–2
Cockman, P   295
Cohen, P   282
cold war   248–50
collectivity in learning   15
Collins, M   94, 95
Comenius   250
Committee for Learning in Aotearoa/New Zealand (CLANZ)   171, 176
communication, Habermas on   92–4
Communist Party, Chinese   130, 131, 132
communitarian   83, 84
community education   45, 51–3, 116, 181–2
competency based education   10, 49, 105, 250, 251–2
competitiveness   186–7
Confucius   126
Conner, D   283
Conservative government (UK)   199
consumer society   63–4
Continuing Education Committee (Finland)   156
Cookson, P   49

Council of Canadians   12
Country Produce   270–9
credit transfer   242
Crew, M   201
Cropley, AJ   13, 21, 250–51
Crowley, D   14, 17
Cultural Revolution (China)   124–5, 126
cultural shift   73
Cunningham, I   74
curriculum   48–50, 143, 145
   in work-based learning   217–18, 222

Dausien, B   39
Dave, RH   13
Davidson, S   355
Davis, E   72, 73
Deetz, A   350
Delors, J   5, 236, 240
democracy   4, 11–13, 15, 96, 97, 98, 245
   in adult education   168–70
   in Hong Kong   144–6
Deng, X   124
Denison, EF   109–110
Denmark   138
Department for Culture Media and Sport (UK)   263
Department for Education and Employment (UK)   5, 21, 26, 29, 30, 199, 200, 256
Department of Education (South Africa)   104
Department of Education and Science (UK)   258
Department of Employment (Germany)   120
Department of Finance (South Africa)   107, 108, 109
Department of Labour (South Africa)   108, 109, 345, 346, 347
Department of Manpower (South Africa)   346
Department of National Heritage (UK)   261
Derrida, J   327, 332, 334
Dewey, J   233, 250, 251
Dilworth, R   281
distance learning   48, 116, 148–9, 216
Dohmen, G   29, 30
Dominice, P   40

Donald, J   69, 75
Dong, M   132
du Gay, P   75, 76, 82
Duke, C   14, 17, 21

East Africa   17
Ecologist, The   7
Eder, K   85, 86
Education and Manpower Bureau (Hong Kong)   149
Education and Training Support Agency (New Zealand)   174, 176, 177
Education Department (Hong Kong)   149
education,
   and democracy   98–8
   and equity   108–09, 111–13
   compared with learning   8–9
   emancipatory   47, 50, 92–8, 245–6
   formal   10, 11
   informal   10, 11
   initial, in Hong Kong   138–9, 141
   liberal   317–25
   non-formal   11
   see also adult education, lifelong education
educational thought, binary and organic logic in   229–32
Edwards, R   12, 16, 17, 59, 63, 76, 110, 228, 247, 251
Elsey, B   354
employee development and assistance programme (EDAP) (Ford UK)   202
Employees Retraining Board (Hong Kong)   138, 149, 150
employment companies   118–21
equity   108–09, 111–13, 340, 341, 353
ethics   82, 322, 326–35, 349–56
European Commission   x, 21, 29, 30, 32, 33, 34, 147
European Social Fund   120, 121
European Union (EU), European Community   viii, 4–5, 32, 198, 199, 201, 237, 241, 242, 292, 295
European Year of Lifelong Learning   4–5, 15, 26 , 30, 33, 198, 262
Evans, B   22, 355
Ewart, W   257
Eyerman, R   37

Fabianism 169
face-to-face relations 326–35
Falk, I 306, 311
Fang, X xii, 124, 126
Faure Report xi, 4, 7, 9, 10, 11, 14, 16, 44
Faure, E 5, 13, 15, 21, 45, 46, 47, 48, 49, 51, 52, 54, 250, 251
fear 66
Featherstone, M 82, 84, 88
Federation of Continuing Education in Tertiary Institutions (Hong Kong) 143
Fenwick, T 281, 283
Ferrier, F 189
Field, J 37
Findsen, B 14
Finland 138, 155–67, 292–302
Fisher, D 269, 270–71, 275, 276, 277, 278
flaming 328
flexibility 33–4, 72, 74, 171–2
Ford Motor Co. *see* employee development and assistance programme (EDAP)
Fordism 110–11
Foreman, G 246
Foster, L 73
Foucault, M 28, 228, 322
Fraser Institute 12
Frasier, J 246
Freire, P 4, 6, 47, 50
French, WL, Bell, CH and Zawacki, RA 276
Freud, S 326, 334
Fromm, E 66
FEDA (Further Education Development Agency (FEDA) (UK) 203, 204
Further Education Funding Council (UK) 201
Further Education Unit 202, 203
Galbraith, JK 247, 249
Gang of Four 124
Gans, S 326, 333, 334
Gates, B 247
Gee, J 70, 73, 286, 287
Gender Task Team (South Africa) 342
General Electric 283, 284, 288
generic skills 219
Germany 115–23
Gibbons, M 38

Gidddens, A 34, 35, 39, 62, 83, 87
Giere, U 104
Gintis, H 52
Glastra, FJ 38
global economy, globalization 5, 14–15, 32, 34, 35, 40, 70, 71–3, 76, 89, 248–9, 253, 284–5
Goldsmiths' College, London 26
Goleman, D 234
Gollan, P 72
Gondek, H 333
Gong, M 134
Goodman, P 4
Gramsci, A 319
Greece 27
Greider, W 284
Griffin, C ix, 14, 353
Grossberg, L 83, 88
Grosz, E 334
Growth, Competitiveness and Employment (EU White Paper) 33
Growth, Employment and Redistribution Strategy (GEAR) (South Africa) 107, 108
Guan, S 125
Gustavsson, B 4, 13, 17

Habermas, J ix, 50J, 66–7, 87, 92–9, 246
Hager, P x, 231
Hall, G 108
Hall, R 71, 73
Hames, R 74
Hamilton, C 72
Hamlet 329, 330, 334
Hampden-Turner, C 275
Hampton, WA 133
Handy, C 37
Harley, A 345
Harley, B 71, 73
Harris, P 173
Hart, M 286
Hastings Boys High School (NZ) 8
Haworth, N 177
Heath, S 45
Heidegger, M 329, 332
Heider, J 272
Hinkson, J 71
Ho, LS 142

Hodgskin, T 47
Hofmeyr, J 108
Holford, J x, 137, 138, 142, 143, 144
Holt, J 4
Hong Kong 137–51
Hood, D 70
horizontal integration 7–8, 9–11
Horn, P 338
Hughes, K 283
human capital theory 109–11, 177
Husen, T 12, 14, 45, 46, 47, 51, 61
Husserl, E 332
Hutchins, R 60–61

Illich, I 4, 9, 53, 61, 62
India 52
individual learning accounts 201, 207–08
individual responsibility 15
individualism, *see* autonomy
individualization 35, 53, 122
Industry Training Act (New Zealand) (1992) 174, 176
information society, age 59, 245–54
Inner London Education Authority (ILEA) 200
International Adult Literacy Survey (IALS) 238, 241
International Journal of Lifelong Education x, 22
International Labour Organization (ILO) 171
International Review of Education 13–14
internet, in teaching and learning 327, 331
Iran 6
Ireland 138
irony, in liberal education 324
Israel 138
Italy 236–44

Jackson, B 52
Jameson, F 248, 254
Jamison, A 37
Jansen, T ix, 88
Japan 17, 137, 180–85
Jarvis, P ix, 60, 63, 66, 156, 162, 166, 201, 243, 332, 349, 350
Jiang, S 134

Jiang, Z 131
job centres (UK) 260–61
Jobs, S 247
justice 326–7

Kallen, D 7, 194, 251
Karpin Report 73, 233–4
Keep, E 174, 177
Kelly, R 73, 74
Kelly, T 257, 258
Kelsey, J 14
Kent Education Department (UK) 201
Kenway, J 74
Kersten, A 350
Kidd, JR 349
Kilpatrick, S 305, 306, 308
Kincheloe, J 280, 287
King, DS 169
King, E 45
Knapper, C 21
Knights, D 75
knowledge organization 38
knowledge society 59
knowledge, tacit and explicit 292–4
knowledge-based economy 32–3
Knox, A 46
Kochan, T 304
Kroker, A 246
Kumar, K 248

La Belle, T 13–14
Labour government, Labour Party (New Zealand) 168, 169, 172
Labour government, Labour Party (UK) 17, 51, 199–200
labour, casualization of 109
Lacan, J 335
Lakatos, I 227, 318
Lam, A 137
Lansbury, R 72, 73
Larsson, S 17
Lash, S 86, 87
Latin America 17
Lau, SK 144, 145, 146
Law, M ix, 171
Lawson, K 227, 228
lean production 292
Learning Age, The vii, 200

364 INDEX

learning
  and communication 87–90
  compared with education 59–60
  contract 274
  cultures 75, 74
learning organization 3, 37–8, 74, 269–79, 280–90, 303–12, 350
  and adult education 281–2
  language of 285–7
learning society 11–13, 59–68
Learning to Be 6, 14, 15 *see also* Faure, E, Faure Report
Learning: The Treasure Within 5
Lee, N 137
Lengrand, P 5, 16, 17, 21, 60
Lester, RK 138, 147
Leung, SW 146
Levinas, E 326–35
Li, P 132
Li, T 131
libraries, public 56–65
life cycle 155
lifelong education 4, 13–14
  and initial education 45–6, 48–50
  and lifelong learning 8, 45, 227–9
  in China 125–6
Lifelong Learning in Europe (journal) 22
Lifelong Learning Research Group (University of Surrey) x
Lifetime Learning – A Consultation Document x, 98
lifeworld, Habermas on 93–4
Limits to Growth 7
literacy 241–3
Littler, C 172
Liu, PW 142, 150
Liverpool 257
Loewenthal, D x
Loewinger, J 269
London,
  City of ix, 200, 203–09
  Corporation of 200, 203, 205, 206, 207
Lowe, DM 78, 246, 253
Lowe, J 16
Luddism 248
Lundvall, B 304, 312
Lury, C 75
Luttrell, W 343

Lyotard, J-F 59, 245, 332

Maastricht 239
MacDermott, K 74
Maffesoli, M 84, 85, 88
Maheu, R 5–6
Maisch, M 215
Malaysia 284
Mali 6
management consultancy 269–79, 291–302
mandatory continuing education 49–50
Maori 168–9, 170, 173, 176, 177, 178
Margate (UK) 262, 264
Marginson, S 72
market, information 64
markets 36, 82, 246
  for continuing education in HK 140, 142, 143
  for education, training, learning 12, 53, 156–8, 164–5, 186–97, 198–208
Marquandt, M 283, 284
Marquardt, J 350
Marsden, D 52
Marshall, R 171
Marsick, V 280, 282–6
Martin, B 166
Martin, E 74
Maslow, A 275
Mathews, J 304
Maynard, A 201
McGivney, V 341
McLennan, A 341
McLeod, D 51
McLuhan, M 230
McNair, S 201
McNay, I 202
mechanics institutes 47, 257
Mezirow, J 94, 95
Middlesex University, National Centre for Work-based Learning Partnerships (UK) 214–15
Mincer, J 110
Ministry of Education (Finland) 157
Ministry of Education (South Africa) 339, 340, 342
Ministry of education, Science, Sports and Culture (MESSC) (Japan) 181, 182, 184

Ministry of Labour (Finland)   162
Ministry of Public Education (Italy)   237
Ministry of Reconstruction Adult Education Committee (UK)   4, 250–1
Minto, J   257
Mirvis, P   277
Mohorcic-Spolar, V   352
Monk, H   356
Moore, R   202
Morgan, G   356
Morgan, RB   74
Motorola   283, 284, 288

Nasta, T   38
National Advisory Group on Continuing Education and Lifelong Learning (UK)   29
National Board of Education (Finland)   162
National Conference on Adult Higher Education (China)   130
National Council on Adult Education (New Zealand)   171
National Council on Educational Reform (Japan)   181, 182
National Party (New Zealand)   168, 173, 174
National Qualifications Framework (New Zealand)   172, 173, 177
National Qualifications Framework (South Africa)   105, 106, 337, 338, 344, 345
National Workplace Development Programme (Finland)   292, 296
NBEET (Australia)   69, 70
neo-liberalism   168, 172, 174, 177, 247
Netherlands   141
New Zealand   8, 14, 61, 137, 138, 168–79
   Council of Trade Unions (NZCTU)   175
   Education Amendment Act 1974   14
Newman, J   319
Niemi, J   14
non-governmental organizations (NGOs)   345
Nonaka, I   292, 293, 294, 295
Nordhaug, O   295
Norway   138
Nuissl, E   115
Nyrere, J   17

Ohliger, J   9, 49
Okamoto, K   137
Opelt, K   121
Open Learning Institute (Hong Kong), see Open University (Hong Kong)
open learning, access to (Finland)   161–2
Open University (Finland)   161
Open University (Hong Kong)   139, 140, 148
Open University (UK)   48, 63–4
Oran   45
Organization for Economic Co-operation and Development (OECD)   4, 5, 13, 14–15, 160, 170, 172
Organization of Petroleum Exporting Countries (OPEC)   251
organizational learning, and tacit and explicit knowledge   292–4
outcomes based education   105, 106,
Owenism   169

Pacific Islanders (in New Zealand)   168–9, 173
paid educational leave   10
   in New Zealand   171
Pakistan   52
Parjanen, L   161
Park, A,
Parkyn, GW   16
participation   12–13
partnerships   52
Passeron, J   52
Patten, C   146
Paulston, R   4, 9
Peng, Z   128
People's Republic of China (PRC), see China
Peperzak, A   327, 328, 329, 330, 333
Perry, W   48
persuasive discourses   69, 75–8
Peters, RS   319
Peukertruth, H   98
Phillips, B   344
Phillips, T   305
Pineau, P   40
Plato   245
Poell, R   295
Polanyi, M   64

policy 21–30
  as discourse 25, 28–30
  community 138, 144–6
  educational, in China 124–33
  educational, in HK 137–51
  educational, in South Africa 103–13
  educational, market–oriented (Finland) 155–66
  in EU 32–43
  in organizations 354
  in UK 198–200
  libraries (UK) 256–65
  macroeconomic, and education 107–13
  South Africa, women and 337–45
post–Fordism 33, 72, 110–11, 253
post–modernism 16, 27–30, 59, 249, 253
  and modernism 82–4
Poster, M 253, 254
prior learning assessment, *see* assessment of prior learning (APL)
private schools 51
private sector of education, in China 126–33
privatization 81
Przeworski, A 169
Psacharopoulos G 106
psychotherapy 333–5

Qayyum, A 8
Qu, Y 134

Rahnema, M 5, 6, 8, 9
Rainbird, H 174, 177
Rameka, N 178
Ranson, S 61, 65
Readings, B 318, 319, 322, 325
Reagan, R 53
real learning 66–7
recognition of prior learning (RPL) 337, 342, 343
recurrent education 4, 14
reflexive modernization 32
reflexivity, reflexive society 34–5, 62–3
Reimer, E 4
research, in continuing education 144
Reynolds, A 283, 284
rhetoric 41, 105, 280
  as logical proof 23–5
  as moral persuasion 25–7
  as style 27–28, 30
  defined 22–23
  see also persuasive discourses
Rifkin, J 288
Rinne, R 45
risk, risk society 32, 35, 36, 38, 66
Robinson, P 74
Roderick, GW 110
Rogers, E 305, 310
Rorty, R 324
Rostock 115–23
Rothwell, W 49
Rover PLC 202
Rubenson, K 10, 13, 353
Ruskin College, Oxford 202
Ryle, G 325

Sakolosky, R 77, 75–6
Salveson, P 201
Saraceno, C 236
Sartre, J-P 332
Saskatchewan (Canada) 51
Savellis, R 74
Scandinavia 17
Schedler, PE 38
Scheler, M 62
Schon, D 37, 62, 231
schools, and lifelong learning 237–43
Schultz, T 109
Schulz, L 77
Schutze, H 353
Scott, M 14
Seddon, T 72
Segal Quince Wicksteed (Asia) Ltd 138
self-disciplinary practices 76
Selman, M xii
Senge, P 198, 250, 280, 285, 305, 350
Shah of Iran 6
Shakespeare, W 329
Sheffield 262, 264
Shoemaker, F 305
Siebert, H 116, 120
Sihvonen, J 163
Simpanen, M 158, 159, 160
Singapore 138, 141
Skills New Zealand 176
Sklair, L 71

Slovenia 351–2
small businesses, learning networks in 303–13
Smith, A 353
Smith, JE 74
Smith, M 175
Smith, R 21, 46
social allocation 35–9, 41
social Darwinism 247
social democracy 51
social forces, school run by 124–33
social movements, new 37, 84, 86, 95, 96,
social responsibility 81
Sopp, P 36
South Africa x, 17, 103–13, 337–48
South America 52
Spender, D 341
State Education Commission (China) 130–4
State, as funder of continuing education 146–7
Stehr, N 59
Stephens, MD 110
Stifter, C 35
Stockley, D 73
Stronach, I 110
substitution effect 121
Sumsion, J 256
Sweden 61

Taggart, R 201
Target Oriented Curriculum (TOC) (Hong Kong) 141, 146
Tawney, RH 16
Taylor, C 324
Teaching and Learning: Towards the Learning Society (EU White Paper) 33, 198
teaching 322–5
TECs (Training and Enterprise Councils) (UK) 199, 202
Tenkasi, RV 292, 293, 294
Thatcher, M 52, 53
Thomas, JE 17
Tiananmen Square 'incident' 139
Titmus, CJ 125, 349
Torbert, WR 269, 270–1, 275, 276, 277, 278
Torres Strait Islander communities (Australia) 189

Torres, C 17
total quality management (TQM) 250, 271, 276
Tough, A 8, 9
Townley, B 74, 76
Trade Union Education Authority (New Zealand) 171, 175
Trade Union Training Board (New Zealand) 171
trade unions, trade union education 169, 171, 173–4, 175–6
training contracts 241–2
transformation, personal, and organizational learning 270–78
transformation, perspective 94
Truscott, K 339, 340
Tuckett, A 15
Tuijnman, A 157, 238
Tung, CH 148
Tunstall, J 48
Tuomisto, J xii, 155, 159

unemployment 5, 115, 117, 118, 119, 162–3
Unipart PLC 202
United Kingdom 138, 141, 256–65
United Nations Conference on the Environment (Stockholm 1972) 7
United Nations Development Programme (UNDP) 6
United Nations Educational, Scientific and Cultural Organization (UNESCO) vii, 3, 4, 5, 14, 15, 22, 44, 104, 125 156, 170–1, 181, 251
  Institute of Education, Hamburg 13
  International Committee for the Advancement of Adult Education 5
  Second World Conference on Adult Education, Montreal 1960 13
  Third World Conference on Adult Education, Tokyo 1972 6, 13, 14
University and Polytechnic Grants Committee (Hong Kong), *see* University Grants Committee
University for Industry (UK) 207
University Grants Committee (Hong Kong) 138–49
University of Brighton (UK) 256, 257, 259, 260

University of Leeds (UK)   214
University of Portsmouth (UK)   214
University of the Third Age (China)   132
unlearning   46
Upton, S   173
Urry, J   86, 87
United States of America   281, 286
Useem, M   304
User Choice   186–97
  enterprise and individual needs in   194–5
Usher, R   16, 17, 63, 76, 228, 247, 251

van der Lans, J   85, 86
Varmola, T   156, 162, 164
Verne, E   61
vertical integration   7–8, 9–10
Vester, M   36
Victoria, Queen   257
Vietnam War   4, 247
vocational education and training   162, 186–97, 236–43
Vocational Training Council (Hong Kong)   138, 149, 150
Vocational Training Council (New Zealand)   170, 171
vocational training, dual system (Germany)   116
vocationalism, new   71
vouchers, and education   201–203, 203–25
Wailes, N   177
Wain, K   21, 104, 227, 228, 232, 233
Walker, D   221
Walker, R   170
Watkins, K   280, 282, 283, 284, 285
Watkins, P   71
Webb, J   74
Wei, Y   129
Weinstein, M   246
welfare state   96, 170–1
Wells, D   287
Welton, M   12, 94, 95
Whirlpool   283–4, 288
Whitwam, D   284
Wild, J   332
Wildemeersch, D   xi, 81, 88
Williams, D   332

Williams, R   47
Willmot, H   75
Wilson, AL   349, 353
Wilson, M   8
Wilson, WJ   39
Winch, C   227
Winnicott, D   335
Winslow, C   38
Winter, R   215
Wittgenstein, L   62
Wolpe, A   345–6
Women's Coalition (South Africa)   338
women, in South Africa   337–47
women, women's education   77, 180
Wong, YC   141, 150
Wood, S   172
Woodhall, M   106
work order, new   70, 73
work   155
work-based learning   15, 73–8, 224–35, 291–302
  access to (Finland)   159–61
  and formal learning   225–7
  and universities   213–22
  importance of context in   221, 230–4
  in Japan   184
  see also Betriebsakademien
  see also learning organization
workers' education   171, 175–6

Workers' Educational Association (New Zealand)   171
Workers' Educational Association (UK)   48
Worth Report (Alberta)   7
Wright Commission (Ontario)   7
Wright, DT   12
Wright, M

Yeaxlee, B   60, 65
You, Q   129, 134
Young, M   201

Zhu, K, 130–31
Zou, T, 128
Zuboff, S, 281

For Product Safety Concerns and Information please contact our EU
representative GPSR@taylorandfrancis.com
Taylor & Francis Verlag GmbH, Kaufingerstraße 24, 80331 München, Germany

www.ingramcontent.com/pod-product-compliance
Lightning Source LLC
Chambersburg PA
CBHW052339230426
43664CB00041B/2209